From
WARFARE STATE
to
WELFARE STATE

MARC ALLEN EISNER

From
WARFARE STATE
to
WELFARE STATE

World War I,
Compensatory State Building,
and the
Limits of the Modern Order

The Pennsylvania State University Press
University Park, Pennsylvania

Library of Congress Cataloging-in-Publication Data

Eisner, Marc Allen.
    From warfare state to welfare state : World War I, compensatory
state-building, and the limits of the modern order / Marc Allen
Eisner.
        p.   cm.
    Includes bibliographical references (p.   ) and index.
    ISBN 0-271-01995-6 (cloth : alk. paper)
    ISBN 0-271-01996-4 (paper : alk. paper)
    1. Political planning—United States—History—20th century.
2. United States—Politics and government—1919–1933. 3. United
States—Politics and government—1933–1945. 4. United States
—Economic policy—To 1933. 5. United States—Economic
policy—1933–1945. 6. World War, 1914–1918—United States.
I. Title.
JK468.P64E57   2000
320.973'09'042—dc21   99-41200
                                                                      CIP

It is the policy of The Pennsylvania State University Press to use acid-free paper for the first
printing of all clothbound books. Publications on uncoated stock satisfy the minimum
requirements of American National Standard for Information Sciences—Permanence of Paper
for Printed Library Materials, ANSI Z39.48–1992.

For Patricia

Contents

Acknowledgments

This book is the product of some five years of research, writing, revision, and rest—a seemingly endless cycle. During this period, I have presented the material to diverse audiences in classrooms, seminar rooms, conference halls, and at the dinner table. I have benefited from the comments (and endurance!) of my colleagues in the Government Department and the John E. Andrus Center for Public Affairs at Wesleyan University, my students at Wesleyan, and fellow panelists and audience members at APSA, NEPSA, and MWPSA conferences. I also benefited from the comments of Ellis Hawley and Peri Arnold, readers for Penn State Press and, more important, individuals that have forever changed the ways in which the larger world understands much of the material addressed in this volume.

As always, I reserve the greatest thanks for my wife, Patricia, and my sons, Benjamin and Jonathan. On a daily basis they provide a foundation upon which all else rests. This book, as so much else, is dedicated to Patricia.

1

Crisis, Continuity, and Political Change

When dividing U.S. history into discrete eras, the Great Depression is often presented, along with the Civil War, as one of those distinctive episodes that permanently changed the nation's developmental trajectory. For many decades, accounts of American political development assumed that the modern American welfare state was born in the New Deal, a child of the Great Depression. The story moved along well-worn lines: Following the bleak days of the Hoover administration, Franklin D. Roosevelt ascended to the presidency to deliver the nation. The shopworn system of the 1920s was replaced wholesale with a new assemblage of innovative policies and agencies designed to reform the economy and discipline capitalism in the name of the "common man." The New Deal state marked the triumph of liberal reform and the realization of the promise of progressivism. Its key innovations provided a firm footing for postwar economic growth and social reform. Many concluded that America's emergence as the central political-economic power in the decades following World War II would have been difficult without the prior creation of the New Deal state. The standard story of Roosevelt's triumphal re-creation of the American system was deficient in one key respect: its accuracy. It may have been a useful fiction. It provided a convenient tool of periodization and a means of interpreting our own history and the significance of

shifting political allegiances in the contemporary period. However, as a growing number of revisionist historians and students of American political development have observed, a careful examination of the historical record reveals
that much of New Deal was less than new. Certainly, the New Deal brought
important changes in patterns of state-society relations. However, there was
much continuity with events of the previous decades. Indeed, any survey of
the twentieth century for the event that changed the trajectory of American
political development should necessarily nominate World War I. The lessons
of war were widely disseminated during the New Era of the 1920s and 1930s.
The New Deal, in this account, must be seen neither in isolation nor as a
reaction to previous decades. Rather, it must be understood as part of the
ongoing evolution of the American state along a trajectory that had already
been put into place. To better appreciate the position of the New Deal in this
trajectory, we must first reflect on the role crisis plays in our understanding
of political change.

Crisis, Continuity, and the New Deal

As the research of recent years reveals, the crisis of the Great Depression
provides a rich opportunity for testing and refining competing theories of
politics and the state. This research suggests that during a crisis the state can
play a far more autonomous role than society-based theories of politics might
predict.[1] During the Great Depression public officials faced popular demands
for recovery and structural reform. Crisis incapacitated business, reducing its
political power, and effectively undermined the threat of a capital strike. Crisis
thus created the political space for policies that would have been impossible
but a few years earlier, when business influence was at its apex. Likewise, one
can explain how the declining business support for the National Recovery
Administration (NRA) after 1934 and the growing importance of labor in the
New Deal coalition created a second opportunity, this time for expanding
the legal recognition of labor rights, creating new institutions for managing

---

1. See Theda Skocpol, "Political Responses to Capitalist Crisis: Neo-Marxist Theories and the Case
of the New Deal," *Politics and Society* 10 (1981): 155–201; Theda Skocpol and Kenneth Finegold, "State
Capacity and Economic Intervention in the Early New Deal," *Political Science Quarterly* 97 (1982): 255–78;
and Kenneth Finegold and Theda Skocpol, "State, Party, and Industry: From Business Recovery to the
Wagner Act in America's New Deal," in *Statemaking and Social Movements: Essays in History and Theory,* ed.
Charles Bright and Susan Harding (Ann Arbor: University of Michigan Press, 1984).

industrial conflict, and introducing welfare initiatives. Crisis, the failure of the NRA, and the formation of the New Deal coalition can provide elements of an explanation of the period's boldest experiments.[2]

The argument presented here is quite different. Although crises create opportunities for change, they are not determinative. There is nothing inherent in a crisis that determines the precise features of the political-institutional response. More important, the drama of crisis may effectively obscure the continuity between the events of the 1930s and those of earlier decades. By focusing on continuity rather than crisis-response, one can identify and explore the connections between the New Deal and earlier episodes in American political development, thus placing this critical period in historical context. In the process, one can better appreciate the importance of the historical inheritance—that is, how existing policy tools, models of administration, and patterns of state-economy relations empowered and constrained policy makers. A greater appreciation for the power of the past can also provide some important insights into the difficulties faced by the welfare state that emerged out of the interwar period.

An Evolutionary Institutional Framework

The concern with continuity and the path-dependent nature of change force us to address broad questions of political-institutional evolution. At a most fundamental level, one can understand institutions as rule systems that translate individual and group actions into collective outcomes in more or less stable and predictable ways. Institutions structure the exercise of human agency by defining roles, relationships, rewards, and sanctions. During the last two decades political science, sociology, history, and economics have all demonstrated a resurgence of interest in institutions. Scholars working at the intersection of Marxist and Weberian perspectives profess to be involved in a "new" institutionalism, as do researchers working in public choice, the new economics or organization, and organizational sociology. The range of theoretical assumptions and methodologies precludes a decisive statement of what theoretical and methodological commitments unite the scholars other than a growing recognition that institutions execute a vital function in shaping individual and collective action. The differences among the sundry variants of institutionalism become somewhat apparent when we note that the schools

---

2. Fred Block, "The Ruling Class Does Not Rule: Notes on the Marxist Theory of the State," *Socialist Revolution* 33 (May 1977): 6–28, and Finegold and Skocpol, "State, Party, and Industry."

would respond rather differently to a few key questions, such as: What factors constrain the play of rationality and self-interest in decision making? To what extent do institutions structure the articulation of human agency? How do institutions shape the aggregation and expression of interests? To what extent are institutions mutable, and what are the forces driving institutional change? Under what conditions are institutions autonomous? To what extent are institutional changes driven by a logic of optimization? Do institutions tend toward equilibrium or remain in a state of disequilibrium?[3] These questions are suggestive, offered only to illustrate the kinds of issues over which strains of institutionalism would arrive at different interpretations.

Given the ambiguity associated with "institutionalism," it is useful to state clearly the assumptions that guide the following analysis. The institutional framework applied in this work draws heavily on the historical institutionalism prevalent in the cross-national studies of political development and the literature in institutional and evolutionary economics. As developed here, the essential elements of an evolutionary institutional framework can be stated as follows:

1. *Bounded Rationality and Information Scarcity.* Individual agents work under the limitations of bounded rationality and information scarcity. The exercise of rational choice is contingent on information. Whereas much work in the choice-theoretical tradition (i.e., "micro-institutionalism") assumes rationality and complete information (assumptions imported wholesale from economics), uncertainty and bounded rationality better describe the constraints operating at the individual level. Limits on rationality and information flows create a bias toward incrementalism and policy making through analogy, while pointing to the need for rather complicated organizational search processes engaged in response to genuinely new challenges. They also help us to understand why mistakes in policy making and institutional design are so common.[4]

2. *Institutional Constraints on Human Agency.* What is the appropriate balance between structure and agency? This question has been the source of much debate and contention in the social and behavioral sciences. At one extreme, one may view human agency as being nonexistent: structure more

3. See Paul J. DiMaggio and Walter W. Powell, introduction to *The New Institutionalism in Organizational Analysis*, ed. Walter W. Powell and Paul J. DiMaggio (Chicago: University of Chicago Press, 1991), 28.

4. See James G. March, "Bounded Rationality, Ambiguity, and the Engineering of Choice," *Bell Journal of Economics* 9 (1978): 587–608, and James G. March and Johan P. Olsen, "The Uncertainty of the Past: Organizational Learning Under Ambiguity," *European Journal of Political Research* 3 (1975): 147–71.

or less determines individual action. Individuals are "situated" in a given network of relationships—those of production, historical processes, and so forth—which shape their behavior in predictable ways. At the other extreme, some micro-institutionalists view all political action as reflecting rational utility maximization in a structural vacuum.[5] This analysis recognizes the ongoing tension and conflict between structure and agency as one of the factors that introduces so much uncertainty and slippage into our explanations of political institutional change. The expression of human agency is structured by institutionally generated rules that define roles, relationships, rewards, and sanctions. State institutions provide a particular configuration of administrative capacities, policy tools, stocks of bureaucratic expertise, and established patterns of state-society relations that both empower and constrain public officials.[6] Yet, institutions are not determinative. Individuals commonly act in defiance of institutional norms. Particular circumstances may lead them to work outside of established routines, thereby altering key features of the institutions themselves. We will return to this issue below.

Once we theoretically recognize institutions and the role they play in structuring human action, the highly stylized portrayal of individual decision making (i.e., as self-interested utility maximization) that has animated much of the literature in public choice no longer seems persuasive.[7] Once again, this is not to say that self-interest is not an important motivating force. Yet, we cannot extract its pursuit from the institutional environment within which individuals interact. Individuals and groups adapt to institutions. Institutions at least partially shape their preferences and the resources they must use in the political process, and meanwhile designate certain patterns of state-society relations as being appropriate. At the same time, individuals and groups strive to adjust institutions to better reflect their needs and interests. In the end—if one can ever identify an end—both structure and agency are reformed through this interaction over time. As Kurt Dopfer notes: "Circular causation is at the very base of an evolutionary approach. Human action is embedded

5. For a fine discussion of the agency-structure issue as it applies to social revolution, see Theda Skocpol, introduction to *Social Revolutions in the Modern World* (Cambridge: Cambridge University Press, 1994).

6. See Peter A. Hall, *Governing the Economy: The Politics of State Intervention in Britain and France* (New York: Oxford University Press, 1986), chap. 1, and Margaret Weir and Theda Skocpol, "State Structures and the Possibilities for 'Keynesian' Responses to the Great Depression in Sweden, Britain, and the United States," in *Bringing the State Back In,* ed. Peter B. Evans, Dietrich Rueschemeyer, and Theda Skocpol (Cambridge: Cambridge University Press, 1985).

7. See Jeff Worsham, Marc Allen Eisner, and Evan Ringquist, "Assessing the Assumptions: A Critical Analysis of the Positive Theory of Political Control," *Administration and Society* 28, no. 4 (1997): 419–40.

in an environment. It shapes the environment, and it is simultaneously and continuously shaped by it."[8]

3. *Institutional Rigidity.* Under normal conditions, the rapidity and extent of institutional adjustment will be limited by institutional tendencies toward inertia. Institutions are geared to reproduce themselves over time by virtue of the ways in which rule systems pattern the action and interaction of individuals and groups. Elites and key beneficiaries of public policies, moreover, have a stake in promoting and protecting institutional designs that will preserve their favored status. As Terry Moe has argued in his work on the politics of structural choice, victorious interest groups and elites will design institutional structures "in such a way that they have the capacity to survive and prosper in an uncertain political future."[9] They will seek to use institutional rigidity to their advantage and will create structures that are biased toward predefined ends, thereby insulating today's victories from the tomorrow's challenges. This may entail selecting biased decision rules, defining the parameters of a policy so as to displace certain issues from the decision-making arena, professionalizing with a particular set of policy intellectuals whose disciplinary norms may shape policy outputs in predictable ways, and strategically structuring group access to sites of policy making.

4. *Path Dependency.* Institutions function and evolve in historical time. Decisions made today shape the opportunity set available tomorrow. Existing administrative capacities, policy tools, stocks of bureaucratic expertise, and established patterns of state-society relations place limitations on alternatives open to officials at any given time. Given the constraints listed above and the path-dependent nature of institutional evolution, we must guard against Panglossian conceptions of institutional evolution. It is simply incorrect to assume that evolutionary processes proceed inexorably toward optimality, efficiency, rationality, democracy, or any other value one chooses.[10] Rather, we must understand existing institutions simply as those that flourished, with all

8. Kurt Dopfer, "The Phenomenon of Economic Change: Neoclassical vs. Schumpeterian Approaches," in *Evolutionary and Neo-Schumpeterian Approaches to Economics,* ed. Lars Magnusson (Boston: Kluwer, 1994), 148.

9. Terry M. Moe, "The Politics of Structural Choice: Toward a Theory of Public Bureaucracy" (paper prepared for delivery at the annual meeting of the American Political Science Association, Washington, D.C., September 1–4, 1988), 8. See also Terry M. Moe, "The Politics of Bureaucratic Structure," in *Can the Government Govern?* ed. John E. Chubb and Paul E. Peterson (Washington, D.C.: Brookings Institution, 1989).

10. See Geoffrey M. Hodgson, *Economics and Evolution: Bringing Life Back into Economics* (Ann Arbor: University of Michigan Press, 1993), 197–213, for a discussion of the limitations of Panglossian accounts of institutional evolution. Although Hodgson is primarily concerned with economic institutions, his insights are applicable to institutional evolution more broadly construed.

their flaws, within the given set of environmental constraints and particular mix of historical antecedents.

This is not to say that an analyst must suspend judgment over the merits of a given set of institutions. One can identify a set of essential state functions and then assess the performance of specific institutions by determining the extent to which they have fulfilled those functions effectively. At a broad level of analysis, we might follow R. Kent Weaver and Bert A. Rockman and examine a state's capacity to execute several basic functions (i.e., the capacity to manage political cleavages in an effort to maintain civil order; to regulate property rights in ways that promote economic growth; to fund the state by extracting resources from civil society; to provide representation for various interests in the policy process—those that are diffuse and poorly organized and those with a preponderance of organizational resources; and to manage international economic and security relations). We might also look to the capacity of state institutions to make and implement policies effectively. That is, we might assess the capacity to set policy priorities and target resources to reflect these priorities; to impose losses on powerful groups; to mobilize the intellectual, administrative, and financial resources needed for effective implementation; to coordinate policy objectives so as to minimize conflict; and to engage search processes and innovate when established policies fail.[11]

5. *Discontinuous Evolution.* Actors seek to address new challenges within existing institutional rule systems. They try to deal with uncertainty and ambiguity "by trying to clarify the rules, make distinctions, determine what the situation is and what definition 'fits.' "[12] When new situations arise, officials will often respond by drawing analogies to problems for which policies and institutions have already been designed. Changes are usually incremental; officials seek to adapt existing institutional capacities to new circumstances. Although gradualism is the norm, periods of relative stability are punctuated by rapid, substantial, institutional changes that recast basic rules, roles, policy tools, and patterns of state-society relations. As a generalization, discontinuous evolution is a response to intense exogenous shocks such as wars, depressions, significant and rapid social changes, and natural disasters. In the United

11. This listing draws on R. Kent Weaver and Bert A. Rockman, "Assessing the Effects of Institutions," in *Do Institutions Matter? Government Capabilities in the United States and Abroad,* ed. R. Kent Weaver and Bert A. Rockman (Washington, D.C.: Brookings Institution, 1993), 6, and Richard Franklin Bensel, *Yankee Leviathan: The Origins of Central State Authority in America, 1859–1877* (Cambridge: Cambridge University Press, 1990), 114.

12. James G. March and Johan P. Olsen, *Rediscovering Institutions: The Organizational Basis of Politics* (New York: Free Press, 1989), 161.

States, notable episodes of discontinuous change have occurred in response to the Civil War, the two world wars, and the Great Depression.[13] The key point is this: the adjustment of institutions to environmental change is not necessarily smooth or efficient. The process tends to lag due to the inertial forces associated with existing institutions, the constraints of information scarcity and bounded rationality, and the tendency for actors to search existing routines in response to new problems. Nevertheless, there are periods of rapid change. Innovations come, as Joseph Schumpeter once noted, in jerks and swarms.[14]

6. *Regimes*. The term "regime" has been used widely in the literature on international relations to describe "a set of principles, norms, rules, and procedures around which actors' expectations converge." They are important because they "constrain and regularize the behavior of participants, affect which issues among protagonists move on and off agendas, determine which activities are legitimized or condemned, and influence whether, when, and how conflicts are resolved."[15] More recently, analysts of domestic policy have applied the regime concept to describe the sets of policies, administrative arrangements, and patterns of state-economy relations that structure politics in a given period.[16] A regime framework is useful, in part, because it forces one to pay attention to continuity across policy areas and over time. As employed in this book, a regime constitutes constellations of policies and institutions in a given period that share a set of goals, values, models of administration, and patterns of state-society relations. This continuity across issue areas reflects distinct intellectual, institutional, and contextual factors that transcend the features of a single policy problem or the difficulties encountered in a given industry. The model of regime change is presented schematically in Figure 1.

13. Several works focus on the political-institutional equivalents of paradigm shifts emerging out of periods of crisis or rapid and significant structural change. See, for example, Martin Shefter, "Party, Bureaucracy, and Political Change in the United States," in *Political Parties: Development and Decay*, ed. Louis Maisel and Joseph Cooper (Beverly Hills, Calif.: Sage, 1978); Walter Dean Burnham, *Critical Elections and the Mainsprings of American Politics* (New York: W. W. Norton, 1970); Robert Higgs, *Crisis and Leviathan: Critical Episodes in the Growth of American Government* (New York: Oxford University Press, 1987); and Marc Allen Eisner, *Regulatory Politics in Transition* (Baltimore: Johns Hopkins University Press, 1993).

14. Joseph A. Schumpeter, *The Theory of Economic Development* (New York: Oxford University Press, 1961), 79.

15. Donald J. Puchala and Raymond F. Hopkins, "International Regimes: Lessons from Inductive Analysis," in *International Regimes*, ed. Stephen D. Krasner (Ithaca, N.Y.: Cornell University Press, 1983), 61–62.

16. For recent works applying different regime frameworks in domestic politics, see Eisner, *Regulatory Politics in Transition;* Robert P. Stoker, *Reluctant Partners: Implementing Federal Policy* (Pittsburgh: University of Pittsburgh Press, 1991); and Richard A. Harris and Sidney M. Milkis, *The Politics of Regulatory Change: A Tale of Two Agencies* (New York: Oxford University Press, 1989).

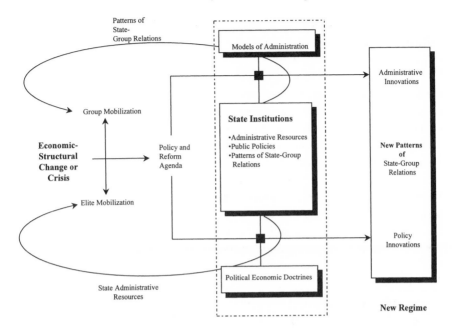

Fig. 1   Regime Change

Economic-structural changes or crises commonly stimulate enormous un-certainty concerning the status of property rights, the distribution of wealth and economic power, and existing relationships between key groups and the state. This uncertainly often stimulates mobilization, as groups demand a redefinition of the state's role or alterations of existing patterns of state-society relations. Either officials may be forced to respond to the mobilization, or they may react to the changes in question in the first instance, seeking to secure the support of various interests for the policy alternatives they embrace. When facing a crisis and the demands it stimulates, public officials may draw on new political-economic and administrative models that suggest a new role for the state and the various means by which expertise and organized interests can be integrated into the policy process. They may draw on recent experi-ences when innovations were necessary (e.g., war, depression) in search of analogies that will assist in formulating a response and building coalitions. Of course, the availability of potential innovations will be conditioned to some extent by the degree to which they can be reconciled with the path-dependent process of institutional development. That is, discretion is constrained by the stock of experience with similar problems, earlier investment and staffing decisions within appropriate agencies, the existing organization of private interests, and patterns of state-group relations, all of which predate the current situation. These very factors may structure the expectations that private interests carry into the policy arena.

When officials face challenges that cannot be readily addressed through incremental adjustments, the stage is set for the kind of rapid, substantial changes in policies and institutions described above as discontinuous. Yet, even here there may be greater continuity than one suspects. First, the raw materials used to construct a new regime—the policies, administrative models, and patterns of state-economy relations—commonly exist already in one form or another. They may be coupled in new ways, reconfigured to meet new challenges or address fundamentally different problems. Second, to the extent that a given crisis demands a response that cuts across policy areas, one may discover significant similarities in the resulting goals, administrative models, and patterns of state-group relations.

7. *Coevolutionary Tendencies*. Given the dense network of linkages connecting public institutions and private-sector actors (e.g., corporations, associations, and unions), and private actors one to another, coevolution is common. Environmental uncertainty often produces organizational isomorphism. That is, organizations commonly search their domain to identify the organizational and strategic responses adopted by other organizations, only to adopt them as their own.[17] Public policies define basic property rights and place limitations on the organization, interaction, and activities of economic institutions. The evolution of private-sector organizations may force accommodative changes in public institutions by stimulating group demands for new public policies or initiating elite efforts to rationalize private- and public-sector activities. At the same time, changes in public institutions and policies may force private-sector institutions to adapt to disturbances in the political-legal environment. Over time, we should expect to see greater coevolutionary tendencies as government regulation of economic activity has addressed more aspects of private-sector activity and the corporate economy has become more dense in interorganizational linkages. There is little evidence that coevolution is symmetrical or that the state has been at the forefront of change. Indeed, the literature on American political-economic development suggests that public institutions tend to lag behind economic institutions, changing reactively and under a variety of constraints.[18]

17. See Paul J. DiMaggio and Walter W. Powell, "The Iron Cage Revisited: Institutional Isomorphism and Collective Rationality in Organizational Fields," *American Sociological Review* 48 (1983): 147–60.
18. See, for example, David Vogel, "Why Businessmen Distrust Their State: The Political Consciousness of American Corporate Executives," *British Journal of Political Science* 8, no. 1 (1978): 45–78.

8. *Disequilibrium.* As a generalization, society-based accounts of politics assume an equilibrium. Public policies are created to reflect with minimal distortion the demands of mobilized or class interests. Similarly, public-choice variants of institutionalism import assumptions of equilibrium from economics to characterize public institutions as oscillating around a point at which political preferences and policies intersect. Although individuals and groups seek to adjust institutions to better reflect their interests and aspirations or create new capacities to address pressing problems, bounded rationality, information scarcity, path dependency, the existence of multiple and potentially irreconcilable demands, and institutional inertia combine to prevent a stable equilibrium from arising. Even when a new regime is introduced, there is a tendency for innovations to lag behind demands, thereby creating ongoing problems for policy makers and groups. In sum, a state of dynamic disequilibrium characterized by tensions and conflicts between the state and private institutions should be understood as the norm rather than as a mere transitional stage to some lasting equilibrium.

When the elements above are brought together, what emerges is a picture of state institutions that are in constant flux, evolving in response to changes in their environment and simultaneously altering this environment. The evolutionary process is not some smooth transition to an ideal final state. Rather, it is a jagged process in which officials draw on a limited array of administrative capacities, policy tools, sources of expertise, and patterns of state–interest-group relations to address problems that may be only dimly understood. The result need not be chaotic. Regimes provide a certain continuity across policy areas and over time. Outside of periods of crisis, institutions tend to adjust to new circumstances in gradual ways, making incremental changes to existing roles and routines.

The New Deal and the Emergence of the Associational Regime

How does an evolutionary institutional perspective allow us better to explore the events of the period in question? Let us return briefly to the New Deal. The New Deal's policies were enacted in response to the structural crisis of the Great Depression. Key economic regulatory initiatives promoted industrial or sectoral stability and adopted an administrative model that integrated interests into the policy process through a system of government-supervised self-regulation. It was believed that such a system could provide a means of managing production, pricing, and employment practices without the conflict and resource demands that would be necessary under more direct forms of planning. Elsewhere, I have referred to the resulting system as the "Associational Regime," reflecting the role of economic associations in the new system and the dissemination of associational doctrines in the wake of the World War I experience.[19] Although we commonly attribute the basic elements of the modern American state to the New Deal, it is in understanding the origins of these innovations—the factors that shaped the response to the crisis of the depression—that the question of historical continuity becomes essential. As Peri Arnold correctly noted some twenty-five years ago: "[T]here lies a grand continuity between the assumptions which underlay policymaking in the 1920s and those which provide the basis for policymaking today. It is this continuity which [the] generally accepted view concerning Hoover and the Great Depression forces us to overlook."[20]

What I wish to argue in the following chapters is not simply that the Roosevelt administration borrowed and benefited from Hoover's legacy. Indeed, such a claim would be trivial. It is true of all presidential administrations vis-à-vis their predecessors. Rather, the Roosevelt administration constructed a recovery program and the welfare state from policies, agencies, and patterns of state-economy relations that originated in World War I mobilization and evolved throughout the 1920s. In the end, the objective is not simply to reexamine the position of the New Deal in the history of the twentieth century but to explore both the way in which the state evolved in this critical period and the unique model of state building adopted in the United States as a response to the demands of war mobilization—something I refer to as *compensatory state building*. According to this model, state capacity was expanded by appending the capacities of private-sector associations on to the state. Whereas in other countries nationalization might have appeared more expeditious, the option was unavailable in the United States due to a combination of historical, institutional, ideological, and political factors. Most important, in this connection, was the severe disjunction between state and corporate development.

The decades preceding the war had witnessed an economic transformation that has been described variously as a managerial revolution and a "corporate reconstruction of American capitalism."[21] Previously, the economic structure

---

19. See Eisner, *Regulatory Politics in Transition,* chaps. 4–5. See also Marc Allen Eisner, "Discovering Patterns in Regulatory History: Continuity, Change, and Regulatory Regimes," *Journal of Policy History* 6, no. 2 (1994): 157–87.

20. Peri Ethan Arnold, "Herbert Hoover and the Continuity of American Public Policy," *Public Policy* 20, no. 4 (1972): 540.

21. See Alfred D. Chandler Jr., *The Visible Hand: The Managerial Revolution in American Business*

was relatively decentralized, and, with a few notable exceptions, corporations were controlled by entrepreneurs or their families. Waves of horizontal and vertical integration and the growing capitalization requirements led increasingly to a separation of ownership and control and the development of more sophisticated managerial systems for making decisions concerning resource allocations, long-term investments, facility siting, technological engineering, the level and mix of output, pricing, domestic and international marketing, wages, and employment practices. The state, in contrast, was woefully underdeveloped. Despite the advances of the Progressive Era, national policy makers had virtually no detailed data on the size and capacities of the nation's industrial plant. The War Department's general staff was incapable of directing a war of any magnitude. Given the vast resources of the largest corporations, the lack of administrative resources within the state, and the severe problems of information scarcity, compensatory state building was largely the product of necessity.

Under these conditions, the appeal of compensatory state building should be clear. It entailed securing voluntary cooperation through the delegation of authority and the provision of benefits. It allowed policy makers access to administrative resources that had never been developed within the confines of the state. Compensatory state building was expedient given the demands of war and the disjunction between private- and public-sector development. This compensatory state building came at a high political and administrative cost. These associations, integral to the functioning of the state, would remain willing participants only as long as participation provided distinct material benefits. State capacity became dependent on the gains of established economic actors, severely compromising state authority and autonomy. It was in the dissemination of this model in the 1920s and 1930s, however, that the real difficulties emerged. In the end, the limits of the modern state as it evolved out of the New Deal could be traced, in large part, to the difficulties inherent in this model of state building.

The mobilization effort embodied a distinctive model of the state, which in turn shaped New Deal state building. First articulated by New Nationalist Progressivism, the model legitimized a greater role for the state in the economy and a quasi-corporatist relationship with key economic interests. The rather dramatic departure from established models of state-economy relations was deemed necessary given the evolution of the large-scale corporate econ-

---

(Cambridge: Harvard University Press, 1977), and Martin J. Sklar, *The Corporate Reconstruction of American Capitalism, 1890–1916* (Cambridge: Cambridge University Press, 1988).

omy. This model lay explicitly or implicitly at the base of major war agencies such as the War Industries Board (WIB). It proved attractive when America entered the war, because it provided a convenient means of compensating for limited state capacities. This model became the core of the Associational Regime. To be certain, it was most evident in the systems created by the National Industrial Recovery Act and the Agricultural Adjustment Act, although it was subsequently extended through the new policies of the Department of Agriculture and the Interstate Commerce Commission, and in the creation of agencies such as the National Labor Relations Board, the Federal Communications Commission, the Civil Aeronautics Board, and the Securities and Exchange Commission. In each case, power was delegated to organized economic interests, which thereupon acted as quasi-public entities, exercising authority to protect or expand their members' claim on national income and maintain industrial stability.

The New Deal's Associational Regime was partially successful in stabilizing the economy, creating new tools for managing production and pricing, thus limiting the competition that might have hastened deflation. It was also politically expedient. Potential opponents were converted into clientele groups dependent in one form or another on state largess. But despite the partial successes of the New Deal initiatives, the new welfare state was plagued by some serious problems. First, the basic tenets of institutional design adopted by New Deal state builders were seriously flawed. The decentralization of power and expertise to the various economic associations at the periphery of the agencies limited the opportunities to direct policy and implementation. Officials could not control policy, and as a result, public policies commonly enriched the most powerful interests and impeded change. With decision making decentralized to the fringes of the state, the policies often worked toward ends that were difficult to reconcile. The problems of overdelegation, dearth of political control, use of policies to aggrandize powerful interests, and lack of coordination would become salient in the postwar period, leading many on the Left to question the progressive legacy of the New Deal and actors of all political stripes to promote deregulation and regulatory reform.[22]

By extension, second, it is commonly acknowledged that the New Deal failed to develop a capacity for planning. This failure has been attributed to the underdevelopment of the American state, the lack of prior experience

---

22. See Theodore Low, *The End of Liberalism* (New York: W. W. Norton, 1979), for the clearest expression of this argument.

with peacetime planning, the existence of multiple and competing visions of
the state within the New Deal, and the declining influence of the planners of
the first New Deal relative to the Wilsonian Progressives who became far
more powerful during the second New Deal.[23] While all these factors undoubtedly played some role, far more important was the tension between the
demands of planning and the demands of compensatory state building. The
success of so many New Deal initiatives depended on the participation of
economic associations, which was contingent, in turn, on the expectation that
the New Deal would provide some tangible economic benefits while not requiring the wholesale surrender of group autonomy. Planning is all but impossible when authority is delegated to private interests whose participation
depends on profitability and when power and expertise are decentralized to
the point where the public and private overlap.[24] To the extent that successful
planning requires the state to impose costs on the most powerful actors, the
adopted model was destined to be problematic.

To claim that the patchwork of the New Deal was made of New Era cloth
is not to assert that the New Deal lacked innovation. It is not to say that
programs did not take on a new significance once combined. Such claims
would be difficult to sustain given the long-term impact of the New Deal in
American politics. However, New Deal state builders recognized the expediency of claiming expansive powers under conditions of crisis and meeting the
emergency situation with programs and models that had established constituencies. Even where this recognition was not explicit, the earlier experiences of
World War I mobilization and the 1920s—experiences shared by the New
Dealers themselves—shaped the dominant understanding of state-economy
relations and conditioned the response to the depression. Thus, returning to
Arnold, we might agree that "both in business and agricultural policy the
New Deal acted to place the tools of coercive power in the hands of private
sector organizations. The impetus was touchingly Hooverian."[25] Thus conceived, the New Deal legacy was as much one of consolidation and rationalization as it was one of revolutionary change.

23. See Ellis W. Hawley, *The New Deal and the Problem of Monopoly* (Princeton, N.J.: Princeton Univer-
sity Press, 1966), and Alan Brinkley, "The New Deal and the Idea of the State," in *The Rise and Fall of the
New Deal Order, 1930–1980,* ed. Steve Fraser and Gary Gerstle (Princeton, N.J.: Princeton University
Press, 1989).

24. Compare the arguments presented by Donald R. Brand, *Corporatism and the Rule of Law: A Study
of the National Recovery Administration* (Ithaca, N.Y.: Cornell University Press, 1988), and Hawley, *The New
Deal and the Problem of Monopoly.*

25. Arnold, "Herbert Hoover and the Continuity of American Public Policy," 541.

Overview

The argument presented briefly above will be developed throughout the following chapters. Part I, "Crisis and the Construction of the Modern State," introduces the role of war in political development (Chapter 2) and provides an overview of the agencies created to manage the mobilization process (Chapter 3). The emergency measures embodied a distinctive model of the state and of state-economy relations that would become quite influential in subsequent decades as it was applied to a host of policy problems. Part II of the book, "Demobilization and the Dissemination of a Model," explores the dissemination of the wartime model in business regulation (Chapter 4), labor relations (Chapter 5), agricultural policy (Chapter 6), and macroeconomic management (Chapter 7). Two things are remarkable when one examines these rather different issue areas: First, it is striking to note the magnitude of change in the 1920s—a point recognized in much of the newer scholarship on the New Era.[26] Second, the impact of the war in each case is rather conspicuous. New models of government organization, new patterns of state-economy relations, new understandings of policy problems, and new expectations concerning state responsibilities combined to force change.

Part III of the book, "Peacetime Mobilization and the Modern State," explores the way in which the model of state building developed in the war was embraced once again as the nation faced a new crisis in the Great Depression. Chapter 8 examines the changes in policy during the Hoover administration. The associationalist system that Hoover had sought to create during the 1920s collapsed under the pressures of the Great Depression, something that could have been quite predictable given the inherent weaknesses of compensatory state building. Chapter 9 turns to the Roosevelt presidency to ask whether the New Deal simply constituted a new deal for an old model—the model developed in World War I. When the New Deal is seen and understood in broader historical context, much of what formerly appeared novel now looks to be but another expression of the wartime model, with problems that were strikingly similar to those which characterized the wartime agencies. The decision to import this model into the new regime essentially constituted a decision to import its structural and political weaknesses as well. The limits this places on the modern state are addressed in the concluding chapter of this book.

26. See, for example, Ellis W. Hawley, "Three Facets of Hooverian Associationalism: Lumber, Aviation, and the Movies, 1921–1930," in *Regulation in Perspective: Historical Essays,* ed. Thomas K. McCraw (Cambridge: Harvard University Press, 1981).

PART I

Crisis and the Construction of the Modern State

Although a given nation may face many obstacles, war poses the most formidable of threats. The failure to prevail can result in the enervation or outright elimination of the state. Even when successful, a nation may have to endure long-term social dislocations and the loss of great human and financial resources. In generic terms, one can identify the challenges that are inherent in any effort to mobilize a society and economy for war. Yet, the manner in which and success with which the challenges are surmounted will vary from state to state and over time. Given the magnitude of the tasks and stakes involved, one should not be surprised that war has a potentially significant impact on a nation's political and institutional development. The administrative models, policy tools, and patterns of state-society relations adopted under conditions of emergency may outlive the crisis, thereby permanently altering the trajectory of political development and giving rise to periods of discontinuous evolution. Similarly, the experience of war can shape popular expectations concerning the role of the state in society. The legacy of war will depend, quite obviously, on the magnitude and ultimate resolution of the conflict. One would not expect the impact of World War II for Germany and the United States to be comparable; one would not expect either of these cases to have the same long-term implications as any of the innumerable minor conflicts that have erupted over human history. Similarly, the legacy of war will depend on the level of state and economic development within a given nation. Development is, after all, path dependent. Even if the trajectory can be altered by crises, there are limits to the plasticity of institutions, policy tools, and patterns of society-state relations.

This study focuses on the impact of the World War I mobilization experience in the United States during the interwar period. To fully discern the legacy of the war, it is essential to preface discussion with an examination of American political development in the decades preceding the conflict. It is also vital to consider the factors that shaped this developmental process and contributed to the deficiency of administrative capacities of the American state, particularly in comparison to its private-sector counterparts. This is the task of Chapter 2. This brief examination of American political development will reveal why, when faced with the immediate demands of war, officials pursued a strategy of *compensatory state building*. That is, it will help explain why the most expeditious means of compensating for the deficit of administrative capacities entailed appending to the state those of more developed private-sector associations. This was accomplished through the creation of decentralized administrative bodies that delegated substantial authority to private associations, thereby vesting them with quasi-public functions. As Chapter 3 reveals, this model was at the core of World War I mobilization in the United States. While it carried a number of obvious benefits, it also imposed considerable costs and biases into the policy process. While these costs were easily justified under conditions of national emergency, they would continue to find expression to the extent that the basic model was apotheosized and disseminated in the wake of the war.

2

War Making, State Making, and American Political Development

> The subordination of the political point of view to the military would be unreasonable, for policy has created the war; policy is the intelligent faculty, war only the instrument, and not the reverse. The subordination of the military point of view to the political is, therefore, the only thing that is possible. —Carl von Clausewitz, 1831

> The mobilization of intelligence and science cannot, in the nature of things, be ordered from above in this country. The necessary organization does not exist, and if it were to be hastily created, it would provoke such antagonism as to defeat its own ends. —*The Nation,* May 10, 1917

The basic argument of this book is relatively straightforward: One cannot understand the New Deal's place in American political history and the strengths and weaknesses of the policy regime at the heart of the modern state without analyzing the events of World War I and the subsequent dissemination of wartime innovations throughout the American political system during the 1920s. They shaped popular and elite expectations, the forms and levels of group organization, and the kinds of administrative and policy tools that were in place at the time of the depression. They shaped the opportunity set from which the Roosevelt administration was compelled to draw. Likewise, if one wants to understand the limits of the modern American state, one must examine the difficulties and biases inherent in the system of wartime management and the ways in which the lessons of war were applied following the cessation of hostilities. On the eve of the Great Depression, the U.S. national government bore very little resemblance to that which existed a generation earlier. While the state would expand significantly over the next decade as part of the New Deal, much of this growth would occur along familiar lines, following a well-established model, a model embraced during World War I under conditions of emergency.

An account of this model's formation, dissemination, and revival will occupy much of this book. But before embarking on this account, we must address three important subjects. First, we must reflect on the state of the state before the Great War. During the nineteenth century, the national government was remarkably underdeveloped for a host of reasons that we shall explore briefly. This underdevelopment is an important part of the story. It created serious impediments to mobilization that had to be negotiated as the nation adjusted to war demands. To explore this point fully, we must pause to consider the impact of war on political development. This is the second goal of the chapter. As many political analysts and historians document, war is one of the most important events in the formation and evolution of the nation state. Some would go as far as to claim that the state is largely a by-product of war. We will consider these arguments and the demands of war with some care. Third and finally, we will examine the impact of war on the development of the American state. Given the underdevelopment of the state, policy makers embraced a uniquely American approach to state development—what I referred to earlier as compensatory state building. We will explore this model of state building and its implications for the development of governmental capacities.

The Longevity of the Lockean State

A nineteenth-century observer of American politics at all familiar with European states would have few difficulties identifying the exceptional features of the U.S. government. On the one hand, the United States was a dynamic nation with an unparalleled level of participation and mobilization. It seemed to be a society in flux, with high levels of group membership and political activity. As James Willard Hurst observed: "[T]he nineteenth-century United States valued change more than stability and valued stability most often where it helped create a framework for change."[1] At the same time, governmental institutions were undeveloped, particularly when compared with their European counterparts. The bureaucracy was unprofessionalized. The executive had few tools of management and indeterminate constitutional authority to exercise anything resembling a leadership role. For most of the nineteenth century, Congress was an assembly of citizen legislators lacking the internal

1. James Willard Hurst, *Law and the Conditions of Freedom in the Nineteenth-Century United States* (Madison: University of Wisconsin Press, 1956), 24.

differentiation, specialization, and professionalization that one might expect of a complex organization.[2] One of the century's most astute students of politics, Alexis de Tocqueville, concluded that "the people often manage affairs very badly."[3] Let us consider briefly his commentary on the American polity and state.

Tocqueville was struck by the equality within American society and the extent to which individuals turned to the political association, a "powerful instrument of action [that] has been applied to more varied aims in America than anywhere else in the world."[4] Here there was a society in motion, a society directed toward political debate and commercial progress and relatively free from the class prejudices and rigid divisions that had long characterized so many European societies. Tocqueville's description is most revealing: "[T]he political activity prevailing in the United States is something one could never understand unless one had seen it. No sooner do you set foot on American soil than you find yourself in a sort of tumult; a confused clamor rises on every side, and a thousand voices are heard at once, each expressing some social requirements. All around you everything is on the move." For the common American, politics was "the only pleasure he knows."[5]

In the federal system, authority was fragmented along vertical dimensions. That is, a good deal of authority was vested in the state and local governments compared with the national government, which was, by design, quite limited. As Tocqueville noted: "[T]he central government is only occupied by a small number of matters." For the most part, these matters have "no more than a questionable influence over individual happiness," while the activities of the states "visibly influence the well-being of the inhabitants." In other words, while "the union secures the independence and greatness of the nation . . . the state preserves liberty, regulates rights, guarantees property, and makes the life and whole future of each citizen safe."[6] With few demands for a greater national presence and, in Tocqueville's opinion, little desire on the part of national officials to expand their responsibilities, the national government's presence was minimal.

2. See, for example, Michael Nelson, "A Short, Ironic History of American National Bureaucracy," *Journal of Politics* 44 (August 1982): 747–78, and Nelson Polsby, "The Institutionalization of the U.S. House of Representatives," *American Political Science Review*, March 1968, 144–68.

3. Alexis de Tocqueville, *Democracy in America*, trans. George Lawrence, ed. J. P. Mayer (New York: Harper & Row, 1969), 243.

4. Ibid., 189.

5. Ibid., 242, 243.

6. Ibid., 262, 366.

In Tocqueville's judgment, the U.S. national government was characterized by a manifest lack of talents: "[G]ood qualities were common among the
governed but rare among the rulers. . . . the most outstanding Americans
are seldom summoned to public office." Indeed, they commonly went into
commerce, which "attracts the attention of the public and fills the imagination of the crowd."[7] He clearly recognized the differences between the more
developed and professionalized bureaucracies of Europe and administration
in the United States, which was "oral and traditional." Tocqueville noted:
"Administrative instability has begun to become a habit . . . by now everyone
has developed a taste for it. Nobody bothers about what was done before his
time. No method is adopted; no archives are formed; no documents are
brought together, even when it would be easy to do so." This too was deemed
to be the product of a society in motion and, more important, reflective of
the overwhelming power of democracy: "American society seems to live from
day to day, like an army in active service. . . . democracy, pressed to its
ultimate limits, harms the progress of the art of government. In this respect,
it is better adapted to a people whose administrative education is already
finished than to a nation which is a novice in the experience of public affairs."[8]

Stephen Skowronek's characterization of the nineteenth-century American
state reinforces Tocqueville's basic observations: "Together, courts and parties
formed the bulwark of the early American state. Their routines lent opera-
tional integrity and internal order to government, allowing it to service a
sprawling and pluralistic nation. . . . At the same time, however, courts and
parties imparted an evanescent or elusive quality to the early American state
that, at least until the 1870s, reinforced the characteristic sense of state-
lessness in early American political culture."[9] Indeed, the national government—Skowronek's state of courts and parties—remained remarkably underdeveloped as an administrative entity despite the fact that the nation
had grown to cover a continent and the national state had expanded its authority significantly during the Civil War and Reconstruction. One indicator
of the state's limited development as an administrative entity—albeit, an
imperfect one—is the distribution of public-sector employees. In 1901, the
federal government had 239,476 civilian employees. Of this number,
136,192, or 58.12 percent, worked in the post office, while another 44,524,
or 18.6 percent, worked in the War and Navy Departments. Setting aside the

7. Ibid., 197, 553.
8. Ibid., 207–8.
9. Stephen Skowronek, *Building a New American State: The Expansion of National Administrative Capacities, 1877–1920* (Cambridge: Cambridge University Press, 1982), 29.

employees from the legislative (5,690) and judicial branches (2,730), one can conclude that a mere 50,340, or 21 percent, of the federal government employees constituted potential administrators.[10] These figures differ somewhat from earlier decades. The post office, for example, accounted for a high of 82.5 percent of civilian employment in 1861, compared with a low of 56.4 percent in 1881. Despite this variation, however, for the bulk of the nineteenth century, the federal government remained something less than a functioning administrative entity and something more than a support system for a post office.

As Chapter 4 shows in some detail, the level of development in the private sector was not at all comparable to that in the state. Over the half century preceding U.S. entry into World War I, something of a revolution in economic organization had occurred in the United States. The multiunit business enterprise emerged initially in the railroads and telegraphs, only to be disseminated into the modern manufacturing industries. The new speed of production made available through mass-production technologies could be combined with regional and national markets. Multiunit corporations integrated mass production and mass marketing. They created their own networks of commodity dealers, wholesalers, and retailers—something that would have been impossible without powerful management tools and access to data. As Alfred Chandler has shown in *The Visible Hand,* the new multiunit firm developed a managerial hierarchy that allowed for rapid expansion, profitability, and productivity-enhancing innovations.[11] By 1917, a distinct managerial class had emerged within the modern corporations, and the separation of ownership and control was almost complete.

The development of large corporate bureaucracies preceded comparable developments in their public-sector counterparts.[12] As William Becker explains:

> In comparative terms of the development of managerial structures, the large-scale corporation was more highly developed bureaucratically than the executive departments of the federal government. The specialization, the division of labor, and the economic rationality of

10. Calculations based on *Statistical History of the United States, Colonial Times to Present,* series Y241–250.

11. Alfred D. Chandler Jr., *The Visible Hand: The Managerial Revolution in American Business* (Cambridge: Harvard University Press, 1977), 484–500.

12. David Vogel, "Why Businessmen Distrust Their State: The Political Consciousness of American Corporate Executives," *British Journal of Political Science* 8 (1984): 45–78.

the largest corporations made them fundamentally more advanced managerially than the government bureaucracies that came into contact with the larger firms in the development of foreign trade. By World War I, major American corporations employed many thousands of employees worldwide. The levels of bureaucratic control were greater and the scale of operations more complex than anything undertaken by the U.S. government at the time. Then, too, most of the major corporations had a longer history as major bureaucratic institutions than the federal bureaucracies.[13]

Managerial capitalism had emerged to become dominant. Bureaucratic professionalization and administrative development lagged in the public sector, whereas the corporate economy stood at the forefront as a world leader. This disjunction between public- and private-sector development would have significant implications with the onset of war.

History, Design, and Ideology

How can one best explain the underdevelopment of the American state? Unfortunately, the underdevelopment of the American state—like so many historical phenomena—is overdetermined. There are several competing explanations, each of which undoubtedly provides part of the answer. To simplify, one can frame explanations in terms of historical inheritance, institutional design, and ideology. Given the nature of the question, it is difficult to arrive at a clear weighing of these competing explanations. Let us consider each in brief, recognizing at the outset that the explanations are not mutually exclusive.

First, one may understand the underdevelopment of the American state as being a product of historical inheritance. In *Political Order in Changing Societies,* Samuel Huntington made a powerful argument concerning the impact of the colonial experience in the United States. According to Huntington's reading of United States history, the nation inherited a Tudor polity based on sixteenth-century assumptions, thus avoiding the rationalization of authority, the functional specialization, and the bureaucratic centralization that would occur across Europe. "Political modernization in America," Huntington writes, "has thus been strangely attenuated and incomplete. In insti-

---

13. William H. Becker, *The Dynamics of Business-Government Relations: Industry and Exports, 1893–1921* (Chicago: University of Chicago Press, 1982), 183.

tutional terms, the American polity has never been underdeveloped, but it has also never been wholly modern."[14] Certainly, the colonial inheritance did not preclude institutional development along the lines witnessed in Europe. It is here, however, that the challenges—or lack thereof—become essential. In Huntington's words:

> In continental Europe, as in most contemporary modernizing coun-
> tries, rationalized authority and centralized power were necessary not
> only for unity but also for progress. The opposition to modernization
> came from traditional interests: religious, aristocratic, regional, and
> local. The centralization of power was necessary to smash the old
> order, break down the privileges and restraints of feudalism, and free
> the way for the rise of new social groups and the development of new
> economic activities. . . . In America, on the other hand, the absence
> of feudal social institutions made the centralization of power unneces-
> sary. Since there was no aristocracy to dislodge, there was no need to
> call into existence a governmental power capable of dislodging it.

Thus, a first answer to the question of America's institutional development is steeped in historical experiences. The colonial legacy was one in which a certain model of public authority was combined with the lack of an aristocracy that needed to be defeated through the application of a new coercive capacity: "[I]n the United States, where the resistance was minimal, so also was the centralization."[15] In the wonderful words of Louis Hartz: "We are confronted, as it were, with a kind of inverted Trotskyite law of combined development, America skipping the feudal stage of history as Russia presumably skipped the liberal stage."[16]

On the related issue of institutional design, one may observe that the institutional fragmentation that characterized the American state in the nineteenth century (and beyond) was not merely the outgrowth of some undirected evolutionary process. Rather, it was a product of calculated constitutional design. The disagreeable experience of colonial rule when synthesized with prevailing treatises in the new science of politics provided the justification for a highly decentralized system in which power was assigned to

14. Samuel P. Huntington, *Political Order in Changing Societies* (New Haven, Conn.: Yale University Press, 1968), 98.

15. Ibid., 126.

16. Louis Hartz, *The Liberal Tradition in America: An Interpretation of American Political Thought Since the Revolution* (New York: Harcourt Brace Jovanovich, 1955), 3.

formally separate institutions. The salient features of the new system were, in the words of Alexander Hamilton, "the regular distribution of power into distinct departments; the introduction of legislative balances and checks; the institution of courts composed of judges holding their offices during good behavior; the representation of the people in the legislature by deputies of their own election: these are wholly new discoveries, or have made their principal progress towards perfection in modern times. They are means, and powerful means, by which the excellences of republican government may be retained and its imperfections lessened or avoided."[17] In Federalist No. 51, James Madison clearly noted that the institutional separation was designed to provide "great security against a gradual concentration of powers in the same department." It was believed that the association of the powers of the branch with those within the branch would lead each to jealously guard its mandate from the infringements of the others: "Ambition must be made to counteract ambition."[18] Finally, such a system would insulate policy from the political demands of the masses. Checks and balances, different electoral calendars and schedules, and limited opportunities for the direct expression of popular demands were all expedients adopted to prevent the republican government from becoming too democratic. The decision to fragment power along vertical and horizontal dimensions was a conscious decision concerning institutional design that would continue to condition development.

Finally, one must consider the role of ideology. American political culture has been strongly influenced by Lockean liberalism, with its belief in the primacy of the individual, the prepolitical nature of property and the market, the consensual foundations of government, the limited scope of public authority, and the right to revolution. The central assumptions of Lockean liberalism have been consistently articulated in American society, even if it has had to compete at times with strands of civic republicanism. Indeed, as James Morone has persuasively argued in *The Democratic Wish,* the tension between a dominant liberalism and "a recurring, subordinate, ideology" of civic republicanism has been at the heart of American political development: "[T]he shared consensus of a united people does not survive the attempt to achieve it. Each effort collapses into the liberal clash of interests organized around a new institutional status quo, which is, itself, eventually challenged in the name of the people."[19]

17. Federalist No. 9, in James Madison, Alexander Hamilton, and John Jay, *The Federalist Papers* (London: Penguin Books, 1987), 119.
18. Federalist 51, in ibid., 319.
19. James A. Morone, *The Democratic Wish: Popular Participation and the Limits of American Government* (New York: Basic Books, 1990), 18.

The Lockean predisposition has created a powerful bias against the expansion and centralization of state power. One of the implications has been the retardation of political development. A predisposition toward the private raises concerns that public institutions would be too quick to impinge on individual action and civil organization. Another implication has been the unwillingness to sanction governmental expansion in any overarching fashion (e.g., the persistent dread of centralized planning) while allowing such expansion in a piecemeal fashion (e.g., the dense network of subsidies, promotions, and regulations that provide support for private interests and associations). As Grant McConnell has argued, the "deep-seated faith in the virtues of small units of social and political organization" and the belief that government is a threat to liberty have directly contributed to the weakness of the American state and the powerful influence of private associations in the political economy.[20]

As this brief discussion suggests, either the historical legacy, tenets of institutional design, or liberal ideology could have been a sufficient cause of the fragmentation of political authority and the slow pace of nineteenth-century political development. When combined, the three forces all exerted a powerful influence. The institutional fragmentation that existed in the nineteenth century would be difficult to overcome and would become a significant liability under the emergency conditions of war. Tocqueville clearly saw that the institutional fragmentation of power in the United States could prove to be a serious problem: "A nation that divided its sovereignty when faced by the great military monarchies of Europe would seem to me, by that single act, to be abdicating its power, and perhaps its existence and its name."[21] In the end, however, war would have the opposite effect. War would stimulate rapid institutional development and the creation of new patterns of state-economy relations, thereby compensating for some (but not all) of the limitations inherent in the original institutional design.

The State, War, and Political Development

In recent decades, scholars from a host of disciplines have devoted much attention to the concept of the state. Even if the debates at times have been

20. Grant McConnell, *Private Power and American Democracy* (New York: Alfred A. Knopf, 1966), 4–6.

21. Tocqueville, *Democracy in America*, 170.

overly absorbed in definitional disputes, they have brought far greater precision to our understanding of the state's position vis-à-vis other political vari-
ables. One can conceptualize state institutions in functional terms, that is, as
structures that emerge to execute some essential function, be it the promotion
of capital accumulation or the transformation of group demands into public
policies. Functionalist definitions commonly fail to account for autonomous
state action, however, which can entail a portrayal of public policies as a
reflection of societal-level factors such as the composition of class forces or
interest-group demands that have been aggregated and expressed through
public actions. A wealth of evidence that the state often functions in opposition to group and class demands, along with greater appreciation for the
complexities of administration, has led to a renewed interest in Weberian
notions of the state that combine the recognition of a core set of necessary
functions with essential structural or institutional features. In Weber's words:

> The primary formal characteristics of the modern state are as follows:
> It possesses an administrative and legal order subject to change by
> legislation, to which the organized activities of the administrative
> staff, which are also controlled by regulations, are oriented. This sys-
> tem of order claims binding authority, not only over the members of
> the state, the citizens . . . but also to a very large extent over all action
> taking place in the area of its jurisdiction. It is thus a compulsory
> organization with a territorial basis. Furthermore, today, the use of
> force is regarded as legitimate only so far as it is either permitted by
> the state or prescribed by it. . . . The claim of the modern state to
> monopolize the use of force is as essential to it as its character of
> compulsory jurisdiction and of continuous operation.[22]

Anthony Smith's definition of the state captures the key features of Weber's
characterization: "Generally, the 'state' comprises a set of differentiated, autonomous and public institutions, which are territorially centralized and claim
jurisdiction over a given territory, including the monopoly over coercion and
extraction."[23] Such a definition leads us to pose questions about variation in
centralization, coordination, and state–interest-group relations that would be

22. Max Weber, *Economy and Society: An Outline of Interpretive Sociology,* ed. Guenther Roth and Claus Wittich (New York: Bedminster Press, 1968), 1:56.
23. Anthony D. Smith, "State-Making and Nation-Building," in *States in History,* ed. John A. Hall (Oxford: Basil Blackwell, 1986), 235.

difficult with a less institutionally rich understanding of the state. These dimensions of the state are directly shaped by the struggles of war.

The Demands of War

Recent scholarship provides important insights into the role that war has played in shaping the evolution of the American state and the political economy. For example, in *Yankee Leviathan*, Richard Bensel skillfully explores the competing models of state building adopted in the North and the South and details how mobilization during the Civil War and reconstruction simultaneously forced a close partnership of the American state, Northern industry, and finance, and created significant barriers to the emergence of a class-based party system.[24] Gregory Hooks's *Forging the Military-Industrial Complex* reveals the ways in which World War II mobilization forged a tight relationship between the Pentagon and monopoly capital, creating a form of planning and compromising the social-policy legacy of the New Deal.[25] While these and other studies address critical episodes in American political development and correctly accentuate the importance of war, there have been no comparable studies of World War I mobilization and the long-term effects of demobilization. This absence is baffling, particularly if—as will be shown—the war played such a key role in shaping the politics and policies of subsequent decades.

The insight that war is a chief force in state development is not new. Analysts have long acknowledged the impact of war on the organization and expansion of public authority. For example, in his 1876 classic *Principles of Sociology*, Herbert Spencer noted the importance of war in social development and the development of the state. "Fulfillment of these requirements, that there shall be complete corporate action, that to this end the non-combatant part shall be occupied in providing for the combatant part, that the entire aggregate shall be strongly bound together, and that the units composing it must have their individualities in life, liberty, and property thereby subordinated, presupposes a coercive instrumentality. No such union for corporate

24. Richard Franklin Bensel, *Yankee Leviathan: The Origins of Central State Authority in America, 1959–1877* (Cambridge: Cambridge University Press, 1990).

25. Gregory Hooks, *Forging the Military-Industrial Complex: World War II's Battle of the Potomac* (Urbana: University of Illinois Press, 1991). See Bartholomew H. Sparrow, *From the Outside In: World War II and the American State* (Princeton, N.J.: Princeton University Press, 1996).

action can be achieved without a powerful controlling agency."[26] German historian Otto Hintze, writing in 1906, identified war as the primary source of institutional development: "[T]he form and spirit of the state's organization will not be determined solely by economic and social relations and clashes of interests, but primarily by the necessities of defense and offense, that is, by the organization of the army and of warfare."[27] More recently, Charles Tilly has suggested that state making is essentially a by-product of war making: "No one designed the principal components of national treasuries, courts, central administrations, and so on. They usually formed as more or less inadvertent by-products of efforts to carry out more immediate tasks, especially the creation and support of armed forces."[28]

War is so consequential because it creates demands that are undeniable and usually cannot be satisfied under existing institutional arrangements and patterns of state-society relations. At the same time, war provides a considerable opportunity for autonomous state action and innovations that may thoroughly recast the relationship between the state and key social groupings. It provides an opportunity for the kind of discontinuous evolutionary periods described in the previous chapter. In their classical presentations, pluralist, elite, and class theories of politics provide little space for state autonomy. The state is the embodiment of societal forces or serves as a more or less neutral mechanism that translates these forces into public policies. Much of the recent literature on the state argues that opportunities for autonomous state action are maximized during periods of crisis. Under the threat of war, state officials may be forced to defy dominant class, elite, or popular interests. Crises such as wars simultaneously stimulate demands for extraordinary measures and weaken the power of dominant forces in society, thus creating the opportunity for creative expansions of state capacity.[29] As Theda Skocpol notes: "[A] state's involvement in an international network of states is a basis for potential autonomy of action over and against groups and economic arrangements

26. Herbert Spencer, *On Social Evolution: Selected Writings*, ed. J. D. Y. Peel (Chicago: University of Chicago Press, 1972), 191. See the discussion in Stanislav Andreski, *Military Organization and Society* (Berkeley and Los Angeles: University of California Press, 1968), 108.

27. Otto Hintze, "Military Organization and the Organization of the State," in *The Historical Essays of Otto Hintze*, ed. Felix Gilbert (New York: Oxford University Press, 1975), 183. See also Ludwig Gumplowicz, *The Outlines of Sociology*, trans. Frederick W. Moore (Philadelphia: American Academy of Political and Social Sciences, 1899). For Gumplowicz, the state is "the organized control of the minority over the majority" (118).

28. Charles Tilly, *Coercion, Capital, and European States: ad 990–1992* (Cambridge: Blackwell, 1992), 26.

29. See Fred Block, "The Ruling Class Does Not Rule: Notes on the Marxist Theory of the State," *Socialist Revolution* 33 (May 1977): 6–28.

within its jurisdiction—even including the dominant class and existing relations of production. For international military pressures and opportunities can prompt state rulers to attempt policies that conflict with, and even in extreme instances contradict, the fundamental interests of a dominant class."[30]

War places a set of rather unique demands on the state and the economy, especially when it is a large-scale war. Such a war, Edward Corwin notes, is a "total war," characterized by its "functional totality." This entails "the politically ordered participation in the war effort of all personal and social forces, the scientific, the mechanical, the commercial, the economic, the moral, the literary and artistic, and the psychological."[31] Such a war mandates the complete mobilization of civil society and the rapid development of new administrative tools to manage the process. To understand more directly what is meant by "complete mobilization," let us consider the economic and managerial demands of total war, particularly as they exist in an industrial context.

First and most obvious, war places extensive demands on the economy in terms of the *quantity of goods produced*. War mobilization requires an expansion of production beyond what would be possible at full capacity. New productive capacity has to be created, forcing policy makers to address explicitly a host of perplexing questions concerning financing, ownership, and the ultimate disposition of war facilities after the cessation of hostilities. It also mandates the creation of new mechanisms to direct the flow of raw materials, fuel, transportation, capital, and labor on an economy-wide basis. Concomitantly, second, there is a *qualitative change in the composition of production*. Given the immediacy of the demands, policy makers cannot vacillate in the hope that market mechanisms will eventually provide the needed incentives. They must immediately develop the tools to redirect resources and capital from peace-related industries to war industries. This can be exceedingly difficult in a market-based system, which relies primarily on capital markets to fund industrial expansion.[32] Policy makers may have to open new channels of finance or create the means to direct the flow of capital. Industries producing goods essential to the war effort must receive preferential access to the capital, raw materials, labor, and transportation needed for production. At the same time, corporations producing nonessential goods may face severe shortages and be

30. Theda Skocpol, *States and Social Revolutions: A Comparative Analysis of France, Russia, and China* (Cambridge: Cambridge University Press, 1979), 31.

31. Edward Samuel Corwin, *Total War and the Constitution* (New York: Alfred A. Knopf, 1970), 4.

32. See John Zysman, *Governments, Markets, and Growth: Financial Systems and the Politics of Industrial Change* (Ithaca, N.Y.: Cornell University Press, 1983), for an excellent discussion of the effects of different systems of corporate finance on the capacity of the state to direct resources toward particular sectors.

forced to convert their facilities to the production of war-related goods or face extinction.

Third, the quantitative and qualitative changes in production are usually combined with *changes in product design and the production process*. Policy makers may be forced to promote standardization to meet military needs. During World War I, for example, a premium was placed on munitions standardization. Corporations had to work closely with the War Industries Board, the branches of the service, and trade associations to develop and implement appropriate standards. Moreover, in hopes of addressing shortages in raw materials and increasing production, the WIB and trade associations pursued efficiency-promoting innovations and eliminated unnecessary product-design features and varieties.[33] During peacetime, detailed questions of product design—like questions of firm ownership and financing—are understood as managerial prerogatives. Under the exigencies of war, however, the boundaries between state and corporate authority are negotiated anew, and public officials exercise the authority normally reserved for corporate management.

Fourth, there is the ever present need to *control prices*. The high production levels required for total war dramatically increase the demand for raw materials, labor, and capital. Furthermore, war normally produces shortages in consumer goods precisely at the time when workers enjoy higher wages as a result of greater intensity in workplace participation. These inflationary forces are combined with the new opportunities for corporations to realize higher profits through price increases. Policy makers can respond to this situation by changing contracting practices, imposing direct price controls, and creating mechanisms to limit the incentives for dramatic price increases (e.g., excess-profits taxes to recoup any "unreasonable" gains). Price controls are administratively complex, requiring the collection and analysis of vast quantities of information on costs and quantities of goods produced. This data may not be readily available, particularly if corporations controlling information do not share the government's enthusiasm for price controls. These activities thus often require the development of new administrative and intellectual tools and changes in the state's relationships with producers.

Fifth, there are *changes in industrial relations*. High levels of production, restrictions on immigration, and the diversion of workers to military service create critical labor shortages. Although they can be partially mitigated by internal migration and the transfer of labor from other uses (e.g., domestic labor, agriculture), shortages remain a critical problem. In addition, in virtu-

33. Rexford G. Tugwell, "America's War-Time Socialism," *Nation,* April 6, 1927, 366.

ally every war, inflation creates pressures for higher wages. Finally, the massive material demands of warfare force policy makers and producers to place a premium on high levels of production. There are no inventories that can insulate an industry from strikes and armed forces from critical shortages. These factors create a situation ripe for labor militancy. As a result, government and business officials have great incentives to eliminate or prevent workplace conflicts. At times, this may take the form of heightened levels of coercion against workers: managers may resort to union busting, policy makers to conscription. In both world wars, however, new agencies were created to resolve conflicts, manage wages and working conditions, and transfer labor to war industries, with the result that new patterns of industrial relations, union growth, and real-wage gains became common products of mobilization.

A sixth and final economic challenge comes in the area of *financing the war effort*. Resources for waging a war can be derived from tariffs, debt, and taxes. The interruption of trade seriously compromises the tariff as a source of revenue. On the taxation side, policy makers may be forced to tax additional sources of income and raise rates well above peacetime levels. The stunning expansion of taxation that often accompanies war requires a host of decisions concerning the assignment of the tax burden and thus the overall distribution of income. Reflecting the need to maintain popular support for the war, wartime has provided one of the few opportunities for major increases in tax progressivity.[34] Although the relative reliance on debt and taxes will vary from war to war, debt commonly plays a central role. For policy makers to raise funds, they must create new debt instruments, organize distributional networks of financial institutions, and initiate patriotic campaigns to create markets for bond issues. The extensive reliance on domestic financial markets may, in turn, stimulate a shortage of private capital for corporate expansion. With military success dependent on maximum production, this capital shortage may create a need for state financing, which introduces an entirely new set of complicated questions concerning the ultimate disposition of production facilities.

War, State Development, and Compensatory State Building

Mobilization and demobilization provide important choice opportunities. At the onset of war, the immediacy of the conflict permits changes that are rapid

34. See John F. Witte, *The Politics and Development of the Federal Income Tax* (Madison: University of Wisconsin Press, 1985), 79–86, 125–29.

and often haphazard. The state of emergency and the prospect that the crisis will be temporary gives officials great latitude. Justified by an emergency, they can execute plans that would normally raise weighty questions about the appropriate role of the state in society, the security of property rights, and the balance of constitutional powers. The freedom afforded by war evaporates with the cessation of hostilities. Yet, demobilization—the conversion of a wartime economy and governing structure to a peacetime status—provides policy makers with a second key opportunity. This time, officials can assess the experiences of the war and modify prewar institutions and governing structures in light of the results. They can purposefully retain some of the emergency measures as permanent features of the postwar economy. This leads to an immediate question: Which features of the wartime system will be retained? Administrators responsible for mobilization, bureaucrats who have discovered solutions to long-standing problems, and interests that have benefited from new policies and patterns of state-group relations all have a stake in the continuation of some of the policies and practices initiated during war. Administrative agencies and their staffs, empowered by new policies to extract greater resources, to expand the regulation of economic activity, and to govern the relationships between competing economic groups, may seek to use these same powers to resolve peacetime policy problems. New agencies created to serve war purposes may prove anxious to survive. As a general rule, the greater the demands of mobilization, the greater the "organizational residue" following the cessation of hostilities and thus the greater the demands for the preservation of wartime institutions.[35]

The Legacies of War

As one might expect, the demands of war mobilization have a significant impact on the evolution of the state. "Total war" can initiate a period of discontinuous evolution, forcing a reconfiguration of institutions, changes in patterns of state-society relations, and the introduction of new policy tools, all of which may well outlive the crisis and permanently alter the trajectory of political development. World War I had several distinct effects on the structure of the state: it resulted in a greater centralization of authority; it required rapid bureaucratic professionalization; and it forced a search for new patterns of interest intermediation. Each of these changes had an impact on

---

35. Charles Tilly, "War Making and State Making as Organized Crime," in *Bringing the State Back In*, ed. Peter B. Evans, Dietrich Rueschemeyer, and Theda Skocpol (Cambridge: Cambridge University Press, 1985), 181.

the capacity of the officials to make and implement policies that would have been impossible a few years earlier. Let us consider each in turn.

War had an immediate impact on the *centralization of authority*. As noted earlier, the American state is rather unique in the degree to which power is fragmented along vertical and horizontal dimensions.[36] This fragmentation—a product of constitutional design and historical evolution—has been one of the more lasting features of the American state. It has considerable implications for state autonomy, institutional coordination, and the possibility of planning. As J. P. Nettl explained in his seminal article on the state: "[I]n the United States the real boundaries of autonomy fall not between state and other institutions but within and between the complex of institutions that elsewhere could be encapsulated within the collectivity of the state." As a result, "we have a sharp disjunction between the well-maintained autonomy of certain federal institutions such as the federal courts, regulatory commissions, and, finally, departments of the federal government; the legislative branch, however, is distinguished by its lack of autonomy and by its constitution as a reflection of cross-pressures and interests."[37] The impact of horizontal fragmentation is exacerbated by vertical fragmentation. The federal system places distinct limitations on national powers by vesting authority in state and local governments; the courts are often forced to adjust the boundaries between national and state jurisdiction. To be certain, the dual federalism of the nineteenth century was transformed in the twentieth century through successive reinterpretations of the commerce clause and the introduction of new national policies that sought to regulate behavior at the subnational level through the imposition of federal mandates and funding programs. At the same time, the exercise of national authority was increasingly contingent on the development of subnational units of government given that proxy administration had become essential to implementing many policies.

The progressive transfer of authority to the executive branch and administrative agencies partially counters this fragmentation. Congress is highly susceptible to localism and interest-group demands because of electoral forces, weak electorally based parties, and the decentralization of the committee system. Legislation is frequently an aggregation of measures designed to appease local constituents. Policy complexity and the difficulties of responding to the demands of multiple interests often leads members of Congress to delegate

36. See the discussion in John L. Campbell, *Collapse of an Industry: Nuclear Power and the Contradictions of U.S. Policy* (Ithaca, N.Y.: Cornell University Press, 1988), 1–17.

37. J. P. Nettl, "The State as a Conceptual Variable," *World Politics* 20, no. 4 (1968): 569.

authority to administrative agencies. While no part of the American state is completely free from group pressures, the executive and bureaucracy are far more insulated than the Congress. From this discussion we can draw a simple generalization: the transfer of authority away from the Congress and to the executive can be considered a key factor promoting the expansion of administrative capacities and lending greater coherence to patterns of state-economy relations.[38]

War promotes precisely this centralization of authority in the executive. The waging of war requires a central command with some capacity to orchestrate the numerous tasks required to deploy and provision forces. In modern warfare, when one cannot depend on soldiers to supply their own weapons and live off the land, government officials must engage a host of complicated technical issues concerning the design and standardization of munitions. This, in turn, entails a greater centralization of authority and economic control. In the words of Stanislav Andreski, "[T]he increasing complexity of armaments favors political centralization."[39] Of course, the complexity of modern nuclear warfare marks the apex of centralized authority in war making. Even the more modest feat of supplying the American Expeditionary Force and allies required the creation of new institutions that could exercise a more centralized control over the distribution of key resources in the economy, the allocation of contracts, and the determination of prices. The War Industries Board, in its odd amalgam of public- and private-sector actors and organizations, may appear decentralized by contemporary standards. Its capacity to direct mobilization often depended on the interpersonal skills of agency elites and the willingness of key economic interests to cooperate. Nonetheless, when seen in historical context, the war brought a remarkable concentration of economic and political authority.

A second factor that contributes directly to the expansion of administrative capacities is *bureaucratic professionalization*. As government evolves from exercising basic police powers to regulating ever more detailed aspects of economic and civil relations, the demand for bureaucratic expertise increases. Indeed, without a measure of bureaucratic professionalism, it is difficult for agencies to function with any semblance of independence. They may remain dependent on private interests for data and analysis; implementation may be

38. See Bensel, *Yankee Leviathan,* chap. 3, for an excellent discussion of state capacity. Bensel provides a very detailed discussion of the features of state development, assessing and comparing the impact of Union and Confederate initiatives on these factors during the Civil War.

39. Stanislav Andreski, *Military Organization and Society* (Berkeley and Los Angeles: University of California Press, 1968), 88.

contingent on the cooperation of regulated parties. Cross-nationally, the United States was a laggard with respect to bureaucratic professionalization because the federal bureaucracy was largely a product of patronage during the nineteenth and early twentieth centuries. Although the coverage of the civil service was initially quite limited following the passage of the Pendelton Act of 1883, it expanded over the course of the next several decades as presidents used civil-service protection opportunistically to limit the patronage available to their successors.[40] This general bureaucratic professionalization was combined with a growing reliance on administrators with specialized expertise in areas relevant to the missions of the specific agencies, a trend that accelerated throughout the Progressive Era.

The quality of policy—and thus the ability of policy makers purposively to address the problems they seek to address—is dependent on the capacity to establish long-term goals, target resources, impose costs, and assess policy performance in light of these goals. The creation of a planning and evaluation function may involve the use of new budgeting procedures. It may require the creation of special planning offices, the development of new intellectual models, or the integration of specialized decision rules into the policy process. In every case, it entails an expanded capacity to collect and analyze data. As one might guess, planning is highly dependent on, and contributes to, agency professionalization. If power is sufficiently centralized and agencies have been professionalized with administrators with relevant expertise, one can expect a movement toward some form of planning and evaluation, assuming that the requisite intellectual models are sufficiently developed to provide some guidance in the task.

The demand for specialists increases dramatically with mobilization, as the government expands its duties to regulate activities for which it has little experience. During World War I, new planning capacity was urgently required to assure that production would match the demands of the services in both quantitative and qualitative terms. This required assigning priority to certain orders and exercising control over the flow of essential raw materials, fuel, labor, capital, foodstuffs, and transportation on a national basis. The creation of such a capacity necessitated the building of new professional staffs and the unprecedented generation of economic data. As Theodore Ropp notes: "Many of the first efforts to measure national potentials in food, manpower, industry, shipping, and gold came out of World War I. . . . The first

---

40. See Nelson, "A Short, Ironic History of American National Bureaucracy."

measurements were for economies under siege."[41] To manage this unprecedented demand for current economic statistics, agencies relied heavily on an influx of economists (including top economists Wesley Mitchell and Edwin F. Gay) and accountants, as well as professionals working for interests that had been integrated into the mobilization apparatus.

Following the war, "those concerned with statistical collection placed a high priority on continuation of wartime advances in economic intelligence," both through expanded data collection by the federal government and through the proliferation of private economic research organizations, such as the National Bureau of Economic Research, the Brookings Institution, the National Industrial Conference Board, and the Twentieth Century Fund, all of which emerged during the period 1916–20.[42] Moreover, a second influx of professionals into government service occurred after World War I. Several agencies were capable of engaging in more expansive policy ventures than they had earlier. They would place a far greater emphasis on the collection of data and the use of new intellectual models in efforts to eliminate problems that had seemed beyond the control of policy makers only a few years earlier. The Department of Agriculture, for example, attempted to shape farmers' selection of crops, based on its forecasts of probable harvests and the resulting market prices. The newly created Bureau of the Budget started considering federal expenditures in a systematic fashion. The Federal Reserve initiated efforts to manage the business cycle using open-market activities. The Commerce Department endeavored to analyze the variety of goods produced and worked to promote standardization and simplification. These efforts would have been unimaginable in the prewar state.

In addition to centralization and bureaucratic professionalization, administrative capacities can be bolstered through measures to structure group participation and introduce *new patterns of interest intermediation,* particularly in a highly decentralized institutional structure. Unimpeded group access to policy makers can dramatically reduce the capacity of officials to engage in purposive policy making, particularly when officials are highly vulnerable to regular elections. At its worst, policy may be the embodiment of disparate group demands. The centralization of authority discussed above may be understood as an important step in modifying the access and influence of interest groups

41. Theodore Ropp, "The Rise of American Military Power," in *Institutions in Modern America: Innovations in Structure and Process,* ed. Stephen E. Ambrose (Baltimore: Johns Hopkins University Press, 1967), 114.

42. Evan B. Metcalf, "Secretary Hoover and the Emergence of Macroeconomic Management," *Business History Review* 49, no. 1 (1975): 67–68.

in the policy process. Policy makers can replace unstructured group access with more structured forms of state–interest-group relations. For example, government officials may seek to create quasi-corporatist arrangements to govern interest-group interaction.[43] For a number of historical, ideological, and institutional reasons, pure corporatism has largely been an impossibility in the United States.[44] During various periods in U.S. history, however, efforts have been made to create such arrangements, integrating trade associations, agricultural associations, and labor unions directly into the policy-making apparatus. The obvious case in point is that of war. Under conditions of war, state managers may seek to use such arrangements to secure the support and technical assistance of key economic groups. Thus, World War I's War Industries Board defined and administered policy through a system of commodity groups and war service committees, the latter organized and certified by the U.S. Chamber of Commerce as being representative of the industry in question. Key positions throughout the WIB were filled with dollar-a-year men drawn from industry, thereby providing another tier of de facto representation. The same model was adopted in other war mobilization agencies such as the Food Administration and the Railroad Administration. During World War II, the War Production Board (WPB), under Director Donald Nelson, employed this same model. Not only were key executive positions staffed with corporate executives drawn from affected industries, the board's twenty-four industrial divisions worked with industrial advisory committees having representatives from key firms and economic associations.[45]

War can have a significant impact on class relations as conscription-related shortages of workers enhance the power of labor relative to capital. As labor gains greater leverage in the economy, businesses function under the credible threat that the state will reduce access to raw materials, finance, transportation, and munitions contracts or commandeer their facilities should they fail to produce munitions. The new patterns of interest intermediation may pro-

---

43. Philippe Schmitter defines corporatism as "a system of interest representation in which the constituent units are organized into a limited number of singular, compulsory, noncompetitive, hierarchically ordered and functionally differentiated categories, recognized or licensed (if not created) by the state and granted a deliberate representational monopoly within their respective categories in exchange for observing certain controls on their selection of leaders and articulation of demands and supports." Philippe Schmitter, "Still the Century of Corporatism," in *Trends Toward Corporatist Intermediation,* ed. Philippe Schmitter and Gerhard Lehmbruch (Beverly Hills, Calif.: Sage, 1979), 13.

44. See Graham K. Wilson, "Why Is There No Corporatism in the United States?" in *Patterns of Corporatist Policy-Making,* ed. Gerhard Lehmbruch and Philippe Schmitter (Beverly Hills, Calif.: Sage, 1982).

45. See Marc Allen Eisner, *The State in the American Political Economy: Public Policy and the Evolution of State-Economy Relations* (Englewood Cliffs, N.J.: Prentice Hall, 1995), 196–204.

vide a key to managing these conflicts. For example, systems of tripartite representation were instituted in a number of war agencies at the time of the Great War. Labor was directly integrated into the mobilization machinery, particularly the National War Labor Board, where a cochairmanship representing business (William Howard Taft) and labor (Frank Walsh) was instituted along with a board providing five representatives each.[46] Labor leaders called on workers to limit strikes in return for official recognition of the right to organize and bargain collectively. The tight wartime labor markets and the administration's pro-labor position resulted in gains for labor, both in terms of union roles and worker incomes.

Compensatory State Building

The model of interest intermediation described above is central to the model of state building adopted of necessity during the war—a model that is best referred to as *compensatory state building*. The demands of war revealed in striking terms the limitations of the American state. Out of necessity, efforts were made rapidly to fill the deficit of administrative capacities. National officials attempted to append to the state the capacities of more developed private-sector institutions such as corporations, trade associations, and agricultural associations. Their cooperation was secured, in turn, not primarily through the compulsion of law but through the incentive of the purse. That is, private interests collaborated in the expectation that cooperation would carry financial benefits (e.g., restrictions on market entry; a high rate of return; access to licenses, contracts, or subsidies).

One might view the phenomenon of compensatory state building through the lens of resource-dependence theory. The key insight from this perspective is that organizations depend on their environments for resources but are constantly seeking to establish control over these resources in hopes of minimizing dependence. As organizations become increasingly interdependent, the task of adjusting to a changing environment becomes far more complicated. As organizations form relationships with other organizations for this purpose, they sacrifice a measure of autonomy.[47] While the resource-dependence perspective has been used primarily to understand the evolution of economic organization, it can be extended to the study of state building, as exhibited

46. See Valerie Jean Conner, *The National War Labor Board: Stability, Social Justice, and the Voluntary State in World War I* (Chapel Hill: University of North Carolina Press, 1983).

47. See Jeffrey Pfeffer and Gerald Salancik, *The External Control of Organizations: A Resource Dependence Perspective* (New York: Harper & Row, 1978).

by Bartholomew Sparrow's examination of World War II mobilization, *From the Outside In*.[48]

During World War I compensatory state building provided obvious political and administrative benefits. On the political side, potential adversaries could be converted into clientele through the provision or promise of benefits. Its voluntarist features partially assuaged ideological concerns over state expansion.[49] On the administrative side, the benefits were equally important. By delegating authority and then defining policies cooperatively with interested parties, policy makers could take advantage of the analytical capacities, experience, and resources of private associations that were often more administratively developed that the agencies in question. To the extent that private interests exercised quasi-public authority in the definition of policy, they were far less likely to impede implementation. The largely positive experience with this model during World War I led to its rapid dissemination in the decades following the war. To state things in the terms introduced in Chapter 1, it became the organizing model for the new regime—a model that would be adopted in a host of agencies seeking to address problems that had few connections to those involved in the war. Its influence would be solidified during the New Deal, as the Roosevelt administration drew analogies between the challenges of the Great Depression and those of wartime mobilization.

Although this model of state building has distinct benefits, they come at a high price. As noted above, organizations trade off autonomy for resources. If state capacities become contingent on the participation of private-sector associations, officials may lack the power or authority to exercise control. The result can be a lack of organizational cohesion and coordination. In this light, Robert Cuff's description of the War Industries Board as "a pluralistic organization" in which "the whole proved a great deal weaker than its constituent parts" becomes an apt representation of the state as a whole.[50] Moreover, because the private-sector associations were voluntarily integrated into agencies in the expectation that participation would bring financial benefits, it was difficult to impose costs on the regulated or to use the state to address questions that had significant consequences for the distribution of power and wealth in the political economy. Attention tended to be focused on "questions

48. Bartholomew H. Sparrow, *From the Outside In: World War II and the American State* (Princeton, N.J.: Princeton University Press, 1996).

49. See McConnell, *Private Power and American Democracy*, 4–5.

50. Robert D. Cuff, "Bernard Baruch: Symbol and Myth in Industrial Mobilization," *Business History Review* 43, no. 2 (1969): 124.

of distribution and conservation, not production and ownership."[51] When
state capacity becomes contingent on corporate profitability and voluntary
cooperation, it becomes both profoundly conservative and far more inflexible
than would be the case had it been developed in accordance with a different
model. This, however, was the model adopted in the war. It was also the
model embraced during the New Deal, as policymakers sought to discover
some means of managing the effects of the Great Depression. It is a model
that carries inherent weaknesses—weaknesses that were incorporated into the
state at a crucial moment, thereby shaping governmental performance in subsequent decades. Indeed, it is a central argument of this book that if one
wants to explain why so many reform efforts failed and so many regulatory
policies benefited the regulated, one must confront the issue of institutional
design and the decisions made in the early decades of the century under the
veil of emergency.

War can have a tremendous impact on the evolution of the state, driving
centralization, bureaucratic professionalization, and forcing a search for new
patterns of state–interest-group relations. Beyond this "organizational residue," there is a residue of popular expectations. The experience of war government creates new expectations concerning the role of the state in society.
Public officials may be expected to manage various problems previously assigned to private-sector actors or deemed to be beyond purposive direction.
As economic historian Jonathan R. T. Hughes writes: "The direct legacy of
war—the dead, the debt, the inflation, the changes in economic and social
structure that come from immense transfers of resources by taxation and
money creation—these things are all obvious. What has not been so obvious
has been the pervasive yet subtle change in our increasing acceptance of federal nonmarket control and even our enthusiasm for it, as a result of the
experience of war."[52] War—like any major crisis—creates new expectations
and a disposition to welcome an expansion of government authority. Thus, it
can have a transformative effect on the state-building process. In the words
of Robert Higgs, "When crisis provoked an extension of governmental powers, the new powers in a fundamental sense never could be merely transitory.
Because the postcrisis society inevitably differed in significant ways, crises are
properly considered historically critical events; they markedly changed the

51. Robert D. Cuff, "Herbert Hoover, the Ideology of Voluntarism, and War Organization During the Great War," *Journal of American History* 64, no. 2 (1977): 369.
52. Jonathan R. T. Hughes, *The Governmental Habit Redux: Economic Controls from Colonial Times to the Present* (Princeton, N.J.: Princeton University Press, 1991), 137.

course of historical development."[53] The changes associated with war are, in many cases, irreversible.

War results in an expansion of the public sector and thus, as Higgs has argued, has a ratcheting effect on the growth of government. The fiscal demands of the state, and the number of public-sector employees—two common indicators of governmental growth—never return to their prewar levels. Governmental authority and expectations concerning the role of the state are expanded permanently as a result of a crisis like war. We must go beyond governmental growth, however, to examine the specific effects of war on patterns of state-society relations and state administrative capacities. How did the experience of war affect the authority of the state in the society after the war? What administrative models and policy tools were adapted to peacetime purposes? How did the war shape the organization of economic interests and patterns of state-economy relations? To answer these questions, we must explore demobilization broadly conceived. Rather than focus merely on the relaxation of wartime controls on prices, wages, and production—often a rapid and haphazard process—we must explore how the innovations of wartime mobilization were preserved and disseminated following the cessation of hostilities. These issues are addressed in some detail in Part II of this book. Before examining the evolution of several policy areas and institutions during the 1920s, however, we must consider the experience of World War I mobilization in greater detail.

53. Robert Higgs, *Crisis and Leviathan: Critical Episodes in the Growth of American Government* (New York: Oxford University Press, 1987), 58.

3

Mobilization, Demobilization, and the Legacy of the Great War

> President Wilson may have conceived the function of this body in military terms, as issuing orders and penalizing their non-fulfillment. If he did, Mr. Bernard Baruch, the chairman, had a different idea. To him the enterprise of war was a vast cooperation. The industrial system was to run as one well-oiled machine, but it was to run on a volunteer basis with plenty of play for individuality. —Rexford G. Tugwell, 1927

> The plan was one of decentralization. So that, as long as we got cooperation, we left the interior organization and control of the particular industry to the leaders of that industry as represented by these committees.
> —Bernard Baruch, 1929

If state making is a by-product of war making, one might not expect World War I mobilization to have had much of an impact on state development.[1] After all, the nation's involvement in the war was brief, lasting under two years. Furthermore, the success of mobilization was mixed. The limited legislative mandate, the weakness of existing institutions, problems of coordination, and ongoing conflicts between agencies involved in the mobilization process took their toll. The experience of war, however, shaped subsequent developments by providing new experiences and expectations concerning the potential role of the state in civil society. It stimulated the development of new state administrative capacities and economic organizations that would reshape the political-economic context during the next several decades.

Mobilization alerted a generation to the potential benefits of planning. It was a fitting culmination of the Progressive Era, with its broad concerns with domestic reform, its faith in scientific knowledge, and its grave dissatisfaction with the performance of many public institutions. For many Progressive re-

---

1. Charles Tilly, *Coercion, Capital, and European States: AD 990–1992* (Cambridge: Blackwell, 1992), 26.

formers, the mobilization agencies appeared to provide a model of what was possible. In the words of Ellis Hawley, many viewed mobilization "as a stepping stone to the social order that a progressive era had envisioned but failed to achieve. A system of war management, they came to believe, could be adapted to the peacetime management of social programs."[2] Government officials, corporate managers, labor leaders, and other group representatives entered the 1920s after playing some role in the mobilization effort. They would draw on the examples of the War Industries Board and other agencies as they encountered new social and economic problems. As Rexford G. Tugwell noted in 1927: "Under war-pressure industry had experimented with a kind of voluntary socialism—and liked it. It liked the substitution of solidarity for suspicion, of unity for compelled disunion, of cooperation for competition, of a common purpose for haphazard growth."[3] These experiences would find their greatest peacetime applications some fifteen years later, in the New Deal.

Second, the war resulted in the hasty creation of new state capacities. A state constructed largely on eighteenth-century assumptions had to be transformed quickly to meet the exigencies of war. New agencies had to be created, and the federal government had to undergo a rapid infusion of expertise. Social scientists and scientists entered public service in numbers that would have been unimaginable only a few years earlier, when many first embraced bureaucratic professionalization as a necessary component of reform. Mobilization decisions required information on potential production levels, costs, prices, and distribution—most of which had never been collected systematically. New policy tools had to be developed with some care if the state was going to exercise extraconstitutional powers over private economic interests. This period of intensive and rapid state building required some significant compromises and a blurring of public and private power that would have some weighty implications.

Finally, despite the brevity of mobilization and the rapidity of demobilization, the war changed the nature of state-economy relations and the political organization of the economy. If administrators had "learned anything from the war, it was not the virtues of collectivism but the potentialities of trade associations."[4] In what would be a model of compensatory state building, the

2. Ellis W. Hawley, *The Great War and the Search for a Modern Order: A History of the American People and Their Institutions, 1917–1933* (New York: St. Martin's Press, 1979), 19.

3. Rexford G. Tugwell, "America's War-Time Socialism," *Nation*, April 6, 1927, 366.

4. William E. Leuchtenburg, "The New Deal and the Analogue of War," in *Change and Continuity in Twentieth-Century America*, ed. John Braeman, Robert H. Bremner, and Everett Walters (Columbus: Ohio University Press, 1964), 129.

War Industries Board's limited resources forced a delegation of authority to commodity sections that, in turn, devolved authority onto business associations and "war service committees." Similar arrangements were forged at other agencies. After the war, many of these associations continued to represent the interests of their sectors and actively sought to nurture close relationships with policy makers and key agencies. As a National Industrial Conference Board report noted in 1925: "The federal governmental machinery was entirely inadequate to assume the responsible management, or even a close technical supervision, of vast industrial enterprises, reaching in many instances across the continent. Accordingly, while primary reliance continued to be placed, for the most part, upon private initiative, the Government undertook to deal in respect to many matters, not with individual business concerns, but entire trades and industries." The demands placed upon trade associations impacted on their development. "As a result of this governmental policy of working through trade associations in dealing with such problems as supply rationing, for example, many of the existing organizations were greatly strengthened and new associations were brought into being."[5]

In the wake of the war, then, new models of state-economy relations and newly developed administrative capacities existed side by side with a new universe of industrial organizations and elites experienced in working with the federal government to control and direct economic activity. The situation was ripe for lasting changes in the organization of the state and its relationship to civil society. This chapter begins with an examination of the fierce debates over the role of the state in the economy and the preparedness controversy that set the context for mobilization. I turn then to address the history, structure, and powers of the central agency in the mobilization process, the War Industries Board. I conclude with a brief discussion of demobilization and its immediate economic and political consequences. The long-term impact of the mobilization experience—the dissemination of policy tools, models of administration, and patterns of state-economy relations—is the subject of the remainder of this book.

Progressivism in Peace and War

The significance of the mobilization experience is best assessed when placed in its historical and intellectual context. A number of new regulatory agencies

5. National Industrial Conference Board, *Trade Associations: Their Economic Significance and Legal Status* (New York: National Industrial Conference Board, 1925), 26. See George Roberts, "The Present Legal Status of Trade Associations and Their Problems," *Proceedings of the Academy of Political Science* 11, no. 4 (1926): 6.

were created during the Progressive Era as policy makers sought to accommodate the emergence of a new corporate-based economy.[6] The role of the state in the economy, however, remained a highly divisive issue. The competing positions over the proper role of the state were presented most clearly during the presidential campaign of 1912. It fixed the intellectual landscape for the next several decades with respect to the competing models of state-economy relations. The incumbent president William Howard Taft—a minor player in the debates—adopted a conservative interpretation of property rights and was highly suspicious of administrative regulation of the economy. He supported an ongoing reliance on the judicial application of the Sherman Act, particularly in light of the recently established rule of reason. In the four years of Taft's presidency, his administration had initiated ninety Sherman Act prosecutions, as compared to Roosevelt's "trust-busting" record of forty-four prosecutions in seven and one-half years.[7]

Rather than propose the creation of some new administrative tribunal to regulate business, Taft argued that the Sherman Act could be made more effective if corporations involved in interstate commerce were required to assume federal charters. Such a system of federal incorporation would furnish benefits to business as well. While it would "subject the business of the concern to the closest scrutiny of government officers," it would simultaneously "save the business from harassment by State authorities."[8] Even if Taft believed that the Sherman Act could be used to regulate the activities of federally chartered corporations, he remained firm in his rejection of social engineering of the kind envisioned by his more progressive counterparts. Taft argued consistently that it "should not be the policy of the Government to prevent reasonable concentrations of capital . . . necessary to the economic development of manufacture, trade, and commerce."[9] Taft's faith in the judicial application of the Sherman Act prevented him from developing a more visionary scheme. His discomfort with campaigning left him in the shadows of the spirited contest between Theodore Roosevelt and Woodrow Wilson.

6. See Marc Allen Eisner, *Regulatory Politics in Transition* (Baltimore: Johns Hopkins University Press, 1993), chaps. 2–3, and Morton Keller, *Regulating a New Economy: Public Policy and Economic Change in America, 1900–1933* (Cambridge: Harvard University Press, 1990).

7. Francis L. Broderick, *Progressivism at Risk: Electing a President in 1912* (New York: Greenwood Press, 1989), 35.

8. William Howard Taft, "Address at the Lincoln Birthday Banquet of the Republican Club of the City of New York, February 12, 1910," in *Presidential Addresses and State Papers of William Howard Taft* (New York: Doubleday, Page & Co., 1919), 1:582

9. William Howard Taft, "Message on Interstate Commerce and Anti-Trust Laws and Federal Incorporation, January 7, 1910," in *Presidential Addresses and State Papers of William Howard Taft,* 1:534.

Roosevelt depicted the emergence of the large corporation as a natural and largely beneficial product of economic evolution: "Combinations in industry are the result of an imperative economic law which cannot be repealed by political legislation." Rather than seek to atomize large corporations through antitrust, Roosevelt's New Nationalism called for the state to play a central role in defining the terms of economic change. "The effort at prohibiting all combination has substantially failed. The way out lies, not in attempting to prevent such combinations but in completely controlling them in the interest of the public welfare."[10] To this end, he called for a national industrial commission, modeled on the Interstate Commerce Commission, that would "have complete power to regulate and control all the great industrial concerns engaged in interstate business."[11] Working cooperatively with large enterprises, it could collect information on production and corporate organization, facilitate agreements among competitors, and supervise labor relations and corporate capitalization. Corporations voluntarily submitting to the commission's authority would do so with the expectation that it would convey a de facto antitrust exemption. "Any corporations not coming under the commission should be exposed to prosecution under the antitrust law, and any corporation violating the orders of the commission should also at once become exposed to such prosecution," with the commission ensuring that court decrees were executed effectively.[12] Thus, the Sherman Act would be reserved for the "bad trusts" that expanded through monopolistic practices.

Taft dismissed TR's distinction between good and bad trusts, arguing that it was unworkable as a matter of law. It would "put into the hands of the court a power impossible to exercise on any consistent principle which will insure the uniformity of decision essential to just judgment." Requiring courts to make these determinations would "give them a power approaching the arbitrary, the atom of which might involve our whole judicial system in disaster."[13] Taft's concern over vesting too much discretionary authority in any body found another expression in his understanding of the presidency—one that stood in clear contrast to that of Roosevelt, who embraced (if not invented) the role of activist president pressing the limits of his constitutional authority. In a lecture given after he left office, Taft argued that Roosevelt's view

10. Theodore Roosevelt, "The New Nationalism," in *The Works of Theodore Roosevelt* (New York: Charles Scribner's Sons, 1926), 17:12.
11. Theodore Roosevelt, "A Confession of Faith," in *The Works of Theodore Roosevelt,* 17:279.
12. Ibid., 280–81.
13. Taft, "Message on Interstate Commerce and Anti-Trust Laws and Federal Incorporation," 531.

ascribing an undefined residuum of power to the President is an un-
safe doctrine . . . it might lead under emergencies to results of an
arbitrary character, doing irremediable injustice to private rights. The
mainspring of such a view is that the Executive is charged with responsibility for the welfare of all the people in a general way, that he
is to play the part of a Universal Providence and set all things right,
and that anything that in his judgment will help the people he ought
to do, unless he is expressly forbidden. . . . The wide field of action
that this would give to the executive one can hardly limit.[14]

This activist conception of the presidency typified by Roosevelt and his expansive New Nationalism found another critic in Woodrow Wilson.

Wilson countered Roosevelt's vision with his New Freedom. His chief
critique of the New Nationalist position was that it would invest power in
the trusts and render the population dependent on the benevolence of large
corporations and the state. In Wilson's words: "Mr. Roosevelt says that the
trusts are a natural development of our economic system, that they are inevitable, that they have come to stay, that we must trust them just as we would
the railroads, and accepting them regulate them, and then see to it that justice
is done . . . through the regulated trusts." Wilson went on to ask: "Is the
government going to make Christians of these trusts? Is the government
going to put bowels of compassion in them? Is the government going to
persuade them to be kind and benevolent to us in the use of their enormous
and irresistible power? Is that all the government is going to do? Is the government going to take us back a hundred years, nay, 150 years, in our development and put us in tutelage again?"[15] Wilson was convinced that
Roosevelt's scheme would lead inexorably to capture: "If the government is
to tell big business men how to run their business, then don't you see that
big business men have to get closer to the government even than they are
now? Don't you see that they must capture the government, in order not to
be restrained too much by it."[16]

Beneath the semantic conflicts, Wilson shared some ground with Roosevelt in his acceptance of large-scale business enterprises ("good trusts," ac-

14. William Howard Taft, *Our Chief Magistrate and His Powers* (New York: Columbia University
Press, 1916), 144–45.

15. Woodrow Wilson, "An Address to Workingmen in Fall River, Massachusetts, September 26,
1912," in *The Papers of Woodrow Wilson* (Princeton, N.J.: Princeton University Press, 1978), 25:261–62.

16. Woodrow Wilson, *The New Freedom: A Call for the Emancipation of the Generous Energies of a People*
(New York: Doubleday, Page & Co., 1913), 201–2.

cording to Roosevelt), which were presented as "necessary and natural . . . and probably inevitable." Nonetheless, he argued that trusts have been "artificially created; they have been put together, not by natural processes, but by the will, the deliberate planning will, of men who were more powerful . . . and who wished to make their power secure against competition."[17] The problem did not compel a momentous increase in the power of the state or the creation of radically new institutions but a simple refinement of the antitrust laws. Wilson explained:

> Everybody who has even read the newspapers knows the means by which these men built up their power and created these monopolies. Any decently equipped lawyer can suggest to you statutes by which the whole business can be stopped. . . . there must be no squeezing out of the beginner, no crippling his credit; no discrimination against retailers who buy from a rival; no threats against concerns who sell supplies to a rival; no holding back of raw materials from him; no secret arrangements against him. All the fair competition you choose, but no unfair competition of any kind.[18]

Wilson called for an extension of antitrust legislation. He wanted "to see to it that competition is so regulated that you won't have to regulate trusts, because there won't be any."[19] This New Freedom was much in keeping with the political-economic doctrines of the Progressive Era. Yet, by the 1920s, the New Nationalist vision of state-economy relations would capture the imagination of New Era economists, policy makers, and business associations. This would be possible only after the crisis of war made a rapid expansion of state capacity necessary.[20]

The Preparedness Controversy

When war erupted in Europe in 1914, the United States had no means to exert military or naval strength an ocean away. The Progressive reform agenda had a distinct domestic orientation: any desire to become actively involved in

17. Ibid., 164–65.
18. Ibid., 172, 173.
19. Wilson, "An Address to Workingmen," 266.
20. See Theodore Roosevelt, *The New Nationalism* (Englewood Cliffs, N.J.: Prentice Hall, 1961), and Wilson, *The New Freedom*. See Martin J. Sklar, *The Corporate Reconstruction of American Capitalism, 1890–1916* (Cambridge: Cambridge University Press, 1988), for a discussion of the debates.

the international arena was subordinated to the immediate goal of eliminating a host of domestic problems. America would stand apart from, and as an example to, the Old World rather than become enmeshed in its corruption. Moreover, many Progressives embraced a politically salient interpretation of the origins of war. As Arthur Link explains: "Wars were mainly economic in causation and necessarily evil because bankers with money to lend, munitions-makers with sordid profits to earn, and industrialists with markets to win were the chief promoters and beneficiaries of war." Link continues: "[T]he path of progressive righteousness led straight to disarmament, an international system based on compulsory arbitration, and an unequivocal repudiation of war."[21]

The lack of popular support for involvement in the European war forced Wilson to strike a position of neutrality, officially proclaimed on August 4, 1914. However, strict neutrality would prove impossible to sustain. The British maritime presence and the blockade of the North Sea threatened to undermine U.S. foreign trade. Although Wilson objected to the British blockade, he did not offer any substantial challenge. Indeed, trade was quickly adjusted away from Germany and Austria and toward the Allies, revealing the hollowness of American neutrality. Between 1914 and 1916, U.S. trade with Germany and Austria fell from $169.3 million to $1.16 million. During the same period, U.S. trade with the Allies increased from $825 million to $3.2 billion. By 1915, shipments of food, raw materials, and munitions were combined with lines of credit to finance allied purchases.[22] Germany sought to impede the free flow of trade to the British Isles with a submarine blockade and the sinking of the British liners Falaba and Lusitania in the spring of 1915. The loss of American life on the undefended ships and the growing submarine menace led Wilson to strongly object to the German policy in a series of letters. Simultaneously, he began a peace initiative to end the war before the United States was forced into the fray. Ultimately, these efforts proved unsuccessful.

Wilson's denunciation of the German submarine strategy was hollow without the requisite military might. While the strong Progressive support for neutrality was ever present, Theodore Roosevelt, Henry Cabot Lodge, Elihu Root, and other Eastern Republicans stressed the importance of national security, predicted an invasion of the United States, and attacked the adminis-

21. Arthur S. Link, *Woodrow Wilson and the Progressive Era, 1910–1917* (New York: Harper & Brothers, 1954), 180.

22. Arthur S. Link, *American Epoch: A History of the United States Since the 1890s* (New York: Alfred A. Knopf, 1955), 177–78.

tration's response to German aggression as pathetically feeble and ineffectual. In *America and the World War,* Theodore Roosevelt's contempt for Wilson's policy could not have been more pronounced. He portrayed the president as "the great official champion of unpreparedness in military and naval matters" and "the great apostle of pacifism." As he noted: "In theory, President Wilson advocates unpreparedness, and in the actual fact he practices, on our behalf, tame submission to wrong-doing and refusal to stand for our own rights or for the rights of any weak power that is wronged."[23] For Roosevelt, the adherence to pacifism was simply fatuous:

> Blessed are the peacemakers, not merely the peace lovers; for action is what makes thought operative and valuable. Above all, the peace prattlers are in no way blessed. On the contrary, only mischief has sprung from the activities of the professional peace prattlers, the ultra-pacificists, who, with the shrill clamor of eunuchs, preach the gospel of the milk and water of virtue. . . . To condemn equally might which backs right and might which overthrows right is to render positive service to wrong-doers. It is as if in private life we condemned alike both the policeman and the dynamiter or black-hand kidnapper or white slaver whom he has arrested.[24]

With the 1916 election on the horizon and the growing threat of German submarines, Wilson responded to his critics while continuing to claim credit for keeping the United States out of the war. In July 1915, he called on the secretaries of war and the navy to develop plans for strengthening national security. The army proposal, a product of planning at the Army War College and Secretary of War Lindley Garrison, was a moderate response given the strident demands of the preparedness bloc. It called for a significant increase in the size of the army, at that time authorized at a strength of 100,000 men, and the creation of a 400,000-man Continental Army. The Continental Army, a volunteer national reserve with professional military training, would replace the National Guard, which would be of little use in international conflicts due to its poor training, patronage-based leadership, and inclusion under the jurisdiction of state governors, who rejected calls for national training standards. While this proposal fell far short of Roosevelt's call for universal conscription and nationalization of munitions industries, it was an improvement

23. Theodore Roosevelt, *America and the World War* (New York: Charles Scribner's Sons, 1915), 184–85, 211.
24. Ibid., 244–45.

over the existing system—unless viewed from the perspective of the National Guard. The navy proposed a grand construction program resulting in naval parity with the British by 1925. The proposal called for a five-year, $500 million program to build a wide array of battleships, cruisers, and submarines.[25]

The preparedness debate became a highly divisive issue, particularly within the Democratic Party. A coalition of thirty to fifty Democrats in Congress, largely from the South and West, formed a formidable antipreparedness bloc. Through their control of the House Military Affairs Committee and support of the House Majority Leader Claude Kitchen, they threatened to prevent passage or seriously modify the president's legislation. Indeed, the antipreparedness bloc countered the proposed creation of a Continental Army by calling for an expansion and "federalization" of the National Guard. Wilson actively courted congressional support for preparedness, albeit with little discernible effect. The opposition to the army-reorganization plan continued unabated. In the end, the Army Reorganization Act of 1916 was a compromise measure. It increased the army to 11,327 officers and 208,338 enlisted men, compared with the existing peacetime contingent of 5,029 officers and 100,000 men. As a concession to the antipreparedness bloc, it expanded the National Guard and integrated it into the national system of defense, in lieu of the Continental Army. Finally, it authorized the War Department's volunteer camps to provide summer training for civilians. While the Army Reorganization Act was weakened by the legislative process, the final naval legislation was strengthened as it passed through the Senate. With the vigorous support of the president, the act accelerated the navy's five-year construction program so that it would be completed in three years. During the first year alone, the navy was authorized to complete construction on four battleships, eight cruisers, twenty destroyers, and thirty submarines.[26] In addition, Congress passed the Merchant Marine Act of 1916, which authorized the creation of the United States Shipping Board to regulate rates and services of ships on interstate, coastal, and international routes. Although it was authorized to own and operate a merchant fleet, to preserve neutrality it was prohibited from purchasing the ships of belligerents.[27]

The expeditious expansion of the army and navy forced policy makers to address the politically hazardous question of finance. Wilson and Treasury

25. George C. Herring Jr., "James Hay and the Preparedness Controversy, 1915–1916," *Journal of Southern History* 30, no. 4 (1964): 383–404.

26. Link, *Woodrow Wilson and the Progressive Era,* 188–91.

27. Link, *American Epoch,* 187.

Secretary McAdoo were united in their commitment to meet most of the expenditures with revenues rather than debt. Although the administration wanted to draw on an increase in customs receipts and taxes on tobacco and alcohol, this regressive tax would have forced the financial burden of preparedness on the lower classes precisely at the time that some congressional Progressives were popularizing the belief that the rich and the large corporations stood to gain from preparedness as they would gain ultimately from war. If this was the case, they concluded, the wealthy should bear more of the costs. The Emergency Revenue Act of 1916 was clearly designed to raise revenue from the wealthiest part of the population. It increased the income tax from 1 to 2 percent. By retaining the existing exemptions, the majority of the population remained free from the new taxes. Moreover, the act raised the surcharge on incomes in excess of $20,000 to a maximum of 13 percent, thereby creating an effective income tax as high as 15 percent. The inheritance tax was increased to a maximum of 10 percent, subject to a $50,000 income exemption. The act also targeted corporations, expanding a variety of corporate taxes and imposing a tax of 12.5 percent on the net profits of armament producers. At the time, the Emergency Revenue Act of 1916 was portrayed as "soak-the-rich" legislation, which appeased the radical and Progressive forces in Congress.[28] Tax policy would continue to contain a strong Progressive element after 1916. However, Congress would decide to place an ever-greater reliance on debt: "[T]he revenue required for the war reached proportions that would have made financing half the cost of the war effort through taxation politically suicidal."[29]

Although the legislation of 1916 authorized an expansion of the armed forces and the generation of new revenues, there was no institutional apparatus to mobilize the economy. Even basic information on economic production and facilities—the most important commodity—was sorely lacking. As Brigadier General Seth Williams recalled: "A need . . . apparent from the first that became more vital every day and that was the cause of great delay and confusion is embodied in the word STATISTICS. A hundred times a day information was necessary that no one could produce quickly. Such questions as: How many looms are there in the United States that can produce heavy duck? How many spindles can make the necessary yarn? Perhaps the trade association had to be requested to procure the answer. Perhaps there was no

28. John F. Witte, *The Politics and Development of the Federal Income Tax* (Madison: University of Wisconsin Press, 1985), 79–81; Link, *Woodrow Wilson and the Progressive Era*, 195–96.

29. Nell Irvin Painter, *Standing at Armageddon: The United States, 1877–1919* (New York: W. W. Norton, 1987), 316.

trade association."[30] The scarcity of information reflected a scarcity of administrative resources. The War Department's general staff was dramatically understaffed, with a mere nineteen officers serving under two major generals. The general-staff shortage and the organizational disarray had direct implications for the War Department's ability to direct a war of any magnitude.[31] Grosvenor B. Clarkson explains that the general staff "had made no study and, as a body, had no comprehension of the fact that in modern war the whole industrial activity of the Nation becomes the commissariat of the army. It had no affiliations with the complex and fecund industrial life of the Nation. It understood nothing of the intertwining ramifications of production. It knew nothing of the economic sequences of new demands, so vast as to exceed existing supplies. Its sole experience in business was the placing of orders for comparatively small quantities of goods in a market so well stocked and so voluminously supplied that they had no appreciable effect on reserves or prices."[32]

The first step in addressing the lack of administrative preparedness was to conduct an inventory of the nation's industrial plant. In 1916, a committee of the Naval Consulting Board conducted an ambitious inventory of approximately eighteen thousand facilities. At the same time, the secretary of war appointed a board to survey munitions resources and determine the need for government production. Most important, however, were the activities of the Council of National Defense, authorized by Congress as part of the Army Appropriations Act of 1916. The council, consisting of six cabinet members (navy, war, interior, agriculture, commerce, and labor), was charged with coordinating industrial demands and overseeing preparation for possible entry into the war. The council's advisory commission united representatives of industry, labor, and the railroads to conduct a survey of American industry. By delegating authority to the representatives of various economic interests, the council could gain access to information superior to the census and the survey of industry conducted every five years.[33]

The council's advisory commission was composed of seven commissioners, each assigned to a specific area of concern for mobilization: transportation,

30. Quoted in E. Elberton Smith, *The Army and Economic Mobilization* (Washington, D.C.: Center of Military History, United States Army, 1991), 37.

31. See Edward M. Coffman, "The Battle Against Red Tape: Business Methods of the War Department General Staff, 1917–1918," *Military Affairs* 26, no. 1 (1962): 1–10.

32. Grosvenor B. Clarkson, *Industrial America in the World War: The Strategy Behind the Lines, 1917–1918* (Boston: Houghton Mifflin, 1923), 111.

33. Bernard M. Baruch, *American Industry in the War: A Report of the War Industries Board, March 1921* (New York: Prentice Hall, 1941), 17.

engineering and education, munitions and manufacturing, medicine and sur-
gery, raw materials, supplies, and labor. To facilitate the collection of information, they worked through committees composed of individuals with an
intimate knowledge of substantive issue areas—often through their commercial ties and activities. In the words of Bernard Baruch, the loose committee
structure provided "a center of contact between the Government and the
industrial life of the Nation. The purpose was to make available . . . the best
thought and effort of American industrial and professional life for the successful prosecution of the war." Although the "council had no administrative
power . . . [i]t consciously or unconsciously served as a great laboratory devoted to discovering and making articulate the new administrative problems
which the war was to involve."[34] Over time, the committees evolved into
some of the key mobilization agencies (e.g., the Railroad Administration, the
Food Administration). Most important, however, was the chain of events that
led to the creation of the War Industries Board.

The War Industries Board

The Council of National Defense established a Munitions Standards Board in
March 1917, under the chairmanship of Frank Scott. The board was initially
responsible for promoting standardization. However, once reconstituted as
the General Munitions Board, it also became a clearinghouse for purchase and
supply. To address difficulties stemming from its unwieldy size, its limited
legislative mandate, and the uneven coverage of various facets of war production, the General Munitions Board was replaced by the War Industries Board
on July 28, 1917.[35] The WIB, composed of five civilians and representatives
of the army and navy, had a smaller executive than the General Munitions
Board to reduce the "need for consultation at the expense of action." Still, the
WIB was not granted any new legal powers. "Extra-legality for the emergency was again invoked to give it powers which were hardly warranted by
the Act that had created the patron bodies of the Council of National Defense
and the Advisory Commission."[36] The new WIB was designed as a coordinat-

34. Ibid., 19.
35. Link, *American Epoch*, 207–8.
36. Frederick Palmer, *Newton D. Baker: America at War* (New York: Dodd, Mead & Co., 1931),
1:353.

ing body, a clearinghouse for the war-industry needs. A lack of executive authority and staffing and the continual attempts of the army and navy to control purchasing created severe administrative problems and rendered the board impotent. Mobilization proceeded by trial and error through the winter of 1917–18, when shortages of rail transportation and coal threatened the war effort.[37]

In the spring, the WIB was reorganized following the near collapse of economic mobilization. At the urging of Treasury Secretary William McAdoo and over the objections of Secretary of War Newton Baker, Wilson appointed the respected financier and WIB veteran Bernard Baruch to the chairman-ship—a man he had come to refer to as "Doctor Facts," reflecting his broad knowledge of American industry.[38] Baruch accepted the position after Wilson agreed to strengthen the powers of the office so that the officeholder might better meet the tasks at hand. Baruch's political loyalty to Wilson and his earlier donation of $35,000 to Wilson's reelection bid did not hurt his chances of securing the position.[39] His strong rapport with business and his skill in creating and nurturing multiple constituencies in and out of government were also decisive.[40] Under the authority granted in the Overman Act, Wilson separated the WIB from the Council of National Defense and increased its power. In the letter offering Baruch the chairmanship of the WIB, Wilson described the board's duties as: "(1). The creation of new facilities and the disclosing, if necessary, the opening up of new or additional sources of supply; (2). The conversion of existing facilities, where necessary, to new uses; (3). The studious conservation of resources and facilities by scientific, commercial and industrial economies; (4). Advice to the several purchasing agencies of the Government with regard to the prices to be paid; (5). The determination, wherever necessary, of priorities of production and of delivery and of the proportions of any given article to be made immediately accessible to the several purchasing agencies when the supply of that article is insufficient, either temporarily or permanently; (6). The making of purchases for the Al-lies."[41] Wilson gave Baruch final authority in all areas except price fixing,

37. See the discussion in Clarkson, *Industrial America in the World War,* 37.

38. For a discussion of the controversies surrounding Baruch's appointment, see Daniel R. Beaver, "Newtown D. Baker and the Genesis of the War Industries Board, 1917–1918," *Journal of American History* 52, no. 1 (1965): 43–58. See Palmer, *Newton D. Baker,* 1:201–2.

39. Neil A. Wynn, *From Progressivism to Prosperity: World War I and American Society* (New York: Holmes & Meier, 1986), 73–74.

40. See Jordan A. Schwarz, *The Speculator: Bernard M. Baruch in Washington, 1917–1965* (Chapel Hill: University of North Carolina Press, 1981), 58–63.

41. President Woodrow Wilson to Bernard M. Baruch, March 4, 1918, reproduced in Baruch, *American Industry in the War,* 24–25.

which was assigned to the WIB's Price Fixing Committee under the directic of Robert S. Brookings.

The WIB exercised a remarkable amount of power despite the fact that it worked with a minimum of statutory authority. It fulfilled a central role in coordinating the demands of the various consuming agencies but lacked the formal authority to assess the validity of service demands or override the purchasing agents of the army and navy. Its real power rested largely in its possession of expertise that the state, working alone, lacked. As George Soule explains: "The real basis of the board's authority, aside from its presidential instructions, lay in the detailed knowledge it accumulated concerning the amount and location of the various supplies that could be obtained, and of the demands being placed upon them."[42] Its power was also derived from its close connections—if not de facto integration—with the commercial interests it was charged with regulating. It appended to the state the administrative capacities of private associations to compensate for its own organizational weaknesses.

The Organization of the War Industries Board

The reconstituted War Industries Board consisted of a board and a number of functional divisions. The board included the heads of the divisions and representatives of the navy and the army under the chairmanship of Bernard Baruch. The functional divisions addressed price fixing, conservation, require- ments, and priorities. Additional divisions "controlled" steel, chemicals, fin- ished products, and labor. Although authority was centralized in Chairman Baruch, two factors hampered the WIB's efforts. First, the WIB was not given the formal sanctions necessary to implement its mandate. It had the power to establish priorities and fix prices, both of which could be used to force some compliance on the part of business and the armed services. And the WIB occasionally threatened to commandeer plants, supplies, and stock- piles, but this was a blunt policy tool. Any concerted attempt at coercing businesses could result in challenges to (or the outright rejection of) the WIB's makeshift legislative authority. Thus, it was forced to rely on coopera- tion. In the end, Baruch was most successful in his use of moral suasion and personal ties to win the voluntary compliance of business.

A second and more significant problem had direct implications for the

42. George Soule, *Prosperity Decade: A Chapter from American Economic History, 1917–1929* (London: Pilot Press, 1947), 15.

organization of the agency. The WIB was required to engage in relatively comprehensive planning activities. Although the nation's involvement in the war was brief, the demands were intensive. The American Expeditionary Force and allied demands claimed about one-quarter of the nation's economic output—no fewer than 9.4 million workers of an active workforce of 37 million were engaged in wartime production.[43] Despite the magnitude and complexity of the tasks involved, the WIB possessed neither the staff nor the technical expertise to coordinate the mobilization process. The WIB compensated for the deficit of administrative capacities by drawing on the expertise of business. Executives from major corporations—the so-called "dollar-a-year men"—staffed most of the major offices in the WIB. Critical, in this respect, were the fifty-seven commodity sections. Each section was composed of a WIB official, commonly a top executive from a corporation working in a related line of business, and officers from each of the consuming agencies (e.g., the army). The sections provided information to the functional divisions and maintained constant communication with the companies in specific lines of business. This communication was facilitated by the creation of war service committees representing industry by line of business. The members of the war service committees were selected by the heads of corporations and trade associations to act as agents in negotiations with the government. Although the war service committees were originally under the supervision of the Council of National Defense, the task was assigned to the U.S. Chamber of Commerce after the fall of 1917. "Where a national organization already existed, the chamber had it appoint a war service committee with authority to represent it, and where a trade was not organized, the chamber took steps to secure its organization and the appointment of such a committee."[44] The U.S. Chamber of Commerce certified the committees as being broadly representative of firms within the industry.[45]

The war service committees and the trade associations provided the WIB with access to a wealth of detailed economic information that would have been impossible to gather independently. When the WIB needed to address problems of supply or develop appropriate conservation measures, it relied heavily on the associations to hold conferences with corporate representatives

43. John Maurice Clark, *The Costs of War to the American People* (New Haven, Conn.: Yale University Press, 1931), 34.

44. Baruch, *American Industry in the War*, 22.

45. See Hugh P. Baker, "Practical Problems of Trade Associations," *Proceedings of the Academy of Political Science* 11, no. 4 (1926): 80, and Robert D. Cuff, "Woodrow Wilson and Business-Government Relations During World War I," *Review of Politics* 31, no. 3 (1969): 404–5.

from the industries. The committees provided a context in which firms in an industry could pool information on production, costs, and pricing. They "granted business far more immunity from the antitrust laws than even the most sanguine advocates of industrial cooperation espoused during the Progressive years."[46] Finally, the associations provided much of the administrative support and staffing for the commodity sections.[47]

The organizational scheme adopted by the WIB conveyed quasi-official status on the trade associations and war service committees. Although this decentralization and devolution of authority gave the WIB access to a new source of expertise and information, it also created distinct but predictable managerial problems. "Technical skill was concentrated along the outer edges of the WIB, within the commodity sections. This had important consequences for the distribution of authority within the organization, for it meant that much of the daily decision making affecting industry took place here through close consultation between industrial representatives and the various section heads. Decisions occurred, in other words, where the territory of the board and of industry overlapped, beyond the reach of central officials." The opportunities for abuse were obvious: "[I]f the commodity chief became a lobbyist for his industry . . . there was little the board could do about it."[48] Indeed, given the extreme decentralization and the obvious conflicts of interest, such activities, when they occurred, were usually beyond detection. Nonetheless, they should have been anticipated. Participation was voluntary and imposed costs. It should come as no surprise that something more than patriotism led businesses to become integrated into the WIB.

The Policy Process

The central responsibilities of the War Industries Board included processing requirements and assigning priorities, controlling prices, and promoting conservation and efficiency in industry. Consider the process adopted by the WIB to execute its central duties, as well as the patterns of state-economy relations that process entailed. The clearance of requirements and the assignment of priorities to the various orders were essential to channel scarce resources to the areas of the war effort where the needs were most immediate. Representa-

46. Paul Koistinen, "The 'Industrial-Military Complex' in Historical Perspective: World War I," *Business History Review* 41, no. 4 (1967): 392.
47. Robert D. Cuff, *The War Industries Board: Business-Government Relations During World War I* (Baltimore: Johns Hopkins University Press, 1973), 158–76.
48. Ibid., 174.

tives of the WIB, the army and navy, the Emergency Fleet Corporation, the Allied Purchasing Committee, the Red Cross, the Railroad Administration, the Food Administration, and the Marine Corps staffed the Requirements Division. Agencies submitted their requirements for raw materials and finished products to the division. These requirements were subsequently turned over to the commodity sections, where they were examined in light of the available resources, facilities, and production schedule. In the end, they were returned to the division, along with some estimate of when the requirements could be met. As the war progressed, the process was hampered by the lack of long-term planning; requirements constantly outpaced the productive capacities of industry. The latter problem could be attributed to the WIB's lack of any independent authority to assess the requirements as presented by the consuming agencies. Under these conditions, it became critical for the WIB to develop some means of processing requirements to give immediate attention to emergency war-related demands and free labor, raw materials, energy, and transportation for defense production. To this end, a priorities system was established.[49]

The Priorities Division assigned each of the orders placed by the services a priority designation. Orders that were of immediate military necessity were assigned the status of AA, whereas other orders were given a designation of declining significance (A, B, C, D). These classifications were combined with numbers (e.g., A-1, A-2) to refine the designations further. Although the priorities system began with critical industries, by July 1, 1918, all industries were placed under WIB regulation. Firms failing to observe the priorities system could be commandeered and operated by the secretary of war, under the authority granted in the National Defense Act of 1916. Short of this drastic measure, the WIB and other mobilization agencies could restrict or eliminate access to transportation and raw materials, making continued production impossible. In large part, the very existence of these sanctions was sufficient to force compliance.

The job of the Priorities Division became increasingly complex as the priorities system was expanded to cover all industries. The demands placed on the division were addressed in several ways. First, a system of automatic classifications was established whereby class A orders placed by the navy, the War Department, and the Emergency Fleet Corporation would be assigned a rating of A-5 upon the submission of a signed affidavit describing the uses of the materials. In addition, an additional organ, the Priorities Board, was cre-

49. Clarkson, *Industrial America in the World War,* 116–27.

ated in March 1918. Under the leadership of Priorities Commissioner Edwin Parker, the board brought together representatives of the services and mobilization agencies to coordinate the ordering and delivery of high-priority goods. In April 1918, the priorities system was expanded on an economy-wide basis to direct the flow of coal, coke, and transportation. By September, the Priorities Board had graded seventy-three industries and some seven thousand plants according to a four-part classification. Class I industries and plants were deemed essential to the war effort; industries in lower classifications could not receive energy and transportation until the needs of the Class I installations had been met. The system for controlling the flow of energy and transportation created clear incentives for companies to convert to defense production.[50] In essence, a system for prioritizing the orders of the armed services had evolved into an experiment in economic planning and coordination on a much broader scale than previously envisioned. Yet, what planning existed proceeded through consultation and bargaining with key economic associations. To understand why, one must examine the WIB's price-fixing activities.

Price-fixing and the WIB's system of priorities worked together as critical components of a single system. With the suspension of the price system, some alternative means had to be found to stimulate the production of urgently needed materials. The price-fixing system provided such a mechanism by establishing prices that would maximize production. Initially, procurement depended on cost-plus contracting. Contracts were negotiated on a firm-by-firm and case-by-case basis by determining the cost of production and adding an acceptable rate of return. As one might expect, this process involved "endless disputes concerning the calculation of costs."[51] Given the difficulties and delays, the WIB needed to set prices on a broader scale through its Price-Fixing Committee, chaired by Robert Brookings, who was, in turn, directly responsible to the president. As a man who had made his fortune in lumber and had been a member of the National Civic Federation, Brookings was strongly predisposed to business-government cooperation.

The price-fixing process—like other activities at the WIB—was consultative and hampered by informational asymmetries. The Federal Trade Commission (FTC) facilitated the determination of prices by conducting investigations of production costs in critical sectors. Although the FTC was a relatively new agency, it had absorbed at its creation analysts from the old Bureau of Corporations experienced in compiling economic data. Neverthe-

50. Baruch, *American Industry in the War*, 53–58.
51. Clarkson, *Industrial America in the World War*, 172.

less, information scarcity continued to constrain the would-be price-fixers and forced ongoing consultation and bargaining with trade association and corporate representatives to set mutually acceptable prices. As Jordan A. Schwarz explains:

> [T]he committee . . . conducted meetings with a great dearth of information basic to industry prices under consideration. Patriotism and intimidation were the committee's chief weapons for arriving at fair prices; but it remained to be proved that industry was patriotic or could be intimidated. Brookings often began sessions with recalcitrant industrialists by lecturing them on their civic responsibilities. In a sense he had no choice, because the meetings were really bargaining sessions in which only one of the two parties knew the facts of costs and inventories. Negotiating for the government required all the bluff and finesse of poker . . . the WIB threatened, cajoled, and pleaded with industrialists to remember a higher cause than their profits. In the end, there was no price-fixing without the consent of the businessman whose price was fixed.[52]

Negotiation and bargaining were essential: "[T]he Administration simply did not possess the organization or the administrative capacity to handle a complicated price-fixing strategy."[53] Negotiations were ongoing: price schedules had to be revised every three months to accommodate the changing costs of labor and inputs. Even as the WIB acquired its own stock of data and expertise, price-fixing continued to be a cooperative enterprise.

Prices commonly emphasized the costs encountered by the smaller producer, who would not be capable of producing with the efficiency of its larger counterparts. The goal was to stimulate high levels of production, even if it had the consequence of expanding the profit margins of the largest firms. The FTC estimated that a price structure high enough to support small steel producers would have yielded profits of 25 to 50 percent for fully integrated or near fully integrated steel firms.[54] Indeed, one might argue that a key difficulty inherent in this system of price-fixing was the existence of dual and potentially contradictory missions. The committee was compelled to create the incentives to maximize production, placing a secondary emphasis on

52. Schwarz, *The Speculator,* 74–75.

53. Robert D. Cuff and Melvin I. Urofsky, "The Steel Industry and Price-Fixing During World War I," *Business History Review* 44, no. 3 (1970): 305. Palmer, *Newton D. Baker,* 2:323.

54. Cuff and Urofsky, "The Steel Industry and Price-Fixing During World War I," 299.

fighting inflation. Nevertheless, President Wilson had committed the government to the latter objective in July 1917, when he had announced that the "just" prices established for military purposes would have to apply to the general population as well.[55]

The WIB's priorities system was created to meet immediate war needs and to channel resources from civilian production to the war economy. The Conservation Division, under the direction of Arch W. Shaw, freed up raw materials, labor, energy, and transportation for war production by promoting greater efficiency in production, shipping, and distribution. The division promoted standardization, convincing commercial interests to reduce the number of styles and varieties. Lacking detailed information or expertise to design engineering standards, the Conservation Division relied heavily on trade associations. Schedules of regulations were issued only after soliciting the suggestions of industry actors concerning areas for potential conservation. Final regulations were also distributed to producers for comment and revision before they were promulgated. In the end, producers were required to pledge their compliance with conservation regulations, conscious of the fact that a failure to comply could result in a loss of access to raw materials, energy, and transportation.[56]

Some of the most successful conservation measures eliminated the "wasteful" variety of goods produced and distributed. A few examples are illustrative. Automobile-tire producers were directed to reduce the styles and sizes of tires from 287 to 9 within two years, saving rubber, labor, and transportation costs. Standardization of farm implements led one manufacturer to reduce the variety of wagon gears from 1,736 to 16. Even seemingly trivial regulations could have a significant impact. A regulation requiring that thread manufacturers place 200 yards of thread on each spool (compared with the industry practice of 100–150 yards) resulted in a 25 percent reduction in labor, wood, packing materials, and shipping space, freeing some six hundred freight cars per year for alternative uses. Similarly, regulations in the woman's clothing industry resulted in a 20 to 25 percent reduction in yards of fabric. A related regulation requiring that knit goods be shipped in paper-covered bales rather than boxes resulted in an estimated annual reduction of 17,312 freight cars and 141 million boxes. These and a multitude of additional regulations left virtually no industry untouched.[57]

55. See Simon Litman, *Prices and Price Control in Great Britain and the United States During the World War*, Carnegie Endowment for International Peace, Preliminary Economic Studies of the War, no. 19 (New York: Oxford University Press, 1920).

56. Baruch, *American Industry in the War*, 65–67.

57. Examples taken from ibid., 67–71.

The War Industries Board provides a perfect illustration of compensatory state building. In each of its activities it relied heavily on the cooperation of regulated industries. While some contemporary champions of the WIB would portray its decentralization and cooperative stance as the products of thoughtful institutional design, they were far more an outgrowth of its limited administrative capacities. As Robert Cuff correctly notes: "[T]he theme of decentralization should be regarded largely as a rationalization for the Board's dependency on oligarchies of private economic power. To find in decentralization an object of praise under these circumstances is essentially to find virtue in the Board's recognition of necessity."[58] Indeed, we might agree with Paul Koistinen's conclusion that "the board was a form of industrial self-regulation writ large."[59] William Leuchtenburg arrives at a similar assessment when he writes that the "outstanding characteristic of the war organization of industry was that it showed how to achieve massive government intervention without making any permanent alteration on the power of corporations."[60] When the WIB faded into history, the economic associations remained, in many cases strengthened from their war experience.

Of course, cooperation was facilitated by the high levels of demand and the opportunities for profitability during the war. As Rexford Tugwell recalled in 1927: "Cautious attitudes toward over-equipment, customary wage-levels, trade secrecy, and hallowed management practices had all been modified. There was an ever-expanding demand; no one needed to worry about markets. Profits were high and certain. All that had to be done was to make the wheels go round and the product come out, faster and faster and faster. If there was any difficulty about technique, technicians, workmen, and plans were provided. On the whole, the war was an industrial engineer's Utopia."[61] With the integration of the WIB and economic associations, it was difficult to locate a line of demarcation separating the state and civil society. The heavy reliance on corporate resources and the expedient of staffing the agency with dollar-a-year men and corporate support personnel raise the serious question whether the WIB constituted a government agency or an odd amalgam of public and private power created under the pressures of war. Whatever the answer, it is clear that this model was applied in the WIB and other mobiliza-

58. Robert D. Cuff, "Bernard Baruch: Symbol and Myth in Industrial Mobilization," *Business History Review* 43, no. 2 (1969): 130.
59. Koistinen, "The 'Industrial-Military Complex' in Historical Perspective," 394.
60. Leuchtenburg, "The New Deal and the Analogue of War," 129.
61. Tugwell, "America's War-Time Socialism," 364.

tion agencies and would continue to find an expression long after the Armistice.

Additional Mobilization Agencies

The War Industries Board was the central mobilization agency during the war. There were, however, a number of other important agencies involved in the mobilization of the civilian economy, including the U.S. Food Administration, the National War Labor Board, the U.S. Railroad Administration, the U.S. Shipping Board, and the U.S. Fuel Administration. Several of these agencies adopted models of administration and patterns of state-economy relations similar to those embraced by necessity at the War Industries Board, whereas others embraced a more statist model. In virtually every case the war experience would continue to shape experience and practices following the war, through the desire either to adopt some of the wartime expedients or, in the case of labor, to avoid at all costs a continuation of federal regulation of industrial relations. Although some of these agencies are examined in greater detail in subsequent chapters, it is useful to explore them briefly at this point.

The U.S. Food Administration

The Food Administration (USFA) was created under the 1917 Lever Food and Fuel Control Act, which gave the president the power to regulate the price, production, and distribution of food and to control all inputs into the production of food, via voluntary agreements with farmers and processors, the licensing of producers and distributors, and the direct purchase and sale of foodstuffs.[62] Administration of food controls was placed under the direction of Herbert Hoover, who had been called back from the Belgian relief agency. The Food Administration's major duty was to maintain the supply of food for the American Expeditionary Force and the Allies. The war made incredible demands on the agricultural sector. In the three years before the war (1914–16) agricultural exports had averaged 6,959,055 tons per year. This figure almost doubled in 1917–18, reaching 12,326,914 tons, and increased again to 18,667,378 tons the next year. The Food Administration had to meet the

---

62. Ronald Schaffer, *America in the Great War: The Rise of the War Welfare State* (New York: Oxford University Press, 1991), 35. George Soule, *Planning U.S.A.* (New York: Viking Press, 1967), 43.

demand of war by promoting maximum production, conservation, and, via a call for voluntary meatless and wheatless days, the substitution of surplus foodstuffs for those that were in high demand. To a limited extent, the administration stabilized prices and promoted production through direct market activity, by buying foodstuffs through the U.S. Grain Corporation and Sugar Equalization Board. Regulation relied primarily on licenses, decentralized administration, and profit incentives. Producers, distributors, and associations were thus provided with licenses upon agreeing to maintain open books, charge "reasonable" prices (i.e., cost plus the prewar average profit), and observe a variety of practices to prevent hoarding, speculation, waste, and the inefficient use of transportation. Many of the Food Administration regulations (e.g., the 1918 50–50 rule requiring the use of wheat substitutes such as potato flour and oatmeal) drew a great deal of protest from farmers, bakers, grocers, and housewives.[63]

The administration of agricultural controls was highly decentralized and relied heavily on voluntarism. The Food Administration's 1,400 workers were vastly outnumbered by "an army of 750,000 volunteers, mainly women, in local committees and organizations."[64] Each state was under the direction of a federal food administrator, who supervised county administrators, who, in turn, supervised special committees at the town level. To account for local variations in prices, boards were created at the county level, where representatives of grocers, retailers, and consumers could negotiate and determine fair prices. These prices were published in local newspapers and used by the county administrators to determine whether licensees were meeting their obligation. Despite the decentralization of the administrative apparatus, new regulations were adopted only after the Food Administration had consulted extensively with the representatives of commodity groups and trade associations. As with the WIB, the decision to staff the agency with individuals drawn from the sector facilitated this consultation.[65] The experiences of the Food Administration played a key role in motivating Hoover's advocacy of associationalism in the 1920s. It also shaped expectations within the agricul-

63. Soule, *Prosperity Decade*, 20–29; Paul Kleppner, *Continuity and Change in Electoral Politics, 1893–1928* (New York: Greenwood, 1987), 147.

64. Wynn, *From Progressivism to Prosperity*, 70.

65. See Robert D. Cuff, "Herbert Hoover, the Ideology of Voluntarism, and War Organization During the Great War," *Journal of American History* 64, no. 2 (1977): 358–72; Litman, *Prices and Price Control in Great Britain and the United States During the World War*, 206–61; Albert N. Merritt, *War Time Control of Distribution of Foods: A Short History of the Distribution Division of the United States Food Administration, Its Personnel and Achievements* (New York: Macmillan, 1920), 29–36.

tural economy by revealing the role regulation could play in securing increases in farm incomes.

The National War Labor Board

As noted in Chapter 2, war creates great problems for labor markets. Labor shortages, accelerated production schedules, and inflation combine to create a situation ripe for labor militancy. Organized labor was integrated into the policy process through participation in a number of agencies during the war. While most mobilization agencies created offices or bureaus to address labor problems, a select set of agencies had a more direct impact on workers. The U.S. Employment Service in the Labor Department worked to place unskilled laborers in essential industries. The Selective Service facilitated these efforts by providing draft exemptions for men working in war industries. The goal was to create incentives to force workers into war production.

The National War Labor Board (NWLB) was the key agency responsible for regulating industrial relations. The NWLB consisted of five business representatives and five labor representatives. It was placed under the cochairmanship of former president William Howard Taft and attorney Frank P. Walsh, the former chairman of the Commission on Industrial Relations. Labor participation in the NWLB reflected a growing consensus concerning the place of organized labor in the political economy. By the time of the war, the leaders of the labor movement—particularly the conservative American Federation of Labor—"accepted the reality and inevitability of the new corporate political economy" and began "to seek accommodation for the national unions within it." Thus, the AFL leadership envisioned a system in which "varying numbers of legally equivalent institutions established temporary or permanent accommodations with each other through voluntarist action and looked to the state simply for ratification of these bargains."[66]

The Wilson administration sought to win labor support for the war effort by recognizing the right of workers to organize and engage in collective bargaining. Indeed, the NWLB operated on an official principle that anticipated the National Labor Relations Act: "The rights of workers to organize in trade unions and to bargain collectively through chosen representatives is recognized and affirmed. This right shall not be denied, abridged, or interfered

---

66. Christopher L. Tomlins, *The State and the Unions: Labor Relations, Law, and the Organized Labor Movement in America, 1880–1960* (Cambridge: Cambridge University Press, 1985), 61, 77. See Clark, *The Costs of War to the American People*, 47.

with by the employers in any manner whatsoever."[67] Although Wilson and the NWLB attempted to strike a conciliatory posture toward organized labor, there was an iron fist inside the velvet glove. Wilson and the agencies adopted a more repressive stance if labor problems persisted after consultation with the war agencies. When strikers refused to return to work, it was not uncommon for federal agents to raid labor union offices, seize union records and equipment, and arrest labor leaders. Wilson went as far as to threaten striking workers in Bridgeport, Connecticut, with the cancellation of their occupational exemptions.[68]

The tight wartime labor markets and the administration's pro-labor position resulted in significant gains for labor—a point explored in greater detail in Chapter 6. Union roles increased dramatically, from 2.77 million in 1916 to 4.125 million in 1919. Moreover, wage rates increased rapidly: the average annual wage for all industrial workers increased from $765 in 1916 to an unprecedented $1,272 by 1919.[69] Even accounting for the wartime inflation, the increase in wage levels was significant. However, unionization rates would plunge precipitously in the 1920s, in the absence of the NWLB. Corporations increasingly created in-house mechanisms for worker representation, internalized industrial relations, and provided a host of benefits that partially replaced the functions of unions with a system of welfare capitalism.

The U.S. Railroad Administration

The WIB, USFA, and NWLB adopted decentralized structures and integrated private associations into the policy process. In certain key areas, however, a more statist model was necessary, giving rise to a form of planning that entailed more intensive government controls than even the New Nationalists would have condoned outside of emergency conditions. This was particularly the case with the U.S. Railroad Administration.

The railroads formed a voluntary Railroads' War Board on April 11, 1917, hoping to prevent a more direct form of rail regulation. This industry effort was problematic from the start. Without government subsidies or guarantees, it proved incapable of imposing costs; it could not compensate lines that lost revenue as a result of the more centralized administration of resources. Moreover, the Railroads' War Board encountered another obstacle in the antitrust

67. E. Jay Howenstine Jr., *The Economics of Demobilization* (Washington, D.C.: American Council on Public Affairs, 1944), 147.

68. Schaffer, *America in the Great War*, 36–37.

69. *Statistical History of the United States*, series D 589–602, 604.

provisions of the Sherman Act and the prohibitions on pooling in the Interstate Commerce Act. Conflict and national emergency were not sufficient justification for a suspension of antitrust provisions absent a framework of direct government control. As Walker D. Hines recalls: "When in November, 1917, the Railroad's War Board announced the putting into effect of a pooling arrangement east of Pittsburgh, the members of the Board were asked to see the Attorney General, who took the position that such action was prohibited by law, and he was unwilling to accede to the view that the Anti-trust Act was suspended. . . . its action was regarded as of doubtful legality by the Department of Justice."[70]

The amount shipped under the direction of the Railroads' War Board in 1917 stood at an unprecedented 398 million ton-miles. Although revenues increased as a result, the higher operating expenses left the rails in worse shape financially than they had been before the war.[71] The railroads also proved incapable of managing competing demands for priority shipments and coordinating rail shipments and merchant marine vessels. This resulted in the near collapse of the rail system and supply effort in 1917, thus effectively ending private control of the industry and legitimizing the direct government control the rails had sought to avoid. The Railroad Administration was created in December 1917.

Under the direction of Treasury Secretary McAdoo, the Railroad Administration pooled the lines to administer the national railways as an integrated system—an achievement that eluded the voluntary Railroads' War Board, which had been constrained by antitrust concerns and an inability to compensate participants. It took control of the lines, terminals, rolling stock, and telegraph companies. Government control of the rails also created an opportunity to address the labor problems that had long affected the railroads. General Order No. 8 facilitated the unionization of railway labor by declaring that "no discrimination will be made in the employment, retention, or conditions of employment or employees because of membership or nonmembership in labor organization."[72] Although the railroads were cautious about such a transfer of authority to public-sector administrators, Wilson and McAdoo

---

70. Walker D. Hines, *War History of American Railroads* (New Haven, Conn.: Yale University Press, 1928), 14–15.

71. *Statistical History of the United States,* series Q-82. Conclusions regarding financial status of the rails is based on a comparison of operating revenues and operating expenses for 1916 and 1917. See *Statistical History of the United States,* series Q-106 and 107.

72. Quoted in D. O. Bowman, *Public Control of Labor Relations: A Study of the National Labor Relations Board* (New York: Macmillan, 1942), 14.

guaranteed an acceptable rate of return (based on the earnings during the period 1914–17) and proper maintenance. Moreover, railroad controls were not comprehensive.

The direct control of the rails was a success. Before the creation of the Railroad Administration, mobilization had been plagued by a shortage of rail transportation. The pooling of freight and the coordination of lines by the administration resulted in an actual surplus of 300,000 freight cars by the end of the war. Following the experience of unified operation, there were many advocates of some form of nationalization. As one observer noted from the perspective of the 1920s: "We are unable to understand why this should be done only in a war emergency. If there are unquestioned benefits to be had from a union of all the railroads in war time, there must be at least some benefits in peace time."[73] Wilson rejected nationalization and an extension of wartime controls, thereby forcing Congress to pass new legislation if it was to make any alteration in the prewar system of regulation. In the end, the Transportation Act of 1920 incorporated some of the features of wartime rail management into the regulatory activities of the Interstate Commerce Commission. Rather than return to its traditional stance of setting maximum prices to protect the shipper—a policy authorized under the Hepburn Act of 1906—the Interstate Commerce Commission was now directed to set *minimum* prices to increase the economic stability of the sector by preventing ruinous price competition.[74]

The U.S. Fuel Administration

Working under the authority granted in the Lever Act, Wilson created the Fuel Administration on August 23, 1917. It sought to increase production by setting prices high enough to force marginal mines into full service while simultaneously promoting conservation, seeking to free up resources by convincing citizens to reduce traveling and heating. The Fuel Administration was placed under the direction of Harry A. Garfield, president of Williams College and personal friend of Wilson. As noted in the discussion of the WIB above, mobilization came perilously close to failing during the severe winter of 1917–18 due, in part, to coal shortages. State and municipal officials commandeered coal shipments for distribution within their jurisdictions, while ships filled with war supplies sat stranded at port for want of fuel. Republicans

---

73. "Merging 12,000 Miles of Railway," *Nation,* February 2, 1927, 107.
74. Soule, *Prosperity Decade,* 33–35.

in Congress charged that Garfield was unfit for his position and argued that the fuel crisis reflected his administrative incompetence. Garfield, in turn, cast blame on the railroads, arguing that the fuel crisis resulted from the breakdown of the transportation system—a point the railroads rejected through reference to the priorities they were forced to meet. The Fuel Administration sought to reduce the impact of the fuel shortage by promoting conservation. It introduced "lightless nights" in November 1917—an unpopular measure that proved most difficult to implement. On January 16, 1918, Garfield ordered all factories east of the Mississippi—with the exception of munitions plants—to cut their fuel consumption during the week of January 18–22 to the levels usually consumed on Sundays. This effort was followed by a mandatory five-day week and the call for reduced fuel consumption on the subsequent nine Mondays (i.e., "heatless Mondays"). Garfield hoped that this would free coal to clear the ports. Although the decision was denounced from many corners, within a week the ports began to clear, allowing for the resumption of the mobilization process and the movement of coal to the cities. Nonetheless, fuel shortages continued to hamper industry through the summer and fall of 1918.[75]

For the remainder of 1918, Garfield promoted conservation and expanded production. Daylight saving time was introduced by Congress in 1918 to conserve on fuel, with estimated savings of more than 1.25 million tons of coal. Similar to the activities of the Food Administration, the Fuel Administration called on drivers to observe "gasless Sundays," beginning September 1, 1918.[76] Despite its difficulties, the Fuel Administration secured increases in production. In 1917, the number of bituminous coal mines stood at 6,939, a number that increased to 8,319 in 1918 under the incentives created by high prices and demand.[77] At the same time, total coal production increased from a prewar level of 503 million tons to 579 million tons in 1918—a level of production that the mining industry would not surpass until 1942, when a new world war once again stimulated a demand for expanded production.[78] Crude-petroleum production increased from a prewar level of 301 million barrels to 356 million barrels in 1918.[79] The historic levels of fuel production

75. Seward W. Livermore, *Politics Is Adjourned: Woodrow Wilson and the War Congress, 1916–1918* (Middletown, Conn.: Wesleyan University Press, 1966), 68–70, 86–89; Kleppner, *Continuity and Change,* 148–49.

76. Wynn, *From Progressivism to Prosperity,* 75–76. Robert Higgs, *Crisis and Leviathan: Critical Episodes in the Growth of American Government* (New York: Oxford University Press, 1987), 138.

77. *Statistical History of the United States,* series M 98.

78. *Statistical History of the United States,* series M-88.

79. *Statistical History of the United States,* series M-133.

suggest that the Fuel Administration was a success, even if it was embroiled in controversy throughout its short history.

The U.S. Shipping Board

When World War I began, the British merchant marine dominated ocean trade, with four times the tonnage registered in the United States. However, the demands of war reduced British ship production to one-third of its peacetime level, while the German submarines claimed a quarter of the existing fleet. When the lack of ocean transportation threatened to become a critical bottleneck in the supply flow, Congress created the U.S. Shipping Board and appropriated $50 million for new construction under the direction of a subsidiary Emergency Fleet Corporation. Although the Emergency Fleet Corporation was chartered on April 16, 1917, its first new ship was not delivered until December 1918.[80] Indeed, the demand for new vessels was apparently met in spite of the efforts of the Emergency Fleet Corporation.

When conflicts between the heads of the Emergency Fleet Corporation and the Shipping Board threatened to derail this critical link in the mobilization effort, President Wilson placed control of the two agencies under Edward Hurley, the chairman of the Federal Trade Commission. Under Hurley's direction, the corporation began building new shipyards along the Atlantic coast, with the goal of producing no less than 15 million tons of new shipping. In the end, this ambitious effort produced little.[81] The Emergency Fleet Corporation also financed projects to facilitate construction indirectly. By the end of the war, it had invested some $64 million to build homes and apartments to house approximately thirty thousand people involved in the shipbuilding industry and improve transportation.[82]

As noted above, the government's construction program was clearly behind schedule. In response to the slow pace of new construction, the U.S. Shipping Board repaired 500,000 tons worth of German ships that had been seized from American harbors. The board added to the fleet by commandeering more than 3 million tons of ships being built in private shipyards and another half million tons of Dutch ships that had been left in port because of the German submarine presence. At the same time, the Shipping Board's Division of Planing and Statistics began operating the entire fleet as a single pool, thus increasing the cargo size and reducing by one-half the time re-

80. Soule, *Planning U.S.A.*, 45.
81. Link, *American Epoch*, 210.
82. Wynn, *From Progressivism to Prosperity*, 119.

quired to load and unload ships. These efforts, when combined with the modest efforts of the Emergency Fleet Corporation, provided the transportation needed to convey troops and matériel from the United States to Europe.[83]

In 1919, 1.1 million tons of merchant vessels were built in the United States, approximately twice the amount built in 1917.[84] At the U.S. entry into the war, the nation had 61 shipyards with 215 ways, employing some 50,000 workers. At the Armistice, there were 341 yards with 1,284 ways in service or close to completion, employing 350,000 shipyard workers.[85] While the Emergency Fleet Corporation and the Shipping Board stimulated the expansion of the nation's shipbuilding capacity, the time lag was so great as to limit its relevance for the war effort, and the waste was colossal. As John Maurice Clark noted, the "Shipping Board and Emergency Fleet Corporation . . . spent 3,316 millions and were left with ships, plants, structures, and materials which were worth only a small fraction of their cost." He concludes: "[T]here could hardly be a more forceful example of the lavishness and inevitable waste—if such a term is permissible—which are almost inseparable from meeting a national emergency which is inexorably sudden, and short, especially in a country of democratic individualism."[86]

The War Finance Corporation

The final war agency to be discussed is the War Finance Corporation. The government absorbed unprecedented amounts of capital for war financing, creating a capital shortage that threatened the expansion of necessary war production facilities. At the urging of Treasury Secretary McAdoo, Congress created the War Finance Corporation (WFC) on April 5, 1918. Under the direction of Eugene Meyer, the WFC was capitalized at $500 million and granted the authority to raise an additional $3 billion through the sale of bonds. The WFC was directed to provide funds to financial institutions, which would distribute capital through loans, and to lend funds directly to critical commodity producers. Through its Capital Issues Committee, the WFC screened new corporate stock and bond issues to limit conflicts with war-bond drives. Created late in the war, the WFC served a very limited role. Overall, it made loans totaling $67.7 million.[87] However, as Robert Higgs rightly

83. Link, *American Epoch*, 210. Soule, *Planning U.S.A.*, 46.

84. *Statistical History of the United States*, series Q-183.

85. Clark, *The Costs of War to the American People*, 43.

86. Ibid., 111, 44.

87. Paul Studenski and Herman E. Krooss, *Financial History of the United States* (New York: McGraw-Hill, 1952), 300.

notes: "At the end of the war, . . . the WFC refused to die; at least it would not stay dead for long. So pregnant with political utility was this all-purpose financial rescue mission that it was destined to be revived, not always under the same name, again and again."[88] Indeed, unlike other war agencies, the WFC continued to have a presence in the nation for more than a decade after the Armistice. In 1919–20, the WFC's primary duty was to assist exporters. During the remainder of the 1920s, it focused on exports from the farm economy. As noted in Chapter 9, the WFC would also play an important role in the federal government's response to the Great Depression, albeit under the name of the Reconstruction Finance Corporation.[89]

The Performance of the Wartime Economy

The War Industries Board and several other mobilization agencies reflected a common pattern of state-economy relations and tenets of institutional design whereby the administrative capacity to mobilize the economy was developed by appending private organizations to the state. The administrative and political benefits were substantial even if the loss of political control over the process, and the potential for exploitation, were considerable. A powerful case can be made against this model of state building: it provided serious problems of political control and oversight, while creating serious conflicts of interest. Nevertheless, given the emergency conditions and the lack of administration capacities, issues of institutional design were of lesser importance than the answer to a simple question: Would the model provide a means of mobilizing the economy for war? If the answer was yes, all else was of secondary importance.

One can adopt various indicators of performance, the relevance of each depending on the goals that one associates with economic mobilization. At the broadest level, one can examine the changes in economic performance during the war years. It should not be surprising that production levels increased dramatically during the war. The annual average gross national product for the five-year period 1912–16, as expressed in 1929 prices, was $62.5 billion, compared with $71.9 billion for 1917–21. Per capita GNP stood at an annual average of $632 for the period 1912–16, increasing to $683 in

88. Higgs, *Crisis and Leviathan*, 142.
89. Wynn, *From Progressivism to Prosperity*, 217.

1917–21, once again adjusted for inflation.[90] Reflecting the highly progressive wartime taxes and increases in manufacturing wage levels, the growing income was not as concentrated in the top of the income distribution as it had been before the war. In 1916, the top 1 percent of the population received 15.58 percent of total national income; three years later, this figure had fallen to 12.84 percent.[91] Increased incomes were also available in the farm economy, largely as a product of heightened war demand for farm commodities. Thus, the parity ratio (an index of prices received and paid by farmers, with a 1910–14 base of 100) reached a high of 120 during the war.[92] Comparable levels would be impossible to achieve in the decades after the war, when politicians and agricultural experts would puzzle over alternative means of achieving parity. Of course, the increases in production stimulated by war and the shortages of labor and key commodities fueled inflation. The cost of living index (1913 = 100) increased from a level of 101.1 in 1915 to 188.7 in 1919. Indeed, by 1920, the index reached 203.7. In some five years, the price level had more than doubled.[93]

Was there success in meeting the demands of war? One indicator of performance is the level of exports to Europe. Given the embargo against Axis powers, this provides a clear picture of the levels of production for the Allies during the war. In 1915, the United States exported $1.97 billion worth of goods to Europe. The average value of exports for the years 1916–19 was $4.37 billion per year, more than double the 1915 level.[94] Unsurprisingly, the largest increases in exports took place in the broad categories of manufactured foodstuffs, semimanufactured goods, and finished manufactures. Comparing the value of merchandise exports in current dollars for 1915 and the average for 1917–19, one finds that the export of manufactured foodstuffs increased from $455 million to $1.39 billion, the value of semimanufactures increased from $356 million to $1.1 billion, and the value of finished manufactures increased from $807 million to $2.45 billion.[95] In each case, the U.S. economy produced and exported amounts that would have been unimaginable absent the demands of war.

As one might expect, the most important export during war takes the form of military personnel and munitions. Over 4.7 million military personnel

90. *Statistical History of the United States*, series F 3, 4.
91. *Statistical History of the United States*, series G 131
92. *Statistical History of the United States*, series K 138.
93. *Statistical History of the United States*, series E 158.
94. *Statistical History of the United States*, series U 123.
95. Calculated from figures in *Statistical History of the United States*, series 64–66.

served during the war, 53 percent of whom were sent overseas.[96] Although some 480 ships were delivered to the Emergency Fleet Corporation to transport personnel, half of the American Expeditionary Force had to be transported in British vessels.[97] Despite the negative assessment of many concerning the levels of direct war-related production, one must note that the brevity of the war and the lack of established defense industries at the beginning of the war placed significant limits on the potential levels of war production. In the words of Ronald Schaffer:

> [T]he Armistice came too soon for industry to reach peak production. A nation whose economy had been operating at near-capacity before April 6, 1917, needed months, if not years, to arrange contracts, build or convert plants, construct machine tools, accelerate munitions production, adapt weapons to changes demanded by people at the front, and deliver the instruments of war. To have armed and supplied all its troops completely in the spring of 1917, the United States would have required, years earlier, a vast military-industrial network that isolationist, antimilitarist taxpayers would not have tolerated and an economy that produced less for civilians.[98]

While the actual production of munitions may have been less than desired, American production did reach its peak near the end of the war. Belligerents intent on the continuation of hostilities had to expect steady increases in U.S. production in each subsequent year, a factor that may have played some role in the decision to end the war.

The seemingly endless demand and the high levels of production created enormous opportunities for corporate profit taking. W. Jett Lauck, an economist working for the brotherhoods and unions of railway employees, conducted a study of wartime profits in 1920. He concluded that corporate profits for the period 1916–18 were $4.8 billion above the level of the three years before the war. The data on returns on investment is quite suggestive of the profitability of the war period. It revealed that

> [t]wo thousand and thirty corporations earned in net profits over 100 per cent per year on their capital stock during the three war years, that 5,724 showed net profits of more than 50 per cent and that

96. *Statistical History of the United States,* series Y 715, 728.
97. Clark, *The Costs of War to the American People,* 44.
98. Schaffer, *America in the Great War,* 61–62.

20,000 earned from 20 to 50 per cent. The average profits during the three war years of all the corporations in the United States with net incomes of $1,000,000 or more approximated 24 per cent on their capital stock. . . . [T]his great group of corporations controlling products essential to daily life made profits sufficient to replace the entire value of their capital stock within a period of slightly over four years.[99]

Despite the claims that the applications of Taylorism, experiments in standardization, and patriotism promoted efficient production in the national interest, the waste and high levels of corporate profitability during the war were not ignored by contemporary observers. As the *Nation* remarked in a 1920 editorial: "Bit by bit facts are emerging which show that our participation in the European War was attended with the same orgy of graft and incompetence that has been present in other conflicts." While the propaganda surrounding the war effort created the impression of efficient war production governed by "higher ideals" and "a better morality in public service," it appeared that the waste and profiteering were veiled by "the shortness of hostilities" and "the fact that the social and legal code which ruled during the war made it impossible for anybody to utter a word of criticism."[100] The high corporate earnings and the problem of waste should come as no surprise given the basic features of the mobilization agencies: delegation of high levels of power to the regulated parties, a lack of meaningful political oversight, and cooperation won through the promise of continued profitability.

From War to Peace

How would the economy return to a peacetime structure after the cessation of hostilities? This question was debated for much of the war. Various economic groups sought to shape the reconstruction efforts to preserve their own interests. Labor hoped to reduce hours, maintain the right to organize, and limit postwar unemployment. Farm associations hoped to secure price and/or export supports to buoy farm incomes. Business representatives wanted the relaxation of antitrust measures combined with support for exports, govern-

99. Charles Patrick Sweeney, "Where Your Money Goes," *Nation*, June 12, 1920, 796. See also "The High Cost of Labor," *Nation*, June 19, 1920, 818.
100. "War, Waste, and Business," *Nation*, November 24, 1920, 582.

ment purchase of surpluses, and other subsidies. As James Mock and Evangeline Thurber correctly note: "Few persons and fewer groups interested in 'reconstruction' had the same definition for the term. All of them talked about the problems the word embraced and about the changes involved, but definitions of reconstruction were as rare in the post-bellum world as specific, constructive war aims had been while we were fighting Germany."[101]

The diversity of demands complicated President Wilson's growing political and physical weakness. When the Republicans realized landslide gains in 1918, the rejection of the Democrats was interpreted as a referendum on Wilson. As Paul Kleppner explains: " 'Wilsonianism,' which two years earlier had represented accomplishment and prosperity, by 1918 symbolized the frustration and resentment that became so widespread during the war. . . . The collective outcome of this process left the Democrats a battered, weakened, and demoralized minority."[102] In this environment, with growing Republican attacks on Wilson's wartime management, the president was simply incapable leading the demobilization efforts and drawing on the wartime gains to promote a progressive agenda.

During the fall of 1918, the U.S. Chamber of Commerce called on Wilson to create a reconstruction commission, with representatives of business, labor, and agriculture, to design a demobilization program. Senate Republicans introduced a bill to create a reconstruction study commission under the control of the Congress. Senate Democrats introduced a proposal calling for a commission that would be controlled by the president. Wilson, however, showed little interest in the possibility of such a commission or in promoting policies to ease the transition into peacetime. There was also a good deal of support for a continued role for the WIB in guiding demobilization and preventing postwar deflation, a consensus within the business community was intent on antitrust revisions. Antitrust exemptions could extend some of the intercorporate relations that had been initiated during the war, thereby providing a means of managing production levels and promoting continued standardization and simplification. While Baruch was fervent in his support for such measures, Wilson's opposition to the various schemes for regulation tempered his eagerness after the Armistice. Certain WIB functions could be transferred to existing departments—the Conservation Division, for example, would find

101. James R. Mock and Evangeline Thurber, *Report on Demobilization* (Norman: University of Oklahoma Press, 1944), 34.
102. Kleppner, *Continuity and Change*, 151.

a new home in the Commerce Department. But without Wilson's assistance, a more ambitious program of reconstruction would be impossible.[103]

In the end, many, including Baruch, argued that the nation had not been fully mobilized and thus reconstruction would not be necessary. Indeed, despite his earlier support for an extended WIB presence, Baruch ultimately accepted the argument that the nation that most rapidly returned to a peacetime structure would have a distinct economic advantage.[104] Those who supported early and rapid reconversion triumphed. Why did demobilization occur so quickly? In part, the answer invokes ideology. Wilson and other New Freedom Progressives were hesitant to support the kind of New Nationalist relations that had been permitted of necessity during the war. Given the nature of the mobilization process, this ideological purity was a bit odd. As Neil A. Wynn suggests, rapid demobilization "was a result of the desire to free business and the economy from direction and regulation as quickly as possible—even more unremarkable given that most of the bodies were, of course, made up of businessmen."[105]

Demobilization occurred hurriedly following the declaration of an armistice on November 11, 1918. Baruch resigned from the WIB on November 28, 1918, in time to attend the peace negotiations in Paris. The agency closed soon thereafter, although a small staff from the WIB was placed in the Commerce Department, where an Industrial Board was created to promote price stabilization and trade expansion. The board was put under the leadership of WIB veteran George Peek, who was himself anxious to return to the private sector. Other mobilization agencies followed the WIB. The Fuel Administration and the National War Labor Board ceased operation in March 1919. The Food Administration closed its doors in early 1920. The WFC, in contrast, continued to exist throughout the 1920s, albeit with a new mission of promoting agricultural exports.[106]

While demobilization occurred quickly, many advocates believed that the nation could not forget the one great lesson of the war, namely, the high costs associated with a lack of preparedness. Baruch would continue to make reference to America's lack of wartime preparation at the onset of the war; he hoped for continued preparedness and called for the maintenance of "a peace-

103. See Robert F. Himmelberg, "The War Industries Board and the Antitrust Question in November 1918," *Journal of American History* 52, no. 1 (1965): 59–74.
104. Mock and Thurber, *Report on Demobilization*, 30–31.
105. Wynn, *From Progressivism to Prosperity*, 199.
106. Ibid.

time skeleton organization based on the experience of the war-making agencies." This agency, staffed by representatives of the armed services and industry, would maintain plans for mobilization and would work with industry
committees so that "it would be possible within a few days to create an
organization which immediately would mobilize all of the industries of the
nation and quickly make available for the Government all of its resources."
More important, Baruch recommended that the government administer an
industrial policy to promote the development of raw materials critical to the
war effort. Such support could take the form of "a protective tariff, a bonus,
an exemption from taxation for a limited period, licensing, or any other effective means." Finally, he called for the preservation of existing munitions production capacities through "outright purchase or by small orders for
munitions and airplanes while at all times there must be kept on hand the
necessary dies, jigs, fixtures, etc., needed for the manufacture of munitions."[107] Lessons concerning the demands of mobilization should have been
one of the enduring lessons of the war. Indeed, as E. Elberton Smith explains:

> The number one lesson brought home for the first time by World
> War I was the importance of the matériel side of modern war and
> the inevitable time lag between the mobilization of troops and the
> mobilization of their all important supporting equipment and sup-
> plies. No longer could the United States rely upon the affirmation of
> William Jennings Bryan that in a national crisis "a million men would
> spring to arms overnight." The fighting of a major war under twenti-
> eth century conditions required elaborate plans for the industrial mo-
> bilization of the entire nation and, when war actually arrived, the
> subjection of the entire economy to a regime of extensive controls.
> More than this it required an indispensable period of time, reckoned
> not in hours or months but in years, before the nation's economic
> potential could be successfully harnessed and converted to producing
> munitions on the scale required.[108]

The demands of mobilization and memories of the preparedness controversy
did not, however, lead to the creation of a permanent apparatus. The lessons
of the war, at least with respect to the demands of rapid mobilization, would
be forgotten for a generation.

107. Bernard M. Baruch to Woodrow Wilson, December 24, 1919, reprinted in Baruch, *American
Industry in the War*, 7–8.
108. Smith, *The Army and Economic Mobilization*, 39.

To assure that the memory of the WIB would not fade (and that its influence would be magnified), Baruch supported Grosvenor Clarkson's writing of *Industrial America in the War* with a major subvention of $38,000, plus expenses. This book, which attributed much of the allied victory to the efforts of the War Industries Board and elevated Baruch as a symbol of the mobilization process, was distributed widely to libraries and individuals.[109] Baruch's *American Industry in the War,* a final report of the War Industries Board, carried a similar message. These publications, along with Baruch's constant presence in policy debates and regular WIB reunions throughout the next several years, were used to publicize and amplify the successes of the board. The wartime experience would have remarkable power in shaping ensuing public-policy debates. New popular expectations concerning the role of the state were wed to a newly organized economy, new agencies, and a network of elites who shared their experience in the mobilization process. In the end, these factors shaped the evolution of the New Deal's Associational Regime and, simultaneously, placed limits on its success.

Toward the Political Economy of the New Era

Given the unprecedented fiscal stimulus of the war, one would rightly anticipate that the elimination of war contracts and the return of so many workers to the civilian economy could send the economy into a deep slump. At the end of World War I, some 25 percent of the workforce was committed to war production. Absent a plan for "reconstruction," rapid demobilization resulted in the wholesale cancellation of war contracts and an immediate surge in unemployment. By the spring of 1919, however, the economy was expanding again, driven by high levels of household savings accumulated during the war, the pent-up consumer demand, and inflationary pressures that created incentives for immediate business investment in new productive capacity. The rapid rise in prices was a source of some concern. In a 1920 article, W. Jett Lauck attributed the rise in prices following the war to an "orgy of profiteering" that had "reached the limits of human endurance." He continued:

> The abnormal conditions created by the war, as was to be expected, greatly increased prices and the cost of living. The war-time era of destruction, restricted production and unproductive consumption reduced pre-existing stocks of goods and made additional accumula-

109. See Cuff, "Bernard Baruch."

tions more difficult, and thus brought about an excess of demand for
commodities over the supply available. The net result has been scarcity values and constant rises in prices during and since the war. . . .
it is evidence that the scarcity situation arising from the war is, and
will continue to be, taken advantage of by conscienceless producers,
distributors, and speculators, to extract huge and indefensible profits
from all classes of the people.[110]

The immediate postwar inflation was short-lived due to shifts in spending
and monetary policies. Large wartime budget deficits ($9 billion in 1918 and
$13.4 billion in 1919) had a strong stimulative effect on the economy. Now
spending reductions and high taxes to buy down the debt placed strong
downward pressures on growth. As the Federal Reserve raised the discount
rate to stem inflation and speculative investment, the combination of a budget
surplus and a tight credit policy induced a sharp decline. The economy entered depression complete with a 50 percent reduction in the price level. This
deflation was particularly problematic for firms that incurred short-term bank
debt to finance inventories that rapidly lost their dollar value with falling
price levels.[111] By the middle of 1921, industrial production had dropped 35
percent, and unemployment had jumped from the 1.4 percent of 1919 to
11.7 percent. The 5 million jobless workers, 30,000 bankruptcies, and almost
500,000 farm foreclosures were most striking when seen in contrast to the
economic boom of the war years. But the new price structure, combined with
unmet consumer demands, brought rapid recovery.[112]

From the fall of 1921 through 1929, the economy entered a period of
expansion, punctuated by mild recessions in the summer of 1924 and the
winter of 1927. As a generalization for the period as a whole, steady economic
growth, productivity gains, and price declines resulted in growing incomes,
high levels of employment, and a prosperity that was broadly enjoyed outside
of the agricultural sector, which witnessed a loss of income following the
expansion and high levels of production during the war. Regardless of the
circumstances, decision makers in the public and private sectors searched

110. W. Jett Lauck, "Changing Prices and the Cost of Living," *Nation*, October 27, 1920, 472–73.
111. Charles H. Schmidt and Ralph A. Young, *The Effects of War on Business Financing: Manufacturing
and Trade, World War I* (New York: National Bureau of Economic Research, 1943), 12.
112. Peter Fearon, *War, Prosperity, and Depression: The U.S. Economy, 1917–45* (Lawrence: University
of Kansas Press, 1987), 15–18; Robert Sobel, *The Age of the Giant Corporations: A Microeconomic History of
American Business, 1914–1970* (Westport, Conn.: Greenwood Press, 1972), 25.

through their wartime experiences to find new ways of addressing problems, promoting high levels of production, and introducing stability. Demobilization from World War I, one might argue, entailed a decade-long process of dissemination, as the model of state building applied under the emergency of war was appealed to in industry after industry.

PART II

Demobilization and the Dissemination of a Model

Total wars require the complete mobilization of society. As hostilities draw to a close, officials must turn to a second portentous task: the return of government, economy, and society to peacetime status. Demobilization requires decisions concerning a host of factors, such as the rate at which conscripts will be returned to the civilian labor force, the lifting of price controls and other wartime regulations, the disposal of stockpiles, the cancellation of munitions orders, and the ultimate disposition of war production facilities. Absent a coherent plan, the end of a war may be highly destabilizing. Those responsible for war mobilization worked without clear precedents. Ad hoc decisions were the order of the day, and insufficient attention was directed to the process of demobilization. We often understand demobilization as the immediate suspension of wartime restrictions. It is useful, however, to extend our time frame to consider the long-term dissemination of wartime experiences. World War I forced the development and adoption of new policies, administrative models, and patterns of state-society relations. It altered popular expectations concerning the potential role of the state. Similarly, it forced changes in the political organization of economy and society. Interests were newly organized and, together with previously organized interests, were integrated into the war apparatus, where they learned quickly the potential benefits that could be derived from public policies. Given the popular expectations concerning a more expansive state role, we should not be surprised that the demands for new public commitments emerged quite rapidly. Government officials and various private-sector elites sought to determine how the innovations adopted during the war might be extended to address a host of problems. In the end, the new policies, administrative models, and patterns of state-economy relations became core components of a new regime.

During the decade of the 1920s, the war experience had a significant impact on the evolution of policy, institutions, and politics in a number of areas. In some cases, developments were a direct extension and application of the war experience. This was certainly true in the area of business regulation (Chapter 4), where associationalist initiatives at the Commerce Department, the Federal Trade Commission, and the Interstate Commerce Commission drew heavily on the wartime experience. In other cases, including industrial relations, agricultural policy, and economic management, the connections were more subtle but nonetheless evident. In industrial relations (Chapter 5), the growing reliance on company unions initiated during the war was extended into the 1920s, albeit in combination with intensified efforts to replace independent union organizations with internal representation through the further dissemination of welfare capitalist benefits. This associational response to the "labor problem" made representation and welfare contingent on business voluntarism, which was itself contingent on economic profitability. In farm policy (Chapter 6), high wartime incomes juxtaposed with the postwar collapse of the farm economy stimulated debates on how the state might inflate and stabilize the farm economy by inducing scarcity. This was a departure from traditional USDA practices, which were tailored to promote ever-higher farm production. In all areas, the major policy proposals each required a higher level of private-sector organization. The decisions over policy responses would depend, in the end, on judgments regarding the proper role of the state and its responsibility for facilitating, rather than guaranteeing, outcomes. In economic management (Chapter 7), the Federal Reserve assumed a more activist role following the war. At the same time, debates over fiscal policy and countercyclical spending resulted in efforts to create an associational response to the business cycle, one that would prove contingent on business voluntarism.

In each of these cases, a new emphasis was placed on new institutional designs, voluntary associations, and efforts to introduce stability and extend public authority to altogether new areas. In each case, the developmental path had been redirected by the experience of war. When taken together, the events in these policy areas provided the foundations for a new regime that would take form during the structural crisis of the Great Depression.

4

Associationalism and the Regulation of Business

Mr. Hoover entered the Department of Commerce with his mind made up to reestablish the essence of the plan inaugurated by the War Industries Board, but he had to find a different method. In time of peace the government is not endowed with such great prescriptive prerogatives, and the mere suggestion of that power contravenes the political doctrines of those who were then and are now in authority. Consequently the Secretary of Commerce had to exercise his ingenuity to find another means to the same end. Propaganda and the United States Chamber of Commerce, the American Engineering Council, and various trade associations were instruments at hand. The touchstone of the campaign was the self-interest of the individual producer and merchant.   —George T. Odell, 1925

I believe we are in the presence of a new era in the organization of industry and commerce in which, if property directed, lie forces pregnant with infinite possibilities of more progress. I believe that we are, almost unnoticed, in the midst of a great revolution or, perhaps a better word, transformation of the whole super-organization of our economic life. We are passing from a period of extremely individualistic action into a period of associated activities. . . . I believe that through these forces we are slowly moving toward some sort of industrial democracy. We are upon its threshold, if these agencies can be directed solely to constructive performances in the public interest.
—Herbert Hoover, 1924

War created a new reference point for regulatory politics. During the war, the War Industries Board promoted corporate organization in trade associations through the decentralized network of commodity sections. As shown in Chapter 3, the commodity sections provided an interface between businesses in each sector through the war service committees. Writing from the perspective of 1921, Emmett Hay Naylor recalled:

When the War Industries Board was formed and found it necessary to get into immediate touch with the various industries in this country, the representative trade associations were the bodies to which it turned. If these associations with their fund of information and their well-working organizations had not been in existence, it would doubtless have impeded the progress which the War Industries Board was compelled, as rapidly as possible, to make. Many government officials previous to the war realized the value of trade associations as the best existing medium of direct contact between the government and industry. The war undoubtedly accentuated the appreciation of the trade association in this respect.[1]

In the words of Joseph F. Bradley: "Baruch . . . drew heavily on the technical knowledge of trade association officers. It was an advantage for the Board to be able to deal with an organization that represented a number of companies instead of dealing with each one individually. . . . Baruch's praise for trade associations encouraged leaders in them to expand their activities and it encouraged the formation of a number of new ones."[2] Indeed, during the peak years of war production, 1916–19, no fewer than fifty-four national trade associations were created.[3] Overproduction and surpluses at the end of the war, when combined with the wartime experience, created an environment ripe for the formation of business associations. As Victor Clark explains: "The problem of stabilizing the conditions . . . could be solved only through cooperative action. Therefore, decided impetus was given to the movement which had already begun in 1914, and which would have been encouraged in any case by war experience, toward organizing procedures for the purpose of pooling statistical, trade, and technical information and for collective advertising, sales promotion, and foreign marketing. In these activities they had the benevolent backing of the government." Overall, the period witnessed the "formation of some nine thousand local, interstate, and national trade organizations."[4]

In addition, business executives derived from the mobilization experience new expectations concerning the potential role of the state. In the words of Eric F. Goldman: "Many of the dollar-a-year men went back to their fifty-thousand-dollar-a-year jobs with an idea buzzing in their heads. Perhaps their decades-old battle for 'free competition' and against 'government in business' had not been wise. . . . Why not give up the talk about competition and draw firms together in trade associations, which would standardize products, pool information, advertising, insurance, traffic, and purchases, and draw up codes

1. Emmett Hay Naylor, *Trade Associations: Their Organization and Management* (New York: Roland Press, 1921), 147.

2. Joseph F. Bradley, *The Role of Trade Associations and Professional Business Societies in America* (University Park: Pennsylvania State University Press, 1965), 25.

3. See a chronology of trade-association creation in National Industrial Conference Board, *Trade Associations: Their Economic Significance and Legal Status* (New York: National Industrial Conference Board, 1925), app. B.

4. Victor S. Clark, *History of Manufactures in the United States*, vol. 3, *1893–1928* (New York: McGraw-Hill, 1929), 325.

of proper practices? Why not stop fighting the government and work with it in setting up these trade associations?"[5] Indeed, some feared that war had made business far too dependent on the state. As Hugh Barker observed in 1926, "[T]he necessary war effort almost fixed the bad habit upon certain groups of business men of turning to the government whenever outside help seemed necessary."[6] Yet, even in this setting, support for government intervention was qualified. "The new thinking was all for intervention—provided that businessmen or business-minded politicians conducted the intervention."[7]

This chapter explores the regulatory legacy of World War I as embedded in some of the key initiatives of the 1920s. During the previous several decades, the market provided an important benchmark for policy makers. Progressive Era regulatory policies were designed to protect market mechanisms (e.g., antitrust legislation) or compensate for their absence where the structural features of an industry made market competition impossible (e.g., railroads, public utilities).[8] Yet, the economy that had evolved over the previous quarter century was more a dense organizational network than a decentralized market, a fact not lost on many contemporary analysts. The existence of a large-scale corporate economy and the experiences of the war suggested a new model of state-economy relations, one in which economic associations and state agencies were integrated and public authority was thereby vested in private associations. This model found its clearest expression in the writings and activities of Herbert Hoover, who provided a powerful defense of "associationalism." After we examine the core elements of associationalism, we will survey the activities of the Commerce Department, the Federal Trade Commission, and the Interstate Commerce Commission. When combined, these cases reveal both the promise and limitations of associationalism. First, we must preface our examination with some discussion of industrial organization and economic governance.[9]

5. Eric F. Goldman, *Rendezvous with Destiny: A History of Modern American Reform* (New York: Alfred A. Knopf, 1958), 307–8.

6. Hugh P. Baker, "Practical Problems of Trade Associations," *Proceedings of the Academy of Political Science* 11, no. 4 (1926): 81.

7. Goldman, *Rendezvous with Destiny,* 308.

8. See the discussion of the Progressive Era's "market regime" in Marc Allen Eisner, *Regulatory Politics in Transition* (Baltimore: Johns Hopkins University Press, 1993), chaps. 2–3.

9. The following discussion draws on Marc Allen Eisner, *The State in the American Political Economy: Public Policy and the Evolution of State-Economy Relations* (Englewood Cliffs, N.J.: Prentice Hall, 1995), chap. 2.

Economic Organization and Governance: Beyond the Market

Orthodox economics portrays the economy in very stylized terms as a large number of interrelated markets with consumers and producers executing transactions governed by the price mechanism. If one adopts the market as a benchmark, changes in industrial organization are interesting particularly for the impact they have on market failure and the creation of monopoly power. Changes in industrial organization and governance are particularly important in the period in question, when organizations were replacing markets on a scale previously unseen. It is difficult to make sense of the political economy and policies of the 1920s without considering economic organization.

One key institutional context shaping organizational evolution is internal to the corporate organization. Standard microeconomic accounts of the firm commonly present the corporation as a production function that transforms inputs into outputs in the quest for profit maximization, under conditions of complete information. The simplifying assumptions integral to this account are problematic because, as Yoram Barzel notes, "under conditions that would allow a textbook firm to exist its function would become inconsequential."[10] In recent decades a growing number of analysts have departed from this stylized portrait by returning to Ronald Coase's pathbreaking work on the firm.[11] Coase asked: "Why the corporation?" If markets perform as assumed, how could one explain the decision to replace market transactions with a firm-based set of orders and coordinating mechanisms. Coase reasoned that if corporations internalize transactions, markets must not be costless after all. Indeed, in the market one must devote resources to negotiating, monitoring, and enforcing transactions on a case-by-case basis. The firm can help economize on these costs by internalizing transactions up to the point where the costs are equal to those associated with market exchange.

This basic insight has contributed greatly to our understanding of economic exchange and organization. Transaction costs exist in large part because information is scarce concerning the dimensions of the goods in question and the behavior of the parties involved in the exchange.[12] Information scarcity and uncertainty engender a host of difficulties, including the ever present

10. Yoram Barzel, *Economic Analysis of Property Rights* (Cambridge: Cambridge University Press, 1989), 43.

11. Ronald H. Coase, "The Nature of the Firm," *Economica* 4 (1937): 386–405.

12. Thrainn Eggertsson, *Economic Behavior and Institutions* (Cambridge: Cambridge University Press, 1990), 15. See Oliver E. Williamson, *Markets and Hierarchies: Analysis and Antitrust Implications* (New York: Free Press, 1975).

problem of agency: principals must find the means of arriving at the desired outputs while minimizing the shirking and opportunism of their agents. Actors may reduce their vulnerability to these problems by specifying tasks precisely, introducing new accounting and oversight mechanisms, or imposing ominous penalties for agency failure. Yet, these mechanisms are themselves costly, and their efficacy depends heavily on information that may be difficult to collect, particularly when an exchange involves complex and highly specific goods. Because exchanges occur in a dynamic context, agents may adapt strategically to elude efficient monitoring. In this milieu, firms may strive to manage their environments by adopting nonmarket governance mechanisms (e.g., long-term bilateral contracting, vertical integration leading to unified control). The key insights of transaction-cost economics are clear: with the exception of the exchange of relatively simple goods, the market may be of limited value. Many corporate strategies and arrangements that circumvent the market may be perfectly rational responses to high transaction costs under information scarcity and uncertainty.[13]

The Question of Economic Evolution

Most neoclassical economists are concerned with economic behavior as it occurs within freely operating, self-equilibrating markets. Market forces, it is argued, drive corporate decision making toward maximum efficiency. John S. McGee notes: "If any firm should be larger than efficiency requires, and charges higher prices than the costs of its present and prospective competitors, they and the market will shrink it. If any firm should innovate better techniques, or offer a superior product at the same costs as its competitors, the market will respond and it will grow."[14] This understanding of the economy is best exemplified by George Stigler's survival test: the best guide to what *should* exist is simple observation of the firms, scales of production, and techniques that have survived the market process.[15] The argument that the market selects firms on efficiency grounds is difficult to accept, however, once we view corporate structures and intercorporate relations as organizational

13. This discussion draws on Oliver E. Williamson, *The Economic Institutions of Capitalism: Firms, Markets, Relational Contracting* (New York: Free Press, 1985).

14. John S. McGee, "Efficiency and Economies of Size," in *Industrial Concentration: The New Learning,* ed. Harvy J. Goldschmid, H. Michael Mann, and J. Fred Weston (Boston: Little, Brown, 1974), 94. See Melvin W. Reder, "Chicago Economics: Permanence and Change," *Journal of Economic Literature* 20 (March 1982): 1–38, and Spiro J. Latsis, "A Research Program in Economics," in *Method and Appraisal in Economics,* ed. Spiro J. Latsis (Cambridge: Cambridge University Press, 1976).

15. George J. Stigler, *The Organization of Industry* (Homewood, Ill.: Richard D. Irwin, 1968), 72–74.

responses to transaction costs. Once we suspend market supremacy and the Panglossian assumption inherent in the survival test, new questions arise: How do corporations adapt to an environment characterized by information complexity and resource scarcity? Why do they develop such variation in institutional arrangements to manage complexity and minimize their own vulnerability? In short, how do we explain the evolution of the corporate economy?

As suggested above, a first response may be found in transaction-cost economics. Oliver Williamson and others have sought to identify how economic actors organize transactions to reduce their uncertainty.[16] Shirking, opportunism, and miscommunication may abound and become more severe as the complexity of the goods increases. Actors can manage uncertainty and reduce monitoring costs by introducing specialized governance structures or nonmarket forms of interfirm relations. The costs of such governance structures may be prohibitive, however, if transactions are infrequent. By entertaining different combinations of transaction frequency and asset specificity (characterized as nonspecific, mixed, or idiosyncratic), Williamson has explained a good deal of variation in governance structures.[17] Markets are the institutions of choice for transactions involving nonspecific investments. When transactions are occasional and/or require high levels of investment specificity, however, other forms of governance are common. Trilateral governance (e.g., when a firm contracts with a third party to supervise performance) and bilateral governance (e.g., two parties cement a long-term relationship with joint investments, reciprocal sales, or multiyear contracts) persist when transactions are frequent and demand greater asset specificity. In extreme cases, firms may embrace unified governance, internalizing the relationships within a single corporation. While recognizing a great potential for variation, Williamson suggests that one will observe an efficient match between structures and transaction types over time.

Transaction-cost explanations have been rightly criticized for assuming that governance structures arise as efficient solutions to market failure. Critics have identified several difficulties. First, as Mark Granovetter has argued, economic behavior is embedded in a dense network of social relations. The "conflict, disorder, opportunism, or malfeasance" that supposedly necessitates alternative governance structures should not exist "where a stable network of relations mediates complex transactions and generates standards of behavior

16. Williamson, *The Economic Institutions of Capitalism*, 52–63.
17. Ibid., 72–84.

between firms."[18] Second, transaction-cost explanations assume efficiency from survival without specifying the selection mechanism that would make this possible or recognizing that "in order to explain the existence of a structure it is neither necessary nor sufficient to show that it is efficient. Inefficient structures do happen to exist and survive, and many possible efficient structures will never actually be selected."[19] Finally, the transaction-cost accounts are usually framed in a political void, neglecting theoretically the legal, political, and historical factors that contribute heavily to the evolution and dissemination of various models of corporate organization and intercorporate relationships. Although it is clear that transaction-cost accounts carry important implications for policy (particularly antitrust policy), it is equally clear that larger political-economic forces are given little or no causal importance.[20]

Evolutionary economics has also contributed to our understanding of economic change. Of particular importance in this regard is *An Evolutionary Theory of Economic Change,* by Richard R. Nelson and Sidney G. Winter. Their account has three key components. First, there are routines, the embodiment of organizational memories that convey the notion that "organizations have built into them a set of ways of doing things and ways of determining what to do." By theoretically elevating routines, the authors "recognize that the flexibility of routinized behavior is of limited scope and that a changing environment can force firms to risk their very survival on attempts to modify their routines." Second, they introduce the idea of search processes that are engaged when firms seek to evaluate, modify, or replace existing routines: "Routines in general play the role of genes. . . . search routines stochastically generate mutations."[21] The final component is the "selection environment," factors endogenous and exogenous to the sector of the economy that place pressure on routines and force the initiation of the search process. Routine rigidity and the disjunction between changes in the selection environment and organizational responses gives rise to a system in which groping processes of adaptation replace the instant movement toward equilibrium cherished by orthodox theories of the firm.[22] Nelson and Winter, and other evolutionary theorists,

18. Mark Granovetter, "Economic Action and Social Structures: The Problem of Embeddedness," *American Journal of Sociology* 91, no. 3 (1985): 503.

19. Geoffrey M. Hodgson, *Economics and Evolution: Bringing Life Back into Economics* (Ann Arbor: University of Michigan Press, 1993), 201.

20. See Charles Perrow, "Markets, Hierarchies and Hegemony," in *Perspectives on Organizational Design and Behavior,* ed. Andrew Van de Nen and William Joyce (New York: Wiley, 1981).

21. Richard R. Nelson and Sidney G. Winter, *An Evolutionary Theory of Economic Change* (Cambridge: Harvard University Press, 1982), 400.

22. For a well-developed critique of Nelson and Winter, see Jack J. Vromen, *Economic Evolution: An Enquiry into the Foundations of New Institutional Economics* (London: Routledge, 1995), 65–129.

acknowledge that public policy plays an important role in shaping the environment in which economic change occurs. This is a welcomed departure from the neoclassical depiction of markets as extrapolitical or prepolitical entities driving economic change free from the larger political and institutional context.

The separation of state and market becomes at best artificial once one acknowledges that market transactions rest on a system of property rights established through public policy.[23] Rather than entertain the notion that the state "intervenes" in the market, one must understand the market as a mechanism of property exchange that would be impossible without legally established property rights and institutions to adjudicate disputes over the exercise of these rights. There is, moreover, little reason to suppose that policy makers will establish efficient systems of property rights, particularly in a decentralized system such as that which prevails in the United States.[24] Policy changes affecting the assignment, transfer, and exercise of property rights fundamentally alter market actions and thus impact on the "selection environment," to use the term adopted by Nelson and Winter. Monetary policy, capital-market regulations, fiscal policy, exchange-rate policy, antitrust policy, and regimes governing trade and industrial relations all function at the macro level. A dense network of regulatory policies, subsidies, tax provisions, and government contracting relations function on the sectoral level. These policies, when taken together, limit the availability of certain governance mechanisms while creating a bias in support of others. The environment may be so chaotic as to preclude a clear understanding of property rights on the part of any of the actors. The combination of transaction frequency and asset speci-

23. See Karl Polyani, *The Great Transformation: The Political and Economic Origins of Our Times* (Boston: Beacon Press, 1944), chap. 12; Fred Block and Margaret Somers, "Beyond the Economistic Fallacy: The Holistic Social Science of Karl Polyani," in *Vision and Method in Historical Sociology*, ed. Theda Skocpol (New York: Cambridge University Press, 1984); Fred Block, "Political Choice and the Multiple 'Logics' of Capital," *Theory and Society* 15, nos. 1–2 (1986): 175–92; and John L. Campbell and Leon N. Lindberg, "Property Rights and the Organization of Economic Activity by the State," *American Sociological Review* 5, no. 5 (1990): 634–47.

24. Douglass C. North, *Structure and Change in Economic History* (New York: W. W. Norton, 1981). North writes: "[T]he more diffuse the distribution of political control as a result of the ability of groups of constituents to capture an interest in the state, the more difficult it becomes to predict or explain the ensuing forms of property rights which will develop. It is not too difficult to account for economic organization of the redistributive societies of the ancient dynasties in Egypt; it is much more difficult to explain the complex economic organization in modern democratic societies where many interests compete with each other in controlling the state and modifying property rights and, hence, economic organization" (43–44).

ficity (to use Williamson's key dimensions) might suggest that a specific set of governance mechanisms would be particularly appropriate in a political-institutional vacuum. Existing patterns of state-economy relations combined with established routines at the level of the firm, however, render firms' adoption of these mechanisms uncertain.

Functionalist explanations of economic evolution tend to be difficult to affirm once economic activity is placed within a richer political-institutional context. This is particularly the case when we consider economic change in the United States, given the organizational complexity of the American state. As noted in Chapter 2, high levels of vertical and horizontal fragmentation result in complicated and convoluted patterns of state-economy relations. Economic actors function in an environment defined by policies implemented by the national government and competing state governments. At the national level, multiple veto points, high levels of interest-group access, and a lack of elite cohesion and independence from electoral and group pressures result in high levels of policy instability.[25] Legislation, regulatory rules, executive orders, and court rulings are implemented in a decentralized bureaucratic system where agencies have different routines, embedded policy preferences, financial resources, and stocks of expertise. Moreover, agencies have varying levels of autonomy; many are forced to function within rigid networks of agency-interest-group relations. The chaotic environment is given greater coherence through the emergence of regimes that cut across multiple policies and institutions, although even under the best of circumstances great variation should be seen as the norm.[26] Factors shaping economic decision making and the evolution of governance are not beyond comprehension. But they must be understood within a specific historical and political-institutional context.

The governance framework developed by John Campbell, J. Rogers Hollingsworth, and Leon Lindberg provides a useful synthesis of the literature on economic governance, economic history, and institutional political economy.[27] They develop a typology of governance mechanisms by considering the degree

25. See R. Kent Weaver and Bert A. Rockman, "When and How Do Institutions Matter?" in *Do Institutions Matter? Government Capabilities in the United States and Abroad,* ed. R. Kent Weaver and Bert A. Rockman (Washington, D.C.: Brookings Institution, 1993).

26. See Robert Solo, *The Political Authority and the Market System* (Cincinnati: South-Western, 1974), and Eisner, *Regulatory Politics in Transition,* chap. 1.

27. See John L. Campbell, J. Rogers Hollingsworth, and Leon N. Lindberg, eds., *Governance of the American Economy* (Cambridge: Cambridge University Press, 1991).

of formal integration (low, moderate, and high) and the range of interaction (bilateral and multilateral).[28] The framework acknowledges the pressures for governance transformation identified by transaction-cost and evolutionary theorists, although it views the search process and subsequent adjustments as less than automatic, due to the constraining effects of existing routines and governance regimes. More important, they explicitly emphasize the role of the state:

> [T]he state assumes a privileged conceptual position . . . because it is capable of influencing governance in many complex ways, most of which are not available to organizations in civil society. One of the things that is so fascinating about the state is that although its agencies can behave like other organizational actors in an industry, participating directly in production and exchange relations, other actors cannot behave like the state because they cannot serve as gatekeepers, allocating resources and information, influence and structure property rights, or affect governance transformations in other ways as does the state.[29]

A politically oriented understanding of economic governance—one that divested itself of Panglossian presumptions—would seek to understand the role that public policies play in the evolution of the economy during any period in question. Historically, a host of public policies in the United States created a bias in support of corporate hierarchies engaged in bilateral relationships rather than associations. Decades of antitrust policy directed in part against associations that could establish various horizontal restraints had the paradoxical effect of creating an environment supportive of large corporate hierarchies and a concentration of economic resources. This bias was reinforced by government contracting relationships during the war. Associations, according to Campbell, Hollingsworth, and Lindberg, provide the most appropriate governance mechanism when there are high levels of organizational integration and a multiplicity of actors. They allow for the exchange of infor-

---

28. Campbell, Hollingsworth, and Lindberg associate the following governance mechanisms with different levels of formal integration and ranges of interaction: markets (low levels of integration, bilateral interaction), obligational networks (moderate levels of integration, bilateral interaction), hierarchies (high levels of integration, bilateral interaction), monitoring (low levels of integration, multilateral interaction), promotional networks (moderate levels of integration, multilateral interaction), and associations (high levels of integration, multilateral interaction). Ibid., 14.

29. Ibid., 31.

mation, the coordination of economic decision making, and the development of rules of conduct or fair competition.[30] The limited dissemination of this governance mechanism in previous decades was largely a product of antitrust enforcement patterns. Yet, during the war there was newfound interest in associational forms of governance (see Chapter 2). They became an integral feature of the compensatory state-building strategy pursued by war mobilization elites. Drawing on the experience of war, support for associationalism became a dominant feature of regulatory politics in the 1920s. Antitrust sentiment became far less important a factor, and regulators increasingly designed procedures patterned on those adopted under conditions of emergency just a few years earlier. The result was an increasingly dense network of horizontal restraints linking together many of the large corporations, a network that had evolved as an externality of antitrust policy.

The Economy of the New Era

World War I came in the middle of a critical period in the evolution of the U.S. economy. The local, decentralized market system of the nineteenth century was being superseded by nonmarket mechanisms, and myriad decisions previously executed in markets were now internalized within the corporation or made within the proliferating number of intercorporate associations that linked them together. The period as a whole witnessed tremendous growth in the physical output of the manufacturing industries. As one might expect, the growth rates differed by sector. The growth in physical output during 1919–29 for selected manufacturing industries reflects these differences: petroleum and coal products, 156 percent; chemical products, 94 percent; rubber products, 86 percent; iron and steel, 70 percent; transportation equipment, 64 percent; lumber, 27 percent. Overall, total manufacturing output grew by 64 percent for the decade. Between 1921 and 1929, manufacturing value added increased from $16.88 billion to $30.07 billion.[31]

The growth of the period reflected growing productivity: During the 1920s, the gross national product increased $235 billion over the previous decade. Of this sum, $212 billion—over 90 percent—can be attributed to productivity gains. According to Frederick C. Mills, this decade saw "the

---

30. See ibid., chap. 1, 12.

31. Solomon Fabricant, *The Output of Manufacturing Industries, 1899–1937* (New York: National Bureau of Economic Research, 1940), 60, 636.

greatest productivity gains of the half century."[32] Although the number of
industrial workers employed declined by 4 percent during the period 1922–
29, the physical volume of production increased by 42 percent. This translated into 50 percent productivity growth per worker during the period in
question.[33] It is easy to identify the factors that allowed for these productivity
gains, even if there are disputes over their relative significance. First, large
increases in capital investment per worker resulted in "long-term increases in
labor productivity or, more precisely, the reduction in labor per unit of output."[34] During the war, large companies encountered difficulties floating
securities issues due to the Capital Issues Committee's capital-market regulations; they financed much of their expansion with undistributed profits and
short-term bank debt, although much new investment was simply postponed.
With the exception of the railroads, the postwar expansion in facilities "developed because going concerns launched new business projects, some of which
had been planned during the war years and deferred, some of which were
newly conceived ventures."[35] This expansion was facilitated by the ability to
enter capital markets. As Gardiner C. Means reported, between 1922 and
1927, the largest two hundred nonfinancial corporations added more than
$21.5 billion to their assets. Of this amount, $5.75 billion came from savings
out of earnings, with another $4 billion from mergers. The bulk of the added
assets, more than $11.8 billion, were claimed through securities sales.[36] Capi-
tal markets provided a critical engine for the growth of large firms.

Growth in the capital stock is important as a means of increasing labor
productivity. This is more than a quantitative issue, however. New machines
and equipment are the embodiment of new technology. Capital investment
provides the transmission belt linking technical innovations and the production process.[37] The more rapid the pace of reinvestment, the greater the likelihood that average-practice technology will approximate the best-practice
technology. Accordingly, with respect to the period in question, Mills notes,
it was not simply capital investment that was relevant but the technology

---

32. Frederick C. Mills, *Productivity and Economic Progress* (New York: National Bureau of Economic
Research, 1952), 6.

33. Arthur B. Adams, *Our Economic Revolution* (Norman: University of Oklahoma Press, 1933), 3–4.

34. Daniel Creamer and Martin Bernstein, *Capital and Output Trends in Manufacturing Industries,
1880–1948* (New York: National Bureau of Economic Research, 1954), 76.

35. Charles H. Schmidt and Ralph A. Young, *The Effects of War on Business Financing: Manufacturing
and Trade, World War I* (New York: National Bureau of Economic Research, 1943), 6.

36. Gardiner C. Means, "The Growth in the Relative Importance of the Large Corporation in American Economic Life," *American Economic Review* 21, no. 1 (1931): 34.

37. Angus Maddison, *Phases of Capitalist Development* (Oxford: Oxford University Press, 1982), 52–53.

incorporated in the investments: "Technological improvements as well as innovations of scientific management were widely adopted in the early twenties; such improvements were chiefly manifest in the tools of production."[38]

Although scientific management found its origins in the earlier dissemination of Taylorist doctrines, it was applied with ever greater vigor during World War I and the 1920s. During this period, scientific management's emphasis on intensive supervision, wage incentives, a detailed division of labor, and the routinization of production tasks was paired with the Fordist model of mass production. The use of specialized machine tools and interchangeable parts predated the period in question. Yet, once combined with the moving assembly line (first introduced in 1914) and long production runs, the Fordist model constituted a most potent paradigm for mass standardized production. The Fordist system was disseminated through American industry via high levels of investment and the rapid influx of new personnel managers and business administrators.[39]

A final factor promoting growth was the rapid dissemination of electric motors in the workplace. In the spring of 1929 President Hoover's Conference on Unemployment released a study that sought to explain the patterns of economic growth in the American economy. Although the report attributed the growth to a number of factors, the most important was the revolution in power. Between 1919 and 1927, the number of kilowatt-hours per capita more than doubled, growing from 425 to 860. The number of electric motors increased from 9.2 million to 19.1 million. As a result, over 95 percent of machinery manufacturing was driven by electrical power, displacing the older and less efficient steam-driven machinery.[40]

Growth and productivity increases were combined with changes in industrial organization. The merger wave of the 1920s and its effects on economic structure were most critical in this regard. War mobilization carried a bias in support of larger corporations, as evidenced by the awarding of war contracts. Despite the Wilsonian rhetoric against bigness, these contracting practices were expedient: large corporations could better guarantee the fulfillment of contracts while reducing the administrative complexity of placing orders.

38. Mills, *Productivity and Economic Progress,* 9.

39. Mark Rupert, *Producing Hegemony: The Politics of Mass Production and American Global Power* (Cambridge: Cambridge University Press, 1995), 59–82; Thomas C. Cochran, *The American Business System: A Historical Perspective, 1900–1955* (Cambridge: Harvard University Press, 1957), 68–76. See Michel Aglietta, *A Theory of Capitalist Regulation: The US Experience,* trans. David Fernbach (London: NLB, 1979), 116–22.

40. Robert Sobel, *The Age of the Giant Corporations: A Microeconomic History of American Business, 1914–1970* (Westport, Conn.: Greenwood Press, 1972), 52–53.

Large firms also benefited from the practices of the WIB, both through their dominant position on war service committees and through the practices of the WIB Price-Fixing Committee, which set prices to stimulate production on the part of less efficient firms. War profits, in turn, drove the expansion of capacity, the implementation of new technology, and the subsequent waves of acquisition. Finally, the diversion of resources toward war-related industries forced severe economic problems in the nonessential industries. Those that could not convert facilities to war production were destined for bankruptcy or open to acquisition. The merger wave was also a by-product of prevailing antitrust doctrines, which tended to assess unified concerns differently from associations or arrangements linking otherwise autonomous units. In the words of William L. Thorp: "The courts judge the individual concern on the basis of its actual behavior, the confederacy on the basis of its potential misbehavior."[41]

The 1920s merger wave differed from the great merger wave of 1895–1904. The first wave was driven by horizontal mergers, which created oligopolies in a number of industries and produced industrial giants such as U.S. Steel, American Tobacco, International Harvester, Du Pont, and Anaconda Copper.[42] During the 1920s merger wave, in contrast, the importance of horizontal mergers declined relative to vertical and conglomerate mergers, many of which were engineered by investment bankers.[43] Nonetheless, a number of large corporations expanded through consolidation. Take the example of the steel industry. Bethlehem Steel acquired Lackawanna Steel, Midvale, Cambria, and Pacific Coast Steel. National Steel was created through the combination of Weirton Steel, Great Lakes Steel, and M.A. Hanna. Republic Steel acquired Central Alloy Steel, Donner Steel, and Bourne Fuller. Following this chain of consolidations in the steel industry, the aging U.S. Steel could no longer monopolize the market.[44]

A second and related difference was that the 1920s wave did not result in significant increases in industrial concentration, which was already high as a result of the last merger wave. Indeed, the new mergers in manufacturing often eroded existing monopoly power (e.g., the case of steel) or preserved

41. Willard L. Thorp, "The Persistence of the Merger Movement," *American Economic Review* 21, no. 1, suppl. (March 1931): 81. See Thomas K. McCraw, "Rethinking the Trust Question," in *Regulation in Perspective: Historical Essays*, ed. Thomas K. McCraw (Cambridge: Harvard University Press, 1981).

42. See the discussion of this merger wave in Ralph L. Nelson, *Merger Movements in American History, 1895–1956* (Princeton, N.J.: Princeton University Press, 1959), 71–105.

43. Samuel Richardson Reid, *Mergers, Managers, and the Economy* (New York: McGraw-Hill, 1968), 56–62.

44. Sobel, *The Age of the Giant Corporations*, 30–31.

existing oligopolies. There were modest increases in concentration in the distributive trades as national chain stores claimed an ever greater percentage of the market. But the most dramatic exception to these generalizations was found in the public-utilities sector, especially electricity and gas. The 35 public-utilities companies on the list of 200 largest nonfinancial corporations grew by 194 percent between 1919 and 1929, compared with a growth rate of less than 50 percent for the other 115 corporations that remained among the top 200.[45] By the end of the decade, the generation of electricity was controlled by three giant holding companies that had acquired much of their assets during the 1920s: J. P. Morgan & Company's United Corporation (23 percent of the nation's electricity), Chase National Bank's Electric Bond and Share (17 percent), and the Insull Group (11 percent).[46]

The economic growth of the New Era and the rise of the new corporate economy were ripe with significance. Adolf A. Berle and Gardiner C. Means provide us with one of the best portraits of this corporate revolution. The decade witnessed a tremendous growth in the largest corporations. In 1920, the largest 200 nonfinancial corporations controlled 33.4 percent of the net income of all nonfinancial firms. By 1928, these firms had grown to claim 40.4 percent of the net income. In contrast, the next 800 corporations endured a shrinking share of net income, falling from 19 percent in 1920 to 18.7 percent in 1928. A similar story can be told with respect to gross assets. The gross assets of the 153 nonfinancial corporations that were in the top 200 in both 1919 and 1927 grew by 52.4 percent during the period—an annual rate of 5.3 percent, well above the 4.4 percent realized by all corporations. As one might expect, asset growth was the greatest in the utilities sector, where assets expanded by 157 percent—an annual rate of 12.3 percent.[47] With the growing scale of corporate activity and the dispersion of ownership through well-developed secondary markets for corporate securities, the trends identified by Berle and Means led inevitably to a separation of ownership and control, as argued in the seminal *Modern Corporation and Private Property*.[48] According to Berle and Means, the separation was revolutionary in nature, the hallmark of a new managerial capitalism. There were "opposing groups,

45. Joe S. Bain, *Industrial Organization*, 2d ed. (New York: John Wiley & Sons, 1968), 106–8.

46. Sobel, *The Age of the Giant Corporations*, 54.

47. Means, "The Growth in the Relative Importance of the Large Corporation in American Economic Life," 18, 24.

48. Adolf A. Berle Jr. and Gardiner C. Means, *The Modern Corporation and Private Property* (New York: Commerce Clearing House, 1932), 121. See also Thorstein Veblen, *The Theory of Business Enterprise* (New York: Charles Scribner, 1904), and Edward S. Herman, *Corporate Control, Corporate Power* (Cambridge: Cambridge University Press, 1981), 5–14.

ownership on the one side, control on the other—a control which tends to move further and further away from ownership and ultimately to lie in the hand of the management itself, a management capable of perpetuating its own position."[49]

According to Berle and Means, the "abdication of the state" and the rise of the modern corporation was "not a change in business method, but a major shift in civilization," full of political implications: "As we fought out the principle of absolutism by governments in political affairs, so, it would seem, we must fight out the principle of absolutism in property affairs when exercised by our corporate managements and stewards. The evolution from enterprises which can be carried on by their owners to engines of production so large as to swallow the individual, and inevitably to separate management powers from property rights, means that the economic framework of the country is undergoing a distinct change."[50] Writing in 1931, Myron Watkins arrived at a similar conclusion: "[W]e have evolved, while hardly aware of it, a controlled economic system. The processes of production and consumption do not go on automatically. . . . productive, distributive, and consumptive processes alike are consciously and deliberately manipulated by those who control the great aggregations of resources which are the most striking and distinctive features of the modern industrial system."[51] Indeed, he concluded that the United States, as it had emerged in the decades just past, was no different from that created in the Soviet Union except in one key respect: "[T]hey have established a controlled economic order by conscious imposition, while we have evolved a controlled order by a blindly groping reorganization of industry."[52]

Despite the image of massive productivity gains and steady growth, the corporate policies carried some long-term negative consequences. First, the high levels of investment forced expansion well beyond what could be justified by existing business conditions. Excluding plants already shut down, a 1934 study by the Brookings Institution concluded: "[O]ur productive system as a whole was operating at about 80 percent of capacity in 1929 and slightly less than that if we take the average of the five years 1925–29. If this 20 per cent of our resources not utilized could have been brought into production, it

49. Berle and Means, *The Modern Corporation and Private Property*, 124.

50. Adolf A. Berle Jr. and Gardiner C. Means, "Corporations and the Public Investor," *American Economic Review* 20, no. 1 (March 1930): 70–71.

51. Myron Watkins, "Trustification and Economic Theory," *American Economic Review* 21, no. 1, suppl. (March 1931): 71.

52. Ibid., 74.

would have added goods and services to an amount one-fourth as great as the total which we were already getting during those years." To function at full capacity, however, corporations would have had to employ the entire potential manufacturing workforce and an additional one-million workers.[53] Josef Steindl arrived at similar conclusions: "[T]here were a number of industries in which expansion was going on . . . and in which the degree of capacity use was *decreasing* during the expansion up to 1929: the capacity was increasing ahead of demand."[54] Corporations forced to maintain high levels of fixed capital and excess capacity financed through loans and securities sales would realize diminishing profits, reduced incentives to invest, and greater fragility when confronted with downward movements in the business cycle. This is precisely what occurred when boom turned to bust at decade's end.

The increases in investment and output per worker actually reduced the demand for industrial labor, bringing the connections between mechanization and unemployment increasingly into question. As one commentator noted in 1928: "What has perhaps most tended to obscure the decreasing employment in the country is the fact that industry as a whole still appears to be prosperous. . . . We encounter the paradox that although employment has been decreasing gradually since 1923, the manufacturing output has been increasing." The explanation was to be found in growing capital intensity: "Machines have been ousting men faster than new industries have been absorbing them. We have a new kind of unemployment—unusually inequitable in that the misery of the employees is less than ever shared by their employers."[55] This would become quite important to economists who developed underconsumptionist interpretations of the depression or argued that stagnation was inevitable in mature monopoly capitalism.

For those who remained employed, the situation was not free of difficulty. As Chapter 5 shows, the new scale of corporate activity diminished labor's power to bargain. As Watkins argued, "The progressive concentration of industrial control has made the theory of the marginal adjustment of wage rates in an open market still more of a quixotic delusion than it was under the simple factory system characteristic of the nineteenth century."[56] As in other

53. Edwin G. Nourse and associates, *America's Capacity to Produce* (Washington, D.C.: Brookings Institution, 1934), 416, 307–8.

54. Josef Steindl, *Maturity and Stagnation in American Capitalism* (Oxford: Basil Blackwell, 1952), 4. See also Paul A. Baran and Paul M. Sweezy, *Monopoly Capital: An Essay on the American Economic and Social Order* (New York: Monthly Review Press, 1966), chaps. 4 and 8.

55. "Out of Work," *Nation*, March 14, 1928, 286.

56. Watkins, "Trustification and Economic Theory," 60.

areas of economic life, markets were being replaced by managerial determinations of appropriate wages and working conditions. The "high-wage-prosperity" doctrine (i.e., that high wages are necessary to maintain high levels of consumption) and the provision of welfare capitalism allowed *some* workers to participate in the period's productivity gains. For many others, however, the fruits of the New Era were beyond reach. The decade as a whole witnessed a growing concentration of wealth at the top of the income distribution and high levels of inequality. Following the growth of the decade, "1929 [stood] out as the peak year for inequality."[57]

Thus, the new industrial economy of the interwar period was dominated by large modern corporate enterprises using the profits of the war and the New Era to fund the expansion of capacity, even if such an expansion carried serious consequences for employment patterns. The growing concentration of wealth and inequality would become highly salient issues, particularly once this excess capacity undermined the viability of many corporations during the Great Depression. Much of the wealth generation and capacity building of the period came as a fruit of capital organization, as firms jointly determined what to produce and avoided actions that might threaten to ignite competition. This organization was a product of both public policy and the war.

The Associationalist Model of State-Economy Relations

The war had an important impact on both the organization of the political economy and the prevailing theories of state-economy relations. As noted in Chapter 3, the War Industries Board relied heavily on interest associations organized by the Chamber of Commerce. The war service committees worked closely with the commodity sections to create a vital connection between the war mobilization apparatus and the business community. In his 1922 review of the War Industries Board, Bernard Baruch reflected on the rise and potential functions of the new business associations:

> These associations, as they stand, are capable of carrying out purposes of greatest public benefit. They can increase the amount of wealth

---

57. Robert J. Lampman, *Changes in the Share of Wealth Held by Top Wealth Holders, 1922–1956* (New York: National Bureau of Economic Research, 1960), 14. See also Simon Kuznets, *Shares of Upper Income Groups in Income and Savings* (New York: National Bureau of Economic Research, 1953).

available for the comfort of the people by inaugurating rules designed to eliminate wasteful practices attendant upon the multiplicity of styles and types of articles in the various trades; they can assist in cultivating the public taste for rational types of commodities; by exchange of trade information, extravagant methods of production and distribution can be avoided through them, and production will tend to be localized in places best suited economically for it. By acting as centers of information, furnishing lists of sources to purchasers and lists of purchasers to producers, supply and demand can be more economically balanced. From the point of vantage which competent men have at the central bureau of an association, not only can new demands be cultivated, but new sources of unexploited wealth can be indicated. In case of a national emergency, the existence of these associations at the beginning would be of incalculable aid to the supply organizations. Many of these considerations apply to large individual companies as well as to associations.[58]

Herbert Hoover, among others, drew on his wartime experiences to fashion a distinctive model of the state and state-economy relations. He stated his desire to discover "a plan of individualism and associational activities that will preserve the initiative, the inventiveness, the individuality, the character of man and yet will enable us to synchronize socially and economically this gigantic machine that we have built out of applied science."[59] Following the war, Hoover promoted his associationalist vision of the American system through a series of public addresses and writings. He also served in a number of important positions, including vice-chairman of the President's Second Industrial Conference and president of the Federated American Engineering Societies. Many corporate elites, bureaucrats, and intellectuals shared this associationalist vision. Let us consider it with some care.

This vision of social order found its ideological grounding in individualism. For Hoover, American individualism was "only in part an economic creed."[60] The nation "abandoned the laissez faire of the 18th Century" when it infused individualism with "the ideal of equality of opportunity." A new emphasis was placed on "social and economic justice." Hoover writes: "We have learned

58. Bernard M. Baruch, *American Industry in the War: A Report of the War Industries Board, March 1921* (New York: Prentice Hall, 1941), 106.

59. Herbert Hoover quoted in Edwin T. Layton Jr., *The Revolt of the Engineers: Social Responsibility and the American Engineering Profession* (Baltimore: Johns Hopkins University Press, 1971), 190–91.

60. Herbert Hoover, *American Individualism* (Garden City, N.Y.: Doubleday, Page & Co., 1922), 37.

that the impulse to production can only be maintained at a high pitch if there is a fair division of the product . . . by certain restrictions on the strong and the dominant."[61] If an individualism based in equality of opportunity required that constraints be placed on the exercise of economic power, one was forced to ask: Who would wield this power? How would individualism be preserved?

Thus far, Hoover would seem to have constructed a case for a regulatory and redistributive state. Hoover, however, rejected the required concentration of public authority. In each case, "it necessitates a bureaucracy over the entire population" that "obliterate[s] the economic stimulation of each member." He objected to "the basic foundations of autocracy, whether it be class government or capitalism in the sense that a few men through unrestrained control of property determine the welfare of great numbers." "The will-o'-the-wisp of autocracy in any form is that it supposes that the good Lord endowed a special few with all the divine attributes."[62] Hoover noted that "the American System holds equally that monopoly, group or class advantage, economic domination, Regimentation, Fascism, Socialism, Communism, or any other form of tyranny, small or great, are violations of the basis of Liberty."[63] If equal opportunity and social and economic justice cannot be guaranteed by the concentrated authority of the state, Hoover argued, we must look to voluntary associations.

Hoover saw the "organizations for advancement of ideas in the community for mutual cooperation and economic objectives—the chambers of commerce, trade associations, labor unions, bankers, farmers, propaganda associations"—as vitally important because "in these groups the individual finds an opportunity for self-expression and participation in the molding of ideas, a field for training and the stepping stones for leadership."[64] Moreover, "there are in the cooperative great hopes that we can even gain in individuality, equality of opportunity, and an enlarged field for initiative, and at the same time reduce many of the wastes of over-reckless competition in production and distribution."[65] Hoover was convinced that economic progress could be achieved through changes in the production process: "The only road to further advance in the standard of living is by greater invention, greater elimination of waste, greater production and better distribution of commodities and services, for by increasing their ratio to our numbers and dividing them

61. Ibid., 10–11.
62. Ibid., 17–19.
63. Herbert Hoover, *The Challenge to Liberty* (New York: Charles Scribner's Sons, 1934), 34.
64. Hoover, *American Individualism*, 41–42.
65. Ibid., 44.

justly we each will have more of them."[66] A system of economic associations provided the best context for the realization of these goals.

The associational system envisioned by Hoover was one in which private associations would engage in self-regulatory functions, while the state would be restricted—under normal conditions—to facilitating the formation of associations and coordinating their activities. As James Stuart Olson explains: "[T]he network of associations held out the promise of a form of private government in which the economy was essentially self-regulatory. In emphasizing professional standards, ethical codes of conduct, and rational problem solving, the private associations were self-disciplining and self-improving; and as they policed themselves internally they naturally contributed to social harmony."[67] This vision of an associational order did not originate with Hoover, even if Hoover presented its strongest justification. Indeed, one can find similar arguments in a number of works written before the war.[68] Edward N. Hurley's *Awakening of Business* provides a good example of the prewar arguments for associationalism. Writing in 1916, he noted that "[c]ooperation is the watchword of our day—cooperation among business men, cooperation between employer and employee, cooperation between business and government." Trade associations had a central role to play in the new economy:

> Having put their own houses in order, business men must get together. Shying bricks at each other across the street does not belong to the new era of American business. No business can go far toward true success if suspicion and fear are the impulses which govern its members. Trade associations are the machinery of cooperation. Through them ignorant competition can be destroyed to a larger extent merely by throwing light upon it, and the basis upon which business is conducted can be generally made more intelligent. The best way to cure some sores is not to cover them up but to cut them out, and business men working together in trade associations can, as a rule, perform such operations with less difficulty than any one else. Trade associations are, in a way which we do not yet appreciate in this

---

66. Ibid., 32–33.

67. James Stuart Olson, *Herbert Hoover and the Reconstruction Finance Corporation, 1931–1933* (Ames: Iowa State University Press, 1977), 20.

68. For a comprehensive examination of the business position on cooperation, see Butler Shaffer, *In Restraint of Trade: The Business Campaign Against Competition, 1918–1938* (Lewisburg, Pa.: Bucknell University Press, 1997).

country, the means of salvation for American business. . . . they can help to lift American business to a higher plane of efficiency.

Hurley's conclusions concerning the role of government were striking, given his position as FTC chairman. He argued that government "must abandon the attitude of the policeman and become the sympathetic, constructive counselor of American business life."[69]

A similar argument was put forth by Arthur Jerome Eddy, in his 1912 treatise entitled *The New Competition*. Eddy observed a process of economic evolution leading to ever larger units of production. "Just as the stage-coach, owned and driven by one man, has given way to the railroad, owned and operated by a hundred thousand men, so the individual laborer, farmer, merchant, small manufacturer, merges his identity in that of his union, his cooperative society, his large corporation, his 'trust,' to secure larger results, do things on a larger scale, a scale commensurate with the marvelous developments of the world today." The new competition rested on the conviction that technological progress depended on shared information and cooperation in all spheres of economic activity. The antitrust laws promoted competition but only by impeding indispensable cooperation. As Eddy explained: "Any law that tries to check cooperative growth is a law against maximum efficiency and, therefore, contrary to the spirit of the age which demands, above all things, quantity, which demands labor- and capital-saving devices in all industries, and, in the last analysis, the trust is a labor- and capital-saving device." Rather than seek to preserve the old competition, the government must "remove all restrictions upon the organization of associations and combinations and . . . directly encourage such organizations, encourage men to do for themselves the things that should be done."[70] Eddy believed that the optimal system for regulating cooperation would take the form of a single commission similar to that proposed by Roosevelt under the New Nationalism.

The arguments made by the likes of Hurley and Eddy were reinforced by the mobilization experience. During the 1920s, others articulated the model as well. Consider the volume on trade associations released by the National Industrial Conference Board in 1925. Noting the same tension identified by Hoover, the volume presented the trade-association movement as a response to "the historical problem of reconciling freedom and authority." The authors

---

69. Edward N. Hurley, *Awakening of Business* (New York: Doubleday, Page & Co., 1916), 42, 207–8, 206. See Agnes Dyer Warbasse, "Milestones in Cooperation," *Nation,* November 8, 1922, 499.

70. Arthur J. Eddy, *The New Competition* (New York: D. Appelton & Co., 1912), 35, 47–48, 357. See also E. H. Gaunt, *Co-operative Competition* (Providence, R.I.: Stevens Press, 1917).

identified two economic extremes. First, there was "the individualistic policy of unfettered and unregulated competition," which engendered "much waste and ill-will and . . . such a degree of mastery . . . as to disillusion the most confirmed laissez-faire enthusiasts." In contrast, one could present "the unpromising alternative of authoritative control of industry under official bureaucratic forms," which involved "such danger of inflexibility and stagnation in economic processes as to deter all but the most venturesome from embracing it." Between these two extremes, the trade-association movement was evolving as a "synthesis of freedom and authority in the economic sphere." The authors concluded: "Stimulated by a developing sense of collective responsibility and held in check by the well-established mandates of public policy, the trade association movement may serve to reinvigorate the competitive system and facilitate the fulfillment of its best promise."[71]

For Hoover and many of his contemporaries, then, voluntary associations provided the foundation of a cooperative social order, a form of "self-government outside of formal government."[72] It is vital to recognize that the state had to play a role in the construction of an associational system.[73] By promoting the formation of economic associations and coordinating their activities, it could support a form of planning without simultaneously dictating the activities of industry. It could promote industrial efficiency and social welfare without sacrificing liberty. Hoover envisioned an associational system that would allow for the promotion of efficiency, the elimination of destructive competition, and the management of macroeconomic fluctuations. By restricting its activities to those of coordinator and intermediary, the state would provide wide room for voluntarism and associational activity. In the worlds of Peri Arnold, Secretary Hoover would use his new powers to transform "this set of attitudes into a new involvement of government in business," thus creating "a native American version of corporatism."[74]

Associationalism and the Commerce Department

Throughout much of 1920, Republicans and Democrats alike sought to convince Hoover to run for the presidency. The *Nation* reported that supporters

71. National Industrial Conference Board, *Trade Associations: Their Economic Significance and Legal Status* (New York: National Industrial Conference Board, 1925), 315–16.

72. Hoover, *The Challenge to Liberty,* 41.

73. See ibid., 33.

74. Peri Ethan Arnold, "Herbert Hoover and the Continuity of American Public Policy," *Public Policy* 20, no. 4 (1972): 531.

viewed him "as being everything he ought to be—a statesman, a liberal, a great organizer, a sound business man with greater detailed knowledge of European conditions than is possessed by any living American." However, "there are a multitude of questions which he must answer before a proper judgment can be formed. Have we any proof . . . that Mr. Hoover is really a liberal? How does he stand on the great economic questions of the day? What vision has he of the future? Does he excuse the prevailing hysteria and the deliberate effort to Prussianize America, to rob us of free speech, of a free press, of the right to assembly? Is he a free trader? Is he really a candidate?"[75] Hoover's unwillingness to clearly state his positions on key policies led, ultimately, to a single question: "Has Mr. Hoover done no conclusive political thinking for himself in all these years of his rich and varied life?"[76] Hoover's campaign eight years later would raise many of the same questions.

Following the election of Harding, Hoover was considered for a number of positions. Ultimately, he was asked to become secretary of commerce, a position he assumed in March of 1921, with President Harding's promise that he could contribute to all aspects of national economic policy and that he would be allowed to transform the Commerce Department and use it to address problems of industrial waste, market expansion, and industrial relations.[77] Hoover's efforts at Commerce encountered some formidable obstacles. There were ongoing battles with other departments, which resented Hoover's intervention in their affairs. Contemporaries noted that Hoover was "Secretary of Commerce and Under-Secretary of all other departments." As Oswald Garrison Villard noted in a 1928 review of Hoover's tenure at Commerce, Hoover's intervention was "bitterly resented in the departments in question. He is hated in the State Department because he won the fight to keep control of the commercial attachés of our legations and embassies. . . . At times the Department of Agriculture, the Department of Labor, the Treasury Department, the Interstate Commerce Commission, the Shipping Board, the Federal Trade Commission, were reported to have protested against Mr. Hoover's playing the under-secretary in their shops."[78] In addition, his efforts to construct an associational order raised serious questions concerning the status of his new programs under the antitrust prohibitions. Although the FTC would

75. *Nation,* January 31, 1920, 127.

76. "Mr. Hoover in the Valley of Decision," *Nation,* February 20, 1920, 225.

77. Herbert Hoover, *The Memoirs of Herbert Hoover,* vol. 2, *The Cabinet and the Presidency, 1920–1933* (New York: Macmillan, 1952), 36.

78. Oswald Garrison Villard, "Presidential Possibilities: Herbert C. Hoover," *Nation,* February 29, 1928, 235.

become a key advocate of associationalism, the Justice Department continued in its support of the antitrust tradition. Finally, as one might expect, there were concerns on the part of a multitude of corporations and associations that had not been consulted: Was the new associationalism to cover all corporations, or only a select few? Despite these problems, Commerce was rapidly transformed into the government's central economic policy-making agency.[79]

Hoover's wartime experiences, his professional socialization as an engineer, and his leadership in the Federated American Engineering Societies (later the American Engineering Council) led him to conclude that efficiency provided the key to economic growth and wage stability. The elimination of waste, he believed, could be combined with an expansion of trade to provide the basis for ongoing growth. A 1921 survey of U.S. industry conducted during Hoover's presidency of the American Engineering Council determined that "25 per cent of the costs of production could be eliminated without reduction of wages, increase in hours or strain on workers." Hoover claimed that his goal was to "put this plan into voluntary action on a nation-wide scale through the Department of Commerce."[80] The elimination of waste required both the careful examination of existing industrial practices and the cooperative identification and targeting of wasteful practices. It required, in short, that the Department of Commerce extend the activities of the War Industries Board's Conservation Division.

As secretary of commerce, Hoover became the prime proponent of associationalism. Under Hoover's direction the Commerce Department expanded and entered entirely new areas of activity. By 1924, Hoover was actively promoting associationalism through close contacts with a large number of agencies, including the Department of Interior, the Labor Department, the Agriculture Department, and the Federal Trade Commission. As noted above, this associational evangelism was not always embraced by other departments.[81]

79. Ellis W. Hawley, "Herbert Hoover and Economic Stabilization, 1921–22," in *Herbert Hoover as Secretary of Commerce, 1921–28: Studies in New Era Thought and Practice,* ed. Ellis W. Hawley (Iowa City: University of Iowa Press, 1981), 49–50. See George T. Odell, "Herbert Hoover—Super-Business Man," *Nation,* September 23, 1925, 326.

80. Hoover, *Memoirs of Herbert Hoover,* 2:31.

81. Ellis W. Hawley, *The Great War and the Search for a Modern Order: A History of the American People and Their Institutions, 1917–1933* (New York: St. Martin's Press, 1979). See David F. Noble, *America by Design: Science, Technology, and the Rise of Corporate Capitalism* (New York: Oxford University Press, 1977), 76–83, and Ellis W. Hawley, "Three Facets of Hooverian Associationalism: Lumber, Aviation, and the Movies, 1921–1930," in *Regulation in Perspective: Historical Essays,* ed. Thomas K. McCraw (Cambridge: Harvard University Press, 1981). For a discussion of the evolution of the trade-association movement and its relationship to the New Deal, see Robert F. Himmelberg, *The Origins of the National Recovery Administra-*

Reorganizing the Department of Commerce

The Department of Commerce found its origins in the Department of Commerce and Labor, created in 1903. Although Commerce and Labor were divided in 1913, insufficient attention had been directed to establishing the Commerce Department as an independent entity. When Hoover was appointed secretary, the department was in a state of disarray. As Hoover later recalled: "The Department of Commerce was a congeries of independent bureaus. . . . Each was an inbred bureaucracy of its own. There was little departmental spirit, or esprit de corps. . . . This lack of cohesion was emphasized by the fact that the Bureaus were housed in fifteen different buildings, mostly rented, and some condemned by the District of Columbia fire and health departments."[82] The department that Hoover hoped would become the central clearinghouse for economic policy making was in need of dramatic reform before such a goal could be realized. To better understand the role that a new Commerce Department could fulfill, Hoover immediately initiated conferences with the representatives of various economic groups. By the end of his first month, Hoover had enlisted twenty-five leaders of business, labor, and agriculture to form an advisory board to help determine how the department could best fulfill its role. For the remainder of his tenure, a seemingly endless set of conferences with engineers, statisticians, and business representatives informed the department's activities. By organizing and nurturing this constituency, Hoover fortified his capacity to lay claim to the resources and statutory support needed to convert the moribund agency.[83]

One of Hoover's first steps was to address the department's mediocre leadership and personnel. Much of the department staff were Wilson appointees who lacked the requisite expertise. Qualified members of the technical staff replaced those who were outside of the civil-service system. Others, who had been appointed by Wilson and provided civil-service protection via executive order, presented an altogether different problem. At Hoover's request, President Harding issued an executive order temporarily relaxing civil-service protection. Subsequently, the Civil Service Commission filled the vacancies with individuals who had passed the civil-service examination. Hoover

tion: Business, Government, and the Trade Association Issue, 1921–1933 (New York: Fordham University Press, 1976).

82. Hoover, *Memoirs of Herbert Hoover,* 2:42.

83. E. Pendelton Herring, *Public Administration in the Public Interest* (New York: McGraw-Hill, 1936), 297; Robert K. Murray, "Herbert Hoover and the Harding Cabinet," in *Herbert Hoover as Secretary of Commerce, 1921–28,* 21.

secured salary increases for the remaining employees and staffed key bureau positions with leaders from business and academia.[84]

Many offices and bureaus with functions related to Commerce's mandate were located in other departments. Rather than duplicate their activities, Hoover successfully orchestrated the transfer of statistical, marketing, transportation, and development units from other agencies to the Commerce Department. For example, he acquired the Treasury's Bureau of Custom Statistics in 1923 and the Bureau of Mines and Patents in 1925. Congress contributed to Commerce's expansion by authorizing the addition of a Housing Division (1922), an Aeronautics Division (1926), and a Radio Division (1927).[85] This expansion had budgetary consequences. During Hoover's tenure, Commerce's budget increased from $24.5 million to $37.6 million, including an additional $7.4 million to fund agencies that had been added to the department. Staffing increased as well, from 13,005 employees to 15,850. Despite the budgetary growth, Hoover had to spend his own money to enlist the necessary support staff. According to his own account, he employed two secretaries and three assistants at a personal expense greater than his salary.[86]

There is no question that Hoover was a critical figure in the history of the Commerce Department. He expanded and professionalized the agency while nurturing relationships with key economic associations. Under his direction, a network of public-private relations was designed to produce mechanisms for managing the new economic order. Drawing on his experience at the Food Administration, "Hoover proceeded to organize a parallel structure of industry sections and industrial committees, staffing the former with volunteer specialists on leave from the private sector. As this was organized, it was also interwoven with the department's technical and service bureaus, with cooperating professional and philanthropic bodies, and with a network of local community units, again much as Hoover had structured his war control system." As Ellis Hawley notes, these efforts were combined with "a series of organizational and promotional conferences, campaigns, and follow-ups, out of which the envisioned mechanisms were supposed to come."[87] Hoover's use of the department to promote associationalism and the legacy of the mobiliza-

84. Hoover, *Memoirs of Herbert Hoover*, 2:43.

85. Ibid.

86. David Hinshaw, *Herbert Hoover: American Quaker* (New York: Farrar, Straus & Co., 1950), 126–28; Hoover, *Memoirs of Herbert Hoover*, 2:43–44.

87. Ellis W. Hawley, "Industrial Policy in the 1920s and 1930s," in *The Politics of Industrial Policy*, ed. Claude E. Barfield and William A. Schambra (Washington, D.C.: American Enterprise Institute, 1986), 65.

tion experience is best illustrated by examining the two most important bureaus at Commerce: the Bureau of Foreign and Domestic Commerce and the
Bureau of Standards.

Associationalism and Trade Promotion

Hoover was convinced that trade expansion and efficiency were vital components of growth. Commerce promoted trade with its Bureau of Foreign
and Domestic Commerce. The demands for government services varied within
the business community, largely on the basis of enterprise size. Larger producers had a volume of sales that could support independent efforts at collecting market information. Smaller firms, in contrast, were dependent on
the support services provided by the Department of Commerce and trade
associations.[88] Despite the fact that larger corporations had developed an independent capacity to exploit foreign trade, they remained concerned with
public policies that shaped the general business environment, for example,
the tariff, antitrust regulations, exchange rates. Under Hoover's direction, the
bureau was professionalized and came to play an active role in identifying
trade opportunities and facilitating agreements between U.S. and foreign
firms, thereby winning the support of larger enterprises.

In 1922, the Bureau of Foreign and Domestic Commerce was reorganized,
professionalized, and placed under the direction of economist Dr. Julius Klein.
The newly reconstituted bureau had sixteen different divisions, each specializing in a particular industry. Division heads were nominated by trade associations, and were regarded as de facto representatives of the industry in question
before being appointed to the positions. The number of divisions would subsequently grow to twenty. At the same time, the bureau created district offices,
which increased in number from seven in 1921 to thirty-six by 1932. Under
Hoover's direction, the number of so-called "cooperative offices" also increased. Cooperative offices functioned much as the district offices. However,
they were located in smaller cities, whereas the district offices were located in
the nation's largest centers of commerce. More important, they were officially
sponsored and supported by a commercial organization, usually the Chamber
of Commerce. Additional bureau representatives were placed in various foreign countries to conduct research and facilitate trade agreements, points that
are discussed in greater detail below. As with other aspects of the Commerce

88. William H. Becker, *The Dynamics of Business-Government Relations: Industry and Exports, 1893–
1921* (Chicago: University of Chicago Press, 1982), 181.

Department's development, Hoover created the new commodity divisions and expanded the cooperative offices to strengthen the department's relationship with business. In the process, he further blurred the distinction between public and private.[89]

Reflecting a model that had gained currency during the war, Hoover created advisory committees for each of the commodity divisions in the bureau. These committees, composed of business executives and trade-association representatives, were designed to facilitate the free flow of information between Commerce and business, the dissemination of foreign economic intelligence, and the rapid identification of problems that might have an impact on existing business practices and exports. While it might be convenient to interpret this as a perfect example of agency capture, E. Pendleton Herring notes the role that these committees played in the bureau's efforts to build support for Commerce initiatives: "In theory the industries chose their representative to head the commodity division and then used the advisory committee as a means of directing the attention of the bureau to their business problems. In actual practice, these advisory committees often were little more than stalking-horses for the ideas of the commodity-division chiefs. The initiatives and direction came form the bureaucrats. The committees became useful channels for aligning the support of a particular industry behind the proposals of the civil servants." When conferences were called with business, as they were on hundreds of occasions, the object was "to advance plans of which the department already approved as a result of its own investigation. Officials felt that . . . the average businessman could not think in general terms, but that, once given a concrete problem, he could make recommendations. Advisory committees served to call the attention of businessmen to the broader questions within their industry."[90]

The bureau's activities were wide-ranging. It compiled reports on general economic conditions and foreign markets for specific commodities, drawing on foreign trade journals and the work of those stationed at the Consular Service's 325 offices and the bureau's own twenty-nine fixed posts. These reports were made available to businesses through regularly published Commerce Reports, Trade Information Bulletins, press releases, and monographs. It also provided a wealth of information on foreign tariffs and regulations,

89. Arnold, "Herbert Hoover and the Continuity of American Public Policy," 535; Herring, *Public Administration in the Public Interest*, 299, 302; and Laurence F. Schmeckebier and Gustavus A. Weber, *The Bureau of Foreign and Domestic Commerce: Its History, Activities, and Organization* (Baltimore: Johns Hopkins University Press, 1924), 82–84.

90. Herring, *Public Administration in the Public Interest*, 299, 300.

foreign rules governing the registration of trademarks and patents, and foreign commercial laws addressing such matters as bankruptcy, incorporation,
and debt collection.[91]

The bureau also facilitated contracts between American and foreign firms.
Its agents collected information on foreign businesses that had indicated some
interest in forging ties with American exporters and reported these "foreign-
trade opportunities" in specific terms (i.e., the precise good desired, the quantity, the nation in question) through the Commerce Reports or newspaper
articles. Specific information on the party was reserved for American firms
that had filed a sworn statement with the Commerce Department and thus
had become part of the bureau's "Exporters' Index." In one year alone (1922),
the bureau publicized 2,960 trade opportunities and provided 127,385 addresses to qualified firms upon request. The bureau also compiled trade lists
of dealers for various commodities, providing specific information on the firms
in question (e.g., manner of organization, capital, commercial standing, etc.).
In 1922, some 992,000 lists were distributed in response to business requests.
Information on American firms was also provided to foreign businesses. Bureau personnel also mediated disputes between U.S. and foreign-based firms,
seeking to resolve disagreements or misunderstandings and educate trade associations regarding the special needs that might exist in a given country.[92]
At times, the bureau had to stimulate the commercial infrastructure necessary
for exports. For example, in hopes of increasing the foreign demand for Amer-
ican-made autos, the bureau convinced tire producers and car manufacturers
to create an international network for servicing cars. The Commerce Department's efforts at simplification and standardization (see the discussion below)
reduced the variety of automobile tires, thereby facilitating the creation of
foreign-based services.[93]

The Bureau also worked to minimize the negative impact of foreign trade
practices on the U.S. economy. The most pressing problem was the effects of
foreign cartels designed to control the flow of key commodities. Rubber, qui-
nine, potash, nitrates, hemp, coffee, mercury, and long-staple cotton were
controlled by cartels or trade agreements in other countries. Congress appropriated $500,000 to the department to investigate and address the foreign
cartels; bureau research parties were sent to a number of nations to examine
the costs of production.[94] In the end, the department promoted several differ-

91. See Schmeckebier and Weber, *The Bureau of Foreign and Domestic Commerce*, chap. 2.
92. Ibid., 53–55, 59–60.
93. See the discussion in Hoover, *Memoirs of Herbert Hoover*, 2:80.
94. Schmeckebier and Weber, *The Bureau of Foreign and Domestic Commerce*, 76–77, 90.

ent responses to foreign cartels and trade agreements. First, it advocated greater conservation efforts to reduce the influx of the commodity in question. For example, it called on domestic rubber users to place a greater reliance on reclaimed rubber. Second, the bureau sought to nurture competing sources of the commodity outside of the nation that had organized the cartel. Finally, it promoted the search for domestic reserves or the identification of substitutes. Thus, the bureau secured funds to explore for potash in Texas and New Mexico—a successful venture that ultimately undermined the German cartel. It also promoted the creation of synthetic plants to counter the Chilean control of nitrates. According to Hoover, these efforts were so successful that within five years there were such surpluses of previously controlled commodities that the market prices were often below the costs of production.[95]

Associationalism, Conservation, and Standardization

The close relationships between the Commerce Department and business associations were similar to those adopted during the war. These patterns of state-economy relations, so evident in the case of the Bureau of Foreign and Domestic Commerce, were even more clearly exemplified in the activities of the Bureau of Standards. Here Commerce fully absorbed functions that had been introduced by the WIB to reduce the impact of wartime shortages. During the war, Bureau of Standards personnel provided support to the WIB's Conservation Division and provided advice on standardization and simplification. In the process, they created a demand for their engineering services that led to a significant loss of Commerce Department engineers and analysts, who were drawn away into private-sector employment. The department compensated for the loss of personnel by creating a research-associate program to bring researchers from industry, trade, and professional associations into the bureau for a limited term of service. The corporate-sponsored research associates had access to department facilities and created a unique interface between the agency and corporations while allowing the bureau to pursue a more ambitious mandate during the 1920s.[96]

Drawing on the wartime conservation experiences, Hoover inaugurated a Division of Simplified Practices in 1922, placing it under the leadership of William Durgin. It was created "to cooperate with American industries in furthering a nation-wide program for eliminating waste in commerce and

95. Hoover, *Memoirs of Herbert Hoover*, 2:81–84.
96. This discussion draws on Herring, *Public Administration in the Public Interest*, 317–24.

industry by reducing the number and sizes and types of standard products."[97] The simplification process, established through the joint efforts of the Commerce Department, the U.S. Chamber of Commerce, and the American Engineering Standards Committee, was patterned on the consensual procedures applied by the WIB. After a survey of an industry identified wasteful practices and excessive product varieties, it called a general meeting of producers, distributors, and commercial consumers. During these meetings, participants made recommendations concerning product variations that could be eliminated to save resources, without seriously affecting the consumer. Once formally accepted by firms responsible for 80 percent of production, recommendations were disseminated through Commerce's Elimination of Waste Series.[98] A similar process was observed in the promulgation of commercial standards addressing the grade, quality, composition, and dimensions of a particular good. Upon the request of a trade association, the bureau would collect information and suggest preliminary commercial standards. Following a series of conferences, an official recommendation would become effective upon the formal written acceptance of firms responsible for 65 percent of the production. From the creation of the Division of Simplified Practices, in January 1922, to July 31, 1925, the Bureau held some 188 simplification conferences in Washington, D.C., covering a variety of industries.[99]

As one might expect, Hoover claimed tremendous savings for industry and the economy as a whole as a result of simplification and standard setting. The economies of scale in production and distribution became evident when the varieties of rough brick were reduced from thirty-nine to one, or the varieties of files and rasps were reduced from 1,351 to 496.[100] In Hoover's words: "[M]anufacturers were able to engage more fully in mass production, as they could produce for stocks instead of filling specific orders; the amount of inventories which must be carried by consumers was greatly reduced, and competition was enhanced in such articles."[101]

Despite this enthusiasm, a critic could identify several problems. Simplification often resulted in commercial standards rather than technical standards. Not only did this alienate department engineers who saw their mission as scientific, it politicized the process. The effects of simplification on competi-

97. Gustavus A. Weber, *The Bureau of Standards: Its History, Activities, and Organization* (Baltimore: Johns Hopkins University Press, 1925), 75.
98. Noble, *America by Design*, 81. Herring, *Public Administration in the Public Interest*, 323.
99. Weber, *The Bureau of Standards*, 172–75.
100. Ibid., 173.
101. Hoover, *Memoirs of Herbert Hoover*, 2:66.

tion and consumers were less than benign. The creation of new standards could result in the elimination of a competitor and the opportunity for large producers to capture a greater market share. Some of the "eliminated" varieties were the primary products of smaller firms that lacked the resources or political savvy to shape simplification decisions. Because compliance depended on business voluntarism and the Commerce Department lacked the authority to bring legal proceedings against corporations that continued to produce goods that had been formally eliminated, compliance was often much less than Hoover would have hoped.[102] But even with the flaws of the simplification process, there is little question that the Commerce Department had given the wartime conservation efforts a new peacetime footing. The Division of Simplified Practices was essentially a restoration of the WIB's Conservation Division—a perfect example of Hooverian associationalism.

The New Competition Versus the Old Antitrust

Despite the general support for associationalism, antitrust sentiment continued to pose an obstacle to the realization of an associational regime. Before the war, larger firms were the primary advocates for antitrust revisions. "Representatives of smaller concerns were uncommitted or hostile, for they feared that antitrust revision would ultimately benefit the competitive position of the industrial giants more than it would help their own."[103] The wartime experience, however, had revealed that associations could serve a positive role even for the small producer. By the end of the war the National Association of Manufacturers had joined with the larger producers in calling for antitrust revision. Changes in the laws, it was argued, would allow trade associations to play a role in economic governance along the lines suggested by Hoover.

Business associations created a potential problem for antitrust enforcement to the extent that they facilitated the collection and circulation of information concerning production costs and pricing, thereby facilitating price-fixing. During the three decades since the passage of the Sherman Act, antitrust legislation had played a key role in shaping business organization and conduct. The act stated the nation's competition policy in exceptionally broad

102. Noble, *America by Design,* 82. Herring, *Public Administration in the Public Interest,* 323.
103. Robert F. Himmelberg, "The War Industries Board and the Antitrust Question in November 1918," *Journal of American History* 52, no. 1 (1965): 61.

terms, declaring illegal "every contract, combination in the form of trust or otherwise, or conspiracy, in restraint of trade or commerce" and proclaiming that "every person who shall monopolize, or attempt to monopolize, or combine or conspire with any other person or persons, to monopolize . . . shall be deemed guilty of a misdemeanor." The broad prohibitions of the Sherman Act were given greater precision as a result of a long and complicated history of court decisions. The Supreme Court introduced the rule of reason in 1911, under which the applicability of the Sherman Act would be determined by weighing the positive and negative effects of a given restraint and examining the means by which market power was established. While the rule of reason promised to provide greater flexibility for business, no one could be certain how the courts would exercise their newfound discretion. Greater flexibility and a reduction of uncertainty could be achieved simultaneously, it was believed, only through the passage of new antitrust laws and the creation of new institutions.[104]

The Clayton Act brought greater specificity to antitrust policy by identifying various forms of conduct that could contribute to monopoly. The Federal Trade Commission Act created the Federal Trade Commission, an independent regulation commission. The new regulatory procedures and the prohibition of "unfair methods of competition in commerce" in section 5 of the Federal Trade Commission Act were designed to bring much needed flexibility and expertise to antitrust.[105] But the imprecision of the Federal Trade Commission Act opened the door to new difficulties: nowhere did it define exactly what constituted "unfair methods of competition in commerce." As a result, one might interpret the FTC's mandate creatively in light of prevailing doctrines of state-economy relations and existing political challenges. Indeed, this is precisely what happened as the FTC evolved from an embodiment of Wilsonian Progressivism to an advocate of associationalism in the 1920s. The evolution of the FTC's policies constituted, in part, a response to the restrictions imposed by the Supreme Court, as is revealed by a brief review of some of the decade's key decisions addressing the status of trade associations. It also reflected a response to the difficult political environment that confronted the commission in its first decade. Let us address these points in turn.

In *American Column and Lumber Co. v. United States* (1921), the Supreme Court determined that the company's activities constituted a violation of the

104. See Marc Allen Eisner, *Antitrust and the Triumph of Economics: Institutions, Expertise, and Policy Change* (Chapel Hill: University of North Carolina Press, 1991), chaps. 2–3.

105. See George Rublee, "The Original Plan and Early History of the Federal Trade Commission," *Proceedings of the Academy of Political Science* 11, no. 4 (1926): 114–20.

Sherman Act prohibition of price-fixing.[106] The association of hardwood producers operated an "open competition plan." That is, it collected daily reports on sales by kind, grade, and quality, daily shipment reports with copies of all invoices, monthly production and stock reports, and monthly price lists that had to be updated immediately upon a change in prices. This information was circulated to association members before their monthly meetings. According to the association, the plan was designed "to disseminate among members accurate knowledge of production and market conditions so that each member may gauge the market intelligently." The association informed members that "knowledge regarding prices actually made" would be sufficient to "keep prices at reasonably stable and normal conditions." Of course, cooperation could result in stability while enhancing profitability: "Co-operation is a matter of business because it pays; because it enables you to get the best price for your product; because you come into closer personal contact with the market."[107] During the monthly meetings, producers openly discussed prices and output, with an eye to eliminating overproduction and preserving profitability.[108]

While the facts in *American Column and Lumber* were not in dispute and provided for the Court's majority clear evidence of a Sherman Act violation, the decision was not unanimous. Justice Holmes noted that the Sherman Act "did not set itself against knowledge," and found the Court's position surprising "in a country of free speech, that affects to regard education and knowledge as desirable."[109] Brandeis echoed Holmes's concerns over the status of information under the Sherman Act. However, his dissent rested on the fact that the association's arrangement did not have the characteristics of a monopoly (e.g., territorial divisions, coercion, and uniformity of pricing). There were concerns that in such a decentralized industry rational competition and intelligent trade demanded access to information that would otherwise not be available.[110]

The decision in *American Column and Lumber* raised Hoover's concern over the range of legitimate association activities under the antitrust laws. Ultimately, it led him to initiate a chain of correspondence with Attorney General

---

106. *American Column and Lumber Co. v. United States,* 257 U.S. 377 (1921).

107. 257 U.S. 377 (1921), at 392–94.

108. See the discussion in A. D. Neale and D. G. Goyder, *The Antitrust Laws of the United States of America: A Study of Competition Enforced by Law,* 3d ed. (Cambridge: Cambridge University Press, 1980), 45–46.

109. 257 U.S. 377 (1921), at 412–13.

110. 257 U.S. 377 (1921), at 415.

Daugherty in February 1922. Hoover and Daugherty agreed that a specific definition of legal activities would be impossible due to the wide range of association activities and the different features of various industries. However, as a general rule, trade-association activities would be legal "provided always that whatever is done is not used as a scheme or device to curtail production or enhance prices, and does not have the effect of suppressing competition."[111] Most important, however, under an agreement with the Justice Department, Hoover placed the Commerce Department in the position of an intermediary. It would collect and distribute the very information deemed of concern in the 1921 court decision, "in effect turning the department into a central trade association for service to all other associations. . . . It was this set of programs which allowed for the continued development and success of the trade association movement."[112]

While the decision gave pause to many advocates of associational activity, there was partial relief in 1925, when the Supreme Court had the opportunity to address a somewhat similar set of circumstances. In *Maple Flooring Manufacturers' Association v. United States,* the controversy addressed an association that collected information on costs, prices, and sales, distributing average-cost and price figures to its members. The Court found for the defendant, concluding that the "free distribution of knowledge" had not made competition "less free." The decision rested on three factors. First, the information distributed by the association was more general than that provided in the earlier case. Second, there was no evidence that pricing and output were discussed at the association meetings. Finally, because the prices charged by association members lacked uniformity and tended to be below average, there was no way to conclude that the association was functioning as a cartel.[113] The Court's decision concluded with a brief statement of the kinds of activities that associations could legally engage in:

> We decide only that trade associations or combinations of persons or corporations which openly and fully gather and disseminate information as to the cost of their product, the volume of production, the actual price which the product has brought in past transactions, stocks

111. Attorney General Harry M. Daugherty to Commerce Secretary Herbert Hoover, February 8, 1922, reprinted in Franklin D. Jones, *Trade Association Activities and the Law* (New York: McGraw-Hill, 1922), 332.

112. Arnold, "Herbert Hoover and the Continuity of American Public Policy," 539.

113. *Maple Flooring Manufacturers' Association v. United States,* 268 U.S. 563 (1925). See Neale and Goyder, *Antitrust Laws of the United States of America,* 46–47.

of merchandise on hand, approximate costs of transportation from the principal point of shipment to the points of consumption . . . and discuss such information and statistics without, however, reaching or attempting to reach any agreement on any concerted action with respect to prices or production or restraining competition, do not thereby engage in unlawful restraint of commerce.[114]

While strong proponents of cooperative competition could have hoped for more—particularly in the area of coordinated production and pricing—the court clarified the range of legitimate association activities under the antitrust laws.[115] With the broad recognition of trade associations as legitimate entities in industrial governance, it became possible to see the kind of social order that Hoover had envisioned. As one contemporary observer, Gilbert H. Montague, noted in 1926:

> As I look at these Supreme Court decisions, it is not so much the opportunity but the responsibility which they have placed on trade associations and on business that today impresses me. Looking into the future, and seeing how the business cycle can be brought under control of society, I can see all the tremendous social and psychological results which may follow. Business can be maintained on present or even better levels, peaks of over-speculation can be cut down, valleys of undue depression can be filled up, extremes of feast and famine can be avoided, and industry can, with reasonable assurance, be stabilized on fairer price levels.[116]

As Chapter 7 shows, Hoover had already promoted a system of countercyclical management that rested on the voluntary actions of business and trade associations.

These cases, filed by the Department of Justice, were in keeping with traditional Sherman Act prosecutions. Despite Montague's optimism, there remained a good deal of uncertainty regarding the status of associational ac-

114. 268 U.S. 563 (1925), at 586.
115. See a contemporary discussion of these decisions and their implications for trade association activities in William J. Donovan, "The Legality of Trade Associations," *Proceedings of the Academy of Political Science* 11, no. 4 (1926): 19–26.
116. Gilbert H. Montague, "New Opportunities and Responsibilities of Trade Associations as a Result of Recent United States Supreme Court Decisions," *Proceedings of the Academy of Political Science* 11, no. 4 (1926), 30.

tivity under the Court's reading of the antitrust laws. Uncertainly was also increased by the Federal Trade Commission, whose imprecise mandate mixed poorly with the highly conflictive political environment in the years after the war. When the FTC was created, it was staffed with analysts transferred from the Bureau of Corporations in the Department of Commerce. The former bureau economists, accountants, and statisticians who provided the analytical core of the FTC were almost immediately enlisted in the war effort. During the war, the Federal Trade Commission worked closely with the WIB Price-Fixing Committee. It assigned a team of economists and accountants to a variety of industries to conduct studies of the costs of production in high-cost and low-cost plants. This data subsequently provided a basis for determining price schedules through a process that involved representatives of the FTC, the Price-Fixing Committee, the WIB commodity section, the war service committee, and industry actors. The FTC also conducted special industry studies of pricing and production at the request of the president and Congress.[117] Thus, at the end of the war, it conducted an investigation of the meatpacking industry at the request of Wilson. The congressional response to the report would create significant problems for the FTC.

The FTC's report revealed that the big-five meatpackers colluded to erect territorial restrictions and inflate the price of livestock and finished products. New competition was impeded through the beef trust's control of stockyards, warehouses, cold-storage facilities, and rail cars. It recommended governmental control of these facilities: administration as a government monopoly would allow for open competition.[118] The congressional reaction to the investigation—a product of heavy industry lobbying and the Red Scare—was ultimately debilitating. Senator Watson introduced a resolution authorizing an investigation of the FTC because "there is reason to believe that a number of employees of the Federal Trade Commission have been, and now are, engaged in socialistic propaganda and in furthering the organization and growth of socialistic organization."[119] The FTC's Chicago office, the office chiefly responsible for the meatpacking investigation, was described as a center "of sedition and anarchy from which radiated the most baleful influence," and as "a spawning ground for sovietism" where the FTC staff "plotted for the destruction of the businesses they were charged to investigate and for the confiscation and collective ownership of all the means for the creation and redistribution

117. Baruch, *American Industry in the War,* 80.
118. For a summary of the report, see *Annual Report of the Federal Trade Commission* (Washington, D.C.: Government Printing Office, 1918), 22–25.
119. *Congressional Record,* 66th Cong., 1st sess., 1919, 58, pt. 7:7166.

of wealth."[120] Watson was careful to note that his sponsorship of the resolution was "in no wise a defense of the packers." Rather, it was an effort "to call attention . . . to the socialistic activities of some of the employees of the Federal Trade Commission who were chosen to investigate the operation of these corporations."[121]

Watson was successful in securing passage of a resolution for a Senate investigation of the commission and alleged that the eleven employees of the FTC who had been key contributors to the meatpacking study were in fact socialists. Although the employees were exonerated, by the end of 1920 all had been discharged under the pretense of funding reductions. It was alleged by Stuart Chase, then a commission official who had been discharged, that the firings were a concession to Congress and an attempt to gain favor from Senator Watson, who would be able to undermine the FTC's budget requests. In response to the scandal, one commissioner, W. B. Colver, declined reappointment. With the Packers and Stockyards Act of 1921, jurisdiction over the industry was transferred to the Agriculture Department.[122]

Despite the concessions to Congress, FTC appropriations declined from a wartime high of $1.75 million in 1919 to $974,480 in 1923. While this reduction reflected the termination of war duties, it also occurred in the midst of the conflicts over the alleged politicization of the agency. For the remainder of the decade, the budget remained relatively stable, increasing slightly to $1.16 million in 1929. During the war, the FTC staff reached a high of 663 (1918); following the meatpacking controversy, it ranged from a low of 308 in 1923 to a high of 380 in 1929.[123] Reflecting the earlier controversies, Congress in 1925 placed on the FTC's appropriation bill a rider limiting the agency's discretion over investigations. The FTC was now prohibited from initiating investigations unless requested by a concurrent resolution of Congress or directly connected to violations of the antitrust acts.[124] Attempts to strike a more conciliatory posture with business and limit conflicts with Congress are evident in the enforcement record. The FTC filed 116 cease and desist orders in 1921—a number that fell to a low of 44 in 1926.[125]

120. Ibid., 7169.
121. Ibid., 7166–67.
122. Thomas C. Blaisdell Jr., *The Federal Trade Commission: An Experiment in the Control of Business* (New York: Columbia University Press, 1932), 77–79. See George T. Odell, "The Federal Trade Commission Yields to Pressure," *Nation,* January 12, 1921, 36–37.
123. Federal Trade Commission, *Annual Report,* various years.
124. Federal Trade Commission, *Annual Report,* 1925 (Washington, D.C.: Government Printing Office, 1925), 1.
125. Federal Trade Commission, *Annual Report,* 1927 (Washington, D.C.: Government Printing Office, 1927), 105.

Under the constraints imposed by Congress, the FTC increasingly emphasized the use of trade-practice submittals as part of the regulatory process.
The movement in this direction was slow, however. In 1919, before the meatpacking investigation, the FTC began holding trade-practice conferences to
promote industry cooperation in the development of standards of conduct.
They were used primarily to clarify the kinds of activities that would be
considered anticompetitive by the FTC. The Court placed the FTC's authority
on very shaky ground in 1920, however, when it had the opportunity to
decide on the first challenge to a Federal Trade Commission decision. The
dispute in *Federal Trade Commission v. Gratz* was less important than the effects
of the decision on commission discretion.[126] When the commission issued a
complaint under the broad prohibition of section 5 of the FTC Act, the Court
objected. The Court opinion, written by Justice McReynolds, was designed to
obstruct a transfer of judicial power to an administrative agency. The decision
proclaimed: "The words 'unfair methods of competition' are not defined in
the statute and their exact meaning is in dispute. It is for the courts and not
the Commission ultimately to decide what they include. They are clearly
inapplicable to practices never heretofore regarded as opposed to good morals
because characterized by deception, bad faith, fraud, or oppression, or against
public policy because of their dangerous tendency unduly to hinder competition or create monopoly."[127] With this decision, the Court "reduced the Commission's jurisdiction to a repetition of common-law formulas."[128]

The *Gratz* decision came as a blow to supporters of the Federal Trade
Commission. In a dissenting opinion, Justice Brandeis noted that the practices
of the FTC were modeled on those of the Interstate Commerce Commission
and had been agreeable to the Court in the past. Moreover, he argued, the
decision denied the central mission of the FTC: "The task of the Commission
was to protect competition from further inroads by monopoly. . . . [It] was
directed to intervene, before any act should be done or conditions arise viola-
tive of the Anti-trust Act. . . . Its action was to be prophylactic. Its purpose
in respect to restraints of trade was prevention of diseased business conditions,
not cure."[129] Brandeis was concerned that attempts rigorously to apply inflexible legal standards would create great hardship for business while leaving
unfair methods of competition untouched.

The trade-practice submittals carried strategic advantages that became

126. *Federal Trade Commission v. Gratz*, 253 U.S. 421 (1920).
127. 253 U.S. 421 (1920), at 427–28.
128. Nelson B. Gaskill, *The Regulation of Competition* (New York: Harper & Brothers, 1936), 110.
129. 253 U.S. 421 (1920), at 435.

particularly clear in the wake of the *Gratz* decision and the congressional response to the meatpacking investigation. First, because the conferences allowed the FTC to cooperate with business in the definition of standards, they reduced the likelihood that its actions would further enrage Congress. Second, because standards were voluntary, the courts' access to the policy process was limited. As one might expect, there were ongoing tensions between the FTC's role in promoting competition and its support for business activity. The tensions were clearly exacerbated when Coolidge appointed William E. Humphrey to the commission in 1925. Humphrey's appointment created a Republican majority on the commission. As a strong adherent of cooperative regulation and associationalism, he provided critical support for the FTC's new direction. Speaking before the Chamber of Commerce in 1925, he made a promise that invoked Senator Watson's allegations of a few years earlier: "So far as I can prevent it, the Federal Trade Commission is not going to spread socialistic propaganda. In so far as I can prevent it, the commission is not going to be used to advance the political or personal fortunes of any person or party."[130]

Humphrey's position came into conflict with that adopted by progressives on the commission, as illustrated by the trade-practice rules adopted by the producers of anticholera serum and virus in 1925. A majority of producers endorsed rules permitting practices such as the provision of discounts, rebates, and advertising for distributors. Two Democratic commissioners, Huston Thompson and J. F. Nugent, dissented from the commission's acceptance of the trade-practice rules. The practices would "suppress competition in large measure by driving out of the business . . . the smaller concerns which are financially unable to meet the costs occasioned thereby, and enable the financially powerful among the manufacturers to dominate and exercise control over the industry." The Republican commissioners C. W. Hunt, Vernon W. Van Fleet, and William E. Humphrey, had no reluctance in accepting the rules, because, they argued, these practices were tools of competition every bit as valid as price competition. If smaller firms could not compete with rebates, discounts, and other enticements, they could not engage in effective competition. They charged that commission Democrats would "stifle competition in order that the smaller concerns may survive." These kinds of conflicts—between philosophies of regulation and competition—would plague

130. "Remarks of Commissioner W. E. Humphrey at the Annual Meeting of the United States Chamber of Commerce, May 20, 1925, Washington, D.C.," reprinted in *Congressional Record,* 69th Cong., 1st sess. 1926, 67, pt. 6:5968–70.

the commission for much of the decade as associationalism and New Freedom Progressivism came into conflict.[131]

On March 17, 1925—less than a month after Humphrey assumed his position—the FTC publicized new procedures. The changes included new opportunities for informal hearings prior to the issuance of a formal complaint. Businesses were now allowed to settle cases through stipulation, pledging to end the questionable practices and thus avoid prosecution. Significantly, the decision to resolve a dispute through stipulation avoided the publicity associated with a formal complaint and prosecution, since it was the FTC's new policy to refrain from issuing public statements on these cases. Moreover, the use of the stipulation process would prevent the matter from entering the courts.[132] Most important for present purposes, the FTC began placing a greater reliance on trade-practice conferences to establish rules of conduct. After the commission created a Trade Practice Conference Division in 1926, "to encourag[e] closer cooperation between business as a whole and the commission," the reliance on this policy tool increased dramatically.[133] During the next five years, the number of conferences continued to grow, reaching a high of fifty-seven in 1930. In the end, the number of requests for conferences surmounted the practical capacities of the Trade Practice Conferences Division.[134]

The new policies and procedures marked a significant shift in the FTC's relationship with business. The commission's *Annual Report* declared: "The new policies have principally to do with the idea of self-regulation in business and industry, and it has been possible to progress in these directions without over-stepping the bounds of the commission's powers as laid down by law. 'Helping business to help itself' wherever and whenever it can be done consistently without prejudice to the best interests of the public as a whole is the principle of this new policy." The U.S. Chamber of Commerce responded to the new policy by urging the formation of "joint trade relations committees" in every line of business to help define new rules in cooperation with the FTC.[135] But the FTC's pride in the changes in policy and process was not

131. Federal Trade Commission, *Annual Report,* 1925, 78.
132. On the FTC's practice of settling cases through stipulation, see W. H. S. Stevens, "Changes in the Federal Trade Commission's Legal Procedures," *Proceedings of the Academy of Political Science* 11, no. 4 (1926): 136–42.
133. Federal Trade Commission, *Annual Report,* 1926 (Washington, D.C.: Government Printing Office, 1926), 47.
134. Herring, *Public Administration in the Public Interest,* 129–30. Federal Trade Commission, *Annual Report,* 1930 (Washington, D.C.: Government Printing Office, 1930).
135. Federal Trade Commission, *Annual Report,* 1927, 1, 7.

shared by all. Champions of active regulation cited the changes as marking the end of an effective Federal Trade Commission. Indeed, Senator King made the new policies the centerpiece of his calls to cut off all resources for the continuation of the Harding-Coolidge FTC.[136]

The trade-practice conferences were held after the industry actors—typically the trade association or a collection of major corporations—filed an application. At the conferences, the FTC facilitated a discussion of the prevailing practices that were unfair, unethical, or in violation of the antitrust laws. The standards were accepted by the FTC following the positive affirmation of industry actors. The rules effectively fell into two categories. Group I rules prohibited practices that were illegal under the Sherman and Clayton Acts, providing a means of giving the vague legislative prohibitions greater specificity in the context of a particular industry. Group II rules addressed activities that were believed by industry actors to be unfair or unethical. These rules were accepted by the FTC as "expressions of the trade" to be enforced by the trade associations.[137] The trade-practice conferences made the trade associations part of the regulatory process. Not only were the associations responsible for enforcing Group II rules, they commonly initiated formal prosecutions through the submission of complaints. By 1928, trade associations had convinced the FTC to conduct over four hundred investigations into the violation of trade-practice rules. Of these, some one hundred resulted in the issuance of formal complaints and/or cease and desist orders.[138]

The trade-practice conferences held great promise. They allowed the FTC to replace the conflicts of the past with cooperation, thus avoiding the kinds of political controversies to which it had been subject in the past. Moreover, as noted above, the private negotiations involving businesses, trade associations, and the FTC limited the role of the courts. Finally, the trade-practice conferences were far more effective in that they covered all of the actors in the industry rather than the few who might have been subject to a decision under the case-by-case approach.[139] As one might expect, the trade-practice conferences were strongly supported by many commentators and business representatives. The National Industrial Conference Board, for example, re-

136. See *Congressional Record,* 69th Cong., 1st sess., 1926, 67, pt. 7:5944–72. Robert Himmelberg dismisses the importance of the changes and characterizes the excitement over the new procedures as largely misplaced. See Himmelberg, *The Origins of the National Recovery Administration,* 49–51.

137. Herring, *Public Administration in the Public Interest,* 130–31.

138. Blaisdell, *The Federal Trade Commission,* 94.

139. Alan Stone, *Economic Regulation in the Public Interest: The Federal Trade Commission in Theory and Practice* (Ithaca, N.Y.: Cornell University Press, 1977), 59.

ported that the conferences were "promising signs . . . of a more cordial relationship between coercive and voluntary agencies for the regulation of business conduct." The board surveyed existing government-association activities and noted that they kept alive "the expectation of eventually obtaining legal sanction for unified regulation of supply and control of price, when exercised with moderation and self-restraint."[140] This, of course, was precisely the problem. As the codes evolved from the simple application of existing legal prohibitions to particular industries to "practices which had never been recognized as unlawful . . . the interest of the business community increased."[141] It became increasingly common for codes to regulate various facets of commercial activity in order to restrain competition.

A number of factors combined to mark the end of the FTC's reliance on trade-practice conferences. In 1929, the FTC decided to condemn as illegal the secret violation of trade-practice rules, arguing that this was a fraudulent practice. This decision clearly signaled that the FTC was exceeding its authority in enforcing what were essentially trade-association rules. More important, however, were the growing concerns that many of the Group II rules were establishing standards that were essentially restraints of trade and thus liable to prosecution under the antitrust laws. While Assistant Attorney General John Lord O'Brian testified before Congress that he had found no cases where firms were violating the antitrust laws "on the advice" of the Federal Trade Commission, they commonly "operated in defiance of a rule or else used the rule as a cover or pretext for illegal practices."[142] Nevertheless, under pressure from the Justice Department, the FTC announced its decision to reconsider all existing rules. The U.S. Chamber of Commerce reacted to this announcement by organizing a meeting in Washington, D.C., of corporations and trade associations subject to the rules. Although the rapid mobilization of business limited the revisions of existing rules, the FTC's new posture eliminated business support for the trade-practice conferences, and they quickly fell out of use.[143] As noted above, the number of trade-practice conferences peaked at fifty-seven in 1930. The next year, the Federal Trade Commission held nine trade-practice conferences and issued revised rules for sixty-two industries.[144]

140. National Industrial Conference Board, *Trade Associations,* 55, 29.
141. Simon N. Whitney, *Trade Associations and Industrial Control: A Critique of the N.R.A.* (New York: Central Book Co., 1934), 54.
142. Quoted in John D. Clark, *The Federal Trust Policy* (Baltimore: Johns Hopkins University Press, 1931), 242.
143. Herring, *Public Administration in the Public Interest,* 131–32.
144. Federal Trade Commission, *Annual Report,* 1931 (Washington, D.C.: Government Printing Office, 1931), 107.

The unwillingness of the FTC officially to accept specific trade practices as fair methods of competition created great uncertainty for businesses and thus eliminated one of the central incentives for participating in the conferences.[145]

The Limits of Associationalism in Railroad Regulation

The 1920s was the decade of associationalism in business regulation. The bias in support of market governance that characterized earlier decades gave way under the pressures of the wartime experience, the revolution in economic organization, and the prodding of government officials. As Hoover argued repeatedly, associationalism offered the benefits of planning absent the weight of bureaucracy. It promised to provide a means of coordinating production and expansion, of scientifically managing the new corporate economy. In some ways, the allegiance to associationalism and the continued belief in the possibility of government-corporation cooperation and corporate self-governance were remarkable given how the Teapot Dome scandal had only recently revealed the dark possibilities that such cooperation offered. As one contemporary critic noted: "[W]e are getting a delightful picture of what a business government really is and exactly what Mr. Harding had in mind when he declared for a return to 'normalcy.' 'Get the government out of private business' was another slogan, and so from the very outset there was a mad rush to dispose of the property of the American people to speculators, get-rich-quick men, and others of this ilk."[146] That such scandals did not foreclose associationalism as an option stands as testament to the power of the wartime legacy and Hoover's advocacy.

The associational experiments were not limited to the Department of Commerce and the FTC. Take the example of the Interstate Commerce Commission (ICC). Railroad regulation was the first major experiment in national regulation in the United States, dating back to the 1880s, when the Interstate Commerce Commission was created to fill the gap left by the Supreme Court's 1886 Wabash decision, which questioned the constitutionality of state regulation of interstate railroad transportation.[147] Following the Hepburn Act of

145. Blaisdell, *The Federal Trade Commission*, 98.

146. "A Business Administration," *Nation*, February 22, 1924, 220.

147. *Wabash, St. Louis, and Pacific Railway Co. v. Illinois*, 118 U.S. 557 (1886). For background on railroad regulation, see Eisner, *Regulatory Politics in Transition*, 47–58. See also the fine study of U.S. railroad regulation Gerald Berk, *Alternative Tracks: The Constitution of American Industrial Order, 1865–1917* (Baltimore: Johns Hopkins University Press, 1994).

1908, the ICC served as a relatively vigorous regulator, imposing maximum rates in the interest of farmers and other shippers who feared that the concentration of control over the rails would result in monopolistic exploitation. The War Railroad Administration managed the lines during the war, following the collapse of the voluntary Railroad's War Board.[148] Positive experience with unified management led to calls for continued government operations. Railroad Administrator William McAdoo called for a five-year experiment in peacetime federal control. But Wilson never seriously entertained the possibility of railroad nationalization or even a temporary extension of government controls. He simply declared that he would return control over the lines to the owners on March 1, 1920, unless Congress acted positively in the interim.[149] Congress responded to Wilson's timetable by passing the Transportation Act of 1920, returning control of the industry to the owners. At the same time, the act significantly expanded the powers of the ICC and created a new benchmark for railroad regulation. The debates surrounding the passage of the Transportation Act were driven by the potentially conflicting goals of promoting industry profitability while guaranteeing that the rails fulfilled their obligations to provide services as common carriers under increasingly competition conditions.[150]

The key features of the Transportation Act marked a clear expansion of, and departure from, the existing regulatory practices of the Interstate Commerce Commission. Some of the provisions addressed the ICC's power over the organization and structure of the industry. Other provisions dealt with the issue of ICC rate making. First, the act gave the ICC broad new powers affecting the structure of the industry. Control over entry and exit was transferred from the states, which regulated abandonment via charters, to the ICC. This power was of great importance insofar as a more liberal policy on abandonments could facilitate the elimination of unprofitable lines, whereas control over entry could protect lines from potential competition and thus allow for the continuation of high rates. Second, to eliminate weak railroads, the ICC was directed to promote rail consolidations through mergers under a reorganization plan authorized by the act and to design a limited number of lines with equivalent rates of return. The ICC was also authorized to approve

148. See Walker D. Hines, *War History of American Railroads* (New Haven, Conn.: Yale University Press, 1928).

149. Arthur S. Link, *American Epoch: A History of the United States Since the 1890s* (New York: Alfred A. Knopf, 1955), 236–37.

150. This discussion draws on Theodore E. Keeler, *Railroads, Freight, and Public Policy* (Washington, D.C.: Brookings Institution, 1983), 25–26.

pooling agreements that previously had been deemed illegal, and was granted control over the issuance of railroad securities.

Most important, the ICC was directed to set *minimum* rates. This was a direct reversal of the ICC's established policy whereby the commission set *maximum* rates in hopes of maintaining low rates for shippers. Under the provisions of the Transportation Act, the ICC determined the floor rates, thus preventing ruinous rate wars and promoting the stability and profitability of the industry. Rates were to be set to guarantee the specific rate of return of 5.5 percent, with an additional 0.5 percent to fund improvements. Under the act's "recapture clause," railroads exceeding the 6 percent rate of return were required to place half of the sum in a reserve fund to be drawn on by the railroad as needed in lean years, and in a "general railroad contingent fund" that would be drawn on by the ICC to fund weaker railroads through loans or equipment leases. These rates were to be in effect for two years, on the assumption that the ICC would determine the aggregate value of the railways and determine what constituted a fair rate of return.[151]

The Transportation Act was a clear departure from the regulatory system established under the Interstate Commerce Act and subsequent railroad legislation. Unlike earlier policy, which was driven by the fear of railroad abuses and a concern for the rights of shippers to reasonable and just rates, the 1920 act was dominated by a recognition of the financial needs of the railroads and the desire for stability. In part, the shift in focus can be attributed to the changing political environment. As Samuel Huntington argues in his seminal piece on the ICC, the growing urbanization of the nation since the passage of the Interstate Commerce Act reduced the power of the agricultural sector, while high commodity prices during the war had attenuated the farmers' fixation on rail rates. While certainly not absent from the debates, shippers did not prevail over the railroads in defining the new legislation. Indeed, the ICC had found a new constituency in the regulated parties. "These factors dictated not only the shift in public policy which was made in the Transportation Act of 1920 but also a shift by the Commission in the sources to which it looked for support. Continued reliance upon the old sources of support would have resulted in decreasing viability. Therefore the Commission turned more and more to the railway industry itself, particularly the railroad management group."[152]

151. Merle Fainsod, Lincoln Gordon, and Joseph C. Palamountain Jr., *Government and the American Economy*, 3d ed. (New York: W. W. Norton, 1959), 268–71.

152. Samuel P. Huntington, "The Marasmus of the ICC: The Commission, the Railroads, and the Public Interest," reprinted in *The Politics of American Economic Policy Making*, ed. Paul Peretz (Armonk, N.Y.: M. E. Sharpe, 1987), 82.

The Transportation Act of 1920 can be viewed as a watershed event in the history of the ICC. Consider Marver Bernstein's characterization of the ICC's history after the passage of the act: "The ICC provides the most obvious illustration of maturity in the life cycle of a commission. Its major regulatory functions have been crystallized since 1920. The original support from farmers and small shippers no longer exists. The ICC has become an integral part of the structure of the railroad industry; and its record reflects its commitment to the welfare of that industry. . . . Increasingly the Commission has identified itself with the interests of the railroad industry, and it is impossible to deal with the modern evolution of the industry without extensive reference to the ICC."[153] Of course, the change in regulatory focus and the heightened concern for the stability of the regulated industry were shared with other regulatory issue areas, as shown above. Indeed, the close agency–interest-group relations forged at the ICC during the 1920s were similar to those examined above in the cases of Commerce and the FTC.

In arriving at this conclusion concerning the ICC, it is necessary not only to consider the emergence of new goals but to examine the policy process itself. The ICC introduced a Bureau of Informal Cases and a Bureau of Traffic designed to enhance cooperation in the resolution of disputes. The former bureau was created as an intermediary in disputes between railroad companies and shippers, with an eye to resolving tariff issues before formal commission action or litigation. In 1929, for example, the Bureau of Informal Cases received 7,339 informal complaints and an additional 44,000 letters.[154] The Bureau of Traffic was created to resolve various traffic and tariff issues both between carriers and shippers and among carriers. As the ICC described its role in 1920: "[I]ts activities are directed toward the adjustment by informal conferences and correspondence of controversies arising between shippers and carriers, and the settlement of differences between carriers concerning divisions of joint rates, designed to promote harmony between the carriers and the public, facilitate the disposition of urgent matters, and lessen the number of matters eventually brought before us upon formal complaint." The bureau was designed to "promote simplicity" and "materially assist in maintaining a spirit of cooperation between the shipping public and the carriers."[155]

153. Marver H. Bernstein, *Regulating Business by Independent Commission* (Princeton, N.J.: Princeton University Press, 1955), 90–91.

154. Interstate Commerce Commission, *Annual Report of the Interstate Commerce Commission, December 1, 1929* (Washington, D.C.: Government Printing Office, 1929), 13.

155. Interstate Commerce Commission, *Annual Report of the Interstate Commerce Commission, December 1, 1920* (Washington, D.C.: Government Printing Office, 1920), 42–43.

The concern with industry stability and cooperation in resolving disputes and developing new tariffs and policies was warmly received by the railroad industry. The railroads created standing rate committees. Working with the National Industrial Traffic League, they developed a process whereby conferences could be used to bring carriers and shippers together to discuss rate changes. At the same time, the shippers worked through their trade associations and local chambers of commerce to create committees that would hold conferences to resolve controversies. These activities occurred outside the ICC. New rules governing industry safety were often developed by the American Railway Association and accepted by the ICC. This delegation of authority to associations was a necessity, given the complexity of the tasks involved. As E. Pendleton Herring explained in 1936: "[G]overnment officials are confronted with tasks of huge proportions and handicapped by lack of resources. It is impossible for them to rely solely on their own expert knowledge, however profound, and in the administration of the law they must obtain necessary information by sympathetic contacts with those in possession of it. Government experts must supplement their knowledge with the expertness of the interests regulated."[156] Herring questioned whether the ICC could remain objective given its dependence on railroad associations. In the end, he concluded that the associations were broad enough "to counterbalance the forces of sectionalism and partisanship" and that they disposed of "internal disputes between individuals within these associations" before making recommendations to the ICC. As a result, he concluded, "the potentialities for autonomy and responsibility on the part of these organizations" were significant, and they had recognized that "an impartial and completely uninfluenced commission" was to their "ultimate advantage."[157] Hoover could not have asked for a better assessment of associationalism in regulation.

Despite these positive attributes, however, problems of competition among different modes of surface transportation would create insurmountable difficulties for regulators. Established interests, once brought into the administration of policy, would create regulatory barriers to technological change. In the post–World War II era, critics of regulation would look back at the ICC as a clear example of agency capture—a condition characterized by rigidity, lethargy, and regulations designed to nurture the regulated parties. While Marver Bernstein would portray capture as a normal occurrence in the life cycle of regulatory agencies, one might also attribute it to a model of institu-

---

156. Herring, *Public Administration in the Public Interest,* 187.
157. Ibid., 207.

tional design premised on the integration of the regulated into the regulatory structure. Associationalism carried some significant strengths. As the war revealed, public officials, by appending to the state the administrative capacities of private-sector interests, could implement complex public policies even when the state itself lacked the requisite administrative capacities. Moreover, the adversarial relationships that seemed intrinsic to regulation could be avoided by transforming regulated parties into clientele. From the perspective of the corporations involved, associational governance provided a means of limiting uncertainty by replacing market forces with agreements covering a range of corporate activities. This could add greater stability and coordination. However, these benefits would carry costs that were manifested in rigidity, conservatism, and, ultimately, policy failure.

5

From Warfare Crisis to Welfare Capitalism

There is in the American labor movement today sadly little social enthusiasm or constructive energy. . . . The decline in the membership of the American Federation of Labor continues, yet no dramatic or effective drive is made to organize the millions of America's unorganized workers. The militant membership of the unions is absorbed in factional fights carried on with a contemptuous disregard for standards of fair play. The energy of many labor leaders is exhausted in hanging on to their jobs—a task in which they are aided in many of the international unions by as clever devices for political manipulation and as flagrant a system of pocket boroughs as ever an old English aristocracy or a modern political boss could imagine. The natural result is a widely diffused cynicism.   —*The Nation,* February 20, 1924

[T]he most impressive change in the American labor movement since the War consists in the new emphasis on production. The old rough-and-ready trade unionism battled over the division of the product, whereas the new, suave, discreet unionism talks the language of the efficiency engineer and business itself about the ways and means of increasing output.
—Arthur W. Calhoun, 1928

World War I brought great advances for labor. Following steady wartime gains, over five million workers belonged to unions in 1920. Many hoped that the wartime industrial-relations system, premised as it was on the principle that workers had a right to organize and find representation in associations of their own choosing, might be extended after the war. A number of factors explored in this chapter forestalled the application of this model. The depression of 1921 created a large pool of surplus labor. With a dearth of legal protections and vigorous business efforts to stem the tide of labor organization, union membership declined rapidly after 1921. By 1929, union membership had fallen to 3.46 million, despite the steady economic growth of the period.[1] Company unions and various forms of business-controlled employee representation were rapidly disseminated in the 1920s. The largest corporations internalized industrial relations via company unions and provided expansive benefits under the system of welfare capitalism, both of which found clear expression during the war. As in the case of business regulation, voluntarism was at a premium. However, a crucial difference should not go unnoticed. In

---

1. *Statistical History of the United States,* series D-736.

the associationalist system of regulation, state agencies played an important role in organizing interests and facilitating agreements that provided for mutual advantages. In the case of labor, however, the state failed to play a comparable role. Corporations continued to enjoy a legal recognition of their property rights, while workers had to depend on traditional forms of labor militancy or business benevolence if they hoped to share in the gains of the New Era. Before a new regulatory system for industrial relations would be possible, the system of the 1920s would have to collapse.

This chapter begins by placing the wartime experience in a broader historical context, exploring the tensions inherent in industrial relations in the United States. After examining the policies of the War Labor Board and other wartime agencies, we turn to the search for a new institutional framework. The task is to explain why the statist elements of the wartime system were eschewed, while many corporation-based innovations were extended. The explanation rests on a rather complicated combination of political-economic, institutional, and ideological factors. In the end, the system that emerged out of the 1920s was one steeped in business voluntarism and associational premises. While the system promised to provide greater stability than the pure market governance of the past and increase the economic security of workers in select firms, these benefits would prove ephemeral under the pressures of the Great Depression.

Industrial Relations Before the Great War

To fully understand the significance of the wartime experiment in industrial relations and the evolution of industrial relations in the 1920s, it is useful to preface our examination of this period by exploring briefly the labor movement and labor policy—if such an entity existed—before the war. The system of labor representation that existed on the eve of the war had a number of distinctive features. From the nineteenth century onward, the American labor movement had been dominated by craft unions representing the skilled trades.[2] Reflecting its constituency, the American Federation of Labor strongly opposed the introduction of mass-production technologies, which would re-

2. This discussion draws heavily on the discussion of labor in Marc Allen Eisner, *The State in the American Political Economy: Public Policy and the Evolution of State-Economy Relations* (Englewood Cliffs, N.J.: Prentice Hall, 1995), 61–63.

place skilled labor with unskilled workers. It also resisted the calls for greater activism in organizing industrial unions. Dual unionism, which was interwoven with American nativism and strong concerns over the implications of capital-intensive production technologies, created an important fissure in the American labor movement.[3] Additionally, and equally important, under Gompers the AFL adopted a strategy of business unionism wherein the AFL would largely confine its activities to addressing wages, hours of work, and conditions of employment. The focus on bread-and-butter gains, it was argued, would fundamentally change the state of labor over time. Business unionism may have made sense given business's frequent recourse to Pinkertons, labor spies, lockouts, blacklists, and yellow-dog contracts. The AFL strategy, while conservative when compared with those adopted by the Industrial Workers of the World, would strengthen the AFL's claims as a responsible partner during World War I.

The Judicial Regulation of Industrial Relations

When labor disputes were adjudicated through established legal channels, business often discovered a welcomed ally in the courts, which commonly interpreted collective action as a criminal conspiracy and an infringement of property rights, even if unions themselves were not routinely considered illegal conspiracies. As noted in one of the key early decisions in the history of the legal regulation of labor, *Commonwealth v. Hunt* (1842): "The manifest intent of association is, to induce all those engaged in the same occupation to become members of it. Such a purpose is not unlawful. It would give them a power which might be exerted for useful and honorable purposes, or for dangerous and pernicious ones."[4] Ultimately, the determination of what constituted a "dangerous and pernicious" purpose would rest with the courts, which were far more likely to err in the favor of business.

The use of the court injunction grew in frequency after the 1880s and 1890s, when a number of railroads were in receivership and under the control of agents of the courts. To justify the use of the injunction, the courts relied on the argument that strikes could interfere in interstate commerce, thus providing a justification for the exercise of federal authority.[5] Similarly, union actions could interfere in the liberty of contract. That is, unions could insert

3. See Foster Rhea Dulles and Melvyn Dubofsky, *Labor in America: A History,* 4th ed. (Arlington Heights, Ill.: Harlan Davidson, 1984), 211–16.
4. *Commonwealth v. Hunt,* 4 Met. (45 Mass.) 111 (1842).
5. See *In re Debs,* 154 U.S. 564 (1895).

themselves into the wage bargain, thereby interfering in a contract that might otherwise define the relationship between the employer and the individual employee. In addition to the injunction, state labor laws were commonly overturned as violations of Fourteenth Amendment guarantees. Thus, in *Coppage v. Kansas* (1915), the Supreme Court struck down a state law prohibiting yellow-dog contracts.[6] The Court recognized the asymmetries inherent in any labor contract. At the same time, however, the courts interpreted very broadly the Fourteenth Amendment guarantee that states shall not deprive any person of life, liberty, or property without due process of law. State efforts to pass laws to eliminate the inequalities that stemmed from the exercise of property rights (in this case, the legislative ban on the use of yellow-dog contracts) were interpreted as an indirect effort to erode Fourteenth Amendment protections. A similar fate befell congressional efforts to prohibit child labor in *Hammer v. Dagenhart* (1918).[7]

The courts continued to deny unions the recognition they desired. Thus, for example, in *Hitchman Coal and Coke Company v. Mitchell et al.* (1917), the Supreme Court addressed a situation involving a United Mine Workers (UMW) effort to force a mining company to recognize the union even if its employees had signed yellow-dog contracts. As for the status of such contracts, the Court noted:

> That the plaintiff was acting within its lawful rights in employing its men only upon terms of continuing non-membership in the United Mine Workers of America is not open to question. . . . Whatever may be the advantages of "collective bargaining," it is not bargaining at all, in any just sense, unless it is voluntary on both sides. The same liberty which enables men to form unions, and through the union to enter into agreements with employers willing to agree, entitles other men to remain independent of the union and other employers to agree with them to employ no man who owes any allegiance or obligation to the union. In the latter case, as in the former, the parties are entitled to be protected by the law in the enjoyment of the benefits of any lawful agreement they may make. This court repeatedly has held that the employer is as free to make non-membership in a union a condition of employment, as the working man is free to join the union, and that this is a part of the constitutional rights of personal

6. *Coppage v. Kansas*, 236 U.S. 1 (1915).
7. *Hammer v. Dagenhart*, 247 U.S. 251 (1918).

liberty and private property, not to be taken away even by legislation, unless through some proper exercise of the paramount police power.

The Court concluded that a union could not interfere with the contractual relationship between the individual employee and the employer. It rejected "the purpose entertained by defendants to bring about a strike . . . in order to compel plaintiff, through fear of financial loss, to consent to unionization of the mine" as an unlawful purpose. It also rejected the "unlawful and malicious methods" resorted to by the UMW, that is, "the inducing of employees to unite with the Union in an effort to subvert the system of employment at the mine by concerted breaches of the contracts of employment known to be in force there, not to mention misrepresentation, deceptive statements, and threats of pecuniary loss."[8] The continued concern with the individual's freedom to contract, the restrictive notion of collective bargaining, the conservative vision of property rights, and ambivalence concerning the position of the union in the wage bargain provided strong reminders that much had to be done to secure labor's position in the political economy.

Industrial Relations in a New Industrial Order

While labor disputes were being fought out on the shop floor and in the courts, many of the Progressive Era debates questioned how new institutions might be designed to manage the "labor problem." These debates found their clearest expression in the efforts of the National Civic Federation (NCF). The NCF was created in 1900 as a tripartite organization, including at various points distinguished representative of business (e.g., Marcus A. Hanna, Samuel Insull, Franklin MacVeagh, Charles Francis Adams, Andrew Carnegie), labor (e.g., Samuel Gompers, John Mitchell), and the public (e.g., Grover Cleveland, William H. Taft).[9] Participants were united in the belief, however loosely articulated, that organized labor had become a permanent part of the industrial political economy and new mechanisms were needed to manage industrial relations. A failure to institute some form of collective bargaining, it was feared, would exacerbate industrial conflicts and undermine the promise of the evolving capitalist economy. The resistance of the antiunion National Association of Manufacturers and the frequent judicial reliance on the

8. *Hitchman Coal and Coke Co. v. Mitchell,* 245 U.S. 229 (1917).
9. James Weinstein, *The Corporate Ideal in the Liberal State: 1900–1918* (Boston: Beacon Press, 1968),
8. This discussion of the National Civic Federation draws heavily on chapter 1 of Weinstein's fine book.

injunction were interpreted as forces that would contribute to industrial war-fare. The NFC promoted collective bargaining and provided conciliation and mediation services through its Trade Agreements Department. Because major employers and unions often had representatives on the NCF, the department provided a forum for discussing agreements. The federation's support for col-lective bargaining placed it at odds with the National Association of Manufac-turers, which spearheaded the movement for the open shop. However, beginning in 1904, with the formation of the NCF's Welfare Division, the federation became a central advocate of welfare capitalism. Its promotion of business paternalism appealed to employers who wanted an alternative to independent unions.[10]

In appointing the U.S. Commission on Industrial Relations in 1913, Presi-dent Wilson demonstrated his support for the efforts to design new institu-tions to manage industrial relations. The commission was chaired by Frank P. Walsh (after Louis Brandies declined the offer) and was similar to the NCF both in its composition (all except one of its members—Frank Walsh—had been active in the federation) and in its governing assumption that new insti-tutions were necessary to integrate organized labor into the policy process. In its application of social science and its efforts to develop mechanisms for social adjustment, the commission was a perfect expression of Progressivism.[11]

The NCF and the U.S. Commission on Industrial Relations were not act-ing in a static legal environment. Congress joined the search for new institu-tions to govern industrial relations. For example, in 1898, Congress passed the Erdman Act, creating a system of mediation and arbitration in railroad labor disputes. Under the act, the chairman of the Interstate Commerce Com-mission and the commissioner of labor could attempt to mediate disputes at the request of either party. Failing a successful resolution of the conflict, they could initiate voluntary arbitration with binding awards. The act also prohib-ited various forms of antiunion discrimination, including the yellow-dog con-tract. The Supreme Court invalidated these latter features in 1908, however, for reasons that one might easily predict, given the events of the last few decades. In *Adair v. United States* (1908), the Court determined that the inter-state-commerce clause did not authorize Congress to interfere in labor rela-tions.[12] Moreover, the Court decided that the due-process clause of the Fifth

10. Ibid., 18–19.
11. See Valerie Jean Conner, *The National War Labor Board: Stability, Social Justice, and the Voluntary State in World War I* (Chapel Hill: University of North Carolina Press, 1983), chap. 1. Weinstein, *The Corporate Ideal in the Liberal State*, 183–85.
12. *Adair v. United States*, 208 U.S. 161 (1908).

Amendment protected the right of an employer to operate a nonunion shop.[13] By 1913, the mediation provisions of the Erdman Act had been invoked sixty-one times, resulting in forty-five settlements before arbitration. Given the success of mediation and the growing power of the railroad unions, labor joined with the railroads in support of new legislation fortifying the system. The resulting Newlands Act of 1913 created a new Board of Mediation and Conciliation, which was authorized to mediate disputes at the request of either of the parties or at its own discretion.[14] The next year Congress continued to support labor with passage of the Clayton Act, which appeared initially to halt the threat of antitrust prosecutions against labor by declaring that "the labor of a human being is not a commodity or article of commerce. Nothing contained in the antitrust laws shall be construed to forbid the existence and operation of labor [organizations] . . . nor shall such organizations, or the members thereof, be held or construed to be illegal combinations or conspiracies in restraint of trade, under the antitrust laws."[15]

Although the new Board of Mediation and Conciliation was called on to resolve disputes, the growing strength of railroad labor led union leaders to believe that they might accomplish more outside of the established framework. Thus, in 1916, the preparedness debate at its height, they threatened a national rail strike to secure the eight-hour day. President Wilson sought to prevent the strike and appealed to Congress for legislative relief. Although Wilson championed more concessions to railroad management than were ultimately provided, fear that additional proposals and debate would delay action forced the rapid passage of the Adamson Eight Hour Day Act. By giving railroad workers legislative concessions, Congress recognized the power of organized labor while sending the message that benefits might be better realized through legislation than through the traditional channels of workplace militancy. In the past, many labor leaders—including Gompers—had been hesitant to support legislative gains. What Congress provided, it could take away—with or without the assistance of the courts. The willingness to embrace the Adamson Act proved a shift in strategy.[16]

13. See Christopher L. Tomlins, *The State and the Unions: Labor Relations, Law, and the Organized Labor Movement in America, 1880–1960* (Cambridge: Cambridge University Press, 1985), 26–27.

14. Merle Fainsod, Lincoln Gordon, and Joseph C. Palamountain Jr., *Government in the American Economy*, 3d ed. (New York: W. W. Norton, 1959), 184–85.

15. Clayton Act of 1914, § 6. See Harold C. Livesay, *Samuel Gompers and Organized Labor in America* (Boston: Little, Brown, 1978), 167–70, for a discussion of Gompers's views of this exemption.

16. See "The Railway Eight-Hour Day," *Nation*, July 24, 1916, 167; "The Predicament of Organized Labor," *New Republic* December 2, 1916, 114–15; and Stephen Skowronek, *Building a New American State: The Expansion of National Administrative Capacities, 1877–1920* (Cambridge: Cambridge University Press, 1982), 272–73.

The gains for organized labor before the war might appear relatively insignificant when compared with the advances in subsequent decades. Yet, the market governance of industrial relations under the watchful eye of the courts was displaced, albeit gradually, by a system in which a role for labor organizations was recognized, though not universally, and the gains for labor could be realized through legislative action. The provisions of the Newlands Act and Adamson Eight Hour Day Act left the majority of the workforce in largely the same position as before their passage. Yet, legislative intervention in what had been traditionally understood as private commercial relationships opened the door for subsequent efforts to redefine the relationship between corporations, labor, and the state. As the *New Republic* noted, Wilson's support for the Adamson Act "renewed the confidence of organized labor in the national government" in that "it introduced the government into a great labor controversy not merely as a policeman or as a pious missionary, but as an active and decisive influence. . . . a principle has been set going which says that the final decision about hours and wages on railroads is not to be left to bargaining which breaks into violence, but is to be made and enforced by the federal government."[17] This principle would grow in importance with the nation's entry into war.

World War I as a Revolution in Industrial Relations

Labor problems are a perennial feature of war. Heightened economic demands and the loss of large numbers of men to military service create labor shortages, thereby increasing the opportunities for wage gains and exacerbating the economy's vulnerability to strikes. In order to secure continuity of production in essential industries, policy makers must develop some mechanisms for structuring the interplay of management and labor while nudging labor out of civilian production and into vital war industries. During World War I, the need for some new system of industrial relations and a new labor-market policy became clear given the expansion of the armed forces. The number of individuals in the military increased from 179,376 in 1916 to 2,897,167 two years later, this latter figure constituting 10.8 percent of the nonagricultural workforce.[18] Several additional factors exacerbated the labor shortage. The

---

17. "An Ineffective Remedy," *New Republic*, November 25, 1916, 83.
18. *Statistical History of the United States*, series Y-763. Military personnel as a percentage of the nonagricultural workforce was determined using data from series D-48.

war and restrictive policies forced a reduction in immigration. In the period 1910–14, an average of 1,034,940 immigrants entered the United States each year. From 1915 to 1919, the annual average number of immigrants fell to 234,535. One contemporary critic noted that the new restrictions on immigration were difficult to fathom: "Within the past two years two millions of unemployed in America have been absorbed, and wages have risen fast. . . . the labor shortage is beginning to hamper American industry in many fields, and is crippling it in some."[19] The period also witnessed the rapid spread of the eight-hour day. From 1914 to 1919, the percentage of those involved in manufacturing who worked forty-eight hours per week or less grew from 11.8 percent to 48.7 percent.[20] The spread of the eight-hour day may be attributed in part to the Adamson Act, in part to the growth in union power. Union membership increased from 2.7 million in 1916 to over 4 million in 1919.[21] Given the shortage of labor and the rising tide of unionism, war production would depend heavily on the success of wartime labor policies.

During the war, most mobilization agencies and the armed services created units to address labor problems. The National War Labor Board and the War Labor Policies Board, the key agencies responsible for labor policy and the regulation of industrial relations, accepted labor representatives as equal decision makers. Labor was also given representation in most wartime agencies, including the Emergency Construction Board, the Fuel Administration, the Food Administration, the War Industries Board, and district exemption boards of the Selective Service. This level of representation provided, in the words of Selig Perlman, "a degree of national prestige and a freedom to expand which could not have been conquered by many years of the most persistent agitation and strikes."[22] With multiple agencies making labor policy, there was often a good deal of confusion. The central agencies responsible for supervising labor relations and labor-market problems were the National War Labor Board and the War Labor Policies Board. In particular, the NWLB remained at the forefront of labor-market policy making during the war.

19. "Immigration and the Labor Supply," *Nation*, May 10, 1917, 570. The figures preceding the quote were calculated from annual data in *Statistical History of the United States*, series C-88. See Leo Wolman, *The Growth of American Trade Unions, 1880–1923* (New York: National Bureau of Economic Research, 1924), 36–37.

20. Sumner H. Slichter, "The Current Labor Policies of American Industries," *Quarterly Journal of Economics* 43 (May 1929): 395 n. 4.

21. *Statistical History of the United States*, series D-735.

22. Selig Perlman, *A History of Trade Unionism in the United States* (New York: Macmillan, 1923), 234–35.

The National War Labor Board

Labor was initially brought into the war mobilization process through representation on the Council of National Defense (CND). Samuel Gompers
helped draft the National Civic Federation's resolution calling on Congress to
create the council. He had also endorsed Wilson's reelection bid and the
Democratic Party more broadly. In the spring of 1916 Gompers argued before
the NCF and in a letter to the National Security League that workers would
have to be integrated into any "true plan of preparedness" if it were to be
successful and in keeping with democratic norms. "If provisions for national
preparedness are to be constructive, they must be based upon voluntary and
democratic principles. . . . spokesmen for labor ought to be on every commission, committee, or representational body that is entrusted with consideration
of problems and determinations of policy."[23] Wilson responded by appointing
Gompers chairman of the CND's Advisory Committee on Labor, where he
worked to mobilize the support of other labor leaders. He called a conference
with 148 labor officials in March 1917 to secure advocacy for the war effort
and a declaration of loyalty. In the declaration, labor leaders pledged "to
defend, safeguard, and preserve the Republic . . . against its enemies whomso-
ever they may be," and called upon "fellow workers and fellow citizens in the
holy name of labor, justice, freedom, and humanity devotedly and patrioti-
cally to give like service."[24] This statement drew the ire of socialists and
pacifists alike, who interpreted the war as a product of capitalist machinations.
Gompers worked hard to minimize dissent, advocating labor's participation
in all aspects of mobilization, the constitution of the CND Labor Committee
as a final board of arbitration, and supporting the Americanization campaign
of the Committee on Public Information.[25]

The difficulties of organizing workers for the war would be exacerbated
by the divisions inherent in American labor. As George P. West explained in
1917: "In no other country are labor leaders confronted with a working class
so divided by race, language and the prejudices incidental to these divisions.
And in no other country are the basic industries under the centralized control
of corporations possessing anything like the power of effectual resistance to
democratic organization that has been developed by our great industrial cor-

23. Gompers's statement quoted in Malcolm W. Davis, "Labor and the Call to Arms," *New Republic,*
June 10, 1916, 137.
24. Lewis L. Lorwin, *The American Federation of Labor: History, Policies, and Prospects* (Washington,
D.C.: Brookings Institution, 1933), 144.
25. Ibid., 148–53, and *Nation,* April 12, 1917, 420.

porations." West doubted that Gompers could be successful in unifying labor. His "organization is practically without representation or influence in the great basic industries that would be the first to undergo mobilization in time of war." As noted above, the division between craft and industrial labor and Gompers's strategy of business unionism militated against unified action. In West's judgment, "working class coöperation would have to be secured either by high wages, unorganized and fractious patriotism in the individual, or, these failing, the most rigorous use of force."[26] In the end, all of these factors would come into play as part of the war mobilization effort.

In September 1917, President Wilson created a Special Mediation Commission, chaired by Labor Secretary William Wilson, to address growing labor unrest in Western lumber, copper, and other vital industries. Composed of two AFL representatives and two employer representatives, with Felix Frankfurter as secretary and dominant voice, the commission created adjustment mechanisms to resolve disputes in several industries. The commission attributed the recent labor disruptions to the "insistence by employers upon individual dealings with their men. . . . This failure to equalize the parties in adjustments of inevitable industrial contexts is the central cause of our difficulties."[27] As a result, it promoted union recognition and guaranteed the right to organize. Similar tripartite boards were established at this time to mediate conflicts on an industry-by-industry basis. The efforts of ad hoc boards, the War Industries Board, the Labor Department, and the Special Mediation Commission were rarely coordinated and left entire sectors outside of the administration's labor policy. In response, the commission recommended that the administration call a tripartite labor conference to devise a labor policy for the war. Secretary Wilson convened a War Labor Conference Board to meet on January 28, 1918. The board was composed of five representatives of labor selected by the AFL and five business representatives chosen by the National Industrial Conference Board. As a public representatives, the labor contingent selected Frank Walsh, while business chose William Howard Taft.[28]

After several weeks of deliberations, the Labor Conference Board presented a set of principles to guide industrial relations and called for the creation of a National War Labor Board patterned largely on the model of the Mediation Commission. The principles recognized the right of workers and employers to organize and engage in collective bargaining: the right of labor

26. George P. West, "Labor's Unpreparedness," *New Republic,* March 10, 1917, 157–58.
27. Quoted in "Labor in War and Peace," *Nation,* February 21, 1918, 198.
28. Bernard M. Baruch, *American Industry in the War: A Report of the War Industries Board, March 1921* (New York: Prentice Hall, 1941), 89–90.

to organize "shall not be denied, abridged, or interfered with by the employers in any manner whatsoever," and "[e]mployers should not discharge workers for membership in trade-unions nor for legitimate trade-union activities."[29] The board also articulated principles preserving existing gains: where union shops existed, they would continue, along with business recognition of union wages, hours, and working conditions. Similarly, where the eight-hour day was already established by law, it would be observed during the war. Women were to receive "equal pay for equal work," while "the right of all workers, including common laborers, to a living wage" was guaranteed. In determining minimum wages, the board presented the principle that the rate of pay must "insure the subsistence of the worker and his family in health and reasonable comfort."[30] These basic principles of war labor policy would find an expression during the New Deal. As Philip Taft correctly observed, New Deal labor policy "was not so much an innovation as a revival and extension of previously enunciated principles," namely those put forth during World War I.[31]

The National War Labor Board was created in April of 1918 and quickly became the central authority on war labor policy.[32] As with the War Labor Conference Board, the NWLB was placed under the cochairmanship of Taft and Walsh.[33] It consisted of five business representatives chosen by the National Industrial Conference Board and five labor representatives selected by the AFL. Labor participation in the NWLB reflected both a pragmatic understanding of the difficulties that labor militancy could create in a war economy and a growing consensus concerning the place of organized labor in the political economy.[34] The regulation of labor was necessary to limit strikes, to provide an orderly adjustment of wages, and to direct labor to critical industries.[35]

29. Quotes from "Principles to be Observed" from Labor Conference Board Report, March 29, 1918, reprinted in Baruch, *American Industry in the War,* 344–45.

30. See Twentieth Century Fund, *Labor and the Government: An Investigation of the Role of the Government in Labor Relations* (New York: McGraw-Hill, 1935), 155.

31. Philip Taft, "Organized Labor and the New Deal," in *How Collective Bargaining Works: A Survey of Experience in Leading American Industries,* ed. Harry A. Mills (New York: Twentieth Century Fund, 1942), 4. See also idem, "Collective Bargaining Before the New Deal," in *How Collective Bargaining Works: A Survey of Experience in Leading American Industries,* ed. Harry A. Mills (New York: Twentieth Century Fund, 1942), 901, where Taft observes that the National War Labor Board "settled many specific issues and formulated and applied principles most of which were reaffirmed in Section 7a of the National Industrial Recovery Act and the National Labor Relations Act."

32. Charles Whiting Baker, *Government Control and Operation of Industry in Great Britain and the United States During the World War,* Carnegie Endowment for International Peace, Preliminary Economic Studies of the War, no. 18 (New York: Oxford University Press, 1921), 82–90.

33. See Conner, *The National War Labor Board,* chap. 1.

34. Tomlins, *The State and the Unions,* 61, 77.

35. See John Maurice Clark, *The Costs of War to the American People* (New Haven, Conn.: Yale University Press, 1931), 47.

The NWLB demanded that there be no strikes or lockouts for the duration of the war. Although the AFL never accepted the no-strike pledge, Gompers repeatedly urged members not to inaugurate a strike unless "principles are involved equally fundamental as those for which fellow citizens have offered their lives—their all."[36] In exchange for this support, the board recognized labor's right to organize, as expressed in the NWLB's official principles.[37] The board sought to coordinate the efforts of the various labor agencies, boards, and commissions while monitoring wage levels and serving as the ultimate mediator in labor disputes. It adjudicated disputes that could not be resolved via normal channels of collective bargaining and created, where needed, committees or boards to settle local disputes through mediation and conciliation. This complicated universe of actors often created significant problems on its own. The growing number of agencies, commissions, and boards were uncoordinated and adopted policies and awards that led workers to move from job to job in unexpected ways. The extreme decentralization also provided unions with more numerous venues for pursuing changes in wages, hours, and working conditions.[38]

In hopes of reducing the confusion and incoherence in war labor policy, President Wilson created a new War Labor Policies Board in May 1918 and placed it under the direction of Felix Frankfurter. The board was made up of the key officials addressing labor issues in the various war agencies—including Franklin D. Roosevelt, who represented the navy. In the words of Bernard Baruch, "the theory of this board was that of an interlocking directorate. . . . It worked out and agreed upon labor policies, and they in turn were executed through the respective agencies themselves."[39] As with the NWLB, the War Labor Policies Board adopted the principles established by the War Labor Conference Board. Its goal was not to establish new principles but to standardize wage decisions across industries and coordinate the policies of different agencies involved in the war effort. In addition, the board studied the housing and transportation needs on an industry-by-industry basis and considered the various ways in which labor flows might be adjusted to meet the needs of critical industries. In the end, the board failed to fulfill its mandate. Its investigations forced delays and frustrated labor and capital alike; efforts to stan-

36. Samuel Gompers, "United in Spirit and Purpose," *American Federationist* 25, no. 5 (1918): 386–87. See also George L. Berry, "Why Labor Must Support the War," *American Federationist* 25, no. 6 (1918): 481–82.

37. E. Jay Howenstine Jr., *The Economics of Demobilization* (Washington, D.C.: American Council on Public Affairs, 1944), 147.

38. Ronald Schaffer, *America in the Great War: The Rise of the War Welfare State* (New York: Oxford University Press, 1991), 36.

39. Baruch, *American Industry in the War,* 91.

dardize wages were thwarted by the unwillingness of labor and business representatives to cooperate. In response, the War Labor Policies Board created a Conference Committee of Labor Adjusting Agencies in the fall of 1918 to standardize wages, hours, and working conditions. However, because its jurisdiction began only after wage boards had arrived at agreements, it was forced to impose standardization decisions ex post facto. In any event, standardization undermined the use of wage differentials to direct labor into vital war industries. In the end, the committee developed recommendations regarding cost-of-living adjustments, wage differentials, the eight-hour day, paid holidays, night work, and enforcement mechanisms. However, the War Labor Board refused to support the effort, and President Wilson delayed action until after the Armistice, when the historical moment had passed.[40]

Despite Wilson's efforts, the close relationship between Gompers and the administration, and the creation of multiple mediation mechanisms, the number of strikes was high throughout the period, reaching 4,450 in 1917 and 3,353 the next year.[41] Even if labor leaders gave verbal support to the war and encountered progressive business leaders in the war agencies, the rank and file was forced to confront corporate management that often refused to increase wages, reduce hours, and bargain with unions. The Industrial Workers of the World refused to abide by the no-strike pledge, moreover, viewing the war as a ripe opportunity to expand its ranks and demand greater gains than those envisaged by the AFL. Growing levels of membership among migrant farm workers, loggers, and copper miners in the West made the IWW's rejection of the wartime accord an important factor.[42]

The IWW's militancy worked to the benefit of the AFL. Efforts to emphasize its radicalism and cast it as an unpatriotic supporter of Germany were combined with a strategy to limit IWW expansion through the use of strikebreakers, the promotion of company unions, and the direct deployment of federal troops. Always the strategist, Gompers understood that as publicity concentrated on IWW extremism, the AFL's status as a responsible partner in the mobilization process would be elevated. The measures used to undermine the IWW, moreover, could eliminate it as a competing source of organization, thus protecting the AFL's cherished system of craft unionism. With Gompers's support, the Wilson administration moved against the Wobblies

40. Lorwin, *The American Federation of Labor*, 166–69.
41. D. O. Bowman, *Public Control of Labor Relations: A Study of the National Labor Relations Board* (New York: Macmillan, 1942), 8–10.
42. Melvyn Dubofsky, *The State and Labor in Modern America* (Chapel Hill: University of North Carolina Press, 1994), 62–63.

on September 5, 1917. Federal raids on every IWW headquarters were followed within the month by the federal indictment of some two hundred IWW labor leaders on charges of sedition and espionage. As Melvyn Dubofsky notes, this strategy would backfire: "With the IWW eliminated, Gompers had achieved a part of his aims, as had his reformer allies in the administration. Paradoxically, they had also endangered parts of their own more positive program for labor reform. The conservatives, who so gleefully crushed the IWW, did not distinguish AFL unions from subversive ones, responsible labor from irresponsible agitators. Thus the campaign against the IWW threatened to spill over into a general anti-labor offensive."[43] Ultimately, threat would become reality at the end of the war.

Although the NWLB did not have independent enforcement powers, the War and Navy Departments and President Wilson possessed a number of means of forcing compliance. Here the administration revealed that its support for labor was contingent on ever-higher production levels. On occasion, the federal government directly commandeered plants that refused to implement NWLB decisions. It seized union records, arrested labor leaders, used federal agents to keep IWW representatives from organizing in critical sectors, and threatened strikers with the loss of occupational exemptions, that is, with substitution of the trenches of France for munitions production.[44] Moreover, one must note that the NWLB's promotion of collective bargaining was not to be confused with an unshakable commitment to independent unions. Various internal-representation plans were deemed equally legitimate. Although the NWLB adopted the principle that neither labor nor business would use the war emergency to further its relative power (this was necessary for securing the support of the National Industrial Conference Board), it played an important role in furthering company unions:

> The War Labor Board . . . laid the foundation for the company unionism which was to have such a growth during the 'twenties and which was to cause so much difficulty for the various labor boards in later years. With organized labor none too strong, the Board representatives would recognize the need for representation in a plant but would be in a quandary as to how to solve the problem. The shop-committee

---

43. Ibid., 69. Following the arrest of 168 IWW leaders in Chicago, the *Nation* noted that the Wilson administration would have to take great care to avoid "all ground for the charge, which is sure to be made, that it is making use of the war emergency to crush labor organization in the interest of 'capitalism.'" *Nation*, October 4, 1917, 357.

44. Schaffer, *America in the Great War*, 36–37.

which was in existence in a great many instances provided the answer, and often administrators would spend many weeks building shop-committee plans in order that there might be representation. While the Board was opposed to individual bargaining, both organized labor and the shop-committee were envisaged as proper machinery for collective bargaining; and since it did not recognize the shop-committee as a "company union," it would often encourage the shop-committee in order to carry out the objective of maintaining the status quo ante.[45]

We will have the opportunity to examine company unions and welfare capitalism later in this chapter. It is, however, critical to note that the tight wartime labor markets and the administration's labor policy resulted in significant gains for labor. As noted earlier, union membership increased dramatically, from 2.77 million in 1916 to 4.125 million in 1919. In some industries, the gains were phenomenal: between 1915 and 1920, the number of union members grew by 25.7 percent in mining, 66.7 percent in building, 283.1 percent in the metal industries, 565.6 percent in textiles, 113.2 percent in clothing, 113.8 percent in leather, 118.1 percent in transportation, 41.9 percent in paper, 15.6 percent in lumber, 75.4 percent in restaurants, and 78.3 percent in public services.[46] Wage rates grew significantly, as revealed by a comparison of 1916 and 1919 figures. Unionized manufacturing workers claimed weekly pay of $32.43 in 1919, $22.27 in 1916. Bituminous coal miners received $33.83 per week in 1919, $19.56 in 1916. Workers in the building trades saw their weekly wages increase from $26.12 in 1916 to $34.32 in 1919. In the railroads, weekly compensation increased to $26.40 in 1919, from $16.62 three years earlier.[47] At the war's end, workers were far better off economically than they had been at any previous point in U.S. history.

Despite these gains, significant problems would become apparent once the activities of the War Labor Board drew to a close on June 30, 1919. Unions that gained a foothold during the emergency of war would not find the same security in peace. As George Soule explained, the "union"

had not gained a foothold in basic mass production industries like steel and automobiles. Many of its new members were in munitions

45. Bowman, *Public Control of Labor Relations,* 10.
46. Wolman, *The Growth of American Trade Unions, 1880–1923,* 38.
47. *Statistical History of the United States from Colonial Times to Present,* series D 589–602, 604.

and metalworking plants, which were being demobilized. It was weak even in such a great industry as textiles. The newly organized members were unfamiliar with union traditions and union discipline, while many employers had accepted collective bargaining only as a war necessity imposed by government, and were awaiting an opportunity to escape it. . . . It was customary in labor circles to speak of the newly created unions as "war babies"—the same term used for the stocks of war industries in which huge speculative profits had been made.[48]

Industries that enjoyed the greatest gains in unionization during the war would also face the largest subsequent declines either because the unions were organizationally weak or because the demand associated with war orders would disappear.[49] The various sources of weakness would prove crucial in the 1920s. Without a new peacetime institution to replace the NWLB and with employers generally unwilling to watch the expansion of labor organization, the stage was set for crisis and a reversal of union fortunes.

The Search for New Institutions

The crisis of war provided an opportunity to promote progressive reforms in workplace regulation and industrial relations. Many of the labor reforms debated during the Progressive Era found a concrete expression once reformers became war administrators. Organized labor had been granted the respectability it had so long desired. Although Gompers was granted a central role in mobilization, this was largely symbolic. As Harold Livesay noted: "When labor's cooperation was sought, as during the war, 'Mr. Gompers' was trundled out as the venerable emblem of respectable workers. When he had served his purpose, 'Sam' was unceremoniously shoved offstage, as when he was excluded from the peace negotiations."[50] In the end, the true test of whether labor had truly achieved a new position in the political economy would rest less on the exigencies of war than on what would occur with the cessation of

48. George Soule, *Prosperity Decade: A Chapter from American Economic History, 1917–1929* (London: Pilot Press, 1947), 187–88.

49. Wolman, *The Growth of American Trade Unions, 1880–1923*, 39. See also Benjamin Stolberg, "The Predicament of American Labor," *Nation*, September 30, 1924, 352.

50. Livesay, *Samuel Gompers and Organized Labor in America*, 181.

hostilities. One contemporary observer noted "a growing appreciation of the extent to which the public suffers by industrial strife and a growing belief that some government body should act to protect the public interest" and "a new demand that government regulation of labor shall be established on a permanent basis."[51]

The hope that the wartime system of labor-relations regulation would be extended into the peace was eroded as the National War Labor Board moved rapidly into decline. The fragile compromises between employers and employees and the willingness of business to accept a greater state role under conditions of war became the first victims of the peace. Increasingly, members of the board came into conflict, and businesses sought to resist board decisions. As businesses strove to reverse the changes of the last several years, labor sought to secure its gains. Frank P. Walsh resigned from his position in the belief that absent the justification of war, businesses would successfully work in concert to undermine the efforts of the board. Taft stayed on but with growing frustration. When the board ceased operation, there were few surprises and few regrets. It had become an irrelevancy with few remaining duties.[52]

The AFL made some early efforts to design a new peacetime structure when in June 1918 it convened a reconstruction committee to compile a report identifying policies that could preserve and extend the gains of the war. It adopted a program for industrial democracy that contained a host of broad reforms and more traditional demands while restating some of the core principles of the NWLB. The Reconstruction Program declared: "The workers of the nation demand a living wage for all wage-earners, skilled or unskilled—a wage which will enable the worker and his family to live in health and comfort, provide a competence for illness and old age, and afford to all the opportunity of cultivating the best that is within mankind."[53] Unsurprisingly, the program identified labor organization as the key to the living wage, demanding formal legal recognition of the right to organize free from employers interference. It also called for higher wages across the board, the imposition of a universal eight-hour day, improved working conditions, and equal pay for women. In addition, the program called for the abolition of child

51. Baker, *Government Control and Operation of Industry in Great Britain and the United States During the World War*, 90.

52. Conner, *The National War Labor Board*, 158.

53. AFL Reconstruction Program quoted in Philip Taft, *The A.F. of L. in the Time of Gompers* (New York: Harper & Brothers, 1957), 369. My description of the program draws on Taft's discussion on 369–72, and Soule, *Prosperity Decade*, 198–99.

labor, the expansion of workmen's compensation, and a two-year moratorium on immigration as well as a permanent policy of banning immigration in periods of high unemployment. The Reconstruction Program went beyond industrial relations to advocate expanded support for cooperative associations in order to reduce corporate profiteering while increasing popular participation in economic affairs. It also demanded higher levels of public investment in sanitation and public housing, government ownership of public utilities, and extension of tax progressivity. The Reconstruction Program received the unanimous support of the AFL executive and the Federation Conference. In the end, however, it resulted in little more than a symbolic declaration entitled "Labor's Bill of Rights" at the AFL executive council meeting in December 1919.

President Wilson joined in the effort to reconstruct the wartime system when he called a tripartite National Industrial Conference to meet in October 1919 to define principles for a "genuine and lasting co-operation between capital and labor." The business contingent included five representatives chosen by the U.S. Chamber of Commerce, five representatives selected by the National Industrial Conference Board, three agricultural representatives, and two each from finance and the railroads. The labor component included fifteen representatives selected by Gompers and an additional four from the Railroad Brotherhoods. In addition, President Wilson selected twenty-one representatives of the public, a group that included Thomas L. Chadbourne, Bernard Baruch, Robert Brookings, Lillian Wald, Charles Eliot, John D. Rockefeller Jr., and Elbert H. Gary.[54] The proceedings were divided over the question whether the government should intervene in the steel strike. Given that Rockefeller's and Gary's "persistent refusal to deal with organized labor had precipitated the walkout" in the steel industry, these two "public" representatives were not likely to promote a role for the state in mediating the conflict.[55] Divisions over the basic role of organized labor in the economy— divisions so clearly exhibited in the steel strike—placed great stress on the conference. Union representatives struck the position that labor must be organized in autonomous unions and that employers must be legally required to bargain with these representatives. They advocated the key planks of the Reconstruction Program, thus demanding reforms that went well beyond the wartime system. Business representatives, in contrast, were intent on preserving their discretion to adopt various forms of internal employee-representation

---

54. Soule, *Prosperity Decade*, 199; Lorwin, *The American Federation of Labor*, 177.
55. Conner, *The National War Labor Board*, 177.

plans, which they saw as superior to negotiating with independent unions. This issue struck at the heart of industrial relations; there was little room for compromise. Gompers reported on the conference in the *American Federationist,* where he bemoaned the "Bourbon spirit" of the business representatives: "The rights of man still mean to them something that need not be considered seriously. The lessons of the war have passed them by. Thus far they have contested the idea of democracy in industry as bitterly as the tories of a century and a half ago contested the idea of democracy in political life."[56] Labor defected from the proceedings on October 23.

On Baruch's recommendation, Wilson convened a second Industrial Conference without the trappings of tripartism. Dominated by a host of notables, including Herbert Hoover, Frank Taussig, William Wilson, Julius Rosenwald, George Wickersham, Owen D. Young, and Henry Seager, the conference met from December 1919 to the following March. It proposed national and regional mechanisms for adjusting labor disputes. At the same time, it sought to prohibit strikes that would have a great impact on the public, noting: "The plain fact is that the public has long been uneasy about the power of great employers. It is becoming uneasy about the power of great labor organizations. The community must be assured against domination by either."[57] In the end, the conference proposals had no impact on policy. As the *Nation* observed: "[W]ithout inquiring into the primary causes of industrial quarrels the Conference nevertheless goes hopefully at the task of settling them; without studying the origin and history of the disease it confidently prepares a remedy. So far as the proposals of the Conference go, the existing industrial organization, with all its inducements to rupture, to violence, to suspension of necessary production, and to interference with the peace and welfare of the community, is to be left as it is."[58] Reflecting the conference's insignificance, Congress denied funding to reproduce its report. Ultimately, the president's ailing health and preoccupation with the League of Nations took their toll. Industrial relations largely returned to their prewar status, albeit with higher levels of unionization and labor militancy.[59]

With no peacetime system of industrial relations in place and rapid price increases threatening to undermine wage levels, the economy became vulnera-

56. Samuel Gompers, "The President's Industrial Conference," *American Federationist* 27, no. 11 (1919): 1045.

57. Lorwin, *The American Federation of Labor,* 179.

58. *Nation,* January 3, 1920, 843.

59. Howenstine, *The Economics of Demobilization,* 147–61; Bowman, *Public Control of Labor Relations,* 11; Dubofsky, *The State and Labor in Modern America,* 91–93.

ble to a new wave of strikes. In 1919 alone, some four million workers participated in strikes in a number of critical sectors, including railroads, steel, and
bituminous coal. With the wartime mediation mechanism in shambles, business proved quick to resist labor demands. A common but effective political
strategy was to link labor unions to Bolshevism. In response to a general
strike in Seattle and a Boston police strike, business leaders roused concerns
that the radicalism of the Russian Revolution was finding fertile soil in the
United States. When Governor Calvin Coolidge decided to fire police strikers
rather than seek arbitration, he received the praise of the public and President
Wilson. As the strikes spread to major industries, including steel, coal, textiles, food, clothing, and railroads, the concerns heightened and provided a
convenient justification for recalcitrant employers unwilling to meet postwar
wage demands. When steelworkers went on strike seeking the eight-hour
day, labor spies and mounted state troopers were deployed, union meetings
were banned in some locations, and labor leaders were portrayed as Communists.[60]

The AFL did little to stem the Red Scare but once again positioned itself
between the radicalism of the IWW and business, returning to a strategy that
had been successful during the war. Gompers faced growing pressure from
industrial workers critical of the AFL's traditional posture and demanding
changes in the internal structure of the AFL that would provide greater representation for them. At the same time, the AFL actively opposed the efforts to
discard the established unions and create a new large union uniting workers
across industry—the "One Big Union" movement. On the political front, the
AFL continued to resist forays into partisan politics, seeking to maintain formal nonpartisanship while opposing the creation of a National Labor Party.
With labor fragmented and no evidence that the executive branch would
promote an extension of labor regulation, the 1920s became a decade of
retrenchment.

The Railroad Labor Board

While the efforts to establish a peacetime version of the NWLB were unsuccessful, there were some notable advances in railroad labor, which drew on
the wartime experience of railroad regulation. With the signing of the Armistice, some of those involved in the Railroad Administration, including Wil-

---

60. Soule, *Prosperity Decade,* 194; Michael E. Parrish, *Anxious Decades: America in Prosperity and Depression, 1920–1941* (New York: W. W. Norton, 1992), 6–7.

liam McAdoo, treasury secretary and head of the Railroad Administration, became strong advocates of nationalization. A plan drafted by Glenn Plumb, an attorney representing the Railway Brotherhoods, called for the unification of the railroads under the ownership of a government corporation run by a tripartite board of directors. Under the Plumb plan, government securities would be used to purchase the lines from their current owners. To critics on the Right, the Plumb plan appeared to be little more than a blueprint for socialism.[61] To critics on the Left, the plan was equally unacceptable. As one critic wrote in the IWW's *One Big Union Monthly,* the use of securities to purchase the stock was "a most outrageous proposition. The railroads have been built by the workers and are being operated by the workers, but have been stolen from the people by unscrupulous politicians and profiteers." The railroads should be "dispossessed by the people without remuneration at the earliest possible moment."[62]

Wilson and Congress resisted the calls for rail nationalization and rapidly returned the rails to their private owners. In addition to rejecting these labor demands, the Senate entertained a provision in the pending transportation bill to prohibit railroad labor strikes. While this did not survive the conference committee, the Transportation Act of 1920 entangled the right to strike in a complex mediation system to be administered by a newly created tripartite Railroad Labor Board. Under the Transportation Act, the board was authorized to engage in arbitration if disputes could not be resolved through collective bargaining. Railroads and employees were authorized to create boards to interpret agreements, but the act included no prohibition of management interference in the selection of representatives. To make the thrust of the new legislation clear, the writers omitted prohibitions of yellow-dog contracts and gave the board no independent enforcement powers.[63]

Despite the earlier objections, it initially appeared that the new Railroad Labor Board was going to be of some benefit to labor when it approved a 22 percent raise for the shop crafts in July 1920 to cover the increases in the cost of living. As is often the case in the history of labor regulation, appearances can be dreadfully deceptive. With the advent of the brief postwar depression, rail traffic and prices fell into decline, eroding much of the justification for the wage award. Railroad managers attacked the board's decision, albeit with little success until Harding assumed the presidency. Harding moved quickly

61. Soule, *Prosperity Decade,* 196–97.
62. "The Plumb Plan," *One Big Union Monthly* 2, no. 1 (1920): 12, 13.
63. Bowman, *Public Control of Labor Relations,* 15.

to appoint new public representatives on the board, which proved to be far more amenable to railroad interests. The board abrogated the national wage agreement, calling on the railroads and unions to negotiate new contracts on a system-by-system basis. Under the depressed conditions, the results were easy to foresee. Indeed, in July 1921, the Railroad Labor Board ordered a 12 percent wage reduction, with additional reductions the following June—cutbacks that fell harder on the shop-craft unions than on the Rail Brotherhoods, which had gained a certain respectability in the minds of the railroad owners. When combined, these two reductions devoured the gains of 1920.[64]

The labor response to the decisions of the Railroad Labor Board was predictable. In June 1922 the shopwork unions voted to strike July 1 unless the board-mandated wage reductions were recalled. The board refused, and the strikers walked out in ranks that numbered more than 400,000. The board quickly passed a resolution declaring the strike illegal and denying strikers a claim on the positions they vacated and on seniority—a position that met with the full support of President Harding. As the administration searched for a viable compromise in subsequent weeks, the question of seniority for returning strikers forestalled an agreement. Given the intransigence of the parties, Harding lashed out against the strikers. Attorney General Daugherty secured a restraining order in federal district court in Chicago, which prohibited the unions from supporting the strike under the provisions of the Transportation Act of 1920 and the Sherman Antitrust Act. Although the unions and a number of other district court judges objected that the Clayton Act had exempted labor from injunctions, the Chicago federal court declared that the injunction would stand. With the restraining order in place and strikers being replaced by permanent workers, the strike was broken. Agreements were reached with the eleven major systems to reinstate workers, albeit under more restrictive conditions than the unions would have desired. More moderate railroads reinstated workers in their previous ranks; others simply rehired individual workers upon application, with no concessions.[65]

The railroad agreement reached in the Baltimore and Ohio line was the most interesting insofar as it fit well with the new understanding of the relationship between labor and corporations. The union agreed to assist the line in eliminating waste. The management agreed to share the benefits of greater efficiency with the workers. Worker committees would explore various means of improving productivity via changes in established practices and organiza-

---

64. Soule, *Prosperity Decade,* 203–4.
65. Ibid., 204–5; Dubofsky, *The State and Labor in Modern America,* 93–96.

tions. This information would become important in making changes in the organization of the workplace while incorporating workers directly into the deliberations on some issues previously reserved for managers. This agreement reflected what was becoming a growing trend in the railroads and elsewhere in the American economy—the rise of the company union.[66] By 1924, company unions had been created to represent a majority of the nonoperating employees on the eastern railroads and over one-third on the western lines. For these employees, the new era in railroad labor had precious little room for independent unions.[67]

Although the Railroad Labor Board handed down some 2,500 decisions by 1925, it lacked the power to force compliance and lost legitimacy following the strike. Congress passed the Railroad Labor Act of 1926, which eliminated the board and authorized the use of presidential mediation commissions when labor negotiations stalled. While the commissions conducted their investigations, strikes were prohibited, thus effectively eliminating the threat of strikes. In exchange for this concession, the act recognized the right to engage in collective bargaining and placed some restraints on employer coercion. At the same time, however, the new law legitimized the company unions created by the railroads in the last half decade. "It was a bargain in which no one lost. Not a single change in railroad labor relations occurred as a result of the new law. The unions surrendered a right they had never really had. . . . everyone realized that the federal government would not tolerate a national railroad strike. Republicans could point to the Railway Labor Act as evidence of their friendship to workers and their respect for responsible trade unionists."[68]

Despite the difficulties encountered by railroad labor, an important legal victory came in the Supreme Court decision in *Texas and New Orleans Railroad Co. v. Brotherhood of Railway Clerks* (1930).[69] The dispute concerned the railway company's efforts to create for railway clerks a company union known as the Association of Clerical Employees—Southern Pacific Lines. The company attempted to coerce members of the brotherhood to make the association their representative. The brotherhood was successful in winning a temporary injunction in district court, under section 2 of the Railroad Labor Act of 1926, which established that representatives should be chosen "without interference, influence, or coercion exercised by either party over the self-organization or

66. Soule, *Prosperity Decade*, 204–5.
67. Dubofsky, *The State and Labor in Modern America*, 96.
68. Ibid., 100–101.
69. *Texas and New Orleans Railroad Co. v. Brotherhood of Railway Clerks*, 281 U.S. 548 (1930).

designation of representatives by the other." When the railway continued its efforts, the court made the injunction permanent and ordered the railway to disestablish the association until such time as a secret ballot could be used to determine the demand for new representation. The circuit court of appeals affirmed the decree, and the Supreme Court agreed to hear the case.

In appealing the injunction to the Supreme Court, the Texas and New Orleans Railroad Company argued that the Railroad Labor Act violated the First and Fifth Amendments and that the decision to issue an injunction was a violation of section 20 of the Clayton Act, which prohibited the use of injunctions in labor disputes. The Supreme Court affirmed the injunction. The Court's opinion, written by Chief Justice Hughes, declared that the legality of collective action "is not to be disputed. . . . employees are entitled to organize for the purpose of seeking the redress of grievances and to promote agreements with employers relative to rates of pay and conditions of work." In passing the Railroad Labor Act, Congress had decided to make "collective action an instrument of peace rather than strife. Such collective action would be a mockery if representation were made futile by interferences with freedom of choice. Thus the prohibition by Congress of interference with the selection of representatives for the purpose of negotiation and conference between employers and employees, instead of being an invasion of the constitutional rights of either, was based on the recognition of the rights of both."[70] This victory for railroad labor came at decade's end and was not representative of the fortunes of labor in the 1920s.

Barriers to a New System of Industrial Relations

Why did the goal of extending the wartime system prove so elusive? This is an interesting question, particularly given the extent to which the policies and procedures of the NWLB would ultimately find a permanent expression in the New Deal's National Labor Relations Board. One might suggest that any hopes of creating a new system of industrial relations were simply dashed by the conservatism of the 1920s. Such an explanation might be appealing despite the mixed record of the period. To arrive at a better explanation, one must explore the broader political-economic and institutional context. Several factors help us explain the evolution of industrial relations in the 1920s, in-

70. 281 U.S. 548 (1930), at 570.

cluding the weakness of unions in the evolving industrial economy, the rise of the American plan, the continued opposition of the courts, the growing conservatism of the AFL, and the rise of welfare capitalism.

The Economy of the 1920s

Following the great gains in union membership during the war, membership fell dramatically as a result of the high levels of unemployment at the beginning of the decade, a series of unsuccessful strikes, and changes in the composition of the economy. Between 1920 and 1926, the thirty-three union organizations representing manufacturing workers absorbed tremendous losses, with membership falling from 1,220,100 to 532,000.[71] The membership losses were partially offset by the dramatic building boom (the contract construction workers increased from 848,000 in 1920 to 1.61 million by 1928, with 905,000 union members, surpassing all other industries in its contribution to organized labor).[72] All other substantial categories of workers suffered significant declines in membership, however, challenging the earlier assertions of many labor leaders concerning the centrality of labor associations in the new political economy. If organized labor was to act as a full partner, the trends in membership were disturbing. Union authority to speak on behalf of labor became increasingly tenuous.

Although the reversal of union fortunes can be attributed, in part, to the postwar depression and the elimination of some war-related industries that had high levels of union membership, it is even more closely associated with two other economic factors that directly affected unions: changes in production technology and sectional patterns of growth. The AFL was essentially a large confederation of craft unions with a well-established bias against unskilled industrial workers. With the partial exceptions of mining and the garment industry, the AFL extended its bias against unskilled labor through the 1920s, devoting few resources to organizing workers in the steel, rubber, chemicals, and automobile industries, even under the leadership of William Green, whose United Mine Workers affiliation should have had the opposite effect.[73] As noted in Chapter 4, the economy was in the midst of a technological revolution in the 1920s, as corporations increasingly embraced more capital-intensive forms of production and mass-standardized production technologies. Expressed in 1929 dollars, the total capital involved in manufactur-

---

71. Slichter, "The Current Labor Policies of American Industries," 427.
72. *Statistical History of the United States,* series D-50, D-748.
73. Parrish, *Anxious Decades,* 90–91.

ing increased from $46.1 billion in 1919 to $63.3 billion in 1929. This translated into a 37.4 percent increase in the capital invested per worker engaged in manufacturing.[74] Growing capital intensity reduced demand for skilled craftworkers. The AFL's natural constituency was being replaced by machines that could be operated by those who had not been beneficiaries of AFL organizing activities. At the same time, the growing reliance on capital translated into higher levels of productivity and profitability, which were partially channeled into higher rates of compensation, thus undermining the appeals of organization.

Sectional growth patterns are important as well. Although the 1920s witnessed strong economic growth, much of it took place outside of the Northeast and larger industrial cities, where the unions were well established. As Mark Perlman notes: "If the less-unionized areas where the antipathy toward unionism was strong grew much faster than the areas more favorable to unionism, then unionism after a time became on the average . . . relatively weaker in terms of its total or overall strength than it had been 'in the beginning.' It was just this kind of differential regional growth that did occur in the 1920's. Consequently, economic growth as such worked against union success during the decade."[75] Given the sectional pattern of growth, significant union gains would require efforts to organize in relatively nonunionized areas, where greater levels of hostility and higher levels of capital intensity could be expected.

The American Plan and New Mechanisms of Workplace Supervision

One of the most effective means of undermining union gains was promotion of the open shop. Over the decade, business executives presented the so-called American plan as a viable alternative to labor collectivism.[76] Under the American plan employers were under no compulsion to hire union members or bargain with their representatives. Such an obligation, it was argued, interfered with the right of the worker to contract freely for his or her labor, and with the exercise of corporate property rights. By and large, the Supreme

74. *Statistical History of the United States,* series P-82. Capital investment per manufacturing worker was calculated by the author, using data in *Statistical History of the United States,* series P-82 and D-51.

75. Mark Perlman, "Labor in Eclipse," in *Change and Continuity in Twentieth-Century America: The 1920s,* ed. John Braeman, Robert H. Bremner, and David Brody (Columbus: Ohio State University Press, 1968), 121.

76. See W. Harris Cook, "Closed Factories and Open Shop," *Nation,* December 22, 1920, 725, and Dulles and Dubofsky, *Labor in America,* chap. 13.

Court recognized these arguments as valid. Corporate officials often went beyond this position simply to refuse to hire union members and to require employees to sign yellow-dog contracts. A number of trade associations proved decisive in promoting the American plan. The National Conference of State Manufacturers Associations, the National Metal Trades Association, the National Founders Association, the National Erectors Association, and the National Association of Manufacturers were particularly important in this regard.[77] In June of 1920, the U.S. Chamber of Commerce adopted a referendum stressing the right to operate open shops. The National Association of Manufacturers followed suit and in the fall created an open-shop department to provide technical assistance to members through special bulletins.[78] As new sectional patterns of economic development emerged, new facilities were created as open shops, thus frustrating a further expansion of unionism. As the *Nation* noted, corporations were using the "American Plan" label because "it is inevitable that Americans should respond sympathetically to the proposal that all men must have an 'equal chance.' If the open shop actually means an equal chance the open shop propaganda will be easy to conduct." However, "the object of the open shop is to eliminate collective bargaining and to substitute dealings with the individual worker. If collective bargaining is eliminated, the union is killed; a worker might as well join a golf club as a union in an open shop. The open shop, then, becomes a non-union shop and the meaning of the present campaign becomes clear."[79]

Although company unions predated the war, they were rapidly disseminated at this time, as businesses saw their utility for limiting disruptions and increasing productivity. As Robert W. Dunn explained in a 1926 address on company unionism: "The company union movement is a war and post-war growth. The joint committees adopted in industrial establishments by various war boards initiated the practice. The achievement of 'industrial peace' and the speeding up of war production was the immediate purpose of their introduction. After the war the large labor turnover and the general success of the device in meeting certain labor problems induced employers to experiment further with them."[80] According to the National Industrial Conference Board, in 1919 some 225 company unions represented 391,400 workers. Within five years, the number of company unions grew to 814, representing a total of

77. Soule, *Prosperity Decade,* 201.

78. Lorwin, *The American Federation of Labor,* 202–3.

79. "The Fight to Break the Unions," *Nation,* December 1, 1920, 609.

80. Robert W. Dunn, "Company Unionism and Newer Tactics of Employers," in *New Tactics in Social Conflict,* ed. Harry W. Laidler and Norman Thomas (New York: Vanguard Press, 1926), 99.

1,177,037 workers. The list of large corporations with company unions at this time included Armour, Bethlehem Steel, Colorado Fuel and Iron, Cudahy, General Electric, Goodyear Tire and Rubber, International Harvester, Kodak, Phelps Dodge, Pullman, Shell Oil, Standard Oil, Swift, and Western Union Telegraph.[81] The growth of company unions would continue over the course of the next decade. They represented a number of workers equal to 9.8 percent of total trade union membership in 1919; this figure would increase to 40.1 percent by 1932.[82]

Growing capital intensity and the spread of mass-production technology entailed new approaches to workplace supervision that were facilitated by the absence of independent unions. Here, various forms of scientific management were brought into the workplace. The relationship between the Taylorite advocates of scientific management and the unions shifted significantly during the period. Before the war, Taylor and his followers viewed unions with some antagonism, believing that they interfered with scientific adjustments in the production process. Union leaders indicted the Taylorites for the use of time-and-motion studies, the bonus system, and the speedup—all means of extracting as much labor as possible out of the workers. Brought to its logical conclusion, scientific management would transform skilled activities into a series of simple motions that could be accomplished by unskilled labor or machines, thereby eliminating the expertise that allowed workers to claim a bargaining position with their employers.[83] As Robert Franklin Hoxie noted in 1924: "Scientific management . . . tends to the constant breakdown of the established crafts and craftsmanship, and the constant elimination of skill in the sense of narrowing craft knowledge and workmanship."[84]

This antagonism was reduced during the war as advocates of scientific management worked side by side with labor representatives in war agencies and observed that labor organizations could make positive contributions to expanded production. Many became agnostic on the question whether workers should be organized by shop committee or independent union. Following the war, Gompers accepted the need for greater productivity and efficiency in industry. While rejecting company unions, labor grudgingly accepted a closer relationship with scientific management. Thus, *Labor: Its Grievances, Protests,*

81. Ibid., 99–100.
82. Taft, "Collective Bargaining Before the New Deal," 906.
83. See Milton Nadworny, *Scientific Management and the Unions, 1900–1932: A Historical Analysis* (Cambridge: Harvard University Press, 1955), 48–67.
84. Robert Franklin Hoxie, *Trade Unionism in the United States,* 2d ed. (New York: Appleton & Co., 1924), 323. See 296–349 for the broader assessment of scientific management.

and Demands, a statement of AFL policy that emerged out of the 1919 convention, declared: "To promote further the production of an adequate supply of the world's needs for use and higher standards of living, we urge that there be established cooperation between the scientists of industry and the representatives of organized workers."[85] The AFL hoped that greater efficiency and productivity would result in stability in employment, wage increases, and improved working conditions. Whether one could rely on business managers to pass the higher profits on to workers remained a problematic issue. Some critics, like William Z. Foster, would note that the AFL's acceptance of "the entire capitalist speed-up, rationalization program . . . turned the unions into mere instruments of the capitalists' production plans. On the altar of production for less costs they sacrificed hard-won union conditions. . . . Cheaper production became their fetish and the only way to working class well being."[86] The AFL's increasing acceptance of scientific management in the name of productivity and stability was, perhaps, a necessity given the rapid decline in union roles and the loss of the crisis that had justified cooperation a few years earlier.

The Courts and the Unions

Beyond the economic and institutional changes detailed above, one must also acknowledge the continued hostility of the courts to labor demands. The courts retained "their traditional view of employment as a contractual arrangement between boss and worker, in which unions were third parties of uncertain standing."[87] Because the courts persisted in governing the status of organized labor in the economy, it is useful to consider the evolution of doctrine in some detail. Sections 6 and 20 of the Clayton Act supposedly eliminated labor's vulnerability to injunctions and antitrust prosecutions. Yet, in 1923, Selig Perlman's survey of recent court decisions concluded that "the legal position of trade unions has continued as uncertain and unsatisfactory to the unions, as if no Clayton Act had been passed."[88] The labor exemptions in the Clayton Act were interpreted very narrowly by the Supreme Court in the 1920s. In *Duplex Printing Press Co. v. Deering* (1921), the Court considered

85. Quoted in Nadworny, *Scientific Management and the Unions,* 115.
86. William Z. Foster, *American Trade Unionism: Principles and Organization, Strategy and Tactics* (New York: International Publishers, 1947), 90.
87. Morton Keller, *Regulating the New Economy: Public Policy and Economic Change in America, 1900–1933* (Cambridge: Harvard University Press, 1990), 144.
88. Perlman, *A History of Trade Unionism in the United States,* 257.

whether sections 6 and 20 prohibited use of the injunction to stop a secondary boycott.[89] Writing the majority opinion, Justice Pitney directly addressed section 6, noting that the exemption was contingent on the activities in question: "[T]here is nothing in the section to exempt such an organization or its members from accountability where it or they depart from its normal and legitimate objects, and engage in an actual combination or conspiracy in restraint of trade. And by no fair or permissible construction can it be taken as authorizing any activity otherwise unlawful or enabling a normally lawful organization to become a cloak for an illegal combination or conspiracy in restraint of trade, as defined by the Sherman Act."[90]

Because the dispute in *Duplex Printing Press* addressed a secondary boycott, the plaintiff questioned the relevance of section 20. This was particularly important because it entailed defining what was meant by the terms "employer" and "employee." That is, was section 20 addressing disputes involving capital and labor broadly construed? Here the Court once again adopted a very narrow reading: "Congress had in mind particular industrial controversies, not a general class war. . . . it would do violence to the guarded language employed were the exemption extended beyond the parties affected in a proximate and substantial, not merely a sentimental or sympathetic, sense by the cause of dispute."[91] Such a narrow interpretation might even affect the role of unions given that most members might not be directly involved in the dispute at hand. As one might expect, this narrow interpretation raised some concern. As Justice Brandeis noted in his dissent: "Congress did not restrict the provision to employers and workingmen in their employ. . . . If the words are to receive a strict technical construction, the statute will have no application to disputes between employers of labor and workingmen, since the very acts to which it applies sever the continuity of the legal relationship."[92]

The Court also addressed the question whether picketing could constitute a form of intimidation, thereby exceeding the limit of actions exempted by the Clayton Act. In *American Steel Foundries v. Tri-City Trades Council* (1921) the Court considered a dispute in which striking union members attempted to prevent the employer from hiring new workers.[93] After reviewing the facts in the case, Chief Justice Taft noted: "All information tendered, all arguments advanced, and all persuasion used under such circumstances were intimida-

89. *Duplex Printing Press Co. v. Deering,* 254 U.S. 443 (1921).
90. 254 U.S. 443 (1921), at 469.
91. 254 U.S. 443 (1921), at 472.
92. 254 U.S. 443 (1921), at 487–88.
93. *American Steel Foundries v. Tri-City Trades Council,* 257 U.S. 184 (1921).

tion. They could not be otherwise." Although Taft noted that disputes would have to be addressed on a case-by-case basis, the threshold for determining what constituted intimidation was set quite low: "We think that the strikers and their sympathizers engaged in the economic struggle should be limited to one representative for each point of ingress and egress . . . and that all others be enjoined from congregating or loitering at the plant or in the neighboring streets by which access is had to the plant." Taft went on to note that "communication, arguments, and appeals shall not be abusive, libelous, or threatening, and that [strikers] shall not approach individuals together but singly."[94] As one might surmise, the line drawn between legitimate demonstrations and intimidation left little room for many of the strategies traditionally adopted by unions.

While the decision in *American Steel Foundries* was quite conservative in its reading of the Clayton Act, it nonetheless entertained a more expansive notion of what constituted "employees" than that which was presented in the earlier *Duplex Printing Press* decision. Based on the earlier case, one might rightly ask: What is the status of the union, given that most individuals involved in a labor dispute will often be members of a union but employed in another facility? Here, Taft's decision recognized that unions had an important role and that they could not be limited to the facility in question: "The strike became a lawful instrument in a lawful economic struggle or competition between employer and employees as to the share or division between them of the joint product of labor and capital. To render this combination at all effective, employees must make their combination extend beyond one shop."[95]

In a more famous case decided the same year, the Court rejected state-level efforts to limit the use of the injunction in labor disputes. The dispute in *Truax v. Corrigan* (1921) involved the application of an Arizona law prohibiting the use of injunctions in labor disputes.[96] The plaintiff claimed that the strike outside of his restaurant by members of the Cooks and Waiters Union had undermined his business, yet the state law, as interpreted by the Arizona Supreme Court, had denied him equal protection of the law under the Fourteenth Amendment. He could not successfully seek an injunction despite the union's efforts to restrict access his establishment. The U.S. Supreme Court agreed, arguing that the law was invalid because it had denied him equal

94. 257 U.S. 184 (1921), at 206.
95. 257 U.S. 184 (1921), at 209.
96. *Truax v. Corrigan,* 257 U.S. 312 (1921). See "Does Mr. Taft Want Direct Action?" *Nation,* January 11, 1922, 32–33.

protection and thus deprived him of property without due process of the law. While it was recognized that laws of this kind were attempts to adjust public policy to meet new political-economic realities, the Constitution was seen as placing strict limits on the degree of experimentation: "Classification like the one with which we are here dealing is said to be the development of the philosophic thought of the world and is opening the door to legalized experiment. When fundamental rights are thus attempted to be taken away, however, we may well subject such experiment to attentive judgment. The Constitution was intended—its very purpose was—to prevent experimentation with the fundamental rights of the individual."[97]

The Supreme Court addressed the minimum wage in *Adkins v. Children's Hospital* (1923).[98] The dispute involved a law fixing minimum wages for women and children in the District of Columbia. The Court concluded that the minimum wage violated the due-process clause of the Fifth Amendment. More specifically, the law severely restricted the freedom to contract. Justice Sutherland noted: "It is simply and exclusively a price-fixing law, confined to adult women . . . who are legally as capable of contracting for themselves as men. It forbids two parties having lawful capacity—under penalties as to the employer—to freely contract with one another in respect of the price for which one shall render service to the other in a purely private employment where both are willing, perhaps anxious, to agree, even though the consequences may be to oblige one to surrender a desirable engagement, and the other to dispense with the services of a desirable employee."[99] In a clear contradiction of the Clayton Act provision discussed above, the Court once again placed labor on the same plane as any other commodity: "In principle, there can be no difference between the case of selling labor and the case of selling goods. If one goes to the butcher, the baker, or grocer to buy food, he is morally entitled to obtain the worth of his money, but he is not entitled to more. If what he gets is worth what he pays, he is not justified in demanding more simply because he needs more; and the shopkeeper, having dealt fairly and honestly in that transaction, is not concerned in any peculiar sense with the question of his customer's necessities." A law that set minimum wages based on the needs of the worker rather than the work done was deemed "so clearly the product of a naked, arbitrary exercise of power, that it cannot be allowed to stand under the Constitution of the United States."[100]

97. 257 U.S. 312 (1921), at 338.
98. *Adkins v. Children's Hospital,* 261 U.S. 525 (1923).
99. 261 U.S. 525 (1923), at 554–55.
100. 261 U.S. 525 (1923), at 558–59.

Further restraints were placed on unions as a result of the decision in
United Mine Workers of America v. Coronado Coal Co. (1925).[101] The issue was
whether a union could be sued for treble damages under section 7 of the
Sherman Act. That is, could a plaintiff gain access to a union's strike funds to
compensate for the loss resulting from union action. Delivering the opinion
of the Court, Taft concluded that "such organizations are suable in the Federal
courts for their acts and that funds accumulated to be expended in conducting
strikes are subject to execution in suits for torts committed by such unions in
strikes." Taft reasoned that when Congress passed the Sherman Antitrust Act,
it "was passing drastic legislation to remedy a threatening danger to the
public welfare, and did not intend that any persons or combinations of persons
should escape its application." Although the act was directed primarily
toward business associations, Congress had "used language broad enough to
include all associations which might violate its provisions . . . and this, of
course, includes labor unions."[102]

If there remained any belief in a right to strike, it was difficult to maintain
following *Dorchy v. Kansas* (1927).[103] In this dispute, members of District 14
of the United Mine Workers were ordered to strike against a Kansas coal
mine until a former employee was given back pay. Proceedings were brought
under the Kansas Court of Industrial Relations Act, which, in hopes of forcing
the orderly resolution of disputes by arbitration, made it unlawful for an
individual to induce others to strike. Rather than address constitutionality,
the Court questioned the law's application in this case. The Court opinion, as
delivered by Justice Brandeis, stated:

> The right to carry on business—be it called liberty or property—has
> value. To interfere with this right without just cause is unlawful. The
> fact that the injury was inflicted by a strike is sometimes a justifica-
> tion. But a strike may be illegal because of its purpose, however or-
> derly the manner in which it is conducted. To collect a stale claim due
> to a fellow member of the union who was formerly employed in the
> business is not a permissible purpose. In the absence of a valid agree-
> ment to the contrary, each party to a disputed claim may insist that
> it be determined only by a court. . . . To enforce payment by a strike
> is clearly coercion. The legislature may make such action punishable
> criminally as extortion or otherwise. . . . And it may subject to punish-

101. *United Mine Workers of America v. Coronado Coal Co.*, 259 U.S. 346 (1925).
102. 259 U.S. 346 (1925), at 391–92.
103. *Dorchy v. Kansas*, 272 U.S. 306 (1927).

ment him who uses the power or influence incident to his office in a union to order the strike. Neither the common law, nor the 14th Amendment, confers the absolute right to strike.[104]

If the right to strike was not absolute, the states were justified in bringing criminal prosecution against union officials should they call strikes without a legitimate purpose.

The Court unquestionably softened its position by the end of the decade, as shown in the earlier discussion of *Texas and New Orleans Railroad Co*. However, the court decisions reviewed above show that the courts would not provide a venue in which labor could seek to extend its rights and protections. Rather, they would continue to interpret labor rights in the narrowest of terms. If the courts could not be relied upon to meet the historical demands of labor—particularly the most fundamental right to organize and strike— and placed distinct limits on what could be awarded by state legislatures, workers would have to look elsewhere for relief. For many, there was no recourse other than a reliance on the corporation.

Union Conservatism

By the 1920s, Gompers was, in the words of one critic, "old, tired, nearly blind, bitterly disappointed, [and] tethered to an obsolete strategy." His earlier commitment to organize workers across the economy fell victim to "an obsession with the survival of his cherished craft unions and the preservation of his own reputation."[105] By World War I the AFL had come to envision itself as coequal with business in the new political economy. In practical terms, this meant that labor leaders had to moderate their demands so as to retain the appearance of being a partner that could be trusted by government officials and business alike. Under Gompers's direction, the AFL had exploited the opportunities made available by the war, achieving a respectability that would have been unimaginable a decade earlier. Yet, this required a continued adherence to trade autonomy, opposition to industrial unionism and the radicalism that its advocates often embraced, and distance from partisan politics.

As a spokesman for workers, Gompers enhanced the standing of the AFL. Yet, the means he adopted to achieve this end seriously compromised its standing as a leader of the labor movement. As Henry Van Dorn stated in

104. 272 U.S. 306 (1927), at 311.
105. Livesay, *Samuel Gompers and Organized Labor in America,* 179.

1920: "[T]he A.F. of L. has conclusively proven its utter inability to success-fully wage war against the employing class. . . . Being based on the antiquated principle of craft unionism, reeking with corruption from top to bottom, and being controlled by a group of well-to-do self-seeking, old-time, political traders, the American Federation of Labor has lost whatever value it ever possessed as a weapon for fighting the battles of the American working class."[106] In addition to attacking its organizational conservatism, critics charged that the AFL had become cozy with business in search of respectabil-ity. As George P. West noted in 1922, "[L]abor leaders have been led further and further into a sort of whispering backstairs alliance with the political agents of the business community, until today their all is staked on it and they are under the necessity of guarding their speech and conduct."[107] The implications were clear: "A labor movement that trims its political ideas to the measure of Democratic and Republican politicians cannot be expected to keep its freedom of action in the purely industrial field. Its endless compro-mising tends to inhibit action as well as thought."[108]

The conservatism of Gompers stimulated a reaction within the federation as well. During the 1921 convention a number of unions introduced proposals that went well beyond those of the leadership, including rail nationalization, old-age pensions, workers' education, and limitations on the lending activities of the Federal Reserve such that it could only support productive activities. At the same time, Gompers's leadership of the AFL was challenged by many progressives, who offered the United Mine Workers' John L. Lewis as a candi-date for the federation presidency. Although Lewis barely received half the votes claimed by Gompers, this challenge was the first in a decade. Over the course of the next few years labor progressives, following the lead of William Z. Foster and the Chicago Federation of Labor, turned their attention to the effort to amalgamate existing craft unions into new industrial unions in order to provide a united front against recalcitrant employers and well-entrenched shop stewards. The rhetoric that accompanied these efforts—Foster, for exam-ple, attacked "the prevailing intense class collaboration policies of union offi-cialdom"—gave Gompers and the AFL leadership ample opportunity to cast the AFL progressives as Communists and demand their removal.[109] When

106. Henry Van Dorn, "Future of the American Working Class and the I.W.W.," *One Big Union Monthly* 2, no. 8 (1920): 38.

107. George P. West, "American Labor's Political Strategy—A Failure," *Nation*, March 29, 1922, 366.

108. Ibid., 367.

109. Lorwin, *The American Federation of Labor*, 213–18; Taft, *The A.F. of L. in the Time of Gompers*, 453–55. The quote is from a 1927 essay in Foster, *American Trade Unionism*, 110.

Gompers died in 1924 at the age of seventy-four, his replacement, William Green, proved himself to be a highly cautious advocate of "those fundamental principles of trade-unionism so ably championed by Mr. Gompers."[110] Little changed.

Under Gompers and Green, the AFL made some concessions to federation progressives. Some of the key proposals (e.g., railroad nationalization and social legislation) offered in the 1920 and 1921 conventions were ultimately accepted. There were modest movements toward amalgamation. Yet, the Portland Manifesto adopted at the 1923 convention—something David Montgomery correctly described as "a celebration of capitalism and a summons to the movement to drive out its radicals"—reinforced the AFL's skepticism of state intervention, supporting instead the need for greater functional representation and cooperation in an emergent industrial democracy.[111] Such a system of cooperation, it was argued, would allow for greater economic efficiency and productivity. The Portland Manifesto revealed that scientific management and the American plan would not encounter serious resistance from the AFL. In such an environment, company unions appeared far less threatening to labor than they once had. Moreover, voluntarism—the rejection of state intervention and the provision of basic benefits on the theory that unions provided the best mechanism for meeting the needs of workers— would continue to find an advocate in Green even up to the crisis of the Great Depression. This voluntarism would continue to create an opportunity for company unions and welfare capitalist benefits.

Company unions were becoming increasingly important, particularly for industrial workers, who were placing pressure on the old craft unions. Some unions sought to discover a means of coexisting with company unions. For example, in 1928 the Amalgamated Association of Street and Electric Railway Employees of America agreed in their contract with Mitten Management not to disturb company unions on Mitten's Philadelphia and Buffalo lines and to base future compensation increases on a comparison of the performance of the Amalgamated workers and those who belonged to the company union. Such an arrangement was full of implications, as noted by A. J. Muste, the chairman of Brookwood Labor College:

A union which exists where capitalism is the dominant system of ownership; which is organized from the top rather than from the

110. Dulles and Dubofsky, *Labor in America*, 248.
111. David Montgomery, *The Fall of the House of Labor: The Workplace, the State, and American Labor Activism, 1865–1925* (Cambridge: Cambridge University Press, 1987), 406.

bottom; which has for its primary function to see that the workers gear in with the mechanism of production so as to insure efficiency; which tacitly accepts the view that thus its members will automatically benefit, and that, therefore, the function of protecting them and securing advantages for them need not be the point of departure in union policy, as it has been hitherto; which virtually relinquishes the right, or at least the power, to strike—this surely isn't the trade unionism of Brother Samuel Gompers any more than it is that of Comrade William Z. Foster. Is it not a close parallel to the Fascist trade unionism established by Mussolini in Italy? And if so, does it herald the dawn of an industrial and political dictatorship in America?[112]

The AFL responded to the critique and the radicalism of Brookwood Labor College by withdrawing its financial support and denouncing Muste (as well as John Dewey!) as a Communist at its 1928 convention. In the words of Carl Haessler, this revealed that the AFL had come to represent little more than "a passionate middle-aged pursuit of conformity and respectability."[113]

Welfare Capitalism

In 1929, Sumner H. Slichter suggested that the evolution of capital-labor relations in the 1920s was, at first glance, difficult to understand: "[E]very aspect of the post-war labor situation might be expected to cause employers to abandon their newly acquired interest in labor's good will and to revert to pre-war labor policies."[114] A number of large corporations sought actively to confront labor organizations; others sought to eliminate the need for unions through changes in the relationship between the corporation and its workers. Continued adherence to the principal of the open shop was combined with a program of welfare capitalism. Owen D. Young and Gerald Swope of General Electric, among others, provided theoretical justification for a new system of industrial relations, referring to it as the "New Capitalism."

Although welfare capitalism came to fruition in the 1920s, movements in this direction can be traced back to the years before and during the war, when progressive managers were making efforts to manage the labor problem

112. A. J. Muste, "Collective Bargaining—New Style," *Nation,* May 9, 1928, 537–38.
113. Carl Haessler, "The Respectable A.F. of L.," *Nation,* December 12, 1928, 654.
114. Slichter, "The Current Labor Policies of American Industries," 396–97.

scientifically. As Slichter explains: "By the end of 1919, 71 enterprises voluntarily established shop committees through which employees could take up grievances with the management. Many firms began to provide their men with life insurance, and in some cases, with disability and sickness insurance. Sales of group insurance increased from $45,474,000 in 1914 to $178,336,000 in 1917, and $425,574,000 in 1919. Prior to 1914, 145 old-age pension plans had been established in American industry. During the five years ending in 1919, 90 additional plans were instituted."[115] These company unions were created along with mechanisms to provide workers with some voice in the production process. As noted earlier, the company unions that gained a strong foothold during the war proliferated in the 1920s. Some 125 companies had created company unions during the war. The number reached 145 by 1919, with employee-representation plans covering 403,765 workers. By 1926, the number had increased to 432. Some 1.37 million workers belonged to company unions, which provided access to profit sharing, stock bonuses, group insurance, old-age pensions, company housing, and clinics. Personnel offices and suggestion boxes were used to address worker grievances in hopes of limiting the attraction of unions. By 1928, over one million employees owned or subscribed to over one billion dollars of stock in their corporations; some five million participated in company insurance plans.[116]

Welfare capitalism held the promise of reducing the attraction of unions. The public sector did not provide an alternative source for the benefits; the AFL did not have the resources to compete with the largest firms. It would be incorrect, however, to present welfare capitalism solely as a strategy to limit unionization, although it is impossible fully to distinguish rhetoric from intention. Increasingly, corporate officials agreed that the efficiency of production and the demand for products depended, in large part, on the welfare of the workforce. By internalizing the union functions, corporations could stimulate greater worker loyalty and productivity while minimizing disruptions to the production process. The desire to manage industrial relations in this fashion reflected the growing belief in the potential for extending scientific management to all aspects of corporate relations.[117] Indeed, scientific management provided the productivity gains necessary to fund the welfare capitalism—

115. Ibid., 395–96.
116. Dulles and Dubofsky, *Labor in America*, 242–43. Soule, *Prosperity Decade*, 223.
117. See Michael J. Piorie and Charles F. Sabel, *The Second Industrial Divide: Possibilities for Prosperity* (New York: Basic Books, 1984), 124–32. For a discussion of the growing role of engineering in labor relations and corporate practices, see David F. Noble, *America by Design: Science, Technology, and the Rise of Corporate Capitalism* (New York: Oxford University Press, 1977).

leaving, of course, a healthy profit for the corporations. In the words of Michael Parrish: "Corporate welfare programs and rising real wages disguised the fact that the income of most industrial workers did not keep pace with their soaring productivity. The gap between what they produced and what they could buy therefore widened over the course of the decade."[118]

If welfare capitalism rested on the growing industrial productivity of the period, one should not be surprised that the collapse of industrial production during the Great Depression placed it under severe stress. As Stuart D. Brandes notes:

> [T]he Great Depression terminated the movement as it had existed. With the deterioration of business conditions after 1929, welfare companies drew their belts ever tighter and reduced or eliminated expenditures on a variety of welfare activities. The great stock market crash quickly made stock purchase plans expendable. When business profits evaporated in the early thirties, profit sharing programs did likewise. Educational and recreational programs were also cut. Many company dentists, education directors, housing supervisors, recreational directors, and social workers joined the swollen ranks of the unemployed. No activity, save employee representation, escaped the cutbacks.[119]

The Great Depression brought the rapid contraction of welfare capitalism. The New Deal would create a space for independent unions and the opportunity to consider, once again, the possibilities for federal regulation of industrial relations. Ultimately, the National Labor Relations Act of 1935 would foreclose the option of company unions and place the state strongly behind independent unions. At the same time, it would give final expression to the principles first presented by the National War Labor Board, making them the foundation of New Deal labor policy.

For organized labor, the decade of the 1920s was one of triumphs, defeats, and opportunities lost. The wartime system of industrial relations failed to survive the Armistice. Corporate recognition of organized labor as an independent and autonomous entity, and state activism in facilitating a system of industrial relations, proved to be fleeting products of the emergency. The NWLB precedent would be called on in later years but only when justified

118. Parrish, *Anxious Decades*, 89.
119. Stuart D. Brandes, *American Welfare Capitalism, 1880–1940* (Chicago: University of Chicago Press, 1976), 142.

by a new emergency, the depression. Moreover, despite Progressive Era efforts to design a solution to the labor problem and a new role for union organizations during the war, the courts continued to view the wage bargain through the lens of property rights and the attendant constitutional protections. The most important legacy of the war for the 1920s was the proliferation of company unions and welfare capitalist initiatives. Embracing the voluntarism of the age, larger corporations sought to engineer the labor problem out of existence by internalizing schemes of employee representation and providing expansive benefits. The AFL conservatism and the shift in economic activity during the 1920s combined with the harsh verdicts of the courts to increase the attraction of company unions and welfare capitalism.

The events in labor relations parallel those in the area of business regulation. As noted in Chapter 4, regulatory agencies sought to construct an associational system in which businesses would manage common problems and promote efficiency through a system of self-regulation. Similar events occurred in the area of industrial relations, albeit with one key difference. In business regulation, an active role for the state in organizing interests and facilitating agreements was legitimized. It could provide a key to stability and profitability by suspending much of the old-style competition and promoting a movement away from market governance. Unwilling to permit a comparable role for the state in the area of industrial relations, corporations sought to return to the prewar system or internalize labor organization in such a fashion as to maximize their control. As a result, the fortunes of many workers became dependent on corporate benevolence. This goodwill would depend, in turn, on the economic fortunes of the corporations in question. The entire system contained an essential weakness that would become painfully apparent with the onset of the depression. Predictably, just as the emergency of war had stimulated the adoption of new institutions for industrial relations, the emergency of depression would result in a return to this same model, this time as a permanent feature of the American state.

6

Agricultural Adversity and the Curse of the Surplus

> [T]he farmer's position must be safeguarded. He must be assured a workable
> return on his labor and capital. Childish illusions about farm prosperity are
> remote from the truth. There are the few who prosper, while the many hobble
> along painfully. Facility in gathering crops and marketing them at a tangible
> surplus, no profiteering in machinery, packing material, feed, and fertilizer, a
> ready labor market, and less pin-pricking by governmental officials will keep
> the farmer on the land.   —Felix Sper, 1921

> [I]n the long run fundamental changes must take place in agriculture itself.
> Either it must be allied with industry and run as supplementary to it or it
> must be so reorganized as to avail itself of the efficiencies which, in our day,
> are revolutionizing the manufacturing arts. Perhaps it will come to large-
> scale operation with fewer proprietors and more laborers working under
> direction. Or, perhaps, what most students hope but scarcely expect, farmers
> will learn the lessons of cooperation so thoroughly that they can retain what
> is so precious in country life by sacrificing what is inefficient and obstructive.
>   —Rexford G. Tugwell, 1927

The New Era of economic growth was but a dream in the farm country.
Contemporary analysts commonly described the 1920s as a period of agricultural depression that vanquished the gains of previous decades and the war.
World War I marked the climax and the end of an agricultural boom that
had started in the last years of the nineteenth century. The statistical measures
paint an unambiguous picture of rising farm fortunes. Monthly agricultural
wage rates, without board, increased steadily from $19 in 1898 to $33 by
1916, almost doubling to a level of $65 by 1920. The parity ratio, an index
of prices received and paid by farmers (1910–14 = 100), provides a broad
indicator of changes in farm income. Between 1910 and 1915, the parity ratio
fluctuated between a low of 94 and a high of 107. During the war, however,
the parity ratio reached a high of 120 in 1917 and 119 in 1918. The rapid
growth in income and property values created powerful incentives to expand
production, enticing many farmers to invest in new land and capital. Indeed,
between 1910 and 1920, total farm acreage increased from 879 million acres
to 956 million acres. The value of farm machinery more than doubled from
$1.85 billion in 1915 to $3.6 billion in 1920. This expansion of acreage and

machinery had powerful implications for farm debt. In 1916, total outstanding debt stood at $5.3 billion. In five years, it would nearly double to $10.2 billion.[1]

The booming agricultural economy fell into rapid decline following the war. The collapse was the product of many factors, including the absence of war-stimulated demand, domestic economic fluctuations following the war, the recovery of European agriculture after 1922, and a failure to return to stable international monetary and trade regimes to facilitate exports. Cash receipts from farming, which had reached a wartime high of $14.5 billion in 1919, had fallen to $8 billion by 1921 and averaged $10.1 billion per year for the period 1921–29.[2] At the urging of the Agricultural Extension Service, commercial farmers adopted new technologies (e.g., chemicals, improved seed hybrids) that improved productivity but counteracted piecemeal measures to manage production by expanding output. As a result, "five percent fewer workers earned their living on American farms in 1929 than a decade earlier. Farmers took thirteen million acres of land out of production during the twenties. Yet farm output actually grew by 9 percent as the productivity of the remaining agricultural workers rose an extraordinary 15 percent."[3]

Many analysts attributed the agricultural depression to a decline in domestic demand. Others, however, were more concerned with the fluctuations in the costs accruing to the farmer.[4] For example, as War Finance Corporation support for European purchases of U.S. farm products ended, the Transportation Act of 1920 increased railroad rates—costs that the farmers could not easily pass on to consumers. As one contemporary observer, G. F. Warren, explained: "[T]he [agricultural] depression is due primarily to the fact that, when prices fall, wages fall less rapidly, leaving freight rates and other distributing charges and taxes high. Therefore, in an industry with a slow turnover,

1. *Statistical History of the United States,* series K 78, 138, 41, 158, and 162.

2. *Statistical History of the United States,* series K 122.

3. Michael E. Parrish, *Anxious Decades: America in Prosperity and Depression, 1920–1941* (New York: W. W. Norton, 1992), 83.

4. Alvin H. Hansen notes: "It is difficult to see that the low purchasing power of farm products in 1920–22 can be attributed either to the European market or to overproduction. The explanation is to be found rather in the failure of domestic demand. There was indeed a surplus that had to be disposed of in the foreign market, but the surplus was caused not by overproduction but by the demand situation in the home market. Europe, in spite of the post-war situation, was able to absorb a much larger quantity of our products than before the war. It is true that an exceptionally low price was required to induce Europe to take these quantities, but it must not be forgotten that a correspondingly low price prevailed in the United States." Alvin H. Hansen, "The Effect of Price Fluctuations on Agriculture," *Journal of Political Economy* 33, no. 2 (1924): 211.

a prolonged depression is an inevitable consequence of financial deflation."[5]
Whether the conditions in agriculture represented a mismatch of supply and
demand, the stickiness of wages relative to agricultural prices during the postwar dislocation, or a combination of the two, there was little question that
the farm economy had fallen into a desperate state, as reflected by the collapse
of the parity ratio following the war.

Contemporary observers painted a vivid portrait of the postwar agricultural collapse. As Henry Raymond Mussey reported in 1921, "[A]fter making
this year's crop on the basis of the highest wages and other costs known since
the Civil War, farmers are now obliged to sell at prices in many instances
below those of 1914. . . . Last spring he was urged to grow record crops, and
he borrowed heavily in anticipation of the harvest; now with his notes falling
due he is obliged to settle for whatever he can get, or go into bankruptcy."
Mussey feared that the crisis would destroy those "unfortunates who bought
their farms at the top of the market—only to discover that they could not
raise 50-cent corn on 500-dollar land."[6] The *Nation* described the agricultural
economy as being in "veritable panic," fearing that a failure of Congress to
respond would have potentially catastrophic results. "We shall all probably
have to pay a price for the wicked waste and extravagance of the war, and
perhaps those are to be congratulated who are having their reaction now. But
none the less, the plight of our producers of the great crops is such that we
are persuaded the new Congress will have to inquire into the situation at once
and to establish the truth with genuine zeal if the revolutionary farmer out-
bursts at Washington are not to become of grave political significance."[7]

Under these conditions, farmers, agricultural associations, farm-state representatives, Department of Agriculture bureaucrats, and agricultural economists entered a debate premised on the need for some form of public
intervention to support farm incomes. In the process, they explored new ways
of understanding the relationship between agriculture and industry and the
state's role in the agricultural economy. Increasingly, analysts questioned what
kind of regulatory tools would be most appropriate. How could farm incomes
be increased without creating new incentives for expansion? How could the
relationship between agriculture and the state be patterned so as to increase
the stability of the farm economy without stimulating demands to support

5. G. F. Warren, "Which Does Agriculture Need—Readjustment or Legislation?" *Journal of Farm Economics* 10, no. 1 (1928): 3. See Kenneth Finegold, "From Agrarianism to Adjustment: The Political Origins of New Deal Agricultural Policy," *Politics and Society* 11, no. 1 (1982): 1–28.
6. Henry Raymond Mussey, "The Farmer and Congress," *Nation*, January 5, 1921, 12.
7. "The Farmers' Distress," *Nation*, November 3, 1920, 492.

incomes in other sectors of society? In this chapter we shall address these questions through an examination of the politics of agricultural policy before the New Deal. As with other policy issues of the period, the agricultural policy debates of the 1920s drew on the example of the most recent experiment in agricultural regulation: the war. Thus, the chapter begins with a survey of the U.S. Food Administration's wartime regulations.

Farm Regulation During the War

The Food Administration was created by President Wilson under the authority granted in the 1917 Lever Food and Fuel Control Act, which granted the president the power to regulate the price, production, and distribution of food and to control all inputs into the production of food. Under Hoover's direction, the Food Administration's major duty was to maintain the supply of food for the American Expeditionary Force and the allies.[8] Hoover emphasized peak production, arguing that it was necessary "to stimulate farm production by every device, for our ultimate success would depend as much upon the farmer as upon reduction of consumption. . . . To stimulate production, we decided to maintain incentive prices in critical farm products." Hoover noted that the USFA attempted to "reduce the farmer's risks by giving guarantees for a period long enough ahead to allow him to market his production."[9] At the same time, it was necessary to reduce consumption and eliminate waste. Hoover opposed a system of rationing and general requisition because it was "the antithesis of American character" and "in a country as large as ours [it] was a practical impossibility without a hundred thousand bureaucratic snoopers." Hoover decided, instead, "to organize the farmers, the housewives, the public eating-places and the distribution trades on a voluntary basis for conservation as a national service."[10]

To maintain high farm commodity prices while preventing inflation generally in consumer prices was inherently difficult. The Food Administration promoted these seemingly irreconcilable goals by applying pressure to reduce

8. George Soule, *Prosperity Decade: A Chapter from American Economic History, 1917–1929* (London: Pilot Press, 1947), 20–29.
9. Herbert Hoover, *The Memoirs of Herbert Hoover*, vol. 1, *Years of Adventure, 1874–1920* (New York: Macmillan, 1952), 242–43.
10. Ibid., 244.

the difference between the sum that farmers received and that which consumers paid. The profit margins of processors and traders had expanded as the nation moved into war, and profiteering and speculation were obscured by the upsurge in prices. The solution, according to Hoover and the Food Administration, was standardization of profit margins for manufacturers and wholesalers.[11] The key to controlling the marketing spread, in turn, was the provision of licenses and the Food Administration's purchase and sale of commodities. Producers, distributors, and associations were provided with licenses upon agreeing to maintain open books, charge "reasonable" prices, and observe a variety of practices to prevent hoarding, speculation, waste, and the inefficient use of transportation.

The Food Administration, as other wartime agencies, relied heavily on government-supervised self-regulation through economic associations. In an early statement on the activities of the Food Administration, Hoover proclaimed: "We can not and we do not wish, with our free institutions and our large resources of food, to imitate Europe in its policed rationing, but we must voluntarily and intelligently assume the responsibility before us as one in which every one has a direct and inescapable interest."[12] In the words of Albert N. Merritt of the Food Administration, "[T]he food trades automatically resolved themselves into an army under Mr. Hoover's leadership. . . . In order properly to capitalize this good will, it was decided to allow the trades to regulate and police themselves so far as possible. Before any important regulation was promulgated, a number of the representative men in each trade were called to Washington . . . [and] asked to make suggestions for the regulation of their particular trades." In the process, "the principle of democracy and voluntary submission to self-made regulations became one of the fundamental principles of the Food Administration, and was at all times the method by which it primarily sought to attain the ends desired."[13] Thus, during the summer of 1917, the Food Administration held conferences with committees representing restaurateurs, hotel managers, clergy, the sugar industry, canners, and key agricultural organizations such as the Potato Associa-

11. James H. Shideler, *Farm Crisis, 1919–1923* (Berkeley and Los Angeles: University of California Press, 1957), 14.

12. Herbert Hoover, quoted in Benjamin H. Hibbard, *Effects of the Great War upon Agriculture in the United States and Great Britain,* Carnegie Endowment for International Peace, Preliminary Economic Studies of the War, no. 11 (New York: Oxford University Press, 1919), 105.

13. Albert N. Merritt, *War Time Control of Distribution of Foods: A Short History of the Distribution Division of the United States Food Administration, Its Personnel and Achievements* (New York: Macmillan, 1920), 6.

tion of America, the International Milk Dealers Association, and the American Association of Refrigerators and Cold Storage Plants.[14]

At Hoover's request, groups responsible for processing, wholesaling, and retailing commodities formed war committees of five or seven individuals to represent their interests and work with the Food Administration. They operated under an antitrust exemption and Hoover's assurance "that our purpose was to win a war, not a mission to bring about social or economic reforms."[15] To this end, the associations played an important role in detecting and punishing violations. Hoover recalled: "[O]ur prime purpose was to give responsibility to the trades and avoid a huge bureaucracy of unskilled persons. It succeeded. . . . These committees were at times even more severe on evil persons than our office would have been. Ofttimes we had to intervene to soften their stern measures which would have put a violator out of business for the duration by cutting off his supplies."[16] As Chapter 4 revealed, these experiences and the understanding of social organization shaped Hoover's subsequent activities in business regulation.

The U.S. Food Administration drew on a highly decentralized administrative system. Each state was under the direction of a federal food administrator and a state food administration. The state food administration supervised county administrators, who, in turn, supervised special committees at the town level. To account for local price variations, county boards were created, where representatives of grocers, retailers, and consumers could negotiate and determine fair prices. These prices were published in local newspapers and used by the county administrators to determine whether various parties were meeting their obligations. Despite the decentralization of the administrative apparatus, new regulations were adopted only after the Food Administration had consulted extensively with the representatives of commodity groups and trade associations at the national level. As with the War Industries Board, consultation was facilitated by staffing the agency with individuals drawn from the sector.[17]

Much of Hoover's effort was directed toward effecting changes in the behavior of consumers and retailers. This required an extensive propaganda

14. Edith Guerrier, *We Pledged Allegiance: A Librarian's Intimate Story of the United States Food Administration* (Stanford: Stanford University Press, 1941), 8.
15. Hoover, *Memoirs of Herbert Hoover,* 1:246–47.
16. Ibid., 247.
17. See Simon Litman, *Prices and Price Control in Great Britain and the United States During the World War,* Carnegie Endowment for International Peace, Preliminary Economic Studies of the War, no. 19 (New York: Oxford University Press, 1920), 206–61; Merritt, *War Time Control of Distribution of Foods,* 29–36.

campaign that included the issuance of over twenty million food leaflets. In this effort, the Food Administration enlisted the support of religious, civic, and women's organizations. An ambitious speaking campaign sent "four-minute men" into every city to give speeches prepared by the Food Administration at events that might attract sizable audiences. Ministers were implored to explain the Food Administration's policies to their congregations. Retailers were compelled to sign pledges to abide by administration rules in exchange for a certificate enrolling them in the Food Administration. Women were given Food Administration bulletins and asked to observe voluntary meatless and wheatless days—thus substituting plentiful foodstuffs for those that were scarce—a practice that would become known as "Hooverizing." They were encouraged to support the efforts of the Food Administration with slogans such as "Slackers in the kitchen are as harmful as slackers in the army—one refuses to fight and the other refuses to help them fight." Some twenty million women signed and displayed pledge cards signifying their support for the war effort and their membership in the Food Administration, even if many complained about the domestic shortages and the "voluntary" substitutions.[18] Following this example, children in Providence were given "A Child's No Waste Pledge," which read:

I pledge allegiance to my flag, in service true I'll never lag.
I'll not despise the crusts of bread nor make complaint whatever fed.
On wheatless days I'll eat no wheat, on other days, eat less of sweet.
I'll waste no pennies, spoil no clothes. And so I'll battle 'gainst our foes.
No slacker I, but a soldier keen to do my best in the year 'eighteen.[19]

While these efforts appear remarkably quaint, they were relatively effective in mobilizing a society for war and creating a broad concern with the conservation of foodstuffs.

The Food Administration was not content with voluntarism but also required that all companies involved in food processing, cold storage, warehousing, mixing, packing, and wholesaling and distributing be licensed, along with retailers with annual revenues in excess of $100,000. Licenses were mandatory and carried important obligations. "The licensee itself puts an obligation upon the licensee whereby he must make reports as to his acts, and must agree under penalty in case of failure, to live up to the demands of the Food

18. See Ronald Schaffer, *America in the Great War: The Rise of the War Welfare State* (New York: Oxford University Press, 1991), chap. 1.
19. Reprinted in Guerrier, *We Pledged Allegiance*, 65.

Administration."[20] The demands of the Food Administration were presented in an extensive list of general and class-specific rules. Rules limited the prices that could be charged to a reasonable profit margin; prohibited hoarding, waste, and various speculative activities; and promoted conservation and efficiency. Licensees were forced to abide by reporting requirements and to open their books to inspection. To facilitate monitoring, licensees were required to print their license numbers on all contracts, bills, quotations, and receipts and were prohibited from trading with firms that had not been licensed.[21] The system was reinforced by the regular publication of information on prices.

To a limited extent, the administration also stabilized prices and promoted production through direct market activity. The Food Administration Grain Corporation, with an initial appropriation of $50 million, was given a monopoly on the authority to purchase wheat in primary markets and distribute it to processors and exporters. Working under the direction of Julius Barnes and Hoover, the Grain Corporation directly determined prices for wheat through its purchases. Similarly, the Food Administration relied on a Sugar Equalization Board, with an appropriation of $5 million, which was placed under the direction of Hoover and George Rolfe. The board purchased the entire crop of sugar produced in the United States, the West Indies, and the Philippines at market prices. However, it sold sugar to processors and exporters at a fixed price. In the case of sugar, campaigns to reduce domestic consumption combined with the activities of the Sugar Equalization Board limited shortages while restraining prices.[22]

The discussion of "reasonable prices" should not veil the fact that price controls were designed to promote production. Farmers would not bring additional land into cultivation without the expectation that the prices would allow them to recapture their costs. Although administered prices could promote production if set sufficiently high, farmers were frequently saddled with disastrous surpluses once regulations were lifted. Consider the case of wheat. When Congress passed the Lever Act in 1917, it set a 1918 price of $2.00 per bushel for wheat but gave the president the authority to adjust the price to stimulate production at a reasonable profit for a period not to exceed eighteen months. Wilson responded by setting the price at $2.20 per bushel

20. Hibbard, *Effects of the Great War upon Agriculture in the United States and Great Britain,* 115.
21. See the list of Food Administration license rules, reprinted in Merritt, *War Time Control of Distribution of Foods,* 30–36.
22. David Hinshaw, *Herbert Hoover: American Quaker* (New York: Farrar, Straus & Co., 1950), 95–97; Soule, *Prosperity Decade,* 20–29; Litman, *Prices and Price Control in Great Britain and the United States During the World War,* 237–48. Hoover, *Memoirs of Herbert Hoover,* 1:245.

in hopes of promoting far higher levels of production than had existed in 1916. With a market price of $1.77 per bushel in 1917, only 651 million bushels were harvested. Under the guaranteed price of $2.20—a price that was officially increased to $2.26 in June—the harvest reached 921 million bushels, almost one-third more than the previous year's harvest. Despite the signing of the Armistice in November 1918, the Food Administration briefly continued to provide price guarantees. As a result, the nation's farms yielded more than 967 million bushels.[23] European demand supported the large harvest for 1919. When price guarantees were lifted on May 31, 1920, however, prices fell rapidly. The bushel price of wheat fell to $1.83 in 1920, $1.03 in 1921, and $.97 in 1922.[24] The acreage harvested did not fall as quickly, thus extending surpluses, which would place downward pressures on farmer incomes. As a contemporary observer noted: "[F]armers, being unable to sell their crops at anything save a heavy loss, are in despair, and cannot pay their loans. In some regions they have been unable to market their crops because the elevators were still full of 1919 wheat and cars were almost impossible to obtain. . . . the farmer is in a blue funk."[25]

A similar but even less fortuitous chain of events occurred when the Food Administration's hog price-fixing committee determined that it cost a farmer some twelve bushels of corn to raise one hundred pounds of live hog. Hoover announced that the price per hundredweight of hog would be set at thirteen bushels of corn or its equivalent of $15.50. This price, announced in November 1917, would be supported for the 1918 spring crop. Hoover did not have the authority or resources to back this price level through purchases—a point he freely admitted. Packers were to agree to this minimum price. By August 1918, however, increases in the price of corn (from $1.19 to $1.72 a bushel) raised the floor price of a hundredweight of hogs to $22.36. This new price, combined with the anticipated record number of hogs, created a serious problem. Hoover retreated from his earlier guarantee. He revised the base price in September, announcing that a hundredweight would be worth thirteen bushels of corn at the average price for the period May–September in eight major corn-producing states—resulting in a reduction of the price per hundredweight from $22.36 to $18. As Hoover was reducing the floor price for hogs, a record number of hogs flowed into Chicago, and hog prices fell below the $18 mark, reaching a low of $16. Hoover responded by calling an additional

23. Theodore Saloutos and John D. Hicks, *Agricultural Discontent in the Middle West, 1900–1939* (Madison: University of Wisconsin Press, 1951), 91–94.

24. *Statistical History of the United States,* series K 271.

25. "The Farmers' Distress," 492.

conference, where packers agreed to observe a floor price of $17.50 per hundredweight, well below what was initially promised.[26] Following the signing of the Armistice in November 1918, Hoover supported the $17.50 hog price through purchases. Under his direction, the Grain Corporation bought some 50 million pounds of pork; the Belgian Relief Commission purchased 20 million pounds. Additional exports of 450 million pounds, facilitated by Hoover, further supported the pork prices, largely because such orders had to be purchased at prices approved by the Food Administration under a requirement imposed by the War Trade Board. When the efforts to stabilize pork prices were officially abandoned in March of 1919, pork prices were driven up by market forces, reaching a high of $21.85 per hundredweight in July, before falling into a rapid decline that would end in 1921, at $6.92.[27]

The U.S. Food Administration was quite successful in stimulating production and conservation, thereby ensuring sufficient exports for the war effort. During the 1918–19 season, the United States had net food exports of 18.6 million tons, almost three times the prewar level of 6.4 million tons. Likewise, the inflation of prices for farm goods remained fairly low. The Labor Department reported that farm prices had risen by approximately 26 percent over the course of the war, an increase comparable with increases in wholesale and retail prices.[28] Hoover was pleased to report that the U.S. Food Administration returned its entire appropriation plus the substantial profits acquired by the Grain Corporation and the Sugar Equalization Board. In Hoover's words: "[T]he Food and Reconstruction Administrations cost the government $50,000,000 less than nothing."[29]

Despite Hoover's declaration of victory, it is clear that the war created a difficult situation for agriculture. The war's termination brought an end to high levels of agricultural demand and profitability. Farmers were left to bear the costs of demobilization with little government assistance. As agricultural economist G. S. Wehrwein explained: "During the World War agriculture was expanded beyond the normal by appeals to patriotism, and by guaranteed prices. Little was done by public action to help agriculture back to normalcy. Some industries were helped in making the transition, others given further protection, and still others, having shifted to the manufacture of war materials, found an undersupplied market for their peacetime goods, and needed no

26. Geoffrey S. Shepherd, *Agricultural Price Control* (Ames: Iowa State College Press, 1945), 19–24.
27. Ibid., 21–22.
28. Figures from Hoover, *Memoirs of Herbert Hoover,* 1:270.
29. Ibid., 271.

help."[30] Agriculture found itself in the unenviable position of producing at levels that exceeded demand and with no systematic public assistance in readjustment.

Just as the war exacerbated the problem of surpluses, it also stimulated new expectations for the role of the state in the agricultural economy. As Eric Goldman notes: "The war had . . . given ideas to the Farm Bureau leaders. Most of them might continue to believe that anything called government intervention smacked of a horrendous Populism. But the lavish governmental aid to agriculture during the war pointed up the possibilities in government interference which interfered in a way that the Farm Bureau leaders liked."[31] In a similar vein, James Shideler notes: "The lesson had been taught that if governmental policy could change the conditions of agriculture during a war emergency, government might also be used on behalf of agriculture during an economic emergency."[32] Given this context, we should not be surprised that the postwar collapse of the farm economy intensified the debate over what role the state might play in the peacetime economy.

New Era Agricultural Regulation

The postwar agricultural crisis and the demands for a new state role were taken up by a much expanded universe of actors from the Department of Agriculture, various commodity groups and farm associations, the growing Farm Bloc in Congress, and various executive-branch agencies outside of the USDA. While the problems of the farm economy engaged an ever growing number of parties, the Department of Agriculture assumed a central position in the policy subsystem. It played a key role both in its efforts to integrate the demands of multiple interests and in its near monopoly on policy-relevant expertise gained through the war, the earlier efforts of the extension service, and the independent research of its Bureau of Agricultural Economics. In contrast to so many other parts of the American state, the Department of Agriculture was characterized by its professionalization and its integration of

30. G. S. Wehrwein, "Which Does Agriculture Need—Readjustment or Legislation? The Case for Legislation," *Journal of Farm Economics* 10, no. 1 (1928): 18–19.

31. Eric F. Goldman, *Rendezvous with Destiny: A History of Modern American Reform* (New York: Alfred A. Knopf, 1958), 308.

32. Shideler, *Farm Crisis,* 17.

research and policy. It was, in the words of Theda Skocpol and Kenneth Finegold, "an island of strength in an ocean of weakness."[33]

The U.S. Department of Agriculture

President Harding appointed Henry C. Wallace as his secretary of agriculture in 1921. Wallace's background as a professor of dairy farming and the publisher of *Wallace's Farmer* predisposed him to view agriculture through the lens of science. He "represented those farmers who were more interested in crop rotation than in social revolution, those who hoped to emulate big business by harnessing the plow to the miracles of science and technology."[34] The technological innovations promoted by the Department of Agriculture over the past few decades, however, had increased agricultural yields and contributed to the farm crisis. "Better methods of farming, better breeds of livestock, better types of seed grain, and more attention to diversification—all preached persistently by the Department of Agriculture and the state colleges of agriculture—might bring an increase in agricultural production, but for even his best efforts the farmer seemed to be only worse off financially each succeeding year."[35] The key question was not whether the USDA could promote new innovations and even higher levels of production—there were few disagreements on this question. Rather, the key question was whether it could find some means of addressing the problems of surpluses and declining farm incomes. How could Wallace's USDA convince farmers to reduce production to meet demand?

Under Wallace's supervision, the department was professionalized and reorganized over the opposition of Hoover, who interpreted these efforts as a challenge to the ascendancy of Commerce as the primary economic agency.[36] A new Bureau of Agricultural Economics was created in 1922 and placed under the direction of Henry C. Taylor, a former head of the Department of Agricultural Economics at the University of Wisconsin. He had been chief of the Office of Farm Management, and later the Bureau of Markets and Crop

33. Theda Skocpol and Kenneth Finegold, "State Capacity and Economic Intervention in the Early New Deal," *Political Science Quarterly* 97, no. 2 (1982): 271.

34. Parrish, *Anxious Decades*, 19.

35. Saloutos and Hicks, *Agricultural Discontent in the Middle West*, 108. See also Gilbert C. Fite, "The Farmers' Dilemma, 1919–1929," in *Change and Continuity in Twentieth-Century America: The 1920s*, ed. John Braeman, Robert H. Bremner, and David Brody (Columbus: Ohio State University Press, 1968), 74–75.

36. Ellis W. Hawley, *The Great War and the Search for a Modern Order: A History of the American People and Their Institutions, 1917–1933* (New York: St. Martin's Press, 1979), 68–69.

Estimates, both of which had been merged to create the new economics bureau.[37] Under Taylor's leadership, the bureau was expanded and professionalized. Its research programs placed it at the forefront of the profession of agricultural economics. As Ellis Hawley notes, the bureau was far more than a research office. It "had managed to establish what amounted to a public research institute, complete with research director, graduate school, and research projects. But this research organization was also linked to and integrated with a centrally coordinated complex of operating divisions, engaged in generally approved lines of production, marketing, financial, organizational, educational, regulatory, foreign relations, rural betterment, and land use work."[38]

The Bureau of Agricultural Economics would, by the end of the decade, employ more social scientists than the remainder of the federal government. It was distinctive in its expertise and the integration of research and administration. What set it apart for Hoover and his compatriots, however, was its advocacy of activities that appeared too close to planning. Thus, the bureau initiated research projects on production planning executed through conferences with farm groups and reports from the agricultural extension offices. In hopes of adjusting farming patterns over time to exploit the advantages of different regions, it conducted research to identify the crops best suited for various parts of the nation. Finally, it began a program to inventory the nation's land in terms of value and use. Ultimately, this information could be used for land-use planning to minimize waste, while providing important information for land purchases.[39] These exercises at planning clearly placed the USDA's Bureau of Agricultural Economics at odds both with Hoover's antistatist visions of cooperative planning and with the commerce secretary's aspirations to expand his own department. Taylor's efforts to professionalize the bureau and establish a separate budgetary line insulated the bureau from political pressures and frustrated Hoover's efforts to diminish its influence.[40]

Wallace worked to advance the agricultural policy debates by assembling

37. Lloyd S. Tenny, "The Bureau of Agricultural Economics—The Early Years," *Journal of Farm Economics* 29, no. 4 (1947): 1017–19.

38. Ellis W. Hawley, "Economic Inquiry and the State in New Era America: Antistatist Corporatism and Positive Statism in Uneasy Coexistence," in *The State and Economic Knowledge: The American and British Experiences*, ed. Mary O. Furner and Barry Supple (Cambridge: Cambridge University Press, 1990), 296–97.

39. Ibid., 297–98.

40. See Tenny, "The Bureau of Agricultural Economics," 1025–26. Harry C. McDean, "Professionalism, Policy, and Farm Economists in the Early Bureau of Agricultural Economics," *Agricultural History* 57 (January 1983): 64–83.

an Agricultural Conference in 1922 to integrate public policy and the activities of farm organizations in hopes of developing cooperative programs for managing fluctuations in the farm economy. The conference brought together 390 participants, including James R. Howard and Gray Silver representing the American Farm Bureau Federation, Judson Welliver representing President Harding, Julius Barnes of the Commerce Department, future vice-president Charles G. Dawes, and conservative New York banker Otto Kahn, who had organized opposition to farm interests in Congress. The conference also included George Peek and Hugh Johnson, former War Industries Board officials, who were actively developing a plan to reduce domestic surpluses through public purchases and sales in foreign markets. Although the conference held the potential to develop detailed proposals, its forty-two recommendations were of questionable value (e.g., the recommendation that "Congress and the President take steps immediately to re-establish a fair exchange value for all farm products with that of other commodities").[41] As Peek would later recall, its "four volumes of facts, figures and diagrams . . . failed to mention the only thing it was appointed to determine—the cause of the agricultural depression."[42]

Wallace was a great policy entrepreneur, actively and successfully pursuing new legislation to regulate various aspects of the farm economy, promote cooperative action, and create greater access to farm credit. He encountered significant resistance, however, to more expansive efforts to regulate the farm economy. In part, this resistance constituted an ideological challenge to Wallace's work to expand the state role in ways that violated the "new individualism" advocated by Hoover and Coolidge. Hoover's opposition to the agriculture secretary was clearly stated in his *Memoirs,* where he noted that Wallace was "in truth a fascist," as exhibited by his "price- and distribution-fixing legislation."[43] Despite this characterization, one suspects that the opposition was closely tied to Hoover's own designs for expanding Commerce to address all aspects of economic activity. Hoover states as much in his *Memoirs,* where he recollects that he accepted the position of commerce secretary with Harding's guarantee that he could be involved in all aspects of the economy. In Hoover's words: "I stipulated to President Harding that I wanted a free

41. Saloutos and Hicks, *Agricultural Discontent in the Middle West,* 378, 331. John D. Black, "The Progress of Farm Relief," *American Economic Review* 18, no. 2 (1928): 270.

42. George Nelson Peek, "Equality for Agriculture with Industry," *Proceedings of the Academy of Political Science* 12, no. 2 (1927): 569.

43. Herbert Hoover, *The Memoirs of Herbert Hoover,* vol. 2, *The Cabinet and the Presidency, 1920–1933* (New York: Macmillan, 1952), 174.

hand to concern myself with the commercial interests of farmers. . . . However, when the Department of Commerce began to be active for the farmers, in promoting exports, and in solving problems of processing and distribution, the Secretary of Agriculture objected, as is the way of all bureaucratic flesh. At once he began to duplicate our work by establishing and expanding the same economic activities." Henry Wallace, whom Hoover described as "a dour Scotsman with a temperament inherited from some ancestor who had been touched by exposure to infant damnation and predestination," was deemed "trouble for the Department of Commerce" and the president.[44] Hoover consistently held that the USDA's work should end with the harvest. Questions of processing and marketing should be assigned to Commerce, Hoover argued, recommending that the USDA's Bureau of Markets be merged into his department. Wallace was unmoved by Hoover's account of departmental jurisdictions.[45]

After Wallace's death, in October 1924, Hoover declined the opportunity to become agriculture secretary and convinced Coolidge to appoint William Jardine, former president of Kansas State College. As Hoover recalled, "[O]ne of [Jardine's] first acts was to pay a public tribute to the Department of Commerce for its service to the farmers. He established at once full cooperation with us."[46] Jardine viewed farming as a business. Through cooperatives and marketing, which he fully supported, he told farmers that their business could be built "along the same lines that industry and other lines of business have found to be effective."[47] As Hawley notes: "Under Jardine the department ceased to be a major center of anti-Hooverism; it purged those who had been guilty of such behavior and became a member of the Hoover team."[48] Thereafter, the department would restrict itself to promoting cooperative action that would not require extensive subsidies and state planning of farm production. It would also acknowledge the Commerce Department's vigorous activities in export promotion and marketing.

The New Political Universe

One of the principal problems facing farmers in the United States was the decentralization of the farm economy. In the words of Kenyon L. Butterfield:

44. Ibid., 109.
45. See the discussion in Shideler, *Farm Crisis,* 141–51.
46. Hoover, *Memoirs of Herbert Hoover,* 2:111.
47. Jardine quoted in Saloutos and Hicks, *Agricultural Discontent in the Middle West,* 290.
48. Hawley, *The Great War and the Search for a Modern Order,* 102.

"[F]arming, as at present practiced, is a highly individualistic business. Instead of a unified management for the entire industry there are 6,000,000 managers. Each farm is a business unit and each farmer is a manager as well as a worker."[49] This decentralization impeded the kinds of joint production decisions that aided manufacturing firms in adjusting production to market conditions. Thus, while many farmers were aware that reducing the supply of commodities would increase prices, absent organization such a strategy would fall victim to the free-rider problem. If organization offered a solution to some of the farmers' problems, why was it so difficult to achieve? One might note the strong individualism of farmers or extreme geographical dispersion as partial answers. However, one must also acknowledge that farmers have never constituted a monolithic bloc. As one observer noted: "The agricultural class, so-called, is cut through by deep seated social, political, and economic differences." As a result, "only dire distress can bring the cotton planter of the South into a political alliance with the wheat grower of the West."[50] Of course, just such a crisis emerged in the years following the war, as farmers of every stripe saw their incomes fall and questioned why the prosperity enjoyed by the industrial economy was not extended to agriculture. Under these conditions, organizational efforts moved ahead far more rapidly than one might otherwise have expected, as new organizations emerged and existing associations expanded.

Wallace and others were forced to consider the question of agricultural regulation in a political context far different than that which had existed only a generation earlier. As Grant McConnell documented in his classic work *The Decline of Agrarian Democracy,* the agrarian populism of the late nineteenth century, focused as it was on broad social reform and majoritarian politics, was displaced by a growing universe of agricultural interest groups during the first decades of the twentieth century.[51] The National Farmers Union had a membership of 107,000 families in 1916 and controlled over 1,600 warehouses for holding crops kept off of the market to elevate prices. In 1915, Arthur Townley founded the Farmer's Nonpartisan League in North Dakota, which demanded low-interest agricultural loans, subsidized insurance, and the creation of publicly owned grain elevators and packing plants. The Nonpartisan League claimed a membership of some 200,000 families by 1918. Its

49. Kenyon L. Butterfield, "The Farm Problem Made Clear," *Current History* 29, no. 2 (1928): 266.
50. E. Pendelton Herring, *Public Administration in the Public Interest* (New York: McGraw-Hill, 1936), 260–61.
51. See Grant McConnell, *The Decline of Agrarian Democracy* (Berkeley and Los Angeles: University of California Press, 1953).

successes, largely limited to North Dakota and surrounding states, included the creation of a bank to provide low-interest loans to farmers and a state-owned North Dakota Mill and Elevator Association to control the storage, processing, and marketing of wheat. In electoral politics, the league was successful in having its candidate elected governor of North Dakota and gaining control of the state legislature. Its achievements were checked during the war, as rising incomes reduced the relevance of the league's message and the Food Administration repeatedly portrayed it as a socialist endeavor.[52]

The Farmer-Labor Party gained support in the Midwest during the 1920s. It sought to disclose the linkages between the plight of the worker and that of the farmer. As Robert M. Buck observed in 1920, the party offered a class interpretation of the current economic ills: "There are two classes—the exploiters and the exploited. At present the exploiters control the two old parties, by financing them equally—supporting them for the purpose of fooling the voters with false issues and thereby keeping the exploited divided so that they cannot function unitedly in politics. . . . The effort of the Farmer-Labor Party is to induce all exploited groups to arise in their political might and unite to throw off the exploiters."[53] Despite the rhetoric, the rural radicals called for a program that was not all that radical after all. As William Hard explained in 1923, "[T]he present rural radical movement wants the price of land to go up. It wants governmental action which, if successful, will inevitably cause the price of land to go up. Philosophically there is absolutely no difference in the end between this endeavor and the parallel endeavor for bringing governmentally created prosperity, and hence artificially enhanced capital value to the silver mines."[54] In the end, the Farm-Labor Party was largely indistinguishable in appeal from other regional third parties that claimed to represent farm interests. It elected members to state government in Minnesota, North Dakota, and Montana, where support was the strongest. Its high point came in the election of Farmer-Labor candidates to the Senate in 1922 and 1923. However, as a third party it had a difficult time competing against others (e.g., the La Follette Progressives, the Nonpartisan League, and the Socialists, among others), all of which remained woefully underfinanced and thus incapable of displacing one of the major parties. While farm parties failed to exert much influence at the national level, they did assume positions

52. Parrish, *Anxious Decades*, 85; Luther G. Tweeten, *Foundations of Farm Policy*, 2d. ed. (Lincoln: University of Nebraska Press, 1979), 70–71.

53. Robert M. Buck, "The Farmer-Labor Party," *Nation*, August 7, 1920, 156.

54. William Hard, "Those Terrifying Farmers," *Nation*, August 1, 1923, 105.

as part of a larger universe of agricultural groups that kept legislators focused on farm issues.[55]

The American Farm Bureau Federation was the largest association created in the wake of the war. It was, in essence, a holding company for the farm bureaus organized by agricultural agents following the passage of the Smith-Lever Act of 1914. In a 1918 meeting of county agents in Chicago, it was decided that state and national federations of farm bureaus were needed. The next year, the American Farm Bureau Federation's constitution was drafted, and in 1920 it was ratified, uniting more than a thousand county and state farm bureaus. By 1921, the federation could claim a membership of 315,000 families, or 1.5 million individuals, in forty-two state federations. The American Farm Bureau Federation appealed to commercial farmers, who were predisposed to adopt new farming technologies and methods disseminated by the county agents. Reflecting these origins, the federation eschewed the older strands of agrarian radicalism and focused on policies that could encourage the business of farming.[56] Thus, it provided a ready clientele for the USDA's agricultural extension activities and a natural audience for the likes of Bernard Baruch, who claimed that farming could be more businesslike if farmers gained access to loans on produce, greater technical support in the form of USDA market reports, and public warehouses where produce could be fairly graded and stored.[57]

Farm interests also began to receive far better representation in Congress. A Farm Bloc, initially consisting of twenty-two senators, was organized largely through the efforts of Gray Silver of the Farm Bureau Federation and other farm-organization representatives, who met with members of Harding's cabinet and members of Congress on May 9, 1921. In a 1922 exposition of the Farm Bloc's goals, Senator Arthur Capper of Kansas noted that "this movement was non-partisan and a recognition of the economic crisis; an endeavor to outline a plan for an economic re-adjustment rather than a scheme to gain partisan advantage." He recalled: "The outstanding reason that brought this group together was the fact that the general public and the majority of Congress had not realized that the nation had passed into a new economic era in which the balance between agriculture and other industries must be more carefully safeguarded."[58] Subsequently, Representative L. J. Dickinson of Iowa would organize the Farm Bloc in the House.

55. Saloutos and Hicks, *Agricultural Discontent in the Middle West,* 342–56.
56. Morton Keller, *Regulating a New Economy: Public Policy and Economic Change in America, 1900–1933* (Cambridge: Harvard University Press, 1990), 152–53.
57. *Nation,* February 23, 1921, 278.
58. Arthur Capper, *The Agricultural Bloc* (New York: Harcourt, Brace & Co., 1922), 10–11.

Under the influence of the Farm Bloc and the new universe of agricultural interests, Congress during the 1920s passed laws regulating packers and stockyards, commodity-futures trading, cooperative marketing, and agricultural credit.[59] As one contemporary observer noted: "If the present Congress has so far favored one class of producers more than another, it is the agricultural class."[60] However, in the words of Gilbert Fite, "none of the legislation passed between 1921 and 1923 got to the heart of the farmers' basic difficulties of surpluses and price disparities. Congress, as well as most farm leaders, advanced the old nostrums of credit, co-operative marketing, and regulation of dealers in agricultural products."[61] If policy makers and farm advocates understood the full dimensions of the agricultural crisis, it was not evident in many of the proposed responses that took the form of short-term solutions to one or another symptom of the problems at hand.

Competing Responses to Agricultural Crisis

The 1920s was a fertile decade for policy debates and initiatives directed toward the goal of ameliorating the farm crisis. Proposals focused on one aspect or another of the farm economy, hoping to extend to farmers some of the devices that had been successfully adopted (or so it was believed) by corporations. Quite naturally, some believed that the tariff could increase farm incomes. Farm associations that had long attacked the tariff as the mother of trusts now embraced it out of the misguided belief that it would bear the same fruits for the farm economy. Other proposals addressed finance. If some means could be found to remedy the perennial lack of farm credit, it was believed, farmers would have a better opportunity to introduce efficiency-promoting innovations. Additional proposals promoted cooperatives under the assumption that decentralization created for the farmers distinctive difficulties that were not to be found in other sectors of the economy, where higher levels of concentration or effective trade associations promoted greater control over the market. In each of these areas, Congress passed legislation, albeit without the expected impact. Indeed, in the case of the tariff and the

59. Keller, *Regulating a New Economy*, 152–53; Tweeten, *Foundations of Farm Policy*, 71–73.
60. "Congress Helps the Farmer," *Outlook*, September 28, 1921, 118.
61. Fite, "The Farmers' Dilemma, 1919–1929," 80, 78.

extension of credit, it could be argued that the net effect was negative.[62] At the same time, a number of competing proposals were debated to alleviate persistent surpluses through the purchase and export of excess commodities or to institute a system of domestic allotments. Although none of these comprehensive proposals were fully implemented during the 1920s, they set the stage for the New Deal initiatives.

Tariffs, Exports, and Agriculture

Farm interests had long been firm advocates of tariff reform. The tariff was denounced as a tool of the trusts, which forced increases in the costs of goods consumed in the countryside. With the collapse of the farm economy in the early 1920s, many reversed their earlier positions and sought refuge in the tariff. In May 1921, Congress passed the Fordney Emergency Tariff Act. The new tariff was designed to protect the "war babies"—war-related industries that had sprung up during the past several years and were deemed in the national interest. While the tariff had a strong industrial bias, agricultural interests benefited as well, reacting to the rapid and substantial reduction in farm prices in 1920–21. As F.W. Taussig notes: "The farmers were as helplessly ignorant concerning the cause of this decline as they had been concerning the previous rise. They clamored vociferously for a remedy." Their demands reflected "the popular debates of the last generation[, which] had inculcated the belief that the mere imposing of a duty served at once to benefit the domestic producer."[63] The Fordney Emergency Tariff Act placed high duties of wheat, corn, meat, wool, and sugar. However, "as a means of meeting the emergency . . . it was hardly more than an amiable gesture. The prices of the several products continued to decline; hardly a better proof could be found of the failure of tariff duties to serve as a remedy of immediate efficacy."[64]

The Fordney Emergency Tariff Act was passed as a interim measure, to remain in effect until Congress could write more comprehensive tariff legislation. The House passed a new tariff bill in July 1921. The Senate Finance Committee, however, took an additional year to make some two thousand

62. For an interesting discussion of various policies that might be adopted to increase the agricultural income, see Charles J. Brand, "The Price Balance Between Agriculture and Industry," *Proceedings of the Academy of Political Science* 11, no. 2 (1925): 157–83.

63. F. W. Taussig, *The Tariff History of the United States*, 7th ed. (New York: G.P. Putnam's Sons, 1923), 452.

64. Ibid. See also F. W. Taussig, *Free Trade, the Tariff, and Reciprocity* (New York: Macmillan, 1924), chap. 11, for a discussion of the impact of the war on the tariff debates.

revisions, many of which reflected the ongoing debates between the Northeastern manufacturing interests and the Farm Bloc. Ultimately, the Fordney-McCumber Act was signed into law in September 1922. Fordney-McCumber placed high tariffs on chemical and metallurgical goods to protect the "war babies" from German competition. High tariffs were also placed on textiles and a host of manufactured goods. New high rates were imposed on meat, wheat, sugar, wool, butter, milk, lemons and other fruits, and flaxseed. Agricultural implements, twine, and potash (used in fertilizer production) were placed on the free list to lower the cost of agricultural inputs. Overall, the average ad valorem rate for free and dutiable imports was 33.22 percent, 38.5 percent for dutiable imports.[65] Except on heavily imported items (e.g., sugar, wool), the imposition of these duties was primarily political.[66]

The tariff would do little to inflate agricultural prices and incomes. Agricultural imports were relatively unimportant as a source of competition and oversupply. Agricultural imports remained fairly steady in the years following the war. Between 1920 and 1932, the dollar value of agricultural imports averaged 4.5 percent of total farm income, ranging from a low of 3.7 percent in 1921 to a high of 5.1 percent in 1926. In addition, the tariff remained primarily industrial in its focus. Higher tariffs increased the cost of manufactured goods in the American market; domestic producers raised prices to capture the windfall from the new protection, while agriculture was forced to accept market prices for its product. As Henry C. Taylor noted in 1926: "The present system is robbing the farmers of the comforts of life and of their accumulated savings in order that those in the protected industries may enjoy an unsurpassed indulgence in the comforts and luxuries of life in this afterwar period when most of the world is sick."[67] On this basis, Taylor and others called for immediate tariff reductions.

To the extent that the new tariffs eroded the ability of foreign nations to raise dollars or encouraged the erection of reciprocal barriers, they actually reduced the foreign demand for American exports. The dollar value of agricultural exports as a percentage of total farm income fell rapidly from the 8.4 percent in 1921 and 4.5 percent in 1922 to an annual average of 2.75 percent for the next decade. The passage of the Fordney Emergency Tariff Act of 1921 and Fordney-McCumber Act of 1922 contributed to the growing economic nationalism, which closed off international markets and limited the ability of

65. Sidney Ratner, *The Tariff in American History* (New York: D. Van Nostrand, 1972), 48–49, 52.

66. Taussig, *The Tariff History of the United States*, 456–57.

67. Henry C. Taylor, "Agriculture and the Tariff," *Proceedings of the Academy of Political Science* 12, no. 2 (1927): 528.

the United States to expand its agricultural exports. Clearly, given the dearth of evidence that the tariff was a successful agricultural policy tool, its use could be justified—if at all—only if it were combined with other policy tools.

As many farm interests were embracing the tariff to enhance farm incomes, Hoover enlisted the Commerce Department in export promotion. For Hoover, part of the solution to surplus agricultural commodities was a vigorous export policy. Farm organizations and agricultural-commodity exporters filed an ever increasing number of requests for export assistance with the Commerce Department, from 42,000 in 1922, to 400,000 by 1927.[68] Commerce actively courted the farmer, advertising its services through a 1923 pamphlet entitled *How the United States Department of Commerce Serves the Farmer*. The pamphlet presented the ways in which the Commerce Department could supply information on foreign markets and intervene in the face of foreign embargoes. Commerce claimed some responsibility for increasing agricultural exports from a prewar level of $1 billion per year to twice that amount in 1922–25. Commerce's role in finding Japanese markets for surplus rice and promoting the purchase of $20 million of corn for Russian famine relief in 1922 provided some support for this assertion.[69]

Despite these successes, the efficacy of these efforts was limited. The erection of new tariff barriers worked at cross-purposes with the export strategy. Moreover, Hoover's efforts could not transform the structure of the farm economy. As Joseph Brandes correctly observes: "In truth, there was not much that Hoover could do for the American farmer. . . . In sharp contrast with business, American agriculture was still characterized by a multitude of independent and unorganized producers. Short of drastic legislative relief, little could be done to alleviate the effects on the American farmer of world market and crop conditions."[70] This decentralization contributed to the perverse fact that as prices declined, production increased, thus further undermining price levels and creating the need to produce ever more. This dynamic of overproduction and falling incomes could not be addressed effectively until the farm economy underwent an organizational revolution. Hence, the importance of cooperative action.

Cooperatives, Credit, and Agriculture

The history of the cooperative movement in agriculture extends back well into the nineteenth century. Cooperatives were of increasing importance fol-

---

68. Hoover, *Memoirs of Herbert Hoover*, 2:110.
69. Joseph Brandes, *Herbert Hoover and Economic Diplomacy: Department of Commerce Policy, 1921–1928* (Pittsburgh: University of Pittsburgh Press, 1962), 10–12.
70. Ibid., 35–36.

lowing the successful examples of dairy cooperatives in Wisconsin (1841) and New York (1851) and the Pchappa Orange Growers Association in California (1888). Associations were created to unite the efforts of local cooperatives and allow for greater control over levels of production. Thus, associations like the Farmers' Educational and Cooperative Union of America and the American Society of Equity were created in 1902 to affect the amount and timing of a commodity flowing to market. Whereas the former focused on cotton producers, the latter worked to create national unions for different crops.[71] The number of cooperatives increased during the expansion of the farm economy in the decades preceding the war, facilitated by an antitrust exemption for nonstock agricultural associations under the Clayton Act of 1914.

During the 1920s, the American Farm Bureau Federation played a decisive role in promoting cooperatives. In 1920, it called a meeting at which Aaron Sapiro, a representative of several successful California cooperatives, explained how the California Marketing Plan developed by the West Coast fruit cooperatives could serve as a model for farmers producing other commodities. As Gustavus Myers noted in 1922: "Its prime requirements are that selling associations must organize by commodity and not by locality, that they must be strictly business and not mere fraternal or sentimental concerns, and that their organization must not be loose, but legally welded. This plan . . . follows that of successful industrial groups of capitalists who are organized on lines of sameness of product."[72] Sapiro suggested that cooperatives employ a system of member contracts to regulate commodity flows and penalize violators. By controlling the warehouses and marketing activities, the cooperatives could eliminate the middleman margins. Sapiro argued that once a cooperative controlled 90 percent of a commodity, it could administer the domestic price by disposing of surpluses in foreign markets.[73] Thus, in a 1924 address before the Indiana Wheat Marketing Conference, Sapiro proclaimed: "We don't say that the purpose of co-operative marketing is to introduce any economy in the physical handling of grain, because we think that particular point is absolutely too trifling to bother about. What are we trying to do? When we talk of co-operative marketing we are saying this: We are interested in raising the basic level of the price of wheat."[74] Sapiro continued to promote cooperatives after 1923, when he became general council for the American Farm Bureau Federation. However, as Luther Tweeten explains, Sapiro's ef-

71. Keller, *Regulating a New Economy*, 153–54. Tweeten, *Foundations of Farm Policy*, 73–74.

72. Gustavus Myers, "The Organized Farmer Steps Forth," *Century Magazine* 103 (1921–22): 24.

73. This account draws heavily on Tweeten, *Foundations of Farm Policy*, 74–75.

74. Quoted in James E. Boyle, "The Farmers and the Grain Trade in the United States," *Economic Journal* 35 (March 1935): 18.

forts bore few fruits: "[G]roups were organized too hastily and with inadequate management. Farmers were yet too numerous, too diversified, and too
independent for these strong measures. One after another, the groups collapsed, and the Sapiro movement for major farm commodities had failed by
1924."[75] One must, however, place the failure of the Sapiro movement in
context. While it is true that the farm economy was not transformed, the
cooperatives had a growing presence, controlling commodities worth approximately $2.2 billion in 1923.[76]

The proliferation of cooperatives was facilitated by the state. The federal
government provided cooperatives with financial assistance via the War Finance Corporation in 1920 and 1921 and passed a number of important
pieces of legislation that were broadly supported by the American Farm Bureau Federation and the Farm Bloc. The Agricultural Credits Act of 1923
authorized the creation of privately operated National Agricultural Credit
Associations. Far more important, it authorized the creation of twelve intermediate credit banks—one in each Federal Reserve district—to provide subsidized loans to farm cooperatives. Each bank would have a capital stock of $5
million, provided by the Treasury, and each bank would function under the
control of the Federal Farm Loan Board.[77] As William R. Camp, a contemporary observer, explained: "This grant of new power to mobilize credit for the
movement of farm products arose from a recognition of the capital limitations
of the small isolated unit country banks, which have made it impossible in
many states for them to expand loans to meet the needs of any one bor-
rower."[78] The cooperative became "a credit mobilizing agency between the
individual grower and the financing institutions."[79]

The intermediate credit system established under the Agricultural Credit
Act was designed to extend credit to cooperative marketing associations while
also providing individuals with access to credit for their farms. Under the act,
the intermediate credit banks made loans to cooperatives based on warehouse

75. Tweeten, *Foundations of Farm Policy*, 75.
76. Milton J. Keegan, "Power of Agricultural Co-operative Associations to Limit Production," *Michigan Law Review* 26, no. 6 (1928): 648.
77. John D. Hicks, *Republican Ascendancy, 1921–1933* (New York: Harper & Brothers, 1960), 194.
For a discussion of the legal status and internal organization of cooperatives, see Gerald C. Henderson,
"Cooperative Marketing Associations," *Columbia Law Review* 23, no. 2 (1923): 91–112.
78. William R. Camp, "Agricultural Pools in Relation to Regulating tne Movement and Price of
Commodities," *Proceedings of the Academy of Political Science* 11, no. 4 (1926): 221–22. Quote from Harry C.
McDean, "Professionalism, Policy, and Farm Economists in the Early Bureau of Agricultural Economics,"
Agricultural History 57 (January 1983): 81.
79. Camp, "Agricultural Pools in Relation to Regulating the Movement and Price of Commodities,"
221.

and shipping receipts. The credit was then distributed to farmers in the form of advances on the commodities placed with the association. During the period 1923 to 1929, the banks extended $471 million to cooperative marketing associations, which distributed the funds as advances to their 960,411 members. This guarantee of credit helped cooperatives leverage funds from other sources as well, allowing for improvements in the physical stock of the associations. Outside of the cooperatives, the intermediate banks guaranteed loans to individual farmers through a variety of institutions, including agricultural credit corporations, national and state banks, savings banks, trust companies, and livestock loan companies. They could either discount the farmer's note with an intermediate credit bank or use it as collateral. However, the individual loan features of the act functioned far less successfully than the extension of credit to cooperatives.[80] In 1929, for example, the intermediate credit banks accounted for a mere 2 percent of the personal and collateral loans made to farmers.

As cooperatives engaged in a form of price-fixing to manage surpluses and enlarge farm incomes, they raised the specter of antitrust prosecutions. Nonstock, nonprofit cooperatives were granted limited antitrust immunity under section 6 of the Clayton Act in 1914. However, because most farm cooperatives used capital stock, the antitrust immunity did not alleviate their legal exposure. Congress responded by placing riders on the Justice Department's annual appropriations, barring it from prosecuting farmers' cooperatives under the antitrust laws. Following some state-level antitrust suits and the vigorous lobbying of agricultural associations, Congress passed the Capper-Volstead Act in 1923, extending antitrust immunity to stock cooperatives and assigning jurisdiction to the Department of Agriculture—their natural patron—rather than the Federal Trade Commission and the Justice Department. This severed the connection between antitrust policy and cooperative activities.[81] With the passage of the Cooperative Marketing Act of 1925, Congress provided cooperatives with an income-tax exemption and authorized the creation of a Bureau of Cooperative Marketing in the Department of Agriculture. By the mid-1920s, some twelve thousand marketing cooperatives were in place, controlling $2.5 billion worth of agricultural commerce.[82]

80. B.M. Gile, "Functioning of the Federal Intermediate Credit Banks," *Journal of Farm Economics* 13, no. 1 (1931): 123–32. For an overview of the core legislation, see Gerald C. Henderson, "The Agricultural Credit Act of 1923," *Quarterly Journal of Economics* 37 (May 1923): 518–22.

81. See James L. Guth, "Farmer Monopolies, Cooperatives, and the Intent of Congress: Origins of the Capper-Volstead Act," *Agricultural History* 56, no. 1 (1982): 67–82.

82. Keller, *Regulating a New Economy,* 155.

While they could provide some limited remedy for the problem of surpluses, effective solutions would require a more active state role.

Domestic Allotments, McNary-Haugenism, and Export Debentures

In addition to the piecemeal solutions to the farm crisis, a number of proposals were developed to regulate agriculture as a whole and address the problem of surpluses. As noted earlier, the difficulties facing the farm economy were partly economic, partly organizational. On the economic side, overproduction resulted in persistent surpluses that lowered prices. With historically high levels of farm indebtedness, this translated into the failure of myriad farms. On the organizational side, high levels of decentralization limited the opportunities for collective efforts to manage production. The importance of the organizational factors becomes clear when one considers the results of previous voluntary crop-reduction programs. In 1919 and 1920, various farm leaders attempted to convince farmers that they should plant fewer acres of wheat, cotton, and tobacco to stabilize incomes. Before assuming the position of agriculture secretary, Wallace had called on corn farmers to limit production. Writing in *Wallace's Farmer,* he beseeched farmers to develop "close-knit organizations" that could restrict production "in the same scientific, businesslike way as labor and capital." By growing more clover or planting legumes instead of corn, Wallace argued, farmers would raise corn prices, enhance the fertility of their lands, and strengthen "the position of the farmer as a class."[83] With no evident response on the part of farmers (and a bumper crop in 1921), Wallace urged state federations of the Farm Bureau to adopt a system of voluntary acreage quotas. Wallace's plan received the endorsement of various farm associations and farm leaders but failed by virtue of its voluntary nature.[84] Voluntary crop reduction posed a perfect free-rider problem: each individual would profit most if all other farmers curtailed their production while he planted a full crop.

As secretary of agriculture, Wallace continued the crusade that he had initiated a few years earlier. Initially, Wallace and Taylor collected information on production and made it available to farmers in the hope that they would adjust their plans regarding what and how much to plant. These efforts, made in 1921–23, were enhanced with the introduction of the Outlook Program in 1923. This program entailed collecting information on future crops through

83. Wallace quoted in Shideler, *Farm Crisis,* 86.
84. Ibid., 86–88.

intention-to-plant reports. On the basis of this information and projections of employment levels and potential demand in export markets, the Bureau of Agricultural Economics would forecast price levels—occasionally in conferences with outside economists—and make planting recommendations concerning levels of production and substitute crops. The forecasting was hampered by a host of political and practical difficulties. However, with the correlation analyses of W. J. Spillman, Howard Tolley, and Mordecai Ezekiel, Taylor was convinced that the bureau's formulas would allow it to "forecast with close to 80 percent accuracy agricultural supplies, demand, and prices."[85] The Outlook Program progressively expanded its reporting efforts. In its first year, it provided projections on wheat, corn, oats, hogs, and cotton. By 1931, the Outlook report would contain projections for forty commodities, statements on domestic and foreign demand, credit, equipment and fertilizers, and farm labor. Despite the growing sophistication of the reports, a key problem remained: information, by itself, was insufficient due to the long lead time necessary to adjust crop decisions and the lack of any mechanism to coordinate the decisions of individual farmers and thus assure that compliance would not yield a lower return. Some means of forcing crop reductions or guaranteeing a return for such actions was desperately needed.[86]

The USDA's W.J. Spillman placed the idea of agricultural adjustment on firmer foundations in 1926 with his domestic allotment plan. The plan went through a number of versions over the course of the next several years, as John D. Black and Beardsley Ruml reworked some of the plan's key features. M. L. Wilson, a professor in the agricultural economics department at Montana State College and veteran of the USDA's Bureau of Agricultural Economics, gave the plan its most influential presentation as the "voluntary domestic allotment plan." Under the plan, a processing tax roughly equal to the amount of the tariff would be collected and distributed among participating farmers on a pro rata basis. Participating farmers would have access to the funds if they signed a contract restricting the size of their crop. The plan carried three important benefits. First, it reduced surpluses at the farm by providing incentive payments and thus directly addressed overproduction. Second, it was voluntary. Farmers who did not participate could plant as much as they desired, although it was believed that the incentives to participate would be great enough to enlist a majority of farmers. Finally, because

85. See Tenny, "The Bureau of Agricultural Economics," 1024–25, and Shideler, *Farm Crisis,* 135–41.
86. H. R. Tolley, "The History and Objectives of Outlook Work," *Journal of Farm Economics* 13, no. 4 (1931): 530.

the tax was placed on those who benefited from production, it was in some fashion self-financing.[87] As shown in Chapter 9, Wilson's active entrepreneurship resulted in the adoption of the voluntary domestic allotment plan as the centerpiece of the New Deal's Agricultural Adjustment Act.

A competing solution to the agricultural problems was formulated by George N. Peek and General Hugh Johnson of the Moline Illinois Plow Company—two veterans of the War Industries Board who would come to play a central role in the New Deal. They attributed the problems facing farmers to surpluses and to the fact that farmers made purchases in markets protected by the industrial tariffs while selling their goods at world prices. The solution for Peek and Johnson was rather straightforward. Rather than place limits on supply through production controls, the government would purchase surpluses to raise prices to a level that would return farmers to the income levels on parity with the baseline of 1910–14. These surpluses would ultimately be sold on international markets at the lower prices. This two-price system would simultaneously raise incomes and dispose of surpluses. Part of the difference between the domestic and international prices would be made up through an agricultural tariff. In the end, the difference between the market and parity prices would be covered through an equalization fee charged to participating farmers.[88]

At roughly the same time, Professor Charles L. Stewart of the University of Illinois developed an export-debenture plan that would not receive serious attention until 1926, when it was backed by the National Grange and introduced as McKinley-Adkins bill. Like the Peek-Johnson plan, this plan was designed to create scarcity by disposing of surpluses on international markets. However, rather than fund the system through an equalization fee, exporters would be given transferable Treasury debentures—or an export bounty— derived from tariffs on imports. These debentures could then be discounted and sold to foreign traders, who could use them to pay import duties. As Joseph S. Davis explained in 1929: "[T]he object of the export debenture system is to stimulate bidding by exporters so that domestic prices will be raised, and this is to be done at an expense to the government. . . . the exporters are expected, not to keep the proceeds of the debentures to offset special costs of their own, but to pass them back to the growers in the form of higher prices paid for farm products." The increase in exports made possible

87. Saloutos and Hicks, *Agricultural Discontent in the Middle West,* 452–55. See W.J. Spillman, *Balancing the Farm Output* (New York: Orange Judd Publishing Co., 1927).

88. Fite, "The Farmers' Dilemma, 1919–1929," 83. See Peek, "Equality for Agriculture with Industry," for Peek's defense of the program.

by the debentures would increase domestic prices for producers via a reduction in domestic supplies. Davis noted that the export-debenture plan was characterized by its administrative simplicity: "Per se, it requires no federal farm board, no stabilization corporations, no government aid to cooperatives, no controversial equalization fee, no revolving fund, no potentially far-flung commercial operations by governmental agencies. It contemplates only a minimum of administrative machinery."[89] Yet, for opponents, the plan was nothing more than a cleverly designed effort to subsidize farm incomes with money earned from the taxes on imports.[90] Stewart wrote a bill incorporating the export-debenture plan and convinced Illinois senator McKinley and representative Atkins to introduce similar bills. Following hearings in the spring of 1926, the bills died in committee.[91]

Of the three major proposals for agricultural regulation, the Peek-Johnson plan attracted the most sustained attention, receiving the backing of much of the Farm Bloc in Congress, a number of agricultural associations, Secretary Wallace, and Bernard Baruch. After 1926, the American Farm Bureau Federation adopted it as well. In 1924, Senator Charles McNary of Oregon and Representative Gilbert Haugen of Iowa introduced legislation to authorize the creation of an Agricultural Export Corporation consisting of the secretary of agriculture and four presidential appointees to purchase and market a host of agricultural commodities, initially including wheat, flour, corn, cotton, wool, beef, pork, sheep, and related foodstuffs. In the end, the McNary-Haugen bill was introduced unsuccessfully on five occasions. In 1924, the bill was defeated in the House of Representatives. In 1925, it failed to come to a vote on the first occasion and was defeated in both chambers in a second attempt. Some Southern Democrats were unenthusiastic because cotton growers exported such a large proportion of their crop that the domestic prices were of little importance. Republican opposition followed the cue of the administration, which rejected the plan as price-fixing.[92] As the *Nation* editorialized, "[T]here was no legitimate reason why it should have been rejected by the Republican Party which has long been committed to the principle and practice of subsidies in the form of the protective tariff." Apparently, "subsidies were ordained for the few, not the many."[93] Similarly, Senator Hen-

89. Joseph S. Davis, "The Export Debenture Plan for Aid to Agriculture," *Quarterly Journal of Economics* 43 (1929): 257, 251.

90. Albert U. Romasco, *The Poverty of Abundance: Hoover, the Nation, the Depression* (New York: Oxford University Press, 1965), 100. See Hicks, *Republican Ascendancy*, 217–18.

91. Saloutos and Hicks, *Agricultural Discontent in the Middle West*, 390.

92. Tweeten, *Foundations of Farm Policy*, 300–301; Hicks, *Republican Ascendancy*, 197–98.

93. *Nation*, July 7, 1926, 1.

rik Shipstead, Farmer-Laborite from Minnesota, noted: "There seems to be no objection to price-fixing except when it is for the benefit of the farmer. . . . We must either repeal all this special price-fixing legislation, or carry it out to its ultimate conclusion and give every industry the same treatment. When special privilege is extended to everyone it ceases to be privilege."[94]

The McNary-Haugen bill passed Congress in 1927 and again in 1928. The support for the legislation came from rural districts, whereas congressmen representing New England, the Middle Atlantic, and cities outside of these regions provided the key sources of opposition. In its final version, the plan covered cotton, wheat, corn, rice, hogs, and tobacco and was to be administered by a Federal Farm Board composed of twelve members (one from each federal land bank district) working with cooperatives that would dispose of surplus crops. As in the original Peek-Johnson variant, the domestic price could be raised up to the level of the tariff. Unlike the original plan, the equalization fee was now to be assigned to processors and transportation companies. Moreover, a stabilization fund would be created to absorb losses. Drawing heavily on memoranda provided by the Commerce Department, President Coolidge vetoed the legislation on both occasions, despite the strong support of the American Farm Bureau Federation, the Farm Bloc, and Southern Democrats who advocated the plan once cotton was included on terms favorable to the export-oriented Southern cotton growers. As one critic noted, following this veto, farmers "ought at last to realize that the Republican Party, which has so long led them around by the nose, is owned body and soul by Big Business."[95] For Coolidge, the correct response to the ongoing problems in agriculture was a further reliance on cooperative marketing and educational services, the former being facilitated by federal credits, which had been advocated by Secretaries Hoover and Jardine.[96]

Advocates of McNary-Haugen saw the proposal as providing an equitable system for managing agricultural surpluses. In the words of George Peek: "The McNary-Haugen plan merely provides a mechanism which the producers of the primary surplus crops can use to regulate the movement of their crops to market, with the cost . . . assessed against all the producers of the commodity affected."[97] Opponents saw the plan as involving a grand subsidy

94. Henrik Shipstead, "Price-Fixing for the Farmer," *Nation*, August 4, 1926, 102.

95. "The President and the Farmers," *Nation*, June 6, 1928, 628.

96. Hicks, *Republican Ascendancy*, 198–99; Hawley, *The Great War and the Search for a Modern Order*, 103. See John D. Black, "The McNary-Haugen Movement," *American Economic Review* 18, no. 3 (1928): 405–27, for an excellent analysis of the political and economic dimensions of the legislation.

97. George Nelson Peek, "The McNary-Haugen Plan for Relief," *Current History* 39, no. 2 (1928): 275.

and a working assumption that the government had the responsibility of maintaining incomes across the economy. Writing in 1925, Benjamin H. Hibbard, a professor of agricultural economics at the University of Wisconsin, attacked what he saw as the underlying logic of the plan and its potential for unending expansion:

> Should the McNary-Haugen bill be enacted there is every reason to believe that all farmers with their many products will demand the direct benefits of it. The tobacco growers will not stand by and see cotton raised in price while their product is allowed to drop to unprofitable levels. The growers of peanuts, potatoes and poultry are surely going to insist on receiving treatment similar to that granted the growers of the favored products. . . . Carried to its logical limit it means that the government shall extend protection to all, which is logically paradoxical. . . . If the government can handle surplus products for farmers, why not for others? The shoe manufacturers, the furniture manufacturers and all the rest are at times confronted with the problem of a surplus. True, they can reduce their outputs, but to do so means unemployment of labor. Why should not the government take the excess products off their hands, dispose of them outside the country, and maintain prosperity at home? This could be shown, by the same reasoning applied to the McNary-Haugen bill, to work more certainly and advantageously than the way in which private enterprise is trying to do the same thing under tariff protection.[98]

Hibbard anticipated that under McNary-Haugen "the government of the United States would become the greatest dealer of the world. . . . The sign to be hung over the place of business would read: 'Uncle Sam, dealer in corn, cotton, wheat, hogs, pork, cattle, beef, sheep, mutton, butter, poultry, eggs,

98. Benjamin H. Hibbard, "Legislative Interference with Agricultural Prices," *Proceedings of the Academy of Political Science* 11, no. 2 (1925): 192–93. See Hibbard's assessment of competing approaches to the problem of agricultural surpluses in B. H. Hibbard, "The Agricultural Surplus," *Journal of Farm Economics* 8, no. 2 (1926): 194–207. Hibbard discounted most approaches to the management of surpluses as failing to provide a comprehensive solution. In the end, he suggested a combination of long-term land planning, improvement of cooperative solutions to managing surpluses, and export promotion via export bounties. However, he also realized that many farmers would be best advised to leave the field altogether: "Farmers should be well enough educated and ready to take advantage of all available opportunities. If they can do better at some other occupation, they should enter it in spite of widespread sentiment to the contrary. They should not leave farming because of bankruptcy but because of opportunity. With a free flow of labor and employment from farming to other industries, and back if necessary, a balance such as we have not recently known may be restored" (206).

wool, tobacco, peanuts and other things too numerous to mention.'" Similarly, Hibbard continued, there was no reason to believe that policy would remain linked to parity: "If the price can be fixed at one ratio to the all-commodity index it most assuredly can be fixed at some other ratio."[99]

Opposition to McNary-Haugen reflected economic concerns as well. Since McNary-Haugen provided no production restrictions, farmers would have a strong incentive to increase the size of their crops and with it their incomes, while forcing the proposed Agricultural Export Corporation to absorb their stocks. There is no reason to believe that farmers would control production voluntarily once they reached parity. Moreover, one must not lose sight of the international context. As the United States raised its tariff levels in the 1920s, it encountered reciprocal increases in tariff barriers. To believe that it could dispose of potentially limitless surpluses in the face of high tariff barriers was little short of fantastic.[100] Treasury Secretary Mellon argued that McNary-Haugen could have additional implications for the long-term economic performance of the nation's competitors. Dumping surpluses in the international market would reduce food prices, subsidizing the costs of production for foreign manufacturers seeking to compete with American firms.[101]

The opposition to McNary-Haugen cannot be attributed solely to a rigid ideological adherence to market liberalism. As shown in Chapter 4, Hoover was committed to finding various means to improve on market mechanisms via state-supervised self-regulation or associationalism. As Eric Goldman correctly observed: "If the business-minded Republican administrations of the Twenties killed the McNary-Haugen bill with frosty vetoes, they certainly did not oppose the larger philosophy behind it. . . . neither Harding, Coolidge, nor Hoover represented the old idea of free enterprise."[102] It was clear, however, that Coolidge and Hoover were strongly aligned with industry. Protective tariffs and equalization fees were both taxes, but they were designed to help different constituencies. The industrial tariff was embraced uncritically, whereas a subsidy for farmers encountered much closer scrutiny.[103]

Agricultural Policy on the Eve of the Great Depression

Farm policy was a key concern for many in the 1928 presidential election.[104] Despite the Democratic overture to the cities, in the selection of Alfred E.

99. Hibbard, "Legislative Interference with Agricultural Prices," 193, 194.
100. See Parrish, *Anxious Decades,* 87–88.
101. Keller, *Regulating a New Economy,* 153.
102. Goldman, *Rendezvous with Destiny,* 308–9.
103. Hicks, *Republican Ascendancy,* 199–200. See Fite, "The Farmers' Dilemma, 1919–1929," 99.
104. See Butterfield, "The Farm Problem Made Clear," for a fine overview of competing proposals and party platforms written on the eve of the election.

Smith, the party platform carried a powerful plank on agriculture that advocated McNary-Haugen or a similarly conceived plan. The platform stated that Coolidge was "primarily responsible for the failure to offer a constructive program," and noted the inconsistency of the Republican posture toward industry and agriculture. "While he has had no constructive and adequate program to offer in its stead, he has twice vetoed farm relief legislation and has sought to justify his disapproval of agricultural legislation partly on grounds wholly inconsistent with his acts, making industrial monopolies the beneficiaries of government favor." The platform went on to explain: "There is a need of supplemental legislation for the control and orderly handling of agricultural surpluses, in order that the price of the surplus may not determine the price of the whole crop. Labor has benefited by collective bargaining and some industries by tariff. Agriculture must be as effectively aided." Thus, the party pledged to pass legislation "to establish and maintain the purchasing power of farm products and the complete economic equality of agriculture."[105] Chester Davis, the author of the agricultural plank, was a close associate of George Peek—an association that was clearly reflected in his explanation of the plight of the farm economy and the role of the public policy. McNary-Haugen also found support in the platform of the Farm-Labor Party.

The Republican Party platform recounted past efforts on behalf of farmers, noting that "the Republican Party and the Republican Administration, particularly during the last five years, have settled many of the most distressing problems as they have arisen, and the achievements in aid of agriculture are properly a part of this record." The Republican platform pledged the party to "the enactment of legislation creating a Federal Farm Board clothed with the necessary powers to promote the establishment of a farm marketing system of farmer-owned-and-controlled stabilization corporations or associations to prevent and control surpluses through orderly distribution," along with ongoing use of the tariff and support for "a Federal system of organization for co-operative and orderly marketing of farm products," albeit "without putting the Government into business."[106] There was, however, no favorable mention of equalization.

Predictably, as Hoover campaigned for the presidency, he courted the support of agriculture without supporting McNary-Haugen. Echoing the party platform, he promised a federal farm board that would help create cooperatives to control surpluses without the government purchases and taxes

105. "Democratic Platform for 1928," in *National Party Platforms, 1840–1960*, comp. Kirk H. Porter and Donald Bruce Johnson (Urbana: University of Illinois Press, 1961), 272–73.
106. "Republican Platform for 1928," in *National Party Platforms, 1840–1960*, 285.

advocated by the McNary-Haugenites.[107] Hoover supported cooperatives in agriculture as he had supported associationalism in business. With respect to the cooperative movement in agriculture, he stated: "I believed it to be one of the most hopeful undertakings, for according to my social theories any organization by citizens for their own welfare is preferable to the same action by the government."[108] B. F. Yoakum, a supporter of the Hoover proposal, stated the justification of the plan in terms that Hoover would have endorsed: "The great need of the farmer is not a Federal board to control his business, or huge Federal appropriations to be fed to him continually, but a law and assistance which will enable him to establish a nation-wide marketing system under which he can market his products efficiently and have some say as to the prices at which they shall be sold, as every other big industry has. Given Federal authority in establishing such a system, the farmers of this country can and will work out their own salvation."[109]

Upon assuming office, Hoover called a special session of Congress to raise agricultural tariffs, rewarding Senator Borah for his support in the presidential contest. He anticipated that tariff revisions would be combined with action on the agricultural reforms he had promised during the campaign. Congressional consideration of the export-debenture plan ended when Hoover stressed his opposition. Mindful of Hoover's rejection of McNary-Haugen, Congress passed the Agricultural Marketing Act of 1929, creating an eight-member Federal Farm Board. The new board administered a budget of $500 million, which was to be loaned to new or existing agricultural cooperatives or crop-stabilization corporations to purchase and store surpluses and thus to elevate farm prices. To this end, the loans could be used to construct or purchase marketing and processing facilities and undertake educational campaigns to convince farmers of the benefits of cooperative action. The board was to work through commodity-specific advisory committees, each composed of seven members selected by the relevant cooperative associations.[110]

The Agricultural Marketing Act was passed in hopes of addressing the organizational dimension of the farm economy that had limited the capacity of farmers to manage production and marketing to meet changing patterns of demand. Alexander Legge, past president of International Harvester and

107. Parrish, *Anxious Decades*, 208.

108. Hoover, *Memoirs of Herbert Hoover*, 2:110.

109. B. F. Yoakum, "Endorsement of the Hoover Plan for Efficient Cooperation," *Current History* 39, no. 2 (1928): 281.

110. Soule, *Prosperity Decade*, 149; Romasco, *The Poverty of Abundance*, 106; Hicks, *Republican Ascendancy*, 217–18.

chairman of the Federal Farm Board, presented the board's duties in this context. He explained that large corporations and chain stores had succeeded as a result of "collective, concerted action, not the action of the individual, not the question of any one mind applied to any one problem, but rather the mature judgment of a large group of trained men, whose job is to determine the policy or program under which the big corporations operate. . . . the disparity in the earnings of agriculture and the workers in some other industry has grown wider" because the farm economy had thus far failed to adopt this principle. Industry must "regulate from day to day the flow of its product to what the consuming demand may be, what its possibilities are." Absent effective organization, each farmer "goes all by himself regardless of what the consuming demand may be, usually in ignorance of what it is, and he goes on producing and wonders why he cannot get a better return for his effort." While cooperation could be promoted by the Federal Farm Board, Legge was skeptical that it could do much to control production levels. Any such controls would have to arise from the private sector. As Legge explained, the control of production "calls for a campaign and it can never be done except as the farmers become organized and where the story can go back home to the farmer. There is no way you can do it by legislation under the constitution of this country, and I doubt if it can be done anywhere. You cannot compel the farmer, but perhaps you can convince him. If he gets more money for producing a little less it may have an argument that will reach him in the course of time but it cannot be done in a hurry."[111] Cooperative organization could provide a means of placing agriculture "on a basis of economic equality with other industries."[112]

Under Legge, the board endeavored to create national cooperatives for each of the major commodities. This task was made far easier by the existence of some 12,500 cooperatives functioning at the local level. In many cases, the board merely facilitated the formation of organizations to represent and coordinate the activities of existing cooperatives. Thus, it worked closely with various grain cooperatives to form a new Farmers National Grain Corporation. Additional national cooperative agencies were created in 1929 to cover wool, cotton, beans, pecans, and livestock. The basic model was for local cooperatives to purchase stock in regional cooperatives, which, in turn, pur-

111. Alexander Legge, "Policy and Program of the Federal Farm Board," *Journal of Farm Economics* 12, no. 1 (1930): 3, 6, and 10.

112. Joseph S. Davis, "Some Possibilities and Problems of the Federal Farm Board," *Journal of Farm Economics* 12, no. 1 (1930): 13.

chased the stock of the new national associations. This allowed farmer control over the new organizations.

While it would be convenient to view the Farm Board as an agency that would orchestrate a highly decentralized universe of cooperative associations, this would be inaccurate. The board hoped to put an end to decentralization by developing centralized national cooperatives each of which would be responsible for the majority of a given commodity and use its market power in its interaction with processors. As David E. Hamilton notes: "For the Farm Board, amalgamation became not just a goal, but an obsession, and stamping out competition between cooperatives its raison d'être." As a result, meetings with the Farm Board "would inevitably mean a lecture on the evils of competition, the need to amalgamate into national sales associations, and the need to 'regulate the flow' of a commodity to market."[113] Until new national associations could form and become self-sufficient, the Federal Farm Board would distribute loans downward through the organizational chain, delegating the final authority to the local cooperatives. The board attempted to use this network to support farm prices. For example, in October 1929, the board announced that the prevailing prices for cotton and wheat were too low. In each case, it called on farmers to withhold crops from the market, pledging $100 million of loans at a rate of up to 90 percent of the value of the stored crop. The board hoped that this would keep farmers from dumping their goods and thus driving down prices.[114] In the end, the efforts to stabilize commodity prices were unsuccessful. The price of cotton fell steadily from 16.8 cents per pound in 1929 to 6.5 cents in 1932; wheat prices fell from $1.05 per bushel in 1929 to 38.6 cents by 1932.[115]

In theory, the board and cooperatives could buy and store surpluses, releasing them to bring the market price to what was determined, in advance, to be a fair price given existing levels of demand. As a countercyclical measure, this plan might have been successful, assuming that the technical difficulties associated with determining the correct price were eliminated.[116] Given the persistence of surpluses, however, the board would need a constant influx of money from the federal government, in sums well above the appropriated $500 million. Indeed, an ongoing direct subsidization of farm incomes would

113. David E. Hamilton, *From New Day to New Deal: American Farm Policy from Hoover to Roosevelt, 1928–1933* (Chapel Hill: University of North Carolina Press, 1991), 57.

114. Romasco, *The Poverty of Abundance*, 112–21.

115. Hicks, *Republican Ascendancy*, 219.

116. See R. B. Heflebower, "Price Stabilization Under the Farm Board," *Journal of Farm Economics* 12, no. 4 (1930): 595–610.

be necessary unless production controls could be imposed. In fact, following the dismal performance in commodity-price stabilization, the board supported efforts to reduce production. With its funds depleted and no authorization to impose mandatory controls, it had little to offer farmers. The limits of cooperation and associationalism were realized in agriculture as clearly as they were in the regulation of the industrial economy.

The unique circumstances of war allowed farmers to enjoy a new level of affluence and fostered positive expectations about the future. Even following the difficult decade of the 1920s, the American farmer was privileged. As historian Fredric L. Paxson noted in 1931: "It is still true that the American farmer has no counterpart among world farmers, past or present. Driving his car over his improved road, with silk stockings on his womenfolk, for purchased entertainment at the nearby town, his social level continues high." It was possible, as Paxson suggested, that the level of wealth created unrealistic expectations, which affected the agricultural policy debates: "The American farmer has assumed too completely that his scale of life is a necessary and eternal matter. . . . no program based upon the assumption that the American farmer type can be made to last forever can be anything but a misleading disappointment if the facts should establish it that the food producer, by the nature of his job, has always lived on the margin of subsistence and always must."[117] Perhaps it was simply the case that farmers would be forced to accept lower incomes outside of those rare moments when demand was stimulated by some exogenous shock.

Expectations concerning future wealth were only part of the story. In agriculture, as in other areas of economic activity, the war aroused a new understanding of the role of the state and the need to bring private economic associations into its administrative structures. The experience with the Food Administration had also created a new awareness of the expansive role the state could play in purposively managing production levels and promoting higher farm incomes. Key participants in the policy debates had been active in wartime administration and had a clear understanding of the ways in which agricultural associations had been integrated into the Food Administration. The proliferation of associations during the conflict and over the decade of the 1920s was a reflection of this wartime experience. The major agricultural recovery plans of the 1920s also provided different but remarkably consistent

117. Frederic L. Paxson, "The Agricultural Surplus: A Problem in History," *Agricultural History* 6, no. 2 (1932): 67, 68.

articulations of this experience. The professionalization and expansion of the Department of Agriculture during the period, and its efforts directly to integrate scientific and economic analysis in its efforts to manage production levels, were an additional expression of the new understanding of the state. Recall that a few years earlier the USDA had been content with developing and disseminating innovations to increase yields. During the 1920s, in contrast, attention shifted to systematic regulatory schemes designed to stabilize the agricultural economy as a whole. Ultimately, one might attribute the failure of policy in the 1920s to the lack of a clear consensus over the appropriate role for the state relative to private interests. The mixture of the public authority and private associations during the war was such that different individuals could have markedly different judgments regarding which proved decisive. The McNary-Haugenites, the supporters of the voluntary domestic allotment plan, and the Hooverian proponents of cooperatives assisted by the Farm Board could all look to the experiences of the war as a source of support.

One might also attribute the difficulties in addressing the agricultural crisis during the 1920s to the substantial changes that were occurring in agriculture relative to other sectors of a growing capitalist economy. Moving beyond Paxson's fatalism, one might attribute the fluctuating fortunes of the farm economy to its changing relationship to the industrial order. As Alvin Hansen explained in 1932:

[A]griculture is more and more becoming a tail tied to the business kite. Agriculture is becoming increasingly dependent upon business for a market, and as this market becomes more and more linked up with a world economy, agriculture becomes peculiarly affected by international forces. This is notably evident in the post-war period and explains in large part the unprecedented swings in agricultural prices, particularly in the depression of 1921 and 1930. Never before, with the possible exception of the first Napoleonic war period, have we witnessed such a frightful collapse in farm product prices. The demand schedules of dealers have, in the past decade, shifted violently owing to the increased uncertainties presented by the world situation. . . . Moreover, agriculture has never before confronted such an extreme dislocation of the industrial life of the whole world as has developed in the post-war period. Finally agriculture is itself becoming more capitalistic and therefore more dependent . . . upon the capital and money markets of the world. Thus agriculture is coming more and more helplessly under the sway of world-wide business cycle forces.[118]

Hansen's message was clear: one could not understand the agricultural economy in isolation from the larger trajectory of economic evolution. Insofar as business cycles impacted upon the welfare of the farm economy, success in agricultural policy would increasingly depend on success in economic management broadly understood.

118. Alvin H. Hansen, "The Business Cycle and Its Relation to Agriculture," *Journal of Farm Economics* 14, no. 1 (1932): 64.

7

Business Cycles, Industrial Stability, and Economic Management

> During the war, when it was to the interest of the government and of the war industries to economize labor, a national system of free labor exchanges was built up to bring the worker and the job together. . . . But after the armistice it was scrapped in response to the demand of selfish interests. Therefore it is not here now to reduce the avoidable unemployment, or to give us a useful measure of the situation. —*The Nation,* January 26, 1921

> Neither the size of real wages nor the growth of national capital is fulfilling the hope raised by our industrial output during the war. . . . Now it really does appeal to one's common sense as preposterous that the laborers should be thoroughly employed at good wages and should enjoy a high standard of living when the nation was wasting fifteen billions a year upon war, but should find it impossible to maintain that standard when the waste of products has ceased. —David Friday, 1920

It is often and mistakenly assumed that the debates over fiscal and monetary policy took form late in the New Deal, coming to fruition in the decades following World War II, when the Keynesian consensus dominated the economic profession and new institutions had been created for macroeconomic management. The decade of the 1920s, in turn, is mischaracterized as a period in which policy makers held fast to classical notions of the economy that failed to recognize a macroeconomy and rejected public intervention in pursuit of full employment or price stability. In reality, the lively theoretical controversies of the 1920s anticipated modern macroeconomic management even if the impact of the debates was muted by the limitations of existing institutions. There were many articulate advocates of a positive state role in economic management. Many of the participants looked back to their experiences in the Great War and tried to provide a theoretical explanation and a practical application of these lessons. These debates were more than an exercise in intellectual speculation: they had an impact on policy and administration.

Placed in historical context, World War I made extraordinary demands on the state, particularly the expenditures, debt, and managerial complexity associated with the mobilization process. On the eve of World War I, the national government had few means of raising revenues other than a tariff that was of declining value in a period of international conflict and a new income tax that was largely untested. Up to that time, the public sector's claim on national resources had been meager. In 1916, the federal government expenditures were $732 million, approximately 1.8 percent of the gross national product. With the war, much changed. In 1919, the federal government spent some $18.5 billion, or 23.5 percent of the GNP. By 1925, the government's claim on the GNP had fallen from the wartime highs but remained more than twice the prewar level.[1] The war forced officials to develop new means of extracting revenues from the population and managing the overall impact of the war's economic stimulus on prices, capital markets, and the flow of vital inputs. The experiences of the war had permanently transformed the minimalist state inherited from the nineteenth century.

The war left several legacies worth addressing. First, the economic demands of the war forced the federal government, for the first time, actively to manage money markets and the fiscal impact of taxation and spending decisions. These experiences suggested a possible role for peacetime economic policy and raised critical questions regarding the potential for a "scientific" management of the economy. For some, the war pointed to a potential for some form of industrial planning. As S. Howard Patterson noted in 1929:

> It is costly to permit industry to function without any broad and comprehensive planning. The World War revealed what a national economic program might do in the matter of improved labor markets and the reduction of human and material wastes. Socialists and other critics of modern capitalism point to the waste and planlessness of economic production on individual initiative and under the lure of private profits. The Russian Gosplan represents an attempt to organize the entire economic system of that county in order to minimize waste and to increase efficiency. Capitalist countries likewise will do well to promote national bureaus of economics, committees of engineers, and industrial councils to consider the reduction of unemployment and other forms of economic waste by improved methods of industrial planning.[2]

David Friday suggested in 1920 that the return to wartime prosperity posed a significant challenge: "Our problem is how to co-ordinate and if necessary

1. *Statistical History of the United States,* series Y 255, 256, and F1.
2. S. Howard Patterson, *Social Aspects of Industry: A Survey of Labor Problems and Causes of Industrial Unrest* (New York: McGraw-Hill, 1929), 301.

remodel our industrial institutions and arrangements [so] that production can be brought to the full without endangering the full employment of labor and without subjecting the business man to the enormous risk of financial extinction to which he has been exposed under the industrial regime of the past."[3] For others, the war experience raised more limited and practical questions. To what extent, for example, could the Federal Reserve use its control over money markets to eliminate inflation and deflation? Would the federal government design strategies of spending to limit unemployment during downturns in the business cycle?

A second and related legacy of the war came in the area of state building. The war had direct implications for professionalization and the status of economic knowledge in the state. As Ellis Hawley explains: "[E]conomic inquiry for purposes of managing the economic system as a whole had its real beginnings during World War I, at least insofar as it was done by credentialed professionals. . . . it was the demand generated by the wartime administrative apparatus that brought dozens of trained economists into government service and put them to work producing the data, tools, and understanding needed for effective performance of the new managerial tasks."[4] The professionalization of the government agencies with economists was a necessary product of the demands of economic mobilization. The economic policy functions assumed by the federal government as part of the mobilization process created a consequent demand for economic data and expertise that, in turn, created the resources for new experiments in economic management.

A third legacy of the war was the economic dislocations that accompanied the end of hostilities. The war forced an immense expansion of credit by the Federal Reserve and an unprecedented outflow of funds to the allies and later to reconstruction. The United States was transformed from a debtor nation into the world's creditor. In late 1919 and 1920, the Federal Reserve concluded that the credit expansion had to cease. In pursuit of this goal, it increased the discount rate greatly, thus putting a stop to the monetary and commercial expansion fueled by the war. In early 1920, the changes in monetary policy were combined with a discontinuation of foreign loans for reconstruction. The loans had played an important role in financing the European demand for American exports. As John Hicks correctly notes: "The results of

3. David Friday, *Profits, Wages, and Prices* (New York: Harcourt, Brace & Howe, 1920), 203.

4. Ellis W. Hawley, "Economic Inquiry and the State in New Era America: Antistatist Corporatism and Positive Statism in Uneasy Coexistence," in *The State and Economic Knowledge: The American and British Experiences,* ed. Mary O. Furner and Barry Supple (Cambridge: Cambridge University Press, 1990), 288–89.

this decision on foreign exchange were so catastrophic as to amount to the creation of an embargo against purchases from the Untied States."[5] The economy fell into a depression that was severe but short-lived. By June 1921, wholesale prices had fallen to 56 percent of the May 1920 level. Real GNP contracted by 12 percent, leaving some 4.75 million unemployed.[6] As George Soule described the situation in 1921:

> We find, strangely, that hundreds of thousands of workmen are clamoring for a chance to produce. And we find that the bankers and manufacturers, who have been talking loudest about the duty of the workers to work harder, are the very ones who are now denying them the opportunity to work at all. The bankers will not give credit, the manufacturers will not manufacture, and the retailers will not buy. It is now the turn of the workman to arise in his righteous anger and say to the masters of the country's business, 'Produce! Produce! Why don't you all get down to work? Your conduct is criminal. You are a lot of unconscionable profiteers, and you ought to be shot at sunrise.' "[7]

In this context a number of intellectuals gave serious reflection to the potential role of public policy in managing economic performance and thus limiting (or eliminating) the fluctuations of the business cycle. Although the most ambitious fiscal policy recommendations were those that emerged out of the 1921 President's Conference on Unemployment, over which Herbert Hoover presided, there were lively debates in the area of monetary policy as well. Both of these are examined at length in this chapter. These debates reflected an appreciation for the possibility of systematic governmental action to control the cycles inherent in a capitalist economy.

The war thus resulted in new state capacities, a shift in the intellectual debates, and a crisis that forced a reconsideration of policy. This chapter examines the legacy of World War I in the area of economic management in some detail. The chapter proceeds in three steps. First, it briefly examines the economic policy innovations associated with the war. Second, it peruses the contemporaneous fiscal policy debates and the attempts, spearheaded in large

5. John D. Hicks, *Republican Ascendancy, 1921–1933* (New York: Harper & Brothers, 1960), 22.

6. Ibid.; Milton Friedman and Anna Jacobson Schwartz, *A Monetary History of the United States, 1867–1960* (Princeton, N.J.: Princeton University Press, 1963), 232; Peter Fearon, *War, Prosperity, and Depression: The U.S. Economy, 1917–45* (Lawrence: University Press of Kansas, 1987), 16.

7. George Soule, "Produce! Produce!" *Nation,* January 5, 1921, 13.

part by Herbert Hoover, to create a system of countercyclical spending that relied heavily on associational tenets—a perfect example of compensatory state building. Finally, the chapter turns to the debates over the role of the Federal Reserve in managing the economy, and the policies adopted by the Fed in the years leading up to the Great Depression.

Wartime Mobilization and Economic Policy

War presents economic predicaments for policy makers. Three difficulties are immediately apparent. First, there is the problem of prices. Consumer-goods shortages, the pressure on labor markets, and the higher levels of money in the economy create strong inflationary pressures. Often, policy makers must work to restrain prices while maintaining prices at a high enough level to stimulate expansion of production by smaller firms that encounter higher costs. Second, there is the problem of funding the war effort. Wars— particularly total wars like World War I—demand levels of funding that would be unimaginable during peace. As a result, wars are accompanied by an expansion of taxation as rates ratchet upward and taxes are extended to goods and activities previously untaxed. The financial demands of modern war are so great, however, that a complete reliance on taxes is both economically and politically unworkable. Thus, policy makers are forced to develop new tools for borrowing funds. Following the war, officials are forced to manage the impact of the resulting debt on the money supply while accepting higher levels of taxation in order to retire the war debt. Third, there is the problem of funding industrial expansion. The transformation of a peacetime economy to a war posture can proceed, in part, through the conversion of existing facilities. Some of this expansion may come automatically as a response to market cues. However, war finance creates shortages of investment capital and thus limits the extent to which, absent direct government investment, such expansion can take place. Thus, policy makers must promote and fund the creation of new factories and the expansion of existing facilities. This, in turn, raises concerns over the ultimate disposition of the facilities following the war.

While these problems may be common to all modern wars, the capacity of governments to address them successfully depends, in large part, on the existence of appropriate policy tools, bureaucratic expertise, and necessary institutional infrastructure. Given the underdevelopment of the American

state at the end of the Progressive Era, the capacity for addressing the problems was woefully inadequate. Although wartime economic policies were reviewed in Chapter 3, it is useful to return to the subject as a preface to our
examination of the macroeconomic policy debates of the 1920s.

The Problems of Price

During the war, some means had to be found to secure control over pricing.
Price-fixing activities were executed by several agencies—with the War Industries Board, the Food Administration, and the Fuel Administration assuming the bulk of the responsibility. The need for a government role in setting
prices was unavoidable. As Herbert Hoover noted, it was "simply the result
of the government being forced in to the issue of becoming the dominant
purchaser and thereby, willingly or unwillingly, the price determiner in particular commodities."[8] Although one might consider the determination of "fair"
prices to be a purely technical matter—there is, hypothetically, a correct price
for any commodity at any given time—price-fixing was rarely conducted according to any firm set of economic guidelines. As Simon Litman concluded
in his 1920 review of wartime price controls: "Government price fixing during
the war was guided little by economic principles. It was not uniform either in
its objects or in its methods, feeling its way from case to case."[9] This was
largely the result of information scarcity. Lacking the data and expertise to
execute this complex task, price-fixers routinely relied on extensive consultation with the affected interest before arriving at a price schedule.

As noted in Chapter 3, the War Industries Board—the body that set
prices for more commodities than any other agency—used two mechanisms:
cost-plus contracting and direct price-fixing. The WIB established a fixed
rate of profit, which was attached to the costs of production. This had the
advantage of integrating the high-cost producer into the war effort and
thereby maximizing potential sources of supply. However, cost-plus contracting created a number of notable economic and administrative problems. As
Grosvenor B. Clarkson, a participant in mobilization, explained: "It was a
policy with manifest defects. It involved the maintenance of enormous and
costly accountancy systems by the Government in order to determine just
what the cost of production was." At the same time, it embroiled participants

---

8. Hoover quoted in Simon Litman, *Prices and Price Controls in Great Britain and the United States
During the World War,* Carnegie Endowment for International Peace, Preliminary Economic Studies of the
War, no. 19 (New York: Oxford University Press, 1920), 318.
    9. Ibid.

in "endless disputes concerning the calculation of costs." Finally, it had the perverse effect of rewarding inefficiency: "[T]he more efficient a producer was, the lower his costs and the less his absolute profits." In Clarkson's judgment, this system, if applied on a government-wide basis, "would have called for an army of accountants almost as large as the army in France."[10]

The technical demands and delays of cost-plus contracting led the WIB to rely increasingly on a consultative process supervised by the Price-Fixing Committee, under the direction of Robert Brookings. The price-fixing activities of the WIB's Price-Fixing Committee were interesting for a number of reasons. First, the WIB often set prices with the goal of stimulating production on the part of the small, high-cost firms while simultaneously restraining inflation. The need to manage the tension between these incompatible objectives raised serious difficulties given that the differences between the average costs of the most efficient firms and those of their least efficient counterparts were often significant. Consider pig iron. The Federal Trade Commission estimated in September 1918 that the cost of producing pig iron was $45.72 per ton in the least efficient firms, compared with $18.14 in the most efficient firms. Given this disparity, what might constitute a reasonable price?[11] The former would provide a considerable profit for the largest corporations; the latter would force the smaller companies into bankruptcy and thus raise a host of potential antitrust concerns. To make matters more chaotic, the armed services were free to negotiate lower prices when possible. In the cases where fixed prices would inflate the profits of the larger producers with distinct cost advantages, it was assumed that the difference would be recaptured through the excess profits tax. Second, following the logic of compensatory state building, price-fixing was accomplished through close interaction with industry actors. "It always took the form of negotiation, and the results were, strictly speaking, agreed rather than decreed prices."[12] In the words of Robert Cuff, "[A] base price for any commodity was whatever the committee and the industry could agree upon."[13]

Without a clear legislative grant of authority to engage in price-fixing, the WIB was essentially incapable of forcing prices against the concerted

10. Grosvenor B. Clarkson, *Industrial America in the World War: The Strategy Behind the Lines, 1917–1918* (Boston: Houghton Mifflin, 1923), 172.

11. Herbert Stein, *Government Price Policy in the United States During the World War* (Williamstown, Mass.: Williams College, 1939), 98.

12. Clarkson, *Industrial America in the World War,* 177.

13. Robert D. Cuff, *The War Industries Board: Business-Government Relations During World War I* (Baltimore: Johns Hopkins University Press, 1973), 236.

resistance of affected firms. Even if it had possessed the authority, it is doubtful that it would have been able to amass the data and deploy the expertise
necessary to execute its mandate. It relied on voluntarism and business participation in the decision-making process to limit the objections to price-fixing
and save the WIB from the arduous task of collecting detailed information
on production costs. Of course, the Price-Fixing Committee had its greatest
success with businesses that were monopolies or oligopolies: they were experienced in administered pricing to promote long-term stability.[14] One result, as
F. W. Taussig noted, was that price-fixing "was opportunist, feeling its way
from case to case."[15] In the end, the WIB could rely on the cheerful cooperation of businesses when they fully expected to acquire more than they sacrificed.

Funding the War

World War I forced unprecedented levels of spending on the part of the
federal government. In 1919, the federal government spent $18.5 billion,
compared with $713 million three years earlier.[16] The critical question was
how to fund such a high level of spending. From a fiscal perspective, the war
could not have come at a better time. The Sixteenth Amendment, ratified in
February 1913, authorized the federal income tax, a new source of revenues.
Before the war, over 90 percent of federal revenues were collected through
excise taxes and customs. While there was an increase in the federal government's reliance on the income tax after 1913—income taxes provided 16
percent of federal revenues by 1916—the war was truly a transformative
event. During the period 1917–20, a majority of government revenues, an
average of 58.6 percent, came from corporate and individual income taxes.
The mainspring of this transformation was the War Revenue Act of 1917, a
highly progressive tax act that lowered exemptions, increased the tax rates,
and placed a surcharge on incomes over $1 million. This act alone increased
federal revenues from $860 million in 1917 to $3.76 billion in 1918. Subsequent revenue acts in 1918 and 1919 brought additional increases in marginal
rates and imposed a war-profits tax based on the change in profits from prewar levels.[17]

14. Ibid., 229.
15. F. W. Taussig, "Price-Fixing as Seen by a Price Fixer," *Quarterly Journal of Economics* 33 (February
1919): 238.
16. *Statistical History of the United States,* series Y 357.
17. John F. Witte, *The Politics and Development of the Federal Income Tax* (Madison: University of
Wisconsin Press, 1985), 75–85.

Although the tax acts of 1917–19 were of enormous national significance and provided much of the funding needed to wage the war, the vast majority of the population experienced no change whatsoever. The reason was simple: the new income tax was remarkably progressive. Indeed, as John Witte notes: "In effect the income taxes were class legislation—a fact explaining some of their appeal. For 1920, the year in which the most returns were filed, there were only 5.5 million taxable returns for a population of 106 million and a labor force estimated at 41.7 million."[18] While the income tax provided the government with a new and powerful source of revenue, the demands of war forced a movement into the bond market. Initially, some, like Treasury Secretary McAdoo, were proponents of a system that built heavily on taxation. McAdoo called for funding 50 percent of the war through taxes—a conservative "pay-as-you-go" approach to war finance that would require imposing taxes on those with lower income, many of whom lived in fear of conscription and resented corporations and the wealthy, who would profit from supplying the war effort. At the same time, a heavy reliance on an income tax that continued to draw on the wealthiest would have required exceptionally high marginal rates, thus discouraging investment. In the end, some 30 percent of the war was funded through taxes, with the remainder raised through the bond market.[19]

Despite cautious predictions of the size of the bond market (estimated in 1917 to be some 350,000 people), patriotic appeals, high yields, low denominations, installment plans, and federal income-tax exemptions dramatically stimulated the demand for war bonds. Moreover, the Federal Reserve provided low rates of interest for member banks, increasing their reserves so that they could purchase government bonds for their own portfolios or lend funds to individual buyers. As a result, the Treasury issued bonds—four Liberty Loans and a Victory Loan—worth $21.5 billion in the period 1917–19. Sales were facilitated by investment bankers, who marketed the bonds through participation in the War Loan Organization, the National War Savings Committee, and Liberty Loan Committees.[20] By 1919, the public debt had grown to $25.5 billion, compared with $1.23 billion in 1916.[21] In the years following

18. Ibid., 86.
19. John Kenneth Galbraith, *Money: Whence It Came, Where It Went* (Boston: Houghton Mifflin, 1975), 141.
20. Vincent P. Carosso, *Investment Banking in America: A History* (Cambridge: Harvard University Press, 1970), 224–27; Paul B. Trescott, *Financing American Enterprise: The Story of Commercial Banking* (New York: Harper & Row, 1963), 163.
21. *Statistical History of the United States,* series Y 368.

the war, this unprecedented level of debt would force the Federal Reserve to play a far greater role in monetary management while forcing the Treasury to run surpluses every year of the 1920s in hopes of paying off the nation's obligations.

Investment Capital and Industrial Expansion

As noted in Chapter 3, the War Industries Board attempted to promote maximum war production through a host of mechanisms. The Conservation Division encouraged changes in product design and varieties to save materials and economize on transportation. The Price-Fixing Committee often set prices relatively high to create incentives for firms to devote resources to war production. The priorities system created similar incentives by threatening to starve firms not so engaged by restricting their access to raw materials, fuel, and transportation. While there were numerous incentives to produce for the war, the success of the Liberty Loan drives created conditions of extreme capital scarcity. Capital flowed out of financial institutions to be invested in the war. At the same time, the tax exemptions created incentives for wealthy investors to substitute the war bonds for commercial bonds and stocks.

To remedy the war-related capital shortage, Treasury Secretary McAdoo and the Investment Bankers Association suggested that the Federal Reserve create a committee to review proposed security issues. In 1918, the Federal Reserve Board responded by creating a Capital Issues Committee (CIC), which passed on proposed securities. These activities were legally authorized in April 1918, with the passage of the War Finance Corporation Act. The CIC consisted of three Federal Reserve Board members and an advisory counsel of investment and commercial bankers. Committees were organized in each Federal Reserve district. Moreover, "Economic Vigilance Committees" were established in each district to collect and disseminate information on parties offering securities without CIC approval.[22] The CIC reviewed capital issues over $100,000 to determine what percentage of the funds would be devoted to war-related activities. Its immediate goal was to channel capital to the war effort. To this end, it reduced the competition for funds during the government's bond campaigns by manipulating the timing of the release of new securities issues so that they would not coincide with Liberty Loan drives. When the Capital Issues Committee suspended operation in December 1918,

---

22. William J. Shultz and M. R. Caine, *Financial Development of the United States* (New York: Prentice Hall, 1937), 562–63. Carosso, *Investment Banking in America,* 230–33.

it had approved securities issues valued at $3.78 billion and rejected issues worth $917 million.[23]

At the same time that the CIC was regulating capital issues with an eye to supplying the war effort, it evaluated the quality of the issues through an examination of the information disclosed in the prospectuses. This latter activity was of great importance even if the CIC lacked the authority to prevent corporations from raising capital. As Vincent P Carosso explains: "The CIC interpreted its duties as extending beyond simple discouragement of the flotation of nonessential or poorly timed issues. Of broader, and in the long run, of much more lasting significance were its efforts to control the sale of fraudulent securities. The experience of the CIC subsequently was cited repeatedly as proof of the urgent need for a federal disclosure law."[24] Indeed, in one of its final reports, the CIC recommended "that federal supervision of security issues, here undertaken for the first time, should be continued by some public agency, preferably by one of the government departments, in such a form as to check the traffic in doubtful securities, while imposing no undue restrictions upon the financing of legitimate industry."[25] Over the course of the next decade, several proposals emerged to extend the activities of the CIC. However, it was only with the market crash of 1929 and the creation of the New Deal's Securities and Exchange Commission that a system for securities regulation was created—one that was modeled explicitly on the example of the CIC.[26]

The same legislation that authorized the Capital Issues Committee created the War Finance Corporation. The WFC was capitalized at $500 million and was authorized to extend an additional $3.5 billion in credit. Working through commercial banks, the War Finance Corporation was authorized to provide credit to essential industries and public utilities that might otherwise have to compete in the market for scarce capital. In this capacity, the WFC would lend its notes to banks, which would make cash loans to targeted enterprises, using the WFC notes as collateral at the Federal Reserve. The banks, under this system, served as intermediaries connecting the WFC and recipient firms. The WFC could also make five-year loans to essential industries that were unable to raise sufficient funds through existing financial mar-

23. Shultz and Caine, *Financial Development of the United States,* 562–63.

24. Carosso, *Investment Banking in America,* 233.

25. Quoted in Joel Seligman, *The Transformation of Wall Street: A History of the Securities and Exchange Commission and Modern Corporate Finance* (Boston: Houghton Mifflin, 1982), 49.

26. Ibid., 49–50, 53. Michael E. Parrish, *Securities Regulation and the New Deal* (New Haven, Conn.: Yale University Press, 1970), 15–16.

kets. In addition, it was authorized to make one-year loans to savings banks, which had suffered from a decline in the value of their securities and a loss of customer deposits to Liberty bonds.[27]

The War Finance Corporation extended credit to a great variety of enterprises, including mining and chemical corporations, manufacturers, public utilities, and electric power plants. Some of the interests received substantial credit lines as a result of WFC activities. The Bethlehem Steel Corporation, for example, received $20 million in credit. However, the greatest contribution came in funding the railroads. Congress authorized the Railroad Administration to purchase equipment or lend money to the railroads from a revolving fund of $500 million. In 1919, the revolving fund was exhausted despite the need for further improvements. The WFC quickly filled the gap by providing some $90 million to railroads—money that they used primarily to reimburse the Railroad Administration for improvements. In the same year, when Congress failed to appropriate an additional $750 million due to a Senate filibuster, the WFC loaned the Railroad Administration $50 million in return for carrier securities that had been provided to the administration as collateral on previous loans. These funds, along with money provided by the War Department and the Navy Department, allowed the Railroad Administration to continue its activities until Congress passed the required appropriation.[28]

Although the War Finance Corporation Act authorized the WFC to continue operations until six months after the end of the war, Congress ultimately replaced its wartime duties with a new set of tasks, thereby extending its life. During the period 1919–20, the WFC provided emergency financial support for exporters in hopes of partially compensating for reductions in orders following the Armistice. The Victory Loan Act of March 1919 authorized the WFC to loan up to $1 billion to assist exporters and U.S. banks that were financing exports. The WFC's activities in the area were limited, however. Congress authorized the War Department to sell surplus stocks on credit. Subsequently, it provided some $1.3 billion of goods to Europe on credit, thus partially relieving the postwar hardship.[29] Although the War Finance Corporation continued to operate from 1921 to 1929, providing agricultural

27. Carosso, *Investment Banking in America*, 228–30; B. M. Anderson, *Effects of the War on Money, Credit, and Banking in France and the United States,* Carnegie Endowment for International Peace, Preliminary Economic Studies of the War, no. 15 (New York: Oxford University Press, 1919), 192–93.

28. E. Jay Howenstine Jr., *The Economics of Demobilization* (Washington, D.C.: American Council on Public Affairs, 1944), 167–69; James Stuart Olson, *Herbert Hoover and the Reconstruction Finance Corporation, 1931–1933* (Ames: Iowa State University Press, 1977), 12–13; Walker D. Hines, *War History of American Railroads* (New Haven, Conn.: Yale University Press, 1928), 133–35.

29. Howenstine, *The Economics of Demobilization,* 270–71.

assistance for farm exports, its tasks were reduced after 1924, when the liqui-dation of the WFC began in earnest. The War Finance Corporation ceased operation in 1929. Yet, it was quickly reborn as the Reconstruction Finance Corporation in the winter of 1931–32, a central component of Hoover's re-covery program.[30]

World War I, then, forced experimentation with economic policies in areas for which there were no clear historical precedents. This experimentation brought with it a great influx of economists—the war bureaucrat of choice in many contexts. Absent the justification of national emergency, however, many were hesitant to support the broad circumvention of the market and the maintenance of a peacetime cadre of economic managers. Thus, "a polity in which power had traditionally been lodged in parties, courts, local units, and organized interests also proved strongly resistant to the idea of a perma-nent managerial establishment. . . . economists who had hoped to institution-alize their wartime position in this manner found that they could salvage little."[31] But economists were not driven from the government wholesale, nor did they abandon public service. Increasingly, economic expertise was fragmented at the agency level. In some cases, such as the Department of Agriculture's Bureau of Agricultural Economics, the connection between the state and the academic discipline was strong and enduring (see the discussion in Chapter 6). In the contrasting case of macroeconomic management, how-ever, economic expertise was diffuse and took many different forms. One result was the lack of a clear message concerning the role of the state in the economy. Another result was an approach to economic policy that emphasized voluntarism while providing little room for the activities of a managerial elite.

New Era Economic Policy

As shown in Chapter 4, Hoover drew on his wartime experiences to promote an associationalist order. Associationalism, he claimed, could provide a form of planning without requiring the large bureaucratic structures that would undermine individualism and national traditions of self-reliance. From Hoo-ver's perspective, a system for planning should depend on cooperation and

30. Hicks, *Republican Ascendancy*, 55; Olson, *Herbert Hoover and the Reconstruction Finance Corporation*, 12–13.

31. Hawley, "Economic Inquiry and the State in New Era America," 290.

the voluntary efforts of business rather than the heavy hand of the state. Although Hoover's justification for associationalism could be compelling, it was also a necessity given the limitations of existing institutions. As one of Hoover's contemporaries observed: "Secretary Hoover with his characteristic vision has done everything within his power to encourage the widespread dissemination of business facts within industries" because "the government has neither the quick-acting machinery nor funds to afford much assistance."[32] While voluntary cooperation was a necessary component of associationalism, it would not be automatic. Businesses would have to be convinced, first, that participation would contribute to their profitability and industry stability and, second, that it would do so without simultaneously increasing their vulnerability to antitrust prosecution. Recall that this fragile system was in tension with the antitrust authorities at the Justice Department, who viewed associationalism as subterfuge for collusion.

The potential benefit of associationalism was not the only lesson to be extracted from the war. Some saw in war mobilization the possibility of extending administrative control over the economy, thereby creating a system of economic management that was not contingent on voluntarism and cooperation. Although there were some failed efforts toward planning in the area of transportation (e.g., the Transportation Act of 1920), the discussion here is limited to the efforts to create a macroeconomic management capacity. The movement toward macroeconomic management was limited by the lack of adequate theory and the resistance of officials who remained wedded to far more traditional fiscal and monetary policies. In the end, the evolution of fiscal policy—as so much else—was easily brought under the sway of Hoover's associationalism, whereas the parallel evolution of monetary policy was dominated by a Federal Reserve that lacked the capacity to execute its new-found duties with the necessary expertise.

Fiscal Policy and the Unemployment Problem

Following the economy's fall into the postwar depression, many drew on their recent experiences to consider how public policies could be designed to prevent similar dislocations in the future. In the fall of 1921, the Commerce Department hosted the President's Conference on Unemployment, chaired by Commerce Secretary Hoover. The Conference brought together policy mak-

---

32. Franklin D. Jones, "Business Statistics as a Means of Stabilizing Business," *Proceedings of the Academy of Political Science* 11, no. 4 (1926), 49.

ers, academic economists, and representatives of labor, finance, manufacturing, mining, and the railroads. President Harding opened the conference by expressing his belief that the economic problems facing the country might be attributed to any of a host of factors: "Liquidation, reorganization, readjustment, [or] re-establishment." However, "all these are a part of the inevitable, and he who thinks they might have been avoided by this plan or that, or this policy or that, only hugs a delusion when reason is needed for a safe council."[33] Under normal conditions, Harding explained, there were about one and one-half million out of work—the so-called parasite percentage. The current crisis increased the ranks of the unemployed to four million. While Hoover suggested that the economy was already in recovery and thus the conference should be concerned primarily with long-term business-cycle management, Harding was far more cautious: "It is difficult to know whether we have reached that bedrock to which reaction runs before the upward course begins." In any event, Harding was firm that the answer should not be found in expansive public spending: the "tonic from the public treasury . . . is to be reckoned a cause of trouble rather than a source of cure."[34]

The conference's mission was to consider plans for eliminating current unemployment and to provide "a long-view study of the business cycle of booms and slumps and their alleviation."[35] Hoover opened the conference by calling on its members to help identify "the measures that would tend to prevent the acute reaction of economic tides in the future." He presented the task in associational terms: "The Administration has felt that a large degree of solution could be expected through the mobilization of co-operative action of our manufacturers and employers, of our public bodies and local authorities, and that if solution could be found in these directions we would have accomplished even more than the care of our unemployed." As a means to this end, the conference was expanded through state branches and subcommittees at the city and county levels to mobilize public and private resources "to look after the destitute."[36]

The immediate concern of the conference was the existing recession, which, by the conference's own imprecise estimates, left between 3.5 and 5.5

33. Harding quoted in "The Nation and the Unemployment Problem," *Outlook*, October 5, 1921, 150.

34. Ibid. See also "The Unemployment Conference," *Outlook*, October 12, 1921, 205.

35. Herbert Hoover, *The Memoirs of Herbert Hoover*, vol. 2, *The Cabinet and the Presidency, 1920–1933* (New York: Macmillan, 1952), 44.

36. Ibid., 44–45. See *Report of the President's Conference on Unemployment* (Washington, D.C.: Government Printing Office, 1921).

million unemployed. A number of predictable recommendations were made for creating employment services, expediting private construction and maintenance projects, and promoting public-works spending. Manufacturers were asked to contribute to the program by reducing hours and days of work rather than laying off workers and, more important, by expanding construction, repair, and production for stocks. Moreover, it was suggested that the Congress move quickly to reduce the wartime income and corporate taxes, conclude the readjustment of railway rates, and complete work on the tariff legislation. Finally, the conference called for "definite programs of action that will lead to elimination of waste and more regular employment in seasonal and intermittent industries . . . in order that the drain upon capital may be lessened and the annual income of workers may be increased."[37]

While the efforts to address the immediate crisis were important, the bulk of the *Report of the President's Conference on Unemployment* was devoted to long-term planning in eliminating the impact of the business cycle. To this end, the *Report* carried a number of recommendations for business. It noted that the "extremes [of the business cycle] are vicious, and the vices of the one beget the vices of the other. It is the wastes, the miscalculations, and the maladjustments grown rampant during booms that make inevitable the painful process of liquidation." As one might expect, the *Report* called on businesses to "check the feverish extremes of prosperity."[38] The federal government, working with trade and commercial associations, should "keep up [the] campaign for simplification of styles and varieties" and "advertise [the] advantages of planning and budgeting." Most important, during the heights of the business cycle, the government and associations should work together to promote the "advantages of withholding postponable projects," thereby creating reserve funds. During a recession, government would have to popularize the "advantage of undertaking some work for the future, especially work of high labor, low material content." It was hoped that these efforts would be combined with a policy on the part of the Federal Reserve and bankers' associations to grant "preferential treatment to loans for productive purposes."[39]

The popular press was making a case for countercyclical spending, albeit without the sophistication of the conference. For example, the *Nation* saw expansive public works as a necessary remedy to the soup kitchens: "While

---

37. *Report of the President's Conference on Unemployment,* 21, 22–23.
38. Ibid., 159.
39. Ibid., 163–65.

money is being prodigally sunk in dangerous armament, the country is in need of roads, of housing, of many public works. . . . Now it is the time of times to undertake such projects. The labor directly employed would affect only a comparatively few trades, but it would throw a switch which would before long start a great many other wheels turning."[40] The conference appealed to the self-interest of the businessman and the government official when it presented its case: "When public works are done in greatest volume during periods of active industry the same men and material are being competed for by both public and private employers. The inevitable result is to raise the height of the crest of the wave of cyclical business inflation and to cause a greater crash when the heightened wave breaks, as it always does."[41] It was far more prudent to defer such projects until a downturn in the business cycle, which would be possible because such programs are "peculiarly suited for consideration as large undertakings covering a long period and capable of elasticity of execution to synchronize with cycles of business depression." Such countercyclical use of public-works spending could exert "a powerful stabilizing influence."[42] It was believed that expanded public-works programs during downturns in the business cycle could result in direct and indirect stimulation. The effects of the public spending would reverberate throughout the economy through a "multiplying effect."[43]

The conference extensively addressed the question of funding countercyclical public-works spending. It developed two competing recommendations. Explored most exhaustively was the option of holding government surpluses in reserve during periods of expansion and then using the reserves to fund public works during periods of contraction. On the assumption that "the year of depression . . . occurs once in about 10 years," the conference recommended that federal, state, and municipal agencies defer at least 10 percent of their average public-works expenditures and place them in reserve. This money was to be released when the Commerce Department provided statistical indicators revealing that the depression year had arrived.[44] This method of funding was presented along with a discussion of the ease of borrowing on bond markets during recessions. The conference concluded that "the credit of a well-managed city or State . . . is less affected by a business depression than the credit or private corporations. Indeed, the supply of loanable credit for investment

40. "More Soup Kitchens?" *Nation,* January 26, 1921, 108.
41. *Report of the President's Conference on Unemployment,* 96.
42. Ibid., 97, 96.
43. Ibid., 103.
44. Ibid., 99.

in municipal bonds is often greatest when industrial and railroad corporations are unable to obtain credit at maximum rates." As a result, "[n]ot only can municipalities borrow more favorably than private borrowers in bad times, but by timing their public work during periods of inactive business and relative unemployment they can also secure a more plentiful and regular supply of materials and labor as an important economy in construction."[45]

In any event, Hoover and the conference believed in the need to identify worthy public-works projects that could be set in motion efficiently and quickly once statistical indicators provided objective evidence of economic downturn. The conference recommended that governments move quickly to prepare for the next downturn in the business cycle. "Public works can not be expanded in large volume on short notice because of the time required for preparing plans, authorizing loans, selling bonds, etc." While construction was to be deferred until recession, officials were cautioned "not [to] defer appropriation for planning and engineering of any work authorized." Moreover, they were advised that public works must be "on a 'commercial' basis, not a 'relief' basis, otherwise waste will result." Moreover, it was suggested that they should consider only those works that would normally be undertaken. There was, in short, no support for make-work programs as a means of providing relief.[46]

It is important to emphasize that the conference did not envision management of the business cycle as primarily the responsibility of the federal government. Indeed, according to the *Report,* the federal government was responsible for some $125 million in public-works construction, compared with $675 million at the state and municipal levels.[47] To be certain, the federal government would continue to fund public works. However, its key responsibility would be mobilizing state and municipal governments and resources. A federal agency—either the Bureau of the Budget or a new Department of Public Works—could coordinate state, county, and municipal efforts and promote the development of sound statistics on business activity and levels of unemployment, which could facilitate spending decisions. However, as Herbert Hoover remarked at the close of the conference:

45. Ibid., 97.
46. Ibid., 98–99; William J. Barber, *From New Era to New Deal: Herbert Hoover, the Economists, and American Economic Policy, 1921–1933* (Cambridge: Cambridge University Press, 1985), 15–21.
47. *Report of the President's Conference on Unemployment,* 103. See "Mobilizing Against Unemployment," *Outlook,* October 19, 1921, 243, and Karen Vega, "Deficit Spending and Relief: A Personal History," unpublished manuscript, n.d.

You have laid out a plan. The plan has been willingly accepted by a large section of the country, and you have erected the machinery to pursue that work, and we will see if we can not get through this crisis without calling on the funds in the public purse for support and subsistence of our unemployed. Whether we can succeed in that will depend greatly upon the coordination and cooperation that we can figure from industries and civic bodies of the United States. That this is a problem for voluntary organization is consonant with the American spirit and American institutions. If we can not secure its solution in that direction we shall have made a distinct step backward in the progress of this country. It is therefore vital that you who return for a term to your own sections of the United States should insist, in season and out of season, that this is a problem that rests upon the voluntary and neighborly action of the American people.[48]

It was hoped that local subcommittees of the conference could be created in every city with a population over twenty thousand. They would play an important role in convincing state and municipal governments of the benefits of public-works investment during periods of contraction and in encouraging business to consider similar policies.

The approach adopted by the Unemployment Conference strongly reflected Hoover's broader vision of economic governance (see Chapter 4). As Evan Metcalf notes: "Hoover still hoped to achieve stability through action by decentralized business decision makers, but the government had a vital role to play in supplying guidance for corporate planners. Indeed the development of government economic statistics in the United States cannot be understood outside the context of this approach to reducing instability." The committees established as a result of the conference "provided a model for future joint public-private economic policy formation, cementing the close relationship among business leaders, policy-oriented academics, and government officials that had grown up during the war, and that outlasted the substance of Hoover's program."[49]

Hoover strongly backed the strategy of countercyclical public-works spending and used every opportunity to win converts. He did so with some initial success. By November 15, 1921, the governors of thirty states an-

48. *Report of the President's Conference on Unemployment,* 34.
49. Evan B. Metcalf, "Secretary Hoover and the Emergence of Macroeconomic Management," *Business History Review* 49, no. 1 (1975): 61.

nounced their plans for road projects that would employ fifteen thousand, financed through bond sales. Beyond the impetus for public works, "the other favorable result of the President's conference seems to be its beneficial effect upon employers who feel an increased responsibility for unemployment."[50] To further study the questions addressed by the conference, Hoover created a Committee on Unemployment and Business Cycles that consisted of leaders of business and industry and was chaired by Owen D. Young, vice-chairman of General Electric. Funded with a $50,000 grant from the Carnegie Corporation, the committee contracted with the National Bureau of Economic Research to conduct a study of the 1921 depression. On the basis of the study, the Committee on Unemployment and Business Cycles published its reports and recommendations in May 1923. Its recommendations echoed those of the original conference report. It called for restrictive monetary policy to restrain expansion, a long-term public-works policy directed toward the alleviation of unemployment over the business cycle, and the production and dissemination of more statistical information that could prove useful to corporations in making investment and production decisions. Although the results of the official report were widely disseminated and popularized, there is little evidence that the business community gave the recommendations widespread consideration.[51]

The debates over a new economic strategy coincided with changes in the management of the budget. A Bureau of the Budget was created under the Budget and Accounting Act of 1921. By providing the president with budgetary authority—an area traditionally guarded by Congress—the act constituted a concrete transfer of power to the executive. The Bureau of the Budget, located in the Treasury but under the direction of the president, provided the president with administrative support in assessing agency claims and developing appropriations targets. The creation of presidential budgetary authority was the realization of recommendations that dated back to the Taft presidency and the 1912 recommendations of the President's Commission of Economy and Efficiency. Presumably, the bureau could facilitate the use of countercyclical public-works spending.[52]

With a new fiscal strategy and new institutions of budgetary control, one

50. *Nation,* January 11, 1922, 30–31.

51. Metcalf, "Secretary Hoover and the Emergence of Macroeconomic Management," 73–77. See Guy Alchon, *The Invisible Hand of Planning: Capitalism, Social Science, and the State in the 1920s* (Princeton, N.J.: Princeton University Press, 1985), chap. 6.

52. Peri E. Arnold, *Making the Managerial Presidency: Comprehensive Reorganization Planning, 1905– 1980* (Princeton, N.J.: Princeton University Press, 1986), 53–55, 37–51.

might have anticipated rapid movement toward the creation of a fiscal-policy-making capacity. However, there were three notable impediments to policy change that would prove decisive. First, for academic economists who viewed the business cycle as a natural expression of economic change, attempts to control it were misguided. It would take the new set of theoretical relationships introduced during the Keynesian revolution to reveal the limits of self-equilibrating markets and legitimize fiscal activism. Second, the economic concerns of the 1920s were focused on the costs of the war. The war resulted in a dramatic expansion of the national debt, which stood at $24.3 billion in 1920, as compared with $1.2 billion four years earlier. The war forced an increase in taxation beyond what most believed prudent given the limited responsibilities of the national government. Following the Armistice, taxes did not return to prewar levels, nor did policy makers gain much more discretion over their spending decisions. The primary concern for Congress and Treasury Secretary Andrew Mellon was debt repayment, followed closely by further tax reductions. Indeed, the federal government ran a surplus every year from 1920 through 1930, reducing the debt to $16.2 billion.[53] Third, the government played a relatively small role in the economy during the 1920s. Spending at all levels of government claimed a bare 5.5 percent of the gross national product—a figure that fell to 3.2 percent by 1929. While the federal government was able to spend at far greater levels than the state and local levels during the war, this emergency violation of federalist principles could not be promoted under conditions of "normalcy." Thus, the new strategies of fiscal management were never enacted—a failure with consequences that would become clear only with the onset of the depression.[54]

Of course, the macroeconomic strategy articulated by Hoover, the Unemployment Conference, and the Committee on Unemployment and Business Cycles envisaged a central role for businesses and trade associations. Presumably, these features of the strategy could be engaged regardless of the macroeconomic priorities of the national government. However, two familiar problems arose. First, the strategy depended on the willingness of businesses to absorb financial sacrifices in order to maintain their workers during times of economic decline, thereby contributing to the management of the business cycle. Individual concerns might find it profitable to reduce the number of employees during a downturn, particularly if other corporations followed

53. *Statistical History of the United States,* series Y 254–57.
54. Morton Keller, *Regulating a New Economy: Public Policy and Economic Change in America, 1900–1933* (Cambridge: Harvard University Press, 1990), 218–19.

Hoover's recommended investment policies. This, of course, created a perfect example of the free-rider problem, in which individual rationality would suggest behaviors that, when aggregated, could effectively undermine the welfare of all parties. Second, there were technical difficulties. Even if businesses and state and municipal governments would be willing to engage in the prescribed policies during economic downturns, clear indicators of economic performance were not widely available—a problem that had been quite evident during the war. As Metcalf explains:

> A key gap in the information necessary for macroeconomic management was the absence of an internally consistent, up-to-date measure of the performance of the economy as a whole. There were a host of business "barometers," reflecting the demand for economic information. The procedures by which their components were weighted and combined, which were critical for relating individual industries' movements to the whole, however, were often unsophisticated or even trade secrets. . . . Annual estimates of Gross National Product did not become regularly available, with less than a year's lag, until 1935.[55]

Herbert Hoover continued his efforts to create this associational system for the remainder of the decade. The relative stability of the economy during the decade and the factors discussed above hindered the creation of a fiscal policy capacity along the lines suggested by the Unemployment Conference. As Chapter 8 reveals, the great tragedy was that Hoover—the chief advocate of this plan for managing the business cycle—would govern during the Great Depression with few policy tools to draw on. Of course, the unwillingness of businesses to abide by their agreements to retain employees following the market crash strongly suggests that the system in question would have collapsed under the weight of the depression regardless of Hoover's success.

Monetary Management and the Quest for Stability

The Federal Reserve Act was passed in 1913, and the Federal Reserve Banks opened for business in November 1914. Under the organic legislation, the Fed was given a limited array of tools to affect monetary activities. Member

---

55. Metcalf, "Secretary Hoover and the Emergence of Macroeconomic Management," 78.

banks were required to submit to Federal Reserve oversight and observe reserve requirements. The Fed could use reserve requirements and the discount window to affect the amount of money in circulation. However, its mandate to facilitate commercial activity did not direct it to use monetary policy in a restrictive fashion and lean against the wind—not that such a directive would have had any practical meaning: during the first several years of the Fed's existence, it was entangled in the exigencies of war. As Harold L. Reed noted in his 1936 study of the Federal Reserve: "[P]olicy prior to 1921 had to be conceived with large regard for treasury requirements, and it was not until the effects of war (not treasury) finance had tended to disappear that the period significantly 'formative' for peace-time operation could begin. As long as war-time necessities were operating little could be done to determine the place the Reserve Banks should occupy in the country's financial machinery and the relative importance in the future of their various powers."[56]

The Federal Reserve was engaged with some of the problems associated with the war in Europe before the United States officially declared war in April 1917. These efforts were largely limited to addressing the stress placed on the international payments system and managing a large loan for cotton producers, who were faced with a record harvest in 1914 and a shortage of shipping, which limited access to markets. Once war was declared, however, attention turned to facilitating the funding of the American Expeditionary Force and allied forces. To this end, the Federal Reserve managed the sale of the five Liberty-bond issues through Liberty Loan committees in each of the Federal Reserve districts, headed by the respective Federal Reserve Bank governors, and facilitated the sale of bonds by promoting loans to the public for bond purchases. In addition, the Fed, as noted above, attempted to regulate corporate access to securities markets through its Capital Issues Committee, which sought to direct resources into essential industries and minimize the conflicts between government bond drives and corporate securities issues. Finally, the Federal Reserve served as the agent for the Treasury in examining and judging applications to ship coin, bullion, and currency to foreign nations, the decision resting on whether the shipment would aid the enemy and whether the resulting imports would be of sufficient worth and necessity to justify the reduction of the gold supply in time of war.[57]

As a direct result of the war, the United States was transformed into a

56. Harold L. Reed, *Federal Reserve Policy, 1921–1930* (New York: McGraw-Hill, 1930), 2.
57. David C. Elliott, "The Federal Reserve System, 1914–29," in *The Federal Reserve System,* ed. Herbert V. Prochnow (New York: Harper & Brothers, 1960), 298–304.

creditor nation with a gold supply that stood at almost twice the prewar level. This gold, combined with the Fed's reduction in reserve requirements for member banks, drove a dramatic expansion of credit. Even if the immediate postwar reduction in war-related production led to a minor slump, this was quickly eliminated by foreign demand for American exports and pent-up consumer demand in domestic markets. Although the Federal Reserve Board was concerned with the growing inflationary forces, it successfully placed the Victory Loan at relatively low interest rates. With the concerns of Treasury financing met, the Federal Reserve Banks turned to the issue of prices: by 1920, wholesale prices stood at more than double their 1914 levels. The Fed increased the discount rate to 6 percent in January, albeit without the desired impact. However, an increase to 7 percent in May was sufficient to end the expansion, as the economy fell rapidly into a depression that was severe but relatively brief. Quite predictably, the combination of a budget surplus and interest-rate increases induced a sharp decline. By the middle of 1921, industrial production had dropped 35 percent, and unemployment had jumped from 1.4 percent (1919) to 11.7 percent. The five million jobless workers, the thirty thousand bankruptcies, and almost half a million farm foreclosures stood in stark contrast to the economic boom of the war years. Fortunately, the decline in production coincided with a 50 percent reduction in wholesale prices, which partially offset the drop in production. The new price structure, combined with unmet consumer demands, brought rapid recovery.[58] Following the 1920–21 depression, the economy entered a new expansionary phase. At the same time, the experience of the war and the immediate postwar depression led members of the Federal Reserve to turn serious attention to the question of the Fed's role in the economy.[59]

Some critics accused the Federal Reserve System of a conspiracy to deflate the farm economy by restricting credit.[60] The attacks prompted the central bank to adopt a highly defensive posture. The Federal Reserve's 1921 *Annual Report* stated: "During the past year, many things have been said and written regarding the Federal Reserve System which are calculated to create entirely false impressions." After describing the core principles of the Federal Reserve Act, the *Annual Report* went on to argue that the Fed could not be held

---

58. Fearon, *War, Prosperity, and Depression,* 15–18; Robert Sobel, *The Age of the Giant Corporations: A Microeconomic History of American Business, 1914–1970* (Westport, Conn.: Greenwood Press, 1972), 25; Paul Studenski and Herman E. Krooss, *Financial History of the United States* (New York: McGraw-Hill, 1952), 330.

59. Studenski and Krooss, *Financial History of the United States,* 305–7.

60. E. A. Goldenweiser, *American Monetary Policy* (New York: McGraw-Hill, 1951), 136.

responsible for intentionally inducing the contraction, because its activities were purely a response to business activities: "There are some who appear to have an impression that the Federal Reserve Board has the power to expand or contract the currency of the country at will. . . . An increase or decrease in the volume of Federal Reserve notes outstanding is not the result of any preordained policy or premeditated design, for the volume of Federal Reserve notes in circulation depends entirely upon the activity of business or upon the kind of activity which calls for currency rather than book credits."[61]

Open-market operations (i.e., the sale and purchase of securities) were authorized in the Federal Reserve Act, although it was generally believed that the discount rate would provide the most important tool of credit policy. This reflected a number of factors, including the lack of theory supporting the creative use of open-market actions, a lack of experience with monetary management, and a realistic recognition of the small federal debt and the limited availability of government securities in the years before U.S. entry into World War I. However, even in the period 1919–20, the Fed's holdings of government securities remained quite limited, at about $300 million. In 1921 and 1922, the Federal Reserve Banks expanded their holdings of securities to increase their earnings in the unstable environment that followed the end of the war. As a result of the decline in 1920–21, the Federal Reserve accumulated a large sum of idle assets. In hopes of realizing greater profits on their portfolios, district banks purchased paper and government securities. Between October 1921 and May 1922, the Reserve Banks purchased some $400 million in government securities.[62] It was discovered at that time that when the Federal Reserve Banks acquired government securities, member banks borrowed less from the Fed.[63] Reductions in Fed holdings had the opposite effect, stimulating a greater reliance on the Fed as a lender of last resort. If open-market operations could have an impact on the lending of banks and the availability of credit in the economy, they could provide an important tool for limiting economic fluctuations.

This insight could have major ramifications, assuming that the organizational infrastructure was in place to translate the insight into practice. In 1921 and 1922, the Federal Reserve's open-market activities were essentially an aggregation of the decisions made by the individual Reserve Banks seeking to increase their earnings. As W. Randolph Burgess explained, this created

61. Quoted in Friedman and Schwartz, *A Monetary History of the United States,* 249–50.

62. Ibid., 251 n. 15; Shultz and Caine, *Financial Development of the United States,* 484–85.

63. C. Richard Youngdahl, "Open Market Operations," in *The Federal Reserve System,* ed. Herbert V. Prochnow (New York: Harper & Brothers, 1960), 116–22.

immediate problems: "Each Bank purchased and sold bankers' bills and government securities in accordance with the decision of its own directors, and executed these orders through whatever channels it chose. One consequence of this procedure was constant danger that the Reserve Banks would be raising prices against themselves by competing with one another in the open market, and, moreover, by creating an artificial market for government securities, would complicate the Treasury's program of financing."[64] Although Benjamin Strong, governor of the New York Federal Reserve Bank (and the de facto head of the Federal Reserve System following the appointment of Daniel Cissinger as governor), tried to convince his fellow governors of the importance of coordinating the purchase and sale of acceptances and securities, open-market activities remained relatively uncoordinated until 1922. At that time, Treasury concerns over the impact of uncoordinated bank purchases and sales on the money market and over the yield on short-term Treasury notes led it to call on the Fed to do more to coordinate its securities purchases and sales. To this end, in June 1922 the governors formed an open-market committee, consisting of the governors of the New York, Boston, Philadelphia, and Chicago Reserve Banks, to coordinate their open-market activities. The governor of the Cleveland Federal Reserve Bank was added in October 1922. Quite naturally, the committee was placed under the leadership of Benjamin Strong.[65]

In 1923, the Federal Reserve Board's Division of Analysis and Research determined that the impact of the Fed's open-market activities in 1922 had been offset by movement in the discount rate. The findings led to the simple conclusion that the open-market activities and discount rate had to be coordinated if the Fed was going to exercise meaningful control over credit. To achieve this coordination, the Federal Reserve replaced the open-market committee with an Open Market Investment Committee (the precursor of the Federal Open Market Committee), to direct "the time, manner, character, and volume of open-market investments purchased by the Reserve banks . . . with primary regard to accommodation of commerce and business, and to the effect of such purchases and sales on the general credit situation."[66] The deci-

64. W. Randolph Burgess, *The Reserve Banks and the Money Market* (New York: Harper & Brothers, 1936), 240.

65. Charles O. Hardy, *Credit Policies of the Federal Reserve System* (Washington, D.C.: Brookings Institution, 1932), 38–39. David C. Whellock, *The Strategy and Consistency of Federal Reserve Monetary Policy, 1924–1933* (Cambridge: Cambridge University Press, 1991), 15–16.

66. Hardy, *Credit Policies of the Federal Reserve System*, 39–40. Shultz and Caine, *Financial Development of the United States*, 586; Eugene Nelson White, *The Regulation and Reform of the American Banking System, 1900–1929* (Princeton, N.J.: Princeton University Press, 1983), 115–25.

sion to use open-market activities, along with discount rates, to stabilize the economy marked an important turning point in the history of the Federal Reserve, even if its efforts to stabilize the economy were tempered by doubts regarding the magnitude of its impact and concerns over the use of additional funds either for productive activity or speculation. However, the new committee was little more than the old committee—its old members under the continued leadership of Benjamin Strong—with expanded responsibilities. In the fall of 1923, further movement was made toward strengthening the Fed's open-market activities through the creation of an open-market investment account that allocated funds among the Reserve Banks on the basis of a formula that took account of the size and holdings of the individual banks. The size of the account could be increased or decreased at the discretion of the committee and the Federal Reserve Board. It was hoped that such an account would unify the open-market activities of the member banks.[67] But before we address the performance of the Federal Reserve, let us consider the debates over the role of monetary policy in managing the economy.

The Monetary-Policy Debate

The new institutional apparatus at the Fed was created at a time when the prevailing understanding of monetary policy was undergoing significant revision. The new thinking concerning the positive role of the Federal Reserve found its clearest expression in the writings and activities of Yale economist Irving Fisher and fellow members of the Stable Money Association. The association was formed in 1921 "to ascertain the most effective method of preventing the vast, though subtle evils arising from unsound and unstable money, and to promote a better understanding thereof, in the expectation that crystallized public opinion will result in constructive congressional action." It contained an impressive list of intellectuals, business executives, and key figures in the economics profession, including John M. Clark, Wesley Claire Mitchell, George Soule, and Henry Wallace.[68] Fisher and his colleagues promoted the quantity theory of money—a well-established economic argu-

---

67. Burgess, *The Reserve Banks and the Money Market*, 242; Youngdahl, "Open Market Operations," 120.

68. The quote from the organization's charter and an extensive list of officers are presented in *Stabilization: Hearings Before the Committee on Banking and Currency, House of Representatives on H.R. 7895*, 69th Cong., 1st sess., 1927, 108–9.

ment whereby the quantity of money was the primary factor affecting price levels.[69]

The quantity theory of money was rather straightforward and served, potentially, as an important intellectual justification for the expansion of Federal Reserve duties. Under the quantity theory of money, one can explain changes in price levels (P) through the interplay of the money in circulation (M), the velocity (V) of monetary circulation, and the volume of trade (T). Stated as an equation: $MV/T = P$. If one accepts the equation as correct, the role of the Federal Reserve becomes relatively clear. Policy makers cannot freely manipulate the volume of trade in both directions in the hope of changing the price level. Likewise, public policy can do little to shape the velocity, or circulation, of money. The only remaining lever for changing the price level is the quantity of money. The Federal Reserve, it was argued, should use its power over discount rates, reserve requirements, and, most important, open-market activities to maintain price stability, thereby limiting fluctuations in the business cycle.[70]

Responding to the dogged advocacy of Fisher and his compatriots and sweeping concerns over the capacity of policy makers to promote economic stability, the House Committee on Banking and Currency held hearings in 1926 and 1927 to consider amendments to the Federal Reserve Act that would direct the Fed to promote stabilization as a primary goal. The proposed bill, the Goldsborough Bill (H.R. 7895), would have directed the Federal Reserve to "promot[e] a stable price level for commodities in general," emphasizing this task by noting that "all of the powers of the Federal reserve system shall be used for promoting stability in the price level."[71] The Goldsborough Bill, and variations on it, had been discussed periodically since 1922. However, at the 1926–27 hearings, the notion of directing the Federal Reserve to promote price stability as its primary goal received extensive consideration. A mélange of prominent economists and members of the Federal Reserve testified on the question of stabilization. Their statements provide an excellent summary of the prevailing arguments for and against active management of the money supply.

Irving Fisher was a careful observer of Federal Reserve activities and the credit market. He recognized that Benjamin Strong's experiences and his own theoretical reflections pointed to similar conclusions. He testified in support

69. Barber, *From New Era to New Deal*, 23–27.
70. Hardy, *Credit Policies of the Federal Reserve System*, 206.
71. *Hearings on H.R. 7895*, 1.

of amending the Federal Reserve Act, since the new legislation would be in keeping with what the Fed was already striving to do. It would merely "authorize and direct the Federal Reserve Board to do what they are doing and commend them for doing what they have been doing, and prevent them from being tempted by any interests in this country from doing otherwise. They could then say, 'The law says we shall not have deflation or inflation.' "[72] Through the active use of the discount rate, open-market operations, and moral suasion, the Fed could maintain a stable currency, thus ending the pattern of inflation and deflation that promoted broader economic instability.

For Fisher and others, monetary stabilization carried important economic and political justifications. While Fisher recognized the demands placed on the Federal Reserve during the war, he believed that a provision along the lines that were being debated might have led it to prevent the postwar inflation and the brief depression that followed. Monetary management could tame the fluctuations in the business cycle that create unemployment, deflation, and bankruptcies, followed by inflation and speculative investments.[73] As Fisher noted: "You have unemployment following deflation quite regularly. . . . Wherever we have index numbers to show the changes in price levels and statistics of unemployment, we find this relationship between instability of money and unemployment." Moreover, the redistributive impact and effects on the purchasing power of the dollar could be the source of political instability. Fisher explained:

> Whenever there is inflation you will find socialism thrives, because the socialist, with his suspicious mind, believes that the great corporations are grabbing, and thus you have the word "profiteer" and other nicknames applied to people into whose laps fall the profits which inflation takes away from others; and, on the other hand, you will find when there is deflation the farmers and others blaming Rockefeller and Morgan and others personifying Wall Street as the cause of their troubles when as a matter of fact the cause is an impersonal one. One of those unjust accusations that the creditor class controls the price level, or the debtor class, and you have the evils of distrust and suspicion and ill feeling and class warfare and sometimes bloodshed.

Fisher concluded: "This is not a radical measure, therefore, that is proposed here; it is a way to fight radicalism. It is one of the most conservative measures

72. Ibid., 66.
73. See Hardy, *Credit Policies of the Federal Reserve System,* 204.

you have had. It is not a hair-brained dreamer's idea; it is something that will prevent the kind of upset that they had in Russia."[74]

Fisher was not the only one to connect monetary management and political stability. John R. Commons, for example, testified that his concerns over the effects of instability on labor led him to support a monetary rule embedded in legislation. He noted that the "fluctuation of prices" is "the most serious of the evils that affect labor in this country. It, first, by this inflation of prices, demoralizes labor; they lose all sense of responsibility for their jobs. Then in the deflation it pauperizes them. So, we have an alternation of demoralization and pauperization which affects our labor class owing only to this fluctuation of prices."[75] Similarly, a number of witnesses testified on behalf of farm interests and suggested that amendments to the Federal Reserve Act would play an important role in providing stability for the farm economy by preventing panics. Andrew Shearer, representing the Kansas State Farm Bureau, the Farmers' Union of Kansas, and the Kansas Grange, noted: "[I]t would be a wonderful assurance to us men, isolated as we are, scattered on the farms of the United States of America . . . that here at last, after so long a time, is a power to prevent panics, to prevent lowering our price level, to prevent ruining our business, which has been done so often."[76] Thus, economists and representatives of various economic interest groups argued that the scientific management of the money supply by the Federal Reserve provided the key to economic and political stability. Given that it could be executed with the tools and data on hand and that it had, in recent years, become the Federal Reserve's practice, the justification for amending the Federal Reserve Act seemed irresistible.

In this context, it is perhaps surprising that the strongest objections came from within the Federal Reserve System. The greatest and most influential opposition to the amendments came from New York Fed governor Strong. He agreed with Fisher that the Federal Reserve had furthered the goal of price stability in the past several years. As he noted: "I personally think that the administration of the Federal reserve system since the reaction of 1921 has been just as nearly directed as reasonably human wisdom could direct it toward that very object." Nevertheless, Strong opened his testimony by noting his concerns over the prudence of legislatively assigning the goal of price

74. *Hearings on H.R. 7895*, 62, 56, 64.
75. Ibid., 1075.
76. *Stabilization: Hearings Before the Committee on Banking and Currency, House of Representatives on H.R. 11806*, 70th Cong., 1st. sess., 1928, 203.

stabilization to the Federal Reserve: "Is it possible that the farmers of the country will interpret this as an effort by Congress to place the responsibility upon the Federal reserve system for attending to the particular problem of prices in which they are interested? . . . Well, if this language is employed in an amendment to the Federal reserve act, may not that somewhat intensify that belief by the farmers that the Federal reserve system can exercise some power over the prices of a particular commodity?"[77]

Strong's key objection, however, was tied to his belief that monetary management was more an art than a science, one that relied heavily on the experience and judgment of central bankers. As Strong explained: "[T]here is no magic formula that can be introduced into the Federal reserve act to control prices. You can not eliminate human judgment in the administration of these matters. . . . Our examination of the past produces the most accurate knowledge of past action and reaction, but when it comes to a decision as to what we are going to do for the future, then just human judgment has got to govern. There is no mathematical formula for the administration of the Federal Reserve System or the regulation of prices."[78] Legislation of the kind proposed, Strong feared, would eliminate the discretion of the Federal Reserve Board on the spurious belief in the existence of some simple technical guide to monetary policy, be it an economic formula or an index. Strong wanted to maximize the Fed's discretion rather than place Congress in the business of monetary management.

Despite Fisher's active advocacy throughout the 1920s, the independence of the Federal Reserve was deemed too important to allow for political direction of its activities. Moreover, at least until the stock-market crash of the 1929, economic performance was positive enough to attenuate anxieties over the Federal Reserve's capacity to manage credit free from new legislation. If one believed, as many suggested, that the price level was driven by a host of forces over which the Fed could exercise little control (e.g., poor harvests, new technologies), the wisdom of placing a legislatively defined rule over the judgment of experienced bankers seemed questionable. Thus, while the exigencies of stabilization provided an opportunity for the careful examination of the Federal Reserve's credit policy and revealed the new theoretical underpinnings of monetary policy, it did not lead to the passage of new legislation.[79]

77. *Hearings on H.R. 7895*, 307, 294.
78. Ibid., 302.
79. Barber, *From New Era to New Deal*, 59–61.

Federal Reserve Performance

Interpretations of Federal Reserve performance during the 1920s and early 1930s vary wildly, assigning to the Fed differing amounts of responsibility for the Great Depression. What was the Federal Reserve's policy during the 1920s? Some suggest that the Fed exercised very little discretion during the period. Rather than use policy to promote stabilization, it is argued, the Federal Reserve pursued unrestrained expansion largely in response to political pressures. If prosperity could be promoted through easier credit, it might be pursued indefinitely through ongoing expansion via the Fed's purchase of government securities. This expansionary policy—supported wholeheartedly by Coolidge, Hoover, and European allies fearful of the potential impact of tight credit—fueled the speculative boom of the decade. As John Hicks explains:

> What were the banks to do with all the money they had on hand? They loaded up freely with government securities, and so added still more to the credit they could make available. They lent to investors in stocks and bonds, which they took as collateral, with much the same result; they provided the necessary backing for installment financing, another principal means of promoting the boom; and they underwrote long-term real estate investments to an alarming degree. Easy credit also contributed to heavy purchases by American investors of European securities—over a billion dollars a year during the Coolidge ascendancy. Americans thus furnished Europeans the extra money they needed to buy American goods; in so doing they contributed greatly to both the European and American booms, but they also added dangerously to the imposing volume of uncollectable debts.[80]

The Fed's policy of easy credit had this impact only after it affected the behavior of corporations and, in turn, banks. Because businesses realized high profits and had access to a rapidly growing market for corporate stocks and bonds, they reduced their demand for commercial loans. Thus the banks simultaneously had to pay interest on an ever growing pool of demand deposits and lacked the means to recycle the funds at a sufficiently high rate of return via loans to corporate borrowers. They therefore used their funds to expand securities investments and loans made for real estate and securities collateral. "Member banks of the Federal Reserve System increased their investments by

80. Hicks, *Republican Ascendancy,* 109.

two thirds between 1921 and 1929, more than doubled their loans on securities in the same period, and expanded their loans on urban real estate about 3½ times. All other loans—mainly commercial—remained stationary in these nine years."[81] In the end, it is argued, the easy credit and high levels of speculative investment created a financial system that was highly vulnerable to shocks. Indeed, the fragility of a financial system built on easy money and speculative investments provided the key link between the crash of 1929 and the Great Depression.

There is another possible interpretation of Federal Reserve performance that deserves some attention, in large part because it forces different conclusions concerning the role of the Federal Reserve in the onset of the depression. Simply put, one might argue that stabilization was not the primary goal of the Federal Reserve during the 1920s. Hence, any interpretation of performance associated with that goal misinterprets the intentions of those involved. This position is struck primarily by those who see the Fed as struggling to maintain the gold standard throughout the 1920s. In essence, it is argued that members of the Fed were skeptical that they could effectively promote domestic price stability through the manipulation of discount rates and open-market activities. Rather, they focused on maintaining a stable gold standard and subordinated any domestic policy goals to this larger international objective when the two came into conflict. Under this interpretation, the question is not, Why did the Fed fail to exercise consistency in its stabilization efforts? The question is, Why did the Fed favor maintenance of the gold standard over stabilization?[82]

Hicks's position is in the minority, and most interpretations of Fed performance in the 1920s recognize the success of Fed policy and its evolving appreciation of the ways in which credit policy could be used to promote stabilization. Despite the concerns over the Fed and stabilization, there is evidence that the Fed engaged in some limited open-market activities to counter the economic impact of the influx of gold into the American economy during the 1920s and to stabilize the business cycle. The Fed's 1923 *Annual Report* emphasized the need to coordinate open-market activities as part of a general credit policy. However, in the Fed's "Guides to Credit Policy," it presented decision rules full of ambiguities. The Fed argued that no simple rule could adequately guide policy. Rather, decisions had to be based on complete evidence. As Milton Friedman and Anna Jacobson Schwartz observe in

81. Soule, *Prosperity Decade*, 155–56.
82. See Whellock, *The Strategy and Consistency of Federal Reserve Monetary Policy*.

their *Monetary History of the United States:* "Despite the skill and acuity with which this section of the report is written, it is yet most unsatisfactory as a guide to credit policy. . . . [It] offers little beyond glittering generalities instructing the men exercising the judgment to do the right thing at the right time with only the vaguest indications of what is the right thing to do."[83]

The Fed began purchasing securities in the open market in December 1923, thereby pumping money into the economy. As a result of this activity, the Federal Reserve Banks increased their holding of government securities from $84 million to $582 million. The Federal Reserve Bank of New York also reduced its rediscount rate from 4 to 3 percent. The easy-money policy of the Fed was a response to a minor downturn that was taking shape in winter of 1923–24, although the policy was also an attempt to reduce imports of foreign capital that would have impeded the return of Great Britain and Germany to the gold standard. In November 1924, with the economy expanding once again, the Federal Reserve Banks began disposing of securities, selling some $260 million worth by March of 1925. This, combined with an increase in the rediscount rate, suggests that the Fed was actively attempting to stabilize the business cycle.[84]

In 1927, the Federal Reserve responded in a similar manner to a business slowdown and financial circumstances in Europe. It promoted credit expansion through a reduction in the rediscount rate and an unprecedented purchase of bonds. The Fed's holdings of bonds increased by $270 million, exceeding $600 million by November. The easy-money policy, it was feared by many, was resulting in a wave of speculative buying on the stock market, which was clearly evident in the meteoric rise of prices on the exchanges. These fears resounded within the Fed. The Chicago Federal Reserve Bank, for example, refused to reduce its rediscount rate from 4 to 3.5 percent until it came under direct order from the board, at which time it complied with protest. Senator Carter Glass, author of the Federal Reserve Act, argued that the organic legislation did not provide for board determination of discount rates. Rather, the system provided for the district banks to set discount rates in response to local credit conditions, with the board exercising its power of "review and determination" only in response to a bank's failure to respond reasonably to these conditions. Nevertheless, the experience of the past several years had revealed to many the importance of coordination in discount rates.[85]

83. Friedman and Schwartz, *A Monetary History of the United States,* 253.
84. Studenski and Krooss, *Financial History of the United States,* 331–32.
85. Ibid., 333–34, and Goldenweiser, *American Monetary Policy,* 146–48.

Finally, by the beginning of 1928, the board responded to the speculative boom by restricting credit. In the first half of 1928, the Fed increased the rediscount rate and sold securities on the market, reducing its holding from $617 million to $235 million. Additional sales of $145 million took place in the first half of 1929. However, the board refused to approve any additional increases in the rediscount rate by the New York Fed. Rather than continue quantitative controls, it shifted to qualitative controls and attempted to restrict the Federal Reserve System's role in financing market speculation. Thus, in February 1929, it released a circular that instructed the member banks regarding the Federal Reserve Board's policy. It stated: "The Federal Reserve Act does not, in the opinion of the Federal Reserve Board, contemplate the use of the resources of the Federal Reserve Banks for the creation or extension of speculative credit. A member bank is not within its reasonable claims for rediscount facilities when it borrows either for the purpose of making speculative loans or for the purpose of maintaining speculative loans." Although the Fed's policy was clear, its impact was negligible.[86]

If the Federal Reserve was relatively successful in managing the economy for extended periods during the 1920s, one must question why the record deteriorated at the end of the decade, as the nation fell into depression. As one might expect, there are several competing positions. A first position focuses on the untimely death of Benjamin Strong and the change in leadership at the Federal Reserve, along with changes in the composition of the open-market committee. No less an authority than Irving Fisher repeatedly stated that the depression would not have occurred if Benjamin Strong had lived and continued to direct monetary policy through the New York Federal Reserve Bank. As Fisher testified before Congress: "I myself believe very strongly that this depression was almost wholly preventable, and that it would have been prevented if Governor Strong had lived." Fisher explained that Strong "discovered . . . that open-market operations would stabilize . . . and for 7 years he maintained a fairly steady price level in this country, and only a few of us knew what he was doing. His colleagues did not understand it."[87] Similarly, Carl Snyder, in his classic *Capitalism the Creator*, described Strong "as perhaps the most prescient financier this country had produced since Alexander Hamilton." He speculated: "[C]ould this man have had twelve months more of vigorous health, we might have ended the depression in 1930, and

86. Studenski and Krooss, *Financial History of the United States*, 333–34.
87. Irving Fisher quoted in Whellock, *The Strategy and Consistency of Federal Reserve Monetary Policy*, 2.

with this the long drawn out world crisis that so profoundly affected the ensuing political developments."[88]

Strong's leadership was considered particularly important given the structure of the Federal Reserve System. A compelling case can be made for the proposition that the institutional structure of the system and the lack of consensus over the proper objectives for the Fed's policies undermined its capacity to execute policy. As John Kenneth Galbraith notes: "The idea of a decentralized central bank—twelve central banks, each operating in some measure of undefined independence of its fellows and of Washington—did not yet seem a contradiction in terms. Rather, it looked a spacious and democratic idea, somehow appropriate to the spacious democracy which the banks would serve."[89] The decentralization of the Federal Reserve System robbed the board of the influence necessary for coherent policy making. The twelve district banks—particularly the New York bank—actively affected credit through their open-market and loan activities. This decentralization would have been less troublesome if there had been a theoretical orthodoxy guiding their behavior or a genuine consensus over policy goals. In fact, various parties debated whether the Fed should promote price stability, facilitate business expansion, or seek to curb speculation. When the district banks disagreed with the board, they frequently acted unilaterally, thus canceling out the impact of monetary policy. In 1929, for example, the Fed's attempt to limit credit by selling securities was partially nullified by an expansion of district-bank activities. Without institutional coherence or a common theoretical consensus, the Fed's capacity to manage the economy remained painfully limited.

Strong was replaced at the New York Federal Reserve Bank by George L. Harrison, who, according to Friedman and Schwartz, initially "operated in Strong's legacy and sought to exercise comparable leadership. As time went on, however, he reverted to his natural character, that of an extremely competent lawyer and excellent administrator, who wanted to see all sides of an issue and placed great value on conciliating opposing points of view and achieving harmony." He was "too reasonable to be truly single minded and dominant."[90] Harrison's appointment came at a critical time. With Strong's death, the Federal Reserve Board attempted to assert its authority but was simply too divided to do so effectively. Reflecting established institutional relations, the Reserve Banks were unwilling to follow the direction of the board. Thus,

88. Carl Snyder, *Capitalism the Creator: The Economic Foundations of Modern Industrial Society* (New York: Macmillan, 1940), 203.

89. Galbraith, *Money,* 134.

90. Friedman and Schwartz, *A Monetary History of the United States,* 414.

in March 1930, changes were made in the composition of the Open Market Investment Committee so that all twelve Reserve Banks would be represented, albeit with no one exercising the leadership formerly brought to bear by Strong. "Open market operations now depended upon a majority of twelve rather than of five governors and the twelve 'came instructed by their directors' rather than ready to follow the leadership of New York as the five had been when Strong was governor." The results were predictable. In the words of Friedman and Schwartz, "[T]hat shift stacked the cards heavily in favor of a policy of inaction and drift."[91]

The decade that began with the promising development—albeit, in outline only—of a proto-Keynesian policy of aggregate-demand management ended in depression. There was a paucity of public-policy tools appropriate for managing a crisis of any magnitude, and the state's fiscal presence in the economy remained quite modest. By necessity, aggregate-demand management had been fleshed out according to the prevailing doctrines of associationalism and business voluntarism. The ultimate success of any countercyclical policy would depend, as a result, on the voluntary actions of corporations willing to sacrifice their individual profitability in the hope that collective action would unite the business economy, and of subnational governments that had exercised the discipline necessary to maintain a reserve fund. Absent an economic crisis that would have legitimized a more forceful application of the strategy delineated by the 1921 Unemployment Conference, little more was possible. In the absence of a coherent fiscal policy, responsibility for macroeconomic management rested with the Federal Reserve and in the person of Benjamin Strong. Despite Strong's death, a growing restlessness among member banks, and the incapacity of the Federal Reserve Board to provide the requisite guidance, a stabilization rule such as that proposed in the Goldsborough and Strong Bills might have provided the necessary directive. However, the legislation never passed. As in other areas of postwar regulation, all was contingent on voluntarism and the goals adopted by individual officials. New strategies of economic management were never enacted—a failure with consequences that would become clear only with the onset of the depression.

91. Ibid.

PART III

Peacetime Mobilization and the Modern State

During the decade of the 1920s, the lessons of war were disseminated through a number of policy areas. As shown in previous chapters, a new emphasis was placed on associations. Hooverian associationalism rested on the assumption that many of the benefits of a more centralized system of planning could be achieved through the voluntary actions of private-sector associations. Business associations could be trusted to set standards and define fair-trade practices. They could be entrusted with creating reserve funds to be spent during downturns in the business cycle. Farm associations could be relied on to manage surpluses without the system of mandatory production controls, price guarantees, and government purchases envisioned by many of the more statist reform proposals. Corporations could address the labor problem by internalizing mechanisms of industrial relations and providing an expansive array of benefits to workers in exchange for ever greater levels of productivity.

The dense network of associations, the peculiar patterns of state-society relations, and the efforts to promote stability and efficiency were recognizably modern features of the new political economy. They were the legacy of war. While Hoover and others could foster high hopes concerning the performance of the new associational economy, this economy suffered a significant vulnerability stemming from one of the key distinctions between war and peace. Although participation in the war mobilization process was formally voluntary, a refusal to cooperate could foreclose access to capital, labor, transportation, and raw materials; active participation, in contrast, could prove highly profitable. Absent the emergency of war, voluntary participation became more than a formality, and the state retained far fewer coercive mechanisms to prevent defection. One could expect private-sector actors to participate only to the extent that the costs were exceeded by the benefits. As noted in earlier chapters, this was one of the key weaknesses of compensatory state building. Although the state would benefit from the administrative capacities of associations that were integrated into the policy process, it was vulnerable to exit and thus had to maintain some guarantee of material benefits. This reduced a good deal of discretion over policy. The guarantee of profitability would become impossible as the economy fell into depression, as shown in Chapter 8. Hoover witnessed the disintegration of a system he had worked to create through much of the 1920s, one that had once promised the benefits of planning and the virtues of voluntarism. Things would change, however, with the election of Roosevelt. At times drawing explicitly on the last great crisis, Roosevelt combined basic associationalist components with a greater set of state powers. This combination, comparable in many ways to what had been created a decade and one-half earlier, would be less subject to problems of exit. However, other problems of institutional design reasserted them-selves—problems that should have been anticipated given the experiences of war mobilization. Policies emerging from this organizational milieu would continue to contain a strong bias in support of the interests that had been integrated into the process, thereby introducing greater rigidity and conserva-tism. Policies would be used to promote transfer-seeking, enriching the orga-nized at the expense of the unorganized. They would impede technological dynamism wherever it threatened to undermine the position of interests inte-grated into the policy process. Finally, with authority delegated to the fringes of the state—that is, where private associations and public agencies over-lapped—political control inevitably flagged, opening questions of legitimacy. As the basic features of compensatory state building were extended beyond the emergency relief and recovery measures, they became permanent features of the New Deal regime and the modern welfare state.

8

Hoover, the Depression, and the Limits of Associationalism

> Mr. Hoover, setting upon the boldest economic experiment ever undertaken on so grand a scale in peace time, has sought to alter the arithmetic of prosperity and depression. . . . Mr. Hoover used the recent economic emergency, following the speculative collapse, as an occasion for turning the great corporations of the country as well as government agencies into vast economic test tubes for trying out his conceptions for replacing the regimen of blind hunches and narrow-visioned immediate self-interest with a new code of rationalized co-ordination and stabilization in the interest of the larger economic group. —Merryle Stanley Rukeyser, 1929

> The battle to set our economic machine in motion in this emergency takes new forms and new tactics from time to time. We used such emergency powers to win the war; we can use them to fight the depression, the misery and suffering from which are equally great. —Herbert Hoover, 1931

By the end of the 1920s, the American political economy looked far different from that at any other time in U.S. history. A new associational order had been constructed out of the models and experiences of war mobilization. In business regulation, agricultural policy, industrial relations, and economic policy making, new assumptions concerning the positive role of the state were combined with a universe of new economic associations, new policy tools, and a wealth of experience gained from the earlier mobilization effort. Increasingly, associations were asked to play a central role in managing and coordinating the affairs of their members, with an eye to solving some vexing problems. As noted earlier, this was a process of compensatory state building. That is, underdeveloped government agencies sought to compensate for their lack of administrative capacities by appending to the state those of private-sector associations. Hoover could give this form of state building an ideological justification: it could provide some of the benefits of bureaucratic planning without the heavy hand of public bureaucracies. However, one should not lose sight of the practical necessity. Without adopting this path, it would have been impossible to introduce the period's key initiatives.

Interests were willing to participate in many of the associational ventures because it made economic sense to do so. During a period of economic expansion, participation carried few costs relative to the benefits. Of course, one might arrive at the same conclusions concerning war mobilization. When one looks beneath the patriotic rhetoric that accompanied the war, one discovers that business participation in the war effort proved extremely profitable. The key question was whether such a system could survive under conditions of economic decline. One might evaluate any planning process, in part, on its capacity to impose losses, in pursuit of long-term objectives, on the parties integrated into the planning apparatus.[1] Would associationalism—a voluntary form of planning—be able to impose such losses, or would participants defect as soon as the economic rationale for participation dissolved? To the extent that corporations were willing to sacrifice profitability for macroeconomic stability, the system might successfully withstand fluctuations in the business cycle. This was Hoover's hope—one derived from his optimistic reading of American culture and his experience with voluntary associations. However, the limits of the system were tested after 1929. The depression drew attention, quite naturally, to the other great crisis in recent memory. Would the crisis of depression lead Hoover to deploy public resources and extend central state authority as had been done under conditions of war?

The severity of the Great Depression that devoured the Hoover presidency is partially captured by economic statistics. National income fell from $83.3 billion in 1929 to $40 billion in 1932. This drop in national income had a powerful impact on unemployment and the business failure rate. The pool of 1.5 million unemployed workers increased to 12.8 million by the end of the Hoover presidency, an unemployment rate of 24.9 percent. The failure rate for corporations increased from 104 per 100,000 in 1929 to 154 per 100,000 three years later. With the growing pool of surplus labor and resources, the wholesale price index fell from 95.3 in 1929 to 64.8 in 1932. In three short years, the nation was transformed from prosperity to economic ruin.[2] This chapter examines Hoover's presidency and the way in which the depression revealed the weaknesses in the associational system he had created. With the new economic crisis, elites across the political spectrum demanded that the state once again adopt extraordinary measures, particularly once the limits of associationalism became clear. Hoover accepted some of these demands.

1. See R. Kent Weaver and Bert A. Rockman, "Assessing the Effects of Institutions," in *Do Institutions Matter? Government Capabilities in the United States and Abroad*, ed. R. Kent Weaver and Bert A. Rockman (Washington, D.C.: Brookings Institution, 1993).

2. Paul Studenski and Herman E. Krooss, *Financial History of the United States* (New York: McGraw-Hill, 1952), 353; *Statistical History of the United States*, series D-46–47, V-2.

However, the ideological commitments that had led him to promote associationalism would militate against a wholesale adoption of the war model.

Before the Fall

The 1928 campaign for the presidency will not be noted as one of the more memorable campaigns of the century. With a record of prosperity under the past several years of Republican rule, the argument that a vote for Hoover was a vote for continuity carried the day. Alfred E. Smith's Catholicism and opposition to the Eighteenth Amendment mobilized much of the opposition. Despite Smith's support for various progressive causes, he ran a conservative campaign that de-emphasized the distinctions between the Democrats and the Republicans. Hoover repeatedly argued that a continuation of past policies would result in an extension of economic growth, a rising economic tide that would eventually eliminate poverty. In the end, Hoover's victory was an easy one. He received over twenty-one million votes, compared with Smith's fifteen million (Hoover claimed 444 electoral votes to Smith's 87). Hoover received a majority of votes in each section of the country in an election that brought out an unprecedented 58 percent of the electorate, more than thirty-six million voters.[3] Hoover's margin of victory and the record of economic prosperity led, quite naturally, to the conclusion that the new presidential administration would encounter few difficulties in extending the policies of the past.

Agricultural Reform

On the eve of the campaign, it was feared that farmers in the Northwest and Midwest might frustrate Hoover's bid for the presidency due to his earlier opposition to McNary-Haugen. These fears were ill founded: every state in the two regions supported Hoover. This was not the product of chance. Hoover actively courted the farm vote by announcing on October 27, 1928, that if elected, he would "of necessity call an extra session [of Congress] so as to secure early constructive action" on the issue of agricultural relief, "which urgently require[d] solution and should not be delayed for a whole year." He

3. Figures are from "The Presidential Election of 1928," *Current History* 29, no. 3 (1928): 353–55.

called the agricultural crisis "our most urgent economic problem."[4] Indeed, reviews of Hoover's first year in office would identify farm relief as his one clear victory. Debates over the tariff—initially introduced as part of the effort to improve farm incomes—would otherwise occupy Congress, effectively stalling other legislation.[5]

Congress passed the Agricultural Marketing Act of 1929 at the request of Hoover. The events leading up to its passage are detailed in Chapter 6. The act created an eight-member Federal Farm Board. The new board administered a budget of $500 million, which was to be loaned to new or existing agricultural cooperatives or crop-stabilization corporations to purchase and store surpluses to elevate farm prices. To this end, the loans could be used to construct or purchase marketing and processing facilities and undertake various educational campaigns to convince farmers of the benefits of cooperative action. The board was to work through a number of commodity-specific advisory committees, each comprising seven members selected by the relevant cooperative associations.[6] By working through the cooperatives, the board would not be involved in making direct support payments or the wholesale purchase of surpluses to be dumped in international markets. It was an associational response to the curse of the surplus.

The Federal Farm Board, under the direction of Alexander Legge, president of International Harvester, began with centralization: it hoped to create national cooperatives for each of the major commodities. In Legge's words, the role of the Farm Board was that of "encouraging the development of large scale, central co-operative marketing organizations" and "expansioning and strengthening of the co-operative movements" so that farmers could exercise a "voice in establishing the rules, regulations, and conditions under which products were disposed of."[7] To this end, the board worked closely with various grain cooperatives to form a new Farmers National Grain Corporation. Additional national cooperative agencies were created in 1929 to cover wool, cotton, beans, pecans and livestock. The basic model was for local cooperatives to purchase stock in regional cooperatives, which, in turn, purchased the stock of the new national associations. This allowed for the guarantee of

    4. Hoover quoted in ibid., 358.
    5. "Intangibles," *Time*, March 3, 1930, 13–17.
    6. George Soule, *Prosperity Decade: A Chapter from American Economic History, 1917–1929* (London: Pilot Press, 1947), 149; Albert U. Romasco, *The Poverty of Abundance: Hoover, the Nation, the Depression* (New York: Oxford University Press, 1965), 106; John D. Hicks, *Republican Ascendancy, 1921–1933* (New York: Harper & Brothers, 1960), 217–18.
    7. Legge quoted in Edwin Hill, "Alexander Legge Defends the Farm Board," *Forbes*, April 15, 1930, 18.

farmer control over the new organizations. Until the new associations could become self-sufficient, the Federal Farm Board would distribute loans downward through the organization, delegating the final authority to the local cooperatives. The Federal Farm Board attempted to use this network to support farm prices. Thus, in October 1929, the board announced that the prevailing prices for cotton and wheat were too low. In each case, it called on farmers to withhold crops from the market, pledging $100 million to lend farmers at a rate of up to 90 percent of the value of the stored crop. The board hoped that this would be sufficient to keep farmers from dumping their goods on the market.[8] However, the new system for managing surpluses would have little impact under the pressure of the depression. In the end, commodity prices—like so much else—would simply collapse.

The Tariff: Agricultural Reform Forsaken?

Hoover received the strong support of Senator William E. Borah during his presidential campaign. As a Farm Bloc member and strong advocate of agriculture, Borah's support was important given the general perception that Hoover favored industrial development over the farm economy. When Hoover called a special session of Congress to consider new farm legislation, he advocated limited revisions in the tariff, aimed primarily at agricultural commodities, albeit with minor reductions in other products. In the end, neither the limited scope of the revisions nor the agricultural focus held true. The initial increases in farm duties were combined with equal or greater increases in duties for virtually anything that might be subject to imports. The new tariff raised duties to new heights and thereby invited retaliatory tariffs on the part of the nation's trading partners. Although the tariff was initiated as part of a broader agricultural reform, Joseph R. Grundy, recently appointed senator from Pennsylvania and president of the Pennsylvania Manufacturers' Association, created a protectionist coalition to see the act's provisions extended to manufacturing. Eastern support for the high farm duties would be traded for the West's support for higher duties on industrial products. In the end, the act strongly supported the manufacturing interests of the Northeast. The Smoot-Hawley tariff rates stood far above those established under the 1922 Fordney-McCumber tariff.[9]

Hoover also hoped to combine revisions in the tariff with institutional

8. Romasco, *The Poverty of Abundance,* 112–21; Hicks, *Republican Ascendancy,* 219.
9. Hicks, *Republican Ascendancy,* 220.

266   From Warfare State to Welfare State

reforms—the revitalization of the moribund Tariff Commission and the creation of a "flexible tariff." As Hoover explained: "I believed that the only way to get the tariff out of Congressional logrolling was through empowering this bipartisan commission to adjust the different rates on dutiable goods upon the basis of the differences in cost of production at home and abroad, and to make these readjustments after objective examination and public hearings."[10] Under the flexible tariff, the Tariff Commission would be empowered to make alterations in the rates set by Congress, thus making them more responsive to changing economic conditions. Whereas the flexible tariff was a Progressive idea—one much in keeping with Hoover's earlier attempts to introduce a greater reliance on administrative expertise—it encountered some very predictable political problems. Many members of Congress, including Senator Borah, were opposed to the transfer of authority such a provision might entail, although these concerns were veiled by discussions of the reactionary nature of the flexible tariff and questions regarding its constitutionality. Hoover not only advocated the flexible tariff but threatened with veto any tariff legislation without sufficient provisions for the flexible tariff. He was successful in realizing the these provisions—if nothing else—when the Smoot-Hawley tariff became law in June 1930.[11]

Hoover's decision to sign the Smoot-Hawley tariff was supported by the American Farm Bureau Federation, the National Grange, the Farmers' Union, and the American Federation of Labor—groups that had not been strong supporters of Hoover in the past. The decision is even more difficult to understand given the tariff's narrow passage (two votes in the Senate) and the broad opposition to the new legislation by many whose advice one might expect Hoover to have taken very seriously. Hoover was advised to veto the bill by Albert Wiggin of Chase National Bank, Charles H. Sabin of Guarantee Trust Company, Charles E. Mitchell of the National City Bank, Thomas Lamont of J. P. Morgan Company, Oswald Garrison Villard of the *Nation,* Roy Howard of the Scripps-Howard newspapers, John J. Raskob and Jouett Shouse of the Democratic National Committee, Henry Morgenthau, and, in Hoover's words, "a whole group of college professors."[12] Indeed, a month before its final passage, 1,028 economists representing the American Economics Association presented a signed statement urging the president to veto the legislation. The petition presented an indictment of the tariff. It argued that

10. Herbert Hoover, *The Memoirs of Herbert Hoover,* vol. 2, *The Cabinet and the Presidency, 1920–1933* (New York: Macmillan, 1952), 292–93.
11. See Hoover's account of the struggle over the flexible tariff in *Memoirs of Herbert Hoover,* 2:292–97.
12. Ibid., 296.

the tariff would increase prices to domestic consumers, provide few benefits for wage earners, increase unemployment, have negative effects on the export trade, and increase foreign hostility. It was not needed by American manufacturers and it would provide no benefits for farmers. Moreover, "a tariff war does not furnish good soil for world peace."[13] As Hicks notes: "Time was soon to prove the economists right in most of their predictions. Protests against the raising of the American tariff wall began to pour in from foreign nations while the bill was still in Congress; after its passage retaliatory tariffs became the order of the day. . . . If the members of Congress who were responsible for the Hawley-Smoot Tariff had taken careful thought on how they could hurt the United States most economically, they could hardly have done worse."[14]

Hoover realized that the new tariff contained a large number of flaws. However, he was far more troubled by the existing process for revising the tariff. As he stated in a June 15, 1930, analysis of the tariff: "Congressional revisions are not only disturbing to business but, with all their necessary collateral surroundings in lobbies, logrolling, and the activities of group interests, are disturbing to public confidence." Hoover believed that the new flexible tariff was of the greatest importance, however, because it allowed for "prompt and scientific adjustment of serious inequities and inequalities" in the tariff while providing the "great hope of taking the tariff away from politics." In retrospect, Hoover would note that "raising the tariff from its sleep was a political liability despite the virtues of its reform."[15] Indeed, the tariff and its connections to the Great Depression would become an important topic in the 1932 campaign.

The Crash and the Depression

The popular memory of the Great Depression begins with a sudden crash of the stock market that forced a free fall into depression. In reality, the crash unfolded over a period of several weeks, with rapid declines followed by periods of relative stability. Moreover, while a few "lucky" analysts predicted

---

13. *Nation,* May 14, 1930; Michael E. Parrish, *Anxious Decades: America in Prosperity and Depression, 1920–1941* (New York: W. W. Norton, 1992), 247–48.
14. Hicks, *Republican Ascendancy,* 223.
15. Hoover, *Memoirs of Herbert Hoover,* 2:298–99.

that the recession would evolve into a depression, the downward ratchet into depression was such that most were convinced at several points that the bottom had been reached and recovery was under way. Major business publications predicted improvements almost on a monthly basis.

The crash of 1929–30 brought to an abrupt end a prolonged period of unprecedented growth in the stock market. The 1920s witnessed a rapid rise in stock-market prices and the overall volume of securities transactions. Stock prices greatly exceeded the underlying values, creating a speculative bubble. The relationship between prices and values was of some importance. By the end of 1928, brokers' loans—loans with stock for collateral—had reached $6.4 billion, increasing to $8.5 billion by September 1929.[16] A significant reduction in stock prices could result in the recalling of loans on a massive scale. The high level of market activity was significant for another reason. Over the course of the 1920s, the volume of market transactions had increased at a fevered pitch. The New York Stock Exchange, which handled fewer than 175 million shares in 1921, had tripled its volume by 1927 and exceeded one billion shares in 1929.[17] As a result, investors often made decisions without current information on prices. This uncertainty would become of great importance as the market entered the fall of 1929.

With the average price of common stocks at 300 percent of their 1925 values, many analysts concluded that the market was overvalued and a correction was inevitable. Thus, when stock prices began to slip in the last weeks of September 1929, there was no real concern. Indeed, modest declines in business activity in earlier months suggested that a mild recession was on its way. The expectations of a mild recession and market correction were thwarted in October. From October 19 through the end of the month the market experienced an unprecedented volume of trade as investors sought to dump their stocks before they had lost all of their value. On October 24, the infamous "Black Thursday," tickers ran so far behind that investors sought to sell stock with no idea how much they had lost. Things would have been much worse if not for J. P. Morgan and other large banks that joined together to form a $240 million pool of funds to purchase stocks and support values. However, even with this intervention, many speculators were ruined as margin calls

16. *Statistical History of the United States,* series X-385. This 1929 estimate of broker's loans and data on value of stock come from Arthur S. Link, *American Epoch: A History of the United States Since the 1890s* (New York: Alfred A. Knopf, 1955), 355.

17. This discussion draws on William J. Shultz and M. R. Caine, *Financial Development of the United States* (New York: Prentice Hall, 1937), 628–66; John Kenneth Galbraith, *The Great Crash: 1929* (Boston: Houghton Mifflin, 1988); and Robert Sobel, *Inside Wall Street* (New York: W. W. Norton, 1982).

devoured their assets. Investors' best stocks subsequently plummeted in value as they tried to raise funds on the markets to cover the calls. Even the efforts of the banks to stabilize the market through stock purchases proved only to be a temporary solution. After some stability in the first weeks of November, the market plunged again on November 13. By that point, the market had lost approximately half its value. The *Times* industrial average, which stood at 452 on September 3, 1929, fell to 224 by November 13. The decline in the market would continue, albeit at a slower pace, in the spring of 1930, arriving ultimately at a low of 58 in July 1932.[18] The prosperity decade had drawn to a close.

Contemporary analysts had difficulties explaining the crash. Although many had expected a correction, this was the financial equivalent of the apocalypse. What had been the cause of this financial collapse? Alfred Bernheim, director of the Labor Bureau, provided a catalog of causes in November of 1929:

> Attempts to account for the crash of 1929 have been many and varied. That the Federal Reserve Board failed to exercise adequate control, or was not constituted so that it might execute it; that the recalcitrant senators in Washington destroyed confidence by obstructing tariff legislation; that the banks wanted to shake the public out of its holdings so that they could acquire them themselves at lower levels; that a "powerful bear clique" raided the market; that an unwholesome proportion of credit was being absorbed in speculation; that the investment trusts were responsible; that the bankers had dumped a huge amount of "undigested" securities on the public; that prices had been driven up beyond all reason through lack of judgment and a false sense of security in the endless continuation of prosperity at an accelerating pace, thereby creating an unhealthy technical condition that had to be corrected—these and still other explanations ranging from the plausible to palpably absurd, have been offered by stock-market apologists.

Bernheim was agnostic when it came to the varied explanations for the crash. He could only conclude that there was "little justification for the belief that the country is about to plunge into a period of depression."[19] In this conclusion, he stood with the consensus—one that would prove dreadfully incorrect.

18. Figures quoted from Galbraith, *The Great Crash*, 135, 145. See Link, *American Epoch*, 356–57.
19. Alfred L. Bernheim, "Wall Street Upside Down," *Nation*, November 27, 1929, 618.

There is little reason to assume that the crash caused the depression. A contemporary account noted that "a combination of fear and mob psychology . . . carried the debacle to the absurd lengths it reached." It was true that "the market must have been extremely vulnerable to offer so little resistance." But, as the *Nation* asked, "[w]hy should this sudden hysteria, this utter lack of confidence, spread like wild fire into ever important financial center at a time when the country as a whole is enjoying at least a normal prosperity?"[20] The answer was deceptively simple: the prosperity rested on shaky foundations that permitted recession to deepen into full-fledged depression.

More than half a century after the onset of the decline there is no consensus on the primary causes of the Great Depression. Although few analysts today identify the market crash as the primary cause of the depression, some see it as part of a larger pattern of monetary mismanagement. This position is best represented by monetarists Milton Friedman and Anna Jacobson Schwartz, who present the depression as the product of failed intervention by the Federal Reserve, which pursued a restrictive policy in 1928–29 in hopes of reducing market speculation. The contraction in the money supply facilitated the wave of bank failures that followed the stock-market crash.[21] In contrast to this argument, many of the most convincing explanations portray the depression as the product of the problems inherent in a mature capitalist economy. Marxist political economists, including Paul A. Baran, Paul M. Sweezy, and Josef Steindl, link the depression to the growth of excess capacity in an increasingly oligopolistic industrial economy. As corporations developed excess capacity (particularly after 1925), they lost a good deal of flexibility in their pricing and reduced investment opportunities. As a result, the mature industrial economy became prone to crisis and depression.[22] Keynes (and Alvin Hansen) also saw depression as a product of a mature capitalist economy, arguing that a high stage of maturation in an economy triggers a commensurate downturn in investment. Moreover, employment levels plummet due to higher levels of capital intensity in the production process, and, as a result, population growth follows. Absent new outlets for investment (e.g., new technologies), the economy would remain in a depressed condition, thereby creating a need for aggregate-demand stimulation via deficit spend-

20. "Wall Street's Crisis," *Nation,* November 6, 1929, 511.

21. See Milton Friedman and Anna Jacobson Schwartz, *A Monetary History of the United States, 1867–1960* (Princeton, N.J.: Princeton University Press, 1963).

22. See, in particular, Paul A. Baran and Paul M. Sweezy, *Monopoly Capitalism: An Essay on the American Economic and Social Order* (New York: Monthly Review Press, 1966), 237–44, and Josef Steindl, *Maturity and Stagnation in American Capitalism* (Oxford: Basil Blackwell, 1952).

ing.[23] When combined, these arguments suggest that the American economy, after prolonged growth and high levels of investment, had reached a point at which there was great vulnerability to exogenous shocks, be they associated with market crashes or policy miscues. As the shock ran through an economy already vulnerable, the contraction deepened and proved highly resistant to the efforts of private- and public-sector actors. Moreover, the depth and dogged persistence of the depression may be linked to another factor: the collapse of the international economy.

Many critics of the Hoover administration argued that the introduction of the new Smoot-Hawley tariff transformed the decline of 1929–30 into a full-blown depression. This explanation, as one might expect, proved particularly vexing to Hoover, given his role in initiating the tariff. However, he would seek subsequently to justify Smoot-Hawley while discounting its overall significance in the depression. As he explained in his *Memoirs:*

> [L]ater statements implying that the passage of the Smoot-Hawley bill was the cause of the depression seem somewhat overdrawn, as it was not passed until nine months after the crash. Moreover, it was not, as later statements suggested, the beginning of a world movement to increase tariffs. In fact, the American increase took place only after nearly thirty other countries had imposed higher tariffs. This world-wide tariff movement was largely an outcome of World War I. The world generally was seeking "self-sufficiency" as a measure of national defense in an era of international fear. Furthermore, many nations were seeking to prevent recurrence of the hardships imposed by inability to import necessary supplied from abroad, resulting from the export restrictions and blockades during the war.[24]

Hoover's reading of the Smoot-Hawley tariff is understandable, given the conviction on the part of many administration opponents that the new tariff—one that Hoover had introduced in payment for Borah's support—had contributed to the depression. Although some of Hoover's critics claimed that the tariff was a chief factor in turning an adjustment into a depression, there are few adherents to this view today. As Peter Temin argues, "[D]espite its popularity . . . this argument fails on both theoretical and historical grounds."

23. See Peter Temin, *Did Monetary Forces Cause the Great Depression?* (New York: W. W. Norton, 1976). This discussion draws on Michael A. Bernstein, *The Great Depression: Delayed Recovery and Economic Change in America, 1929–1939* (Cambridge: Cambridge University Press, 1987).

24. Hoover, *Memoirs of Herbert Hoover,* 2:291–92.

As Temin explains, the tariff is an expansionary tool insofar as it diverts demand from imports to domestically produced goods. If the argument is refined to state that Smoot-Hawley reduced the demand for American exports via retaliatory tariffs abroad, the ultimate impact is limited by the magnitude of U.S. exports relative to the overall GNP. Exports accounted for some 7 percent of GNP in 1929 and fell a mere 1.5 percent of 1929 GNP by 1931. During the same time, however, real GNP declined by 15 percent. As Temin concludes: "With any reasonable multiplier, the fall in export demand can only be a small part of the story. And it needs to be offset by the rise in domestic demand from the tariff. Any net contractionary effect of the tariff was small."[25]

While not the primary cause, the international component to the depression was unquestionably powerful. The international economy rested on remarkably shaky foundations following World War I due to the combined impact of war debt and reparations, on the one hand, and high U.S. tariffs on the other. As of December 31, 1919, the total private and public debt owed to the United States was in excess of $17 billion.[26] The United States was initially unwilling to cancel the intergovernmental debts and reparations, thereby making it a constraint on the international system throughout the 1920s. At the same time, the return to high tariffs during the 1920s created severe difficulties for foreign nations seeking to acquire the dollars needed to service this debt. The record of U.S. trade surpluses throughout the decade of the 1920s is a testament to the effectiveness of the tariff during this period. With tariffs in place and the debt payments an unavoidable reality, foreign nations relied heavily on U.S. bank loans and U.S. investment. As pressure from the crash on bank and corporate assets grew, capital from abroad fled. In light of this withdrawal of funds, as well as the impact of Smoot-Hawley on international trade and the erection of retaliatory trade barriers, it is clear that the new tariff played some contributory role. However, as with the market crash itself, the impact was magnified by underlying structural weaknesses.

Associationalism Redux

Hoover's response to the stock-market crash and the subsequent economic decline reflected both the limited tools at his disposal and his philosophy of

25. Peter Temin, *Lessons from the Great Depression* (Cambridge: MIT Press, 1989), 46.
26. Link, *American Epoch*, 283.

economic governance. On the first count, analysts commonly look negatively at Hoover's response to the depression without recognizing that the federal government was quite small, certainly incapable of executing on its own the kind of program recommended almost a decade earlier, during the Unemployment Conference. Even accepting the limited fiscal footprint of the national government, one must not lose sight of Hoover's ongoing belief in balanced budgets. If in abstract he realized the benefits of a more expansionary fiscal policy—the only conclusion one can derive from the Unemployment Conference—he was ideologically committed to balanced budgets. As spending targeted toward relief and public works expanded, he consistently sought to achieve balance through the promotion of greater economies in government. Given the lack of developed policy tools for dealing with a crisis of this magnitude, Hoover had little option but to fall back on the associational system he had so vigorously promoted in earlier years. Of course, Hoover was philosophically predisposed toward an associationalist response. Short of war (and, perhaps, even under circumstances of war), Hoover was unwilling to assign a great power to the bureaucracy. He was committed to the proposition that key responsibilities could be executed by private economic associations acting in concert.

In November 1929, Hoover began holding a series of conferences with representatives of industry, finance, labor, agriculture, construction, public utilities, and railroads in hopes of fostering cooperation in meeting the impact of the crash. On November 19, Hoover met with the railroad presidents to advocate the maintenance or expansion of construction work. Similarly, on November 21, at a meeting with a group of industrial leaders, he argued that wages should be maintained through continued construction and, where necessary, corporations should shorten the workweek rather than eliminate workers. Hoover did not entertain the possibility that the crash constituted a serious crisis; he assured conferees: "In market booms we develop over-optimism with a corresponding reverse into over-pessimism. They are equally unjustified."[27] Later that day, Hoover met with labor leaders to secure their agreement to withdraw existing wage demands and prevent strikes. A press release reflected the key features of these conferences: "[T]he President was authorized by the employers . . . to state on their individual behalf that they will not initiate any movement for wage reduction, and it was their strong recommendation that this attitude should be pursued by the country as a whole." It was believed that such a measure would maintain "the consuming

27. "Action Counts," *Time*, November 25, 1929, 11.

power of the country." The release continued: "The President was also authorized by the representatives of labor to state that . . . no movement beyond
those already in negotiation should be initiated for increase of wages, and that
every co-operation should be given by labor to industry in the handling of its
problems."[28] The next day, Hoover met with leaders of the building and
construction industries to conclude a similar agreement. Additional conferences were held with agricultural leaders on November 25, and representatives of the public utilities on November 27.

Hoover's efforts to organize and mobilize the private associations to stabilize the economy found their clearest expression in December. At the November 21 meeting, Hoover had asked the chairman of the U.S. Chamber of
Commerce, Julius H. Barnes, to create an executive committee of business.
The resulting National Business Survey Conference—a group consisting of
some 400 business and trade-association representatives and an Advisory
Committee of 150—met in Washington on December 5, 1929.[29] In addressing the conference, Hoover called on business "to create a temporary organization to counteract the effects of the recent panic in the stock market." He
stressed that there should be "no movement to reduce wages." Rather, "the
greatest tool of stability is construction and maintenance work. . . . All of
these efforts have one end—to assure employment." Hoover also stressed the
need for the continued purchase of raw materials and promoted vigorous
exports without dumping.[30] Although Hoover had a broad agenda for the
Chamber of Commerce representatives, he was careful to explain that the
government would not take control of business activities. Rather, he issued
"a request from the government that [the conference's representatives] cooperate in prudent measures to solve a national problem. A great responsibility and a great opportunity rest upon business and economic organizations of
the country."[31]

As one might expect, the business response to Hoover was quite positive.
In the words of Merryle Stanley Rukeyser, "Private corporations are organized
for profit, and can achieve their corporate purposes only by going ahead."
Individually, they may be hesitant to pursue policies that will prevent further
decline—for example, retaining their employees, building up stocks. How-

28. Press release of November 21, 1929, reprinted in William Starr Myers and Walter H. Newton,
The Hoover Administration: A Documented Narrative (New York: Charles Scribner's Sons, 1936), 28.
29. See Julius H. Barnes, "The President's Conference Means BUSINESS," *Forbes,* January 15, 1930,
21.
30. "Good Old Word," *Time,* December 16, 1929, 11.
31. Herbert Hoover, quoted in Myers and Newton, *The Hoover Administration,* 34.

ever, "they are willing to proceed as soon as they realize that others are willing to do so."[32] Hoover had unified their efforts through his conferences. As Merle Thorpe wrote in the *Nation's Business,* the journal of the U.S. Chamber of Commerce, government and business "stand together. Through the President, the Government has spoken. Through a host of its leaders, Business pledges its resources and resourcefulness to maintain the momentum of industry. *The two forces are working hand in hand, as in wartime.*"[33]

Hoover's overtures to business in the weeks following the crash were given some emphasis by critics on the Left who attached far greater significance to the conferences than would a generation of post–New Deal historians. A November 1929 editorial in the *Nation,* for example, observed: "What Mr. Hoover is really trying to do, apparently without knowing it, is to create a Supreme Council of National Economy in the United States, and it will be interesting to see how far he can go in our topsey-turvey capitalist economy. He is right in wanting a planned economy."[34] As a contemporary critic noted, the effort to move toward some sort of planning in the United States would be highly problematic:

> The immediate policy that Mr. Hoover is urging is one that requires great financial strength, uncommon foresight, and an unusual willingness to wait for gains. . . . The attempt to plan and direct the economy of a communist state like Russia, where the sole aim may be abundant production wisely distributed, is an undertaking of appalling difficulty. The task of directing and coordinating the economic activity of a capitalist state like the United States, where the social end of production is constantly interfered with by certain activities of private industries seeking immediate profit, is immensely more difficult.[35]

In a similar assessment, Leo Wolman of the Amalgamated Clothing Workers of America characterized Hoover's conferences as a "Supreme Economic Council or Americanized Gosplan." He was doubtful that Hoover would be successful, in part because of the poor state of knowledge concerning the economy. More important, the administration could not "act like war govern-

---

32. Meryle Stanley Rukeyser, "What the World of Finance Talks Of," *Nation's Business* 18, no. 1 (1930): 166.

33. Merle Thorpe, "Partners for Prosperity," *Nation's Business,* 18, no. 1 (1930): 9, emphasis added.

34. *Nation,* November 27, 1929, 611.

35. "Business to the Rescue," *Nation,* December 4, 1929, 652.

ment and create a rapidly expanding market for all goods and services by systematic and continuous inflation."[36] War mobilization must address problems of expansive demands and shortages. How does one allocate scarce resources and control inflationary pressures? During depression, surpluses exist throughout the economy. Deflation replaces inflation. In the end, the two problems are not comparable. Unfortunately, this insight, that the demands of depression and those of war posed much different challenges, would be lost on both Hoover and his successor.

Hoover would have repudiated any effort to associate his conferences with state planning. Hoover's faith in private-sector cooperation was strong, as revealed by his earlier associational efforts. Hoover did not seek to eliminate some flaw inherent in capitalism or introduce reforms that would guarantee economic stability. Rather, he sought to promote a return to the high levels of production that had characterized so much of the decade. Nevertheless, Hoover did not believe that the task of recovery was to be assigned to the market and private associations. The state had a vital role to play. Thus, in the early days of the market crash, Hoover met with Treasury Secretary Mellon, Undersecretary of the Treasury Ogden Mills, and Federal Reserve Board governor Ray Archibald Young to forge an agreement on reducing corporate and personal income taxes for 1929, payable in 1930, by 1 percent. The $160 million tax reduction was approved through meetings with Senate and House leadership. The tax cut, ultimately passed through a joint resolution of Congress, was large but, in Hoover's mind, fully responsible given the anticipated 1929 surplus gained through increases in government efficiency.[37] Hoover also supported the Federal Reserve's November reductions in the discount rate, on the belief that this would facilitate investments that might increase employment. He also ordered all government departments to expedite public-works projects and sent a telegraph to all state governors urging them to engage in an "energetic, yet prudent, pursuit of public works."[38] On November 18, Hoover met with Treasury Secretary Mellon to propose that Congress increase the funding for the Federal Public Building Program by $423 million. Six days later, he sent telegraphs to the nation's governors and mayors requesting that they cooperate in expanding construction and public works, thus "providing for the absorption of any unemployment which might result from present disturbed conditions."[39] Hoover's proposed budget for the 1930

36. Leo Wolman, "Hoover's Fillip to Business," *Nation,* December 11, 1929, 710.
37. "Action Counts," *Time,* November 25, 1929, 11.
38. "Mind and Momentum," *Time,* December 2, 1929, 23.
39. Ibid., 28.

fiscal year, presented to Congress on December 4, 1929, reallocated resources to provide more to the Farm Board and public works without jeopardizing the overall balance of expenditures and revenues.

With a new and broadly supported network of conferences linking the government and economic associations pledged to take steps to stabilize the economy, and with what was, at least by contemporary standards, a notable fiscal-stimulation program in place, Hoover might have had reason to believe that the impact of the crash would be limited. Indeed, business optimism remained strong, and the stock market showed some signs of recovery. As shown above, the popular appraisals of Hoover's role in the weeks following the crash were largely positive. How different the story would be if it only ended here.

The Vexing Problem of Unemployment

Initially, there was good reason to believe that Hoover's associational strategy would stimulate corporate investment and end further unemployment and deflation. Broad support for Hoover's policies reflected the president's assurance that joblessness was improving—a claim he began making in January 1930 on the basis of rather flimsy economic data. Despite Hoover's assurances, piecemeal evidence indicated that joblessness was growing in the early months of 1930. Reports of breadlines and full soup kitchens coincided with claims that the unemployment problem in New York was—as New York industrial commissioner Frances Perkins announced—the worst in some fifteen years. The jobless marched in Los Angeles, Seattle, Chicago, and New York with signs that read "Work or Wages." A national strike had been called for March. The response from Washington was, at best, muted. In part, the explanation is tied to a lack of good indicators of joblessness. The Labor Department estimated unemployment using an index based on figures from 1926. The estimates of unemployment were hampered by small samples, infrequent reporting, and a methodology that failed to differentiate part-time and temporary employment from full-time employment. Labor Secretary James John Davis announced in March of 1930 that there were approximately three million unemployed out of a workforce of forty-six million.[40]

As the Labor Department was releasing these estimates, Hoover sought to place a far more positive gloss on the situation. He claimed that unemployment was largely restricted to twelve states, with the remaining thirty-six

40. "How Many Jobless?" *Time*, March 17, 1930, 15–16; *Time*, February 24, 1930, 17.

indicating no departure from normal seasonal unemployment. Hoover assured the nation: "The low point of business and unemployment was the latter part of December and early January. Since that time employment has been slowly increasing. The amount of unemployment is, in proportion to the number of workers, considerably less than one-half (probably only one-third) of that which resulted from the crashes of 1907–8 and 1920–22. All the evidences indicate that the worst effects of the crash upon employment will have passed during the next 60 days."[41] With Hoover's positive appraisal on record, Davis revised downward his original estimates of unemployment. In a cynical ploy that failed to convince serious analysts, Davis now claimed that approximately one million workers were unemployed.

Despite Hoover's claims that the economy had already reached its nadir and recovery would be forthcoming, the Labor Department's estimates of monthly unemployment failed to reveal any real improvement in joblessness in the spring of 1930. The Labor Department estimated that employment fell from 99.3 in September 1929 (1926 = 100) to 89.3 by March 1930— hitting the lowest level since the department began collecting statistics in 1923.[42] Using the Labor Department's estimates of labor-force size, this index would translate into 4.9 million jobless, with a large number of uncounted workers who were no longer fully employed. These figures are comparable to those presented by the AFL's William Green, who testified before the Senate Commerce Committee that in February 1930 there were already 3.7 million jobless—with over $1 billion in lost wages in January alone.[43] Indeed, if Hoover believed his own statements concerning unemployment, his actions suggested a much different judgment. In April, Hoover signed a bill that authorized $575 million for new road construction, thereby employing 100,000 workers. Even when faced with clear evidence that shrinking income taxes would turn a projected surplus of $22 million into a comparable deficit, Hoover asked Congress for an additional $28 million for the construction of new public bridges. Six months after the crash, Hoover proclaimed that "we have now passed the worst and with continued unity of effort we shall rapidly recover." He concluded that the "great economic experiment . . . to stabilize economic forces" had "succeeded to a remarkable degree. . . . The acceleration of construction programs has been successful beyond our hopes."[44] This conclusion—flying in the face of the growing economic evidence and Hoover's own frantic efforts to stimulate further spending—can be interpreted as little

41. "How Many Jobless?" 16.
42. "Spring Slump," *Time*, April 28, 1930, 12.
43. "Dole or Revolution," *Time*, April 14, 1930, 14.
44. "The Presidency: Acting," *Time*, May 12, 1934, 13.

more than an effort to shape expectations and prevent panic from exacerbating existing economic problems.

With growing evidence of economic decline, Hoover's critics became increasingly vociferous. In May 1930, the *Nation* published, under the title "Ballyhoover," a sharp critique of the administration's economic program, seeking to identify Hoover's chief contributions after "the seventh disastrous month of business depression." First, there was "a series of spectacular and enormously advertised conferences with business leaders out of which was to come an impossible stimulation of construction that would have been economically unsound if it could have been brought about." Recall that only a few months earlier the *Nation* had characterized these very conferences as a positive step toward economic planning. Second, there was "a deliberate suppression of the facts of depression and unemployment." The *Nation* reached a conclusion that would be shared by a growing percentage of the population: Hoover's "theory and his action are those of a publicity man, not of the economist or statesman."[45]

By the fall of 1930, recognizing that the winter could prove devastating given the higher-than-anticipated levels of unemployment, Hoover began organizing relief. His response took the form that one might have anticipated. On October 30, 1930, Hoover created the President's Committee for Unemployment Relief and placed it under the chairmanship of Colonel Arthur Woods, who had directed federal unemployment-relief activities under Secretary Hoover's direction in 1922. Woods would serve in this capacity until August of 1931, when he resigned and was replaced by Walter Gifford, president of American Telephone and Telegraph Company. At the national level, the organization had a committee with some sixty members, including Bernard Baruch, Newton Baker, Pierre Dupont, William Green, Edward Hurley, Alexander Legge, and Wesley Mitchell.[46] At Hoover's direction, the new organization worked with governors to establish Unemployment Relief Committees at the state level and, in turn, at the local level, where over three thousand such committees were created. The committees, composed of so-called leading citizens, were charged with the task of coordinating the efforts of federal, state, and municipal programs and those of private organizations. Decentralization and self-help were the guiding principles of the relief effort. Presenting an argument that could have been taken out of the pages of *American Individualism,* Hoover responded to members of Congress who had demanded dramatic increases in federal spending:

45. "Ballyhoover." *Nation,* May 14, 1930, 560.
46. Myers and Newton, *The Hoover Administration,* 113–14.

This is not an issue as to whether people shall go hungry. . . . It is a question as to whether the American people on one hand will maintain the spirit of charity and mutual self help through voluntary giving and the responsibility of local government as distinguished on the other hand from appropriations. . . . My own conviction is strongly that if we break down this sense of responsibility of individual generosity to individual and mutual self help in the country in times of national difficulty and if we start appropriations of this character we have not only impaired something infinitely valuable in the life of the American people but have struck at the roots of self-government. Once this has happened it is not the cost of a few more millions but we are faced with the abyss of reliance in future upon Government charity in some form or another. The money involved is indeed the least of the costs to American ideals and American institutions.[47]

Hoover understood his approach to relief—one that he had applied during the war—as an effort to "summon the maximum of self help" and give the American people "a chance to show whether they wish to preserve the principles of individual and local responsibility and mutual self help before they embark on . . . a disastrous system." Yet, Hoover promised to "ask the aid of every resource of the Federal Government" should the committees, private charities, state and local governments lack adequate resources.[48]

Hoover had reason to believe, once again, that the economy was about to enter recovery and that the Committee for Unemployment Relief would fulfill its duties. The American Economic Association, in its December 1930 meeting, had stated that recovery during the spring of 1931 was assured. The efforts to accelerate public construction had been successful. The Commerce Department reported that the construction projects of federal, state, and municipal governments, when combined with those of public utilities and railways, stood at $6.39 billion for 1930, well above the $5.26 billion of 1929—a boom year.[49] States, as organized by the Committee for Unemployment Relief, reported that private charities and state and local funding were adequate. There were even reports that the breadlines formed during the previous year had been discontinued in several states.

One must be careful to distinguish between the success of relief efforts

47. Hoover's press statement of February 3, 1931, reprinted in Ray Lyman Wilbur and Arthur Mastick Hyde, *The Hoover Policies* (New York: Charles Scribner's Sons, 1937), 375.

48. Ibid., 376.

49. Myers and Newton, *The Hoover Administration*, 60.

and the progress of recovery. The relief efforts had the modest, if essential, goal of preventing starvation, whereas recovery entailed the return to economic growth. The American Economic Association's prediction of a spring 1931 recovery was not fulfilled; things on the employment front actually became far worse. The gradual accumulation of evidence concerning low levels of private construction, growing unemployment, and wage reductions undermined the rosy picture of rapid recovery. New construction—deemed to be the engine of recovery—fell from $10.8 billion in 1929 to $6.4 billion in 1931.[50] Despite the promises of the business community to maintain their employees, the record reveals that unemployment increased rapidly. The unemployment rate, which stood at 3.2 percent in 1929, jumped to 8.7 percent by 1930 and 15.9 percent in 1931.[51] At the same time, average annual earnings per full-time employee fell from $1,405 in 1929 to $1,275 in 1931, thus undermining the hope of bolstering purchasing power.[52] The business press had started asking whether "Hoover luck" had become "Hoodoo Hoover," and warned that an "army of unemployed . . . six million hungry men, though unarmed, constitute a danger of immeasurable gravity."[53] By the fall of 1931, when the United States Steel Corporation led a series of large employers in reducing wages, the failure of Hoover's associational strategy became clear. A successful associational strategy would have required that corporations sacrifice their individual profitability in a period of economic collapse. In the words of Albert Romasco: "[T]he organization of the business community, and its schooling in great co-operative efforts, were insufficiently developed to permit it to meet successfully a major economic crisis."[54]

Hoover sought to mask the aggravation of the unemployment problem with statistical manipulation. His record of cheery statements designed to shape expectations—something his critics would refer to as "Christian Science economics"—stood in contrast with the stark reality.[55] Moreover, his recourse to American individualism and voluntarist strategies led many to question Hoover's competence to manage—or even understand—the crisis. Henry Raymond Mussey, for example, recalled the joy many felt over "the accession to the Presidency of an engineer and business man of wide experience who

---

50. *Statistical History of the United States,* series N-2.

51. *Statistical History of the United States,* series D-47.

52. *Statistical History of the United States,* series D-696.

53. "Fact and Comment," *Forbes,* June 1, 9130, 9; "War Looms! A Call to Arms!" *Forbes,* September 15, 1931, 9.

54. Romasco, *The Poverty of Abundance,* 65.

55. See "Christian Science Economics," *Nation,* February 17, 1932, 185.

would lead this country . . . as an economist." By the summer of 1931, Mussey could with confidence write: "[T]hat illusion has faded. Facts and expert opinions alike are brushed aside when they do not agree with preconceived policies, and it has been generally discovered that the President's economics is the economics, not of the trained student of social affairs, but simply of a successful though not highly intelligent mining engineer. It is, in fact, the economics of 1831, not 1931." The "belated and bastard individualism" that Hoover employed as economic theory led him to view the economic process as "a race between individuals (and a fair race at that) for prizes, not a collective undertaking whereby individual competition is directed to supplying the food and clothing and other things needed by society." Mussey found neither an "utterance disclosing any real comprehension of the underlying causes" of the depression nor "any proposal for action based on a recognition of those causes."[56]

A similar assessment was made by Robert La Follette, a leader of the Progressive Republican opposition to Hoover's policies. La Follette agreed with Mussey that Hoover "lacked either the understanding or the courage to press toward the goal of alleviating the distress of the unemployed." All that one witnessed was a "timidity and disingenuousness," a "bankruptcy of his leadership" that revealed "the tragic failure of rugged individualism" and placed "the major costs of deflation upon those least able to bear it—the unemployed." This came as a grave disappointment to La Follette, given Hoover's efforts a decade earlier in exploring the causes of unemployment and developing policies that might prevent its reemergence. He noted: "The failure of President Hoover during his Administration is revealed by his attitude toward the measures which would have at least partially ameliorated the unemployment crisis, and which have been under discussion since the unemployment conference over which he presided in 1921."[57] As economic conditions deteriorated, along with the associationalist strategies Hoover had adopted, the pressure toward a more activist policy became irresistible.

Beyond Associationalism

The depression became far more desperate through 1931, as noted above. The explanation is partially tied to the failure of Hoover's conferences to yield

56. Henry Raymond Mussey, "The President's Economics," *Nation,* July 18, 1931, 33–36.
57. Robert M. La Follette, "The President and Unemployment," *Nation,* July 15, 1931, 61–63.

long-term changes in corporate policy. However, an equally important part of the explanation is tied to the fact that during the spring and summer of 1931 the international component of the Great Depression fell into place. Ironically, the international economy collapsed precisely when it appeared that the domestic economy had finally entered a period of recovery. During the spring of 1931, the sharp decline of past months leveled off, and various indicators of economic performance began to improve. However, the performance of the U.S. economy was linked to the international economy, which rested, in turn, on the fragile system that emerged out of World War I. The combined demands of debt repayment and high tariffs placed great pressure on the capacity of European nations to raise needed funds. Over the course of the 1920s, they had increased their reliance on short-term loans. In March, French banks began calling for repayment of short-term loans made to the Germans and Austrians. By May, the largest bank in Vienna had failed under the pressure of repayment. Subsequent withdrawals of gold from Germany increased the probability that it would default on its loan and reparation payments. A moratorium negotiated in June provided short-term relief. However, the French turned their focus to the British banks, seeking to withdraw large stores of gold. The demands could not be met; in September the Bank of England defaulted on its gold payments, and the nation suspended the gold standard. The crisis deepened when European banks began withdrawing some $1.5 billion of gold deposits from American banks. The American banks responded to the withdrawals by recalling domestic loans and demanding repayment of short-term loans abroad. The growing insecurity over international economic relations led many once again to dump stocks in the New York exchange, driving down their value. These events forced a significant increase in the number of bank failures: bank suspensions increased from 1,352 in 1930 to a record 2,294 in 1931, accounting for $1.691 billion in deposits.[58] Moreover, the collapse of the international payments system, combined with the ratcheting-up of tariffs in the months following the passage of Smoot-Hawley, virtually stalled international trade. The total value of exports and imports fell from $7.5 billion in 1930 to $5.6 billion in 1931 and $4.1 billion a year later. Despite the passage of a debt moratorium, which relieved fifteen nations from paying $253 million in war debts between July 1, 1931, and June 30, 1932, the damage was done. The depression was now unquestionably a global phenomenon.[59]

58. *Statistical History of the United States*, series X-165, 172.
59. *Statistical History of the United States*, series U-1, 2; Link, *American Epoch*, 368–73; *Time*, January 4, 1932, 9.

The Reconstruction Finance Corporation

In 1929–30, Hoover's great hope was that the cooperative network he had promoted would prove sufficient to eliminate the depression. But the associational strategy was already beginning to fray by early 1931. With the wave of bank failures resulting from the financial crisis in Europe, Hoover finally concluded that a greater state role was justified. As one might expect, Hoover returned to the model of war mobilization. With the various conferences failing to produce the desired results, Hoover expanded expenditures through an increase in government-financed construction projects and the creation of the Reconstruction Finance Corporation. In his annual message to Congress on December 8, 1931, Hoover recommended the creation of "an emergency reconstruction corporation of the nature of the former War Finance Corporation." During the fall of 1931, many had called on Hoover to create a new WFC, including Eugene Meyer, its former director. Hoover's resistance stemmed from his belief that private financial institutions would be able to create a sufficient pool of capital. Hoover floated the idea for the new WFC in an October 4 meeting with Mellon, Meyer, Mills, and thirty financial leaders. The New York bankers offered a quid pro quo: they would contribute the $500 million pool of credit to create a National Credit Association if Hoover requested that Congress authorize a new War Finance Corporation along with an extension of rediscount eligibility for the Federal Reserve.[60] Hoover's faith in voluntarism had been tempered by experience, and the financial community was unwilling to entertain further associationalism without significant shifts in public policy. Under the prevailing economic conditions, he had no choice. He called for the creation of the "new" agency.

As envisioned by Hoover, the agency would strengthen "the weak spots to thus liberate the full strength of the nation's resources. It should be in position to facilitate exports by American agencies; make advances to agricultural credit agencies where necessary to protect and aid the agricultural industry; to make temporary advances upon proper securities to establish industries, railways, and financial institutions which cannot otherwise secure credit, and where such advances will protect the credit structure and stimulate employment." The Reconstruction Finance Corporation was presented as a

---

60. Jordan A. Schwarz, *The Interregnum of Despair: Hoover, Congress, and the Depression* (Urbana: University of Illinois Press, 1970), 88–89. See Gerald D. Nash, "Herbert Hoover and the Origins of the Reconstruction Finance Corporation," *Mississippi Valley Historical Review* 46 (December 1959): 455–68, and Myers and Newton, *The Hoover Administration,* 126–29.

temporary and emergency measure. It would "be placed in liquidation at the end of two years."[61]

Hoover's efforts to recreate the old War Finance Corporation with authority to make loans to public and private ventures encountered resistance from various factions in Congress. Southern Democrats successfully forced concessions for agriculture, demanding that the RFC be authorized to make loans to livestock and agricultural credit corporations and land banks, with an additional $50 million going directly to the USDA for crop loans. Northern Democrats were far less successful in their attempts to get authorization for the RFC to make direct loans to the cities for relief. Similarly, Hoover weathered the criticism of progressives, who objected to the RFC, viewing it as a welfare policy for millionaires and a means of taking money from a hurting population and channeling it to the very institutions that had been to some extent responsible for the current depression.[62] Nevertheless, on January 16, 1932, the bill creating the Reconstruction Finance Corporation passed both houses; differences were reconciled, and it was signed into law on January 22. In the end, the most powerful argument for the RFC was the depression rather than existing political-economic doctrines.

The RFC was capitalized with $500 million and was authorized to borrow an additional $1.5 billion. In addition to the newly described duties, the RFC was to assume the activities of the National Credit Association, which had proved far too slow in meeting the financial crisis. Reflecting the criticisms that had been voiced in the earlier debates, Hoover stated that the RFC "is not created for the aid of big industries or big banks. Such institutions are amply able to take care of themselves. It is created for the support of the smaller banks and financial institutions, and through rendering their resources liquid to give renewed support to business, industry, and agriculture. It should give opportunity to mobilize the gigantic strength of our country for recovery."[63]

The RFC was part of a broader effort to increase liquidity—a necessity given the evidence, delivered in a confidential report of January 1932, that lack of confidence in the financial system had resulted in widespread hoarding of currency. More than a billion dollars had been removed from the nation's financial system, and the rate of withdrawal was increasing. Hoover publicly called on Americans to have greater confidence in the stability of the banking

61. Hoover's message to Congress is reprinted in Myers and Newton, *The Hoover Administration*, 149.
62. See James Stuart Olson, *Herbert Hoover and the Reconstruction Finance Corporation, 1931–1933* (Ames: Iowa State University Press, 1977), 33–39, for a discussion of the legislative debates.
63. Hoover's message is reprinted in Myers and Newton, *The Hoover Administration*, 164.

system. Simultaneously, he asked Senator Carter Glass to assist in passing legislation that would ultimately help to relieve the credit crunch by allowing the Federal Reserve to back its notes with government securities rather commercial paper (which was increasingly scarce) and gold. Following the passage of the act in February 1932, the Federal Reserve undertook a higher level of open-market activity. The Federal Home Loan Bank Act, passed in July, also assisted in increasing liquidity by creating a system of twelve Home Loan Banks that could rediscount small home loans. With greater liquidity, creditors could meet the demands for withdrawal without recalling loans. With these acts and the creation of the RFC, Congress and the administration had gone far to reduce the credit stringency in the financial system. It was passed in the quixotic hope that these measures would ease the path to recovery.[64]

The RFC board of directors was to consist of seven directors, with a maximum of four Republicans. Hoover's discretion in appointing Republicans was limited by the legal requirement that the governor of the Federal Reserve, the Farm Loan commissioner, and the secretary or undersecretary of the Treasury sit on the board. Hoover named Eugene Meyer as chairman of the RFC. Meyer had been a member of the War Industries Board and a member of the War Finance Corporation's board of directors. Later, he had been the director of the Farm Board and chairman of the Federal Reserve. Meyer's expertise and war experience was combined with the prestige of Charles Dawes, whom Hoover named RFC president. Initially, Hoover considered naming Bernard M. Baruch to the RFC. However, Baruch refused the offer once the top two positions had been filled. Other Republican directors included Undersecretary of the Treasury Ogden Mills, and H. Paul Bestor, head of the Federal Farm Loan Board. Harvey Couch, Jesse Jones, and Wilson McCarthy filled the three Democratic slots on the RFC.[65] Although a conscious decision was made to adopt the skeletal organization previously employed by the War Finance Corporation, the RFC was able to draw on the statistical support of the Federal Reserve.

The RFC marked a significant shift from earlier Hoover policies. Some contemporary observers believed that the shift was great enough that positive results would have to be forthcoming: "Certainly if this measure does not

---

64. See Romasco, *The Poverty of Abundance*, 190–95, and Richard Norton Smith, *An Uncommon Man: The Triumph of Herbert Hoover* (New York: Simon & Schuster, 1984), 134–40.

65. In addition to Baruch, Hoover also considered appointing Edward Hurley, former chairman of the Federal Trade Commission and the U.S. Shipping Board. "R.F.C.," *Time*, January 25, 1932, 11–12; "The Presidency," *Time*, February 15, 1932, 9. Biographical information on the RFC board is presented in Olson, *Herbert Hoover and the Reconstruction Finance Corporation*, 39–41.

restore [the economy] nothing will. It puts us financially on a war basis and the power lodged in the board is really unprecedented."[66] Writing in the *American Federationist,* Chester M. Wright noted that the RFC was "the most complete mobilization and propaganda machine the United States has known since the World War. And . . . not in six months were the war authorities able to crate a machine as complete as the one here whipped into shape in six weeks."[67] Yet, to others the shift appeared to address the symptoms of the depression rather than the causes. As one critic noted, "[I]t is essentially a palliative, not a cure."[68] Others noted it was a bit naive to suppose that Hoover had the solution to the depression given the failure of his earlier policies. In Paul Y. Anderson's words: "To suggest at this stage of the depression that Hoover has any plan for curing it would be like taking a pulmotor to a funeral, which would be unseemly."[69] The chief critique focused on the administration's apparent willingness to extend the dole to business while leaving those in poverty to depend on the goodwill of others.

During the winter of 1931–32, political pressure for relief grew dramatically. National Hunger Marchers, numbering 1,670, descended on Washington, followed by another 15,000 marching behind Father James Cox. At the same time, Progressive Republicans and liberal Democrats, rebuffed by the administration's insistence that the proposed RFC should not engage in relief, offered proposals of their own. Thus, in December Senators La Follette and Costigan proposed a disbursement of $375 million to the states, to be distributed as relief to the unemployed. Hoover's objections concerning the budgetary implications of the proposal carried the day. Subsequent proposals introduced through the spring sought to discover a source of funding that would be acceptable to the president. One revision of the La Follette-Costigan bill, advocated by Senator Hugo Black, would provide the funds as a loan. Another version, championed by Senator Robert Wagner, would have made the $375 million an advance on future highway allotments. Hoover was successful in defeating these proposals. Subsequently, the proposals became increasingly bold. By March, Wagner was calling for a $1.1 billion public-works program. Two months later, Costigan proposed legislation that would provide a grant of $500 million to the states.[70]

66. "Washington Notes," *New Republic,* January 27, 1932, 291.
67. Chester M. Wright, "Campaign Against Depression," *American Federationist* 39, no. 3 (1932): 279.
68. "Doles for Industry," *Nation,* February 3, 1932, 131.
69. Paul Y. Anderson, "Is Uncle Sam 'Going Native'?" *Nation,* January 6, 1932, 14.
70. Olson, *Herbert Hoover and the Reconstruction Finance Corporation,* 65–67.

In the name of balanced budgets, Hoover resisted the demands for expanded relief. He also argued that the RFC needed to be given a chance to execute its functions. Yet, the early assessments of the RFC's performance were uniformly negative. On the Left, critics attacked Hoover and the RFC for creating a dole for corporations while refusing relief for the common man. In the business community, critics complained that the RFC would fail to have the intended impact so long as it continued its restrictive lending policies and high interest rates. To make matters worse, conflicts within the RFC itself—many of which were tied to Meyer's narrow interpretation of the agency's mandate—threatened the recovery program. In the end, Hoover found a way out of this political predicament by following the lead of one of his colleagues from war mobilization days—Bernard Baruch.

Baruch, along with General Hugh Johnson and Newton Baker, former colleagues from the War Industries Board, had been considering the issue of relief and how the RFC might facilitate investment without doing permanent damage to the principle of balanced budgets. Baruch concluded that the RFC could lend money to state and local governments, which were sponsoring self-liquidating public works (e.g., water and sewer works, toll bridges, electrical parks) that could be completed on schedule and instantly generate revenues, which could then be used to repay the loans. Working with Senator Joseph Robinson, Baruch convinced Hoover that this plan constituted a means of stimulating public works without violating the principles emphasized earlier in the president's conflicts with Congress.[71]

In May, Hoover held conferences with members of Congress to build support for omnibus legislation that would provide the RFC with a greater role than earlier authorized, combining Baruch's public-works provision and elements of earlier legislative proposals. Under Hoover's proposal, the RFC would lend $300 million to the states for relief—as earlier proposed by Hugo Black. Here, Hoover distinguished between loans to states and direct federal spending for relief. He believed that "responsibility for relief to distress belongs to private organizations, local communities, and the States." The Organization on Unemployment Relief, with its network of over three thousand local committees, would continue to promote the mobilization of state and local funds along with charitable contributions. Although the RFC might underwrite state bonds, it would not get into the business of direct relief. In addition, it would finance self-liquidating public works along the lines suggested earlier by Baruch. As Hoover explained: "The financing of 'income-

71. Ibid., 67.

producing works' by the Reconstruction Finance Corporation is an investment operation, requires no Congressional appropriation, does not unbalance the budget, is not a drain upon the Treasury, does not involve added burdens upon the taxpayer either now or in the future. It is an emergency operation which will liquidate itself with the return of the investor to the money markets." In short, the efforts of the RFC "constitute temporary mobilization of timid capital for positive and definite purposes of speeding the recovery of business, agriculture, and employment."[72] Finally, the RFC would lend funds to businesses that already had orders they could not otherwise fill due to a lack of credit. On this basis, Hoover requested that Congress authorize the RFC to place $3 billion in securities.

The debates and legislative maneuvers of the next two months leading to the passage of the Emergency Relief and Construction Act were complicated; the details need not concern us here. While Hoover was forced to accept some key compromises, the final act closely resembled the administration's bill. The Emergency Relief and Construction Act of 1932 significantly extended the RFC's mission and the resources it was devoting to the task of recovery. First, the act authorized $300 million worth of loans to states. As noted above, this money was to be used for purposes of relief. The loans available to any individual state could not exceed $45 million (i.e., 15 percent of the total) and were made available at a 3 percent interest rate only after governors certified that the funds raised through private charities and taxes were insufficient. Second, the act authorized $1.5 billion of loans for public works that would be income producing, in keeping with the Baruch proposal. Similarly, third, the act authorized the Federal Reserve to make loans to businesses in need of credit. Finally, the act addressed agricultural relief by authorizing the RFC to create an agricultural credit corporation, capitalized at $3 million, in each of the Federal Land Bank districts. The credit corporations would lend money to marketing and financial organizations involved in the sale of farm products. Once new legislation was in place, Hoover turned to the management of the RFC and replaced Meyer, Dawes, and Bestor—a bloc on the RFC that had opposed the expansion of the agency's mandate. With new legislative authority, new funding, and new leadership, the RFC was positioned to play a far more active role in promoting recovery on multiple fronts.[73]

Hoover's conviction that the RFC should not make direct relief expendi-

---

72. Hoover quoted in Myers and Newton, *The Hoover Administration*, 205, 209, 208.

73. Olson, *Herbert Hoover and the Reconstruction Finance Corporation*, 72–74. Fearon, *War, Prosperity, and Depression*, 143.

tures carried a high price. Many members of Congress had wanted the RFC to make direct payments (rather than loans) to the states on the basis of population. Hoover rejected this $300 million pork-barrel fund out of his concern for waste and the obvious impact such a decision would have on the committees on unemployment relief, which still appeared to be a sufficient means of promoting self-help. The RFC would loan money that states might use for relief, but this was all. Congress responded to Hoover's victory by passing in July 1932 a deficiency funding bill that eliminated funding for the president's Organization on Unemployment Relief. The $120,000 required by the organization was a trivial sum—a modest contribution to any effort to balance the budget. Hoover accepted the deficiency bill only to arrange for the RFC to cover the costs of the agency as part of the expenses of administering the $300 million already authorized under the Emergency Relief and Construction Act.[74]

By March 1933, the RFC had authorized more than $2.9 billion in loans. Of this amount, the biggest beneficiaries were banks ($1.138 billion), agricultural credit institutions ($460 million), state and local governments ($453 million), and railroads ($360 million).[75] While some argue that the RFC played a crucial role in stabilizing the financial sector by providing additional liquidity, it is difficult to separate its impact from that of the Federal Reserve, which expanded its open-market operations. Moreover, because the RFC lent relatively small sums of money and, after August 1932, was required to disclose information on the institutions that had borrowed money—information that banks feared would be interpreted as a sign of insolvency—one might argue that its impact was far less than it might have been.[76]

The Reconstruction Finance Corporation was significant for reasons that went beyond its provision of capital. Hoover's "new agency" was not only modeled on the old War Finance Corporation of World War I. It was the old war agency resurrected and staffed with many of the WFC's former employees. The return to the wartime agency was important symbolically, for it revealed a shift from earlier optimism to crisis management. As James Stuart Olson explains: "When he called for the creation of the RFC, Hoover institutionalized the analogue-of-war concept: the RFC was little more than the WFC, which had its origins in the American past—it had served two presidents, Wilson and Harding, and it had dealt effectively with financial diffi-

---

74. Wilbur and Hyde, *The Hoover Policies*, 379–80.
75. Shultz and Caine, *Financial Development of the United States*, 656.
76. Fearon, *War, Prosperity, and Depression*, 116.

culties in the war and postwar years. Therefore, Hoover patterned the RFC after its World War I predecessor, looking on the RFC as the reapplication of an emergency economic measure."[77] A crisis can be used to justify difficult decisions and redraw the boundary between the public and the private. Before, Hoover could invest hope in the cooperative relations he had forged with elites and associations throughout the American economy. Voluntarism along associational lines, he believed, could provide a solution for the depression. Now that crisis had been admitted and the cooperative efforts of the financial community had failed to perform as expected, a more statist role could be justified—albeit as a temporary expedient.

Hoover's RFC was also significant because it marked a turning point in the relationship between the state and the economy. For the first time, the government assumed responsibility for economic performance. As Jordan Schwarz notes:

> When Hoover agreed to the Wall Street bankers' demands for the Reconstruction Finance Corporation, he opened the floodgates to a torrent of demands for federal relief legislation. He had admitted that the means of reconstruction was less important than the objective. Also, by giving relief to capital institutions, he had sanctified the claims of other sectors of the community to federal relief. Moreover, he had given Congress a license for legislating recovery and relief. Before the RFC, laws could no more change the business cycle than Congress could alter the weather; in 1932 they became as effective as medical science against disease.[78]

The decision to create the RFC was, as shown above, forced on Hoover. His acceptance of the RFC was a concession to the financial community and a recognition that the old associationalism would no longer be sufficient. For the remainder of the decade, the state would play a far more central role than it had in the past. New laws and policies would be introduced in many cases to displace the old private-sector initiatives that had given Hoover such hope in the 1920s.

77. Olson, *Herbert Hoover and the Reconstruction Finance Corporation*, 45. See William E. Leuchtenburg, "The New Deal and the Analogue of War," in *Change and Continuity in Twentieth-Century America*, ed. John Braeman, Robert H. Bremner, and Everett Walters (Columbus: Ohio State University Press, 1964).

78. Schwarz, *The Interregnum of Despair*, 233.

A Return to War Government?

As Hoover was witnessing the failure of associationalism and seeking to extend the state's role—albeit, with some timidity—a growing body of critics from across the political spectrum began calling for a more comprehensive response to the depression. To be certain, the plans differed, and often significantly. However, they shared an important feature. In virtually every case, the plans looked backward to the war governance as a model of how state-economy relations could be reconfigured to meet the new crisis. On September 17, 1931, Gerald Swope, president of General Electric, published his recovery plan—a plan that bore a clear resemblance to the arrangement put into place during war mobilization. The Swope plan would have required all companies with fifty or more employees and engaged in interstate commerce to join trade associations, their activities being facilitated by antitrust liberalization. The trade associations, in turn, would be supervised by a federal agency. The corporations would provide their workers with a uniform workman's compensation act, life and disability insurance, old-age pensions, and unemployment insurance, each to be privately funded. In addition, Swope wanted all companies to adopt uniform accounting plans and provide earnings statements. This plan combined key elements of the War Industries Board and welfare capitalism.[79]

The Swope plan received the immediate support of many business leaders, including Owen Young. As one commentator noted: "The palpable truth is that some sort of action will be taken by somebody. . . . if industry remains idle and indifferent, steps will be taken by the politicians. This should have been clear to our financial and industrial leaders long ago."[80] The plan also received qualified support on the Left. The *Nation,* for example, noted that the Swope plan was "at once the most comprehensive, the most far-reaching, and the most detailed plan . . . so far put forth by any responsible 'captain of industry.'" The plan was "a recognition by one of our most intelligent industrialists that the capitalist system is now on trial and seriously threatened; it is an attempt to preserve that system by a drastic reorganization of it."[81] In contrast, the nation's leading socialist, Norman Thomas, did not have as supportive an interpretation. He predicted that the plan would be more likely to create "a curious semi-syndicalist form of capitalism than to give us

79. Eliot A. Rosen, *Hoover, Roosevelt, and the Brains Trust: From Depression to New Deal* (New York: Columbia University Press, 1977), 63.
80. "Will Swope Plan Bring Salvation?" *Forbes,* October 1, 1931, 10.
81. "Stabilizing Business," *Nation,* September 30, 1931, 232.

planned production and distribution for use rather than profit." After reviewing an impressive set of practical problems with the Swope plan, Thomas arrived at his final objections: "[I]t is consciously dedicated to the preservation of private profit. . . . The plan is weak because Mr. Swope's underlying philosophy is still weaker. For the immense mass of workers with hand and brain the question of purpose precedes the question of plan." Swope was merely advocating a "scheme for plastering a plan on to the essential planlessness of the profit system."[82]

Hoover's assessment of the Swope plan was as harsh as that of Norman Thomas, despite the fact that it had strong business support and was largely analogous to the wartime mobilization system of which he had been a part. A memorandum written in response to the Swope plan reveals Hoover's assessment:

> This plan provides for the consolidation of all industries into trade associations, which are legalized by the government and authorized to "stabilize prices." There is no stabilization of prices without price-fixing, and this feature at once becomes the organization of gigantic trusts such as have never been dreamed of in the history of the world. This is the creation of a series of complete monopolies over the American people. It means the repeal of the entire Sherman and Clayton Acts, and all other restrictions on combinations and monopoly. In fact, if such a thing were ever done, it means the decay of American industry from the day this scheme is born, because one cannot stabilize prices without protecting obsolete plants and inferior managements. It is the most gigantic proposal of monopoly every made in history.[83]

In Hoover's judgment, the Swope plan was no more than a blueprint for fascism. Whereas the combination of business under the guise of associationalism had been considered appropriate in earlier years, when this was combined with a more central role for the state and forays into the areas of pricing decisions and production levels, it crossed a distinct ideological line.

Many of the key elements of the Swope plan were echoed in the plan put forth by the U.S. Chamber of Commerce's Committee on Continuity of Business Employment. The committee of nineteen business leaders appointed by

82. Norman Thomas, "A Socialist Looks at the Swope Plan," *Nation*, October 7, 1931, 357–59.
83. Hoover's memorandum of September 17, 1931, is reprinted in Myers and Newton, *The Hoover Administration*, 119.

the Chamber announced its conclusions in November 1931. It called for a National Economic Council, created by business, to act as an advisory board. The council, with three to five members representing all of business, would be formally independent from the Chamber of Commerce. Following the Swope plan, the Chamber called for a revision of the antitrust laws to facilitate the management of production. Similarly, it supported Swope's plan for unemployment insurance and other welfare capitalist programs.[84] The Chamber of Commerce held a referendum on the proposals and released its results on December 19, 1931. Its members agreed that the antitrust laws should be revised to allow a broader role for combinations to manage production levels. That is, corporations should be allowed to collude to reduce production in areas where overproduction was a problem. Trade associations would serve as economic councils to forge agreements among their members, with a superior economic council governing the process under government supervision.[85]

One should not believe that business saw such a plan as marking a wholesale departure from the existing capitalist order. Consider the position adopted by Julius H. Barnes, chairman of the Chamber of Commerce and the man Hoover named to head the National Business Survey Conference. In his "platform for American business" released in November 1931, he reaffirmed some of the key features of the plan put forth by Swope and the Chamber of Commerce. At the same time, he argued that business must "reassure the individual American that we shall preserve the tradition of private enterprise and that Government shall act as an umpire only, to preserve fair play between its people." He called on business and those in poverty alike to eschew excessive dependency on the government. For relief, he said, we must rely on "the great reservoir of American sympathy" and "avoid, in any form, domination from the national treasury as charity goals, but maintain employment in justified public works until private industry can reabsorb its full quota."[86]

Although the Swope plan and the Chamber of Commerce plan assigned a great deal of authority to businesses—as one might rightly expect given their origins—plans that emerged from outside of the corporate world shared a similar model, one that could be traced back to the experience of war mobilization. Consider the plan conceived by J. M. Clark, J. Russel Smith, Edwin Smith, and George Soule, functioning as a subcommittee for the National

---

84. "Planning Business Stability," *Nation's Business* 19, no. 11 (1931): 56–58.

85. Myers and Newton, *The Hoover Administration,* 155. See Sumner H. Slichter, "Unemployment Relief by Business," *New Republic,* December 30, 1931, 181–84.

86. Julius H. Barnes, "A Twelve-Plank Platform for American Business," *Nation's Business* 19, no. 11 (1931): 15.

Progressive Conference. Their plan, released in January 1932, proposed a National Economic Board composed of experts in finance, scientific management, labor relations, agricultural economics, and a support staff of economists and statisticians. This board, to be appointed by the president, was to organize councils to create permanent planning organizations on an industry-by-industry basis. These new organizations would represent capital, labor, consumers, and small business, taking advantage of whatever planning capacities were already in place in existing organizations. These organizations, in turn, would be federated to create regional planning councils.[87]

In a clear departure from the Swope plan, the National Economic Board and the regional planning councils would seek to maximize production. "The true objective of planning is not less production but more. It is not stabilization at any given fixed level, but regularized growth . . . in order that our consumption might grow accordingly." The board would also promote "a nationally organized labor market with a nationwide employment service, vocational guidance and vocational reeducation for workers displaced from their jobs," along with unemployment insurance. In the process, there would be efforts to redistribute income toward those at the bottom, "who will spend more of it for the products of mass production." This would entail raising the lowest wage rates and eliminating high-cost businesses, which compensated for inefficiency through low wages. Finally, the board would institute "an elastic system of public works" that would absorb the unemployed during downturns in the business cycle.[88] Where did the authors of the National Progressive Conference plan find their models? According to the authors, they found precedent in the Swope plan and existing mechanisms used in industrial planning in U.S. firms. However, one of the chief sources was "the experience of the World War when centralized control was needed in the interest of efficient mobilization of the nation's resources." The other chief source was "the Russian Five Year Plan, which applies the methods of centralized control to ordinary peace-time production, but under a system of compulsory socialism which we are not ready to initiate."[89] Regardless of the sources, Hoover would not give this plan even the limited attention received by the earlier

87. See J. M. Clark, J. Russell Smith, Edwin S. Smith, and George Soule, *Long Range Planning for the Regulation of Industry* (report of a subcommittee of the Committee on Unemployment and Industrial Stabilization of the National Progressive Conference, published as a supplement to the *New Republic*, January 13, 1932).

88. Ibid., 4–8.

89. Ibid. See George Soule's writings supporting a system similar to that proposed in the National Progressive Conference Report, in "Chaos or Control: Learn from War," *New Republic*, March 23, 1932, 152–58, and "A Challenge to Inaction," *New Republic*, April 6, 1932, 199–204.

business-based plans. The business plans would lead to fascism—this plan to socialism. Both would violate key constitutional and philosophical principles.

The pressures for a new planning mechanism and a movement from the old associationalism of the 1920s to a more statist variant continued throughout 1932. Stuart Chase called for a "Peace Industries Board" modeled directly on the War Industries Board. Robert La Follette introduced legislation to create an economic council of fifteen members to collect and analyze data on the economy and recommend broader relief legislation. Charles Beard introduced what was perhaps the most ambitious proposal: the creation of a new national council, which would formulate a five-year plan for industrial recovery. According to Beard, the national council would "repeal the antitrust acts and declare all industries affiliated with the national economic council public-service enterprises subject to principles of prudent investments and fair returns." The council would survey "productive facilities and consumption capacity" as a basis for planning. It would "give each industry . . . the form of a syndicate of associated corporations with large directional and service powers."[90] In April 1932, Bernard Baruch, Federal Reserve governor Owen Young, and Herbert Bayard Swope, the brother of Gerald Swope, joined in the calls for a national planning board. The trend continued on June 10, 1932, when a committee of business representatives met with Hoover and publicized its recommendation that the old Council of National Defense be resurrected as an advisory body representing key economic interests. As noted in Chapter 3, the Council of National Defense was the body created by Wilson that gave birth to the key war mobilization agencies. Hoover rejected the request, noting in some detail the large number of bodies (e.g., the RFC, the Federal Reserve, the Federal Farm Board, the President's Organization for Unemployment Relief, and the newly created joint committees of industry and finance) with representatives of various economic interests. "Comprised of men of both political parties . . . they constitute the most effective economic council that could be devised because they have behind them both authority and cooperation."[91]

The pressure on Hoover to adopt a more ambitious recovery program continued as the election of 1932 approached. On September 23, 1932, Henry I. Harriman, president of the Chamber of Commerce, urged Hoover to accept the plan supported by the earlier chamber referendum and to pro-

90. "A Panorama of Economic Planning," *Nation's Business*, February 1932, 29–32.

91. Hoover's press statement of June 10, 1932, reprinted in Myers and Newton, *The Hoover Administration*, 217–18.

mote it as a part of his reelection campaign.[92] Hoover's intransigence held fast. His associationalism and reading of American individualism were simply incompatible with a more expansive role for the state. Consider Hoover's defense of his policies, delivered in a campaign speech on October 31, 1932:

> There is one thing I can say without any question of doubt—that is, that the spirit of liberalism is to create free men; it is not the regimentation of men. It is not the extension of bureaucracy. . . . you cannot extend the mastery of government over the daily life of a people without somewhere making it master of people's souls and thoughts. Expansion of government in business means that the government, in order to protect itself from the political consequences of its errors, is driven irresistibly without peace to greater and greater control of the nation's press and platform. Free speech does not live many hours after free industry and free commerce die. It is a false liberalism that interprets itself into government operation of business. Every step in that direction poisons the very roots of liberalism. It poisons political equality, free speech, free press, and equality of opportunity. It is the road not to liberty but to less liberty. True liberalism is found not in striving to spread bureaucracy, but to set bounds to it.

Hoover's position was not based on the practical problems that the various plans would present: "Even if the government conduct of business could give us the maximum of efficiency instead of least efficiency, it would be purchased at the cost of freedom."[93] In the end, Hoover's rejection of the various recovery plans found firm philosophical foundations and could not be bargained away in the name of political expedience.

As Hoover faced the 1932 campaign, the differences from his campaign four years earlier could not have been more pronounced. In 1928, high levels of employment and sustained growth had given the nation great confidence in the economy. The great engineer would provide the expertise to extend the fruits of economic growth to those who had yet to benefit from the system he had worked to forge in the years since the war. Some of Hoover's critics did not attribute the depression to the administration, although for many the connection was too attractive to resist in an election year. Yet, even if responsi-

92. Wilbur and Hyde, *The Hoover Policies*, 311.
93. Herbert Hoover, "America vs. the 'New Deal,' New York, October 31, 1932," reprinted in Myers and Newton, *The Hoover Administration*, 516–21; quote from 520.

bility could not be assigned to Hoover, the failure of associationalist responses and the president's unwillingness aggressively to extend the reach of the state brought him a certain measure of blame for the length and depth of the crisis. By the fall of 1932, a Democratic victory appeared all but certain. Hoover had adopted a defensive posture, began making expansive promises to varied constituencies, and warned that a Roosevelt victory would carry dire consequences for the possibility of recovery. Although Roosevelt was remarkably inconsistent in his campaign rhetoric, he at least hinted at a more intensive form of government-industry cooperation and planning than had Hoover.[94] In the end, the election of 1932 would provide another opportunity for compensatory state building and for a return to the model of wartime government.

94. Kim McQuaid, *Big Business and Presidential Power: From FDR to Reagan* (New York: William Morrow, 1982), 24.

9

A New Deal for an Old Model

There is no choice presented to American business between intelligently planned and controlled industrial operations and a return to the gold plated anarchy that masqueraded as rugged individualism. There is only the choice presented between private and public election of the directors of industry. If the privately elected boards of directors and the privately chosen managers of industry undertake this task and fulfill their responsibility, they will end all talk of dictatorships and governmental control of business. But if they hold back and waste these precious hours, if they take counsel with prejudice and doubt, if they fumble their great opportunity, they may suddenly find that it has gone forever.   —Donald Richberg, 1933

Not even Franklin Roosevelt, armed with the powers of a Czar, can compel any individual or corporate employer to pay out in wages money that has not first been earned. Something cannot be exacted or extracted from nothing. The whole "New Deal" must collapse unless it can be made possible for industry and business to exist, to meet its bills. Of what avail is Revolution if it begets only Receivership. . . . Dictators must not kill dividends: That would decree defeat.   —*Forbes*, August 15, 1933

The 1932 presidential election is commonly presented as a central turning point in American history, comparable perhaps to the Civil War in its impact on politics and public policy. To retell the *popular* story of the New Deal is relatively easy. At the nadir of the Great Depression, Roosevelt constructed a new policy regime premised on a fundamentally new understanding of the role of the state in the economy and the responsibilities of the government to the citizens. The new policies and institutions were reinforced by a new electoral coalition—itself a product of a party-system realignment—that would support a prolonged period of experimentation and change. Stated more simply: the sharp turn in policy forced by the Roosevelt administration marked the emergence of the modern American state and a new regime of policies, agencies, and patterns of state-economy relations that constituted a sharp break with those of the 1920s, when a series of Republican presidents provided for business while blessing the rest of the nation with the hollow comforts of self-reliance.

Such an account of the depression and the New Deal obscures more than it reveals, masking the numerous connections between the real accomplishments of the Roosevelt presidency, World War I, and the New Era. Of course, the core argument of this book is that the New Deal is best understood as part of a larger history, one that dates back at least to U.S. entry into World War I. The models of state-economy relations and administration developed during the war, new patterns of state-group relations, and the experiences of those who were involved in the mobilization process constituted the core elements out of which the New Deal regime was constructed. In essence, this places the war and the 1920s in a more important place than many contemporary histories would allow when seeking to identify the origins of the modern state and to determine what, in reality, was "new" about the New Deal. As Peri Arnold observed more than two decades ago: "Typically, pre-Rooseveltian public policy is brushed aside as largely laissez-faire in character. . . . that time prior to the New Deal has been so distorted that we fail to see the link it has to contemporary public policy." Arnold continues:

> Herbert Clark Hoover, not Franklin Roosevelt, is the father of modern public policy. Hoover, as Secretary of the U.S. Department of Commerce, provided the rationale and policy formations which were to compose the essential character of our public policy. During the early and middle 1920s Herbert Hoover consciously provided the official rationale and organization for a public policy which brought government into areas once deemed wholly private. He, in this period, became the father of "big government." Our problem has been that we all missed this point. We honored (or castigated) F.D.R. with that title and then were stymied by the degree to which big government was Hooverian after all.[1]

As shown in previous chapters, the associationalism of which Hoover was a key proponent was one of the central legacies of the war. As it evolved throughout the 1920s, finding a variety of expressions, it offered a distinctive vision of state-economy relations and economic organization. In this chapter we will explore the ways in which Roosevelt and his advisers drew freely on this history, refining, rather than rejecting, the associational legacy of the 1920s and adopting its key features, albeit with some significant modifications, as the core of the New Deal.

As one might guess, there are critics who dismiss the contention that the

---

1. Peri Ethan Arnold, "Herbert Hoover and the Continuity of American Public Policy," *Public Policy* 20, no. 4 (1972): 526. Many of these connections have been developed in Colin Gordon, *New Deals: Business, Labor, and Politics in America, 1920–1935* (Cambridge: Cambridge University Press, 1994), and in David M. Hart, "Herbert Hoover's Last Laugh: The Enduring Significance of the 'Associative State' in the United States," *Journal of Policy History* 10, no. 4 (1998): 419–44.

New Deal's contributions are best weighed in the context of a larger history. There is strong opposition to the argument that Roosevelt dug deeply into the legacy of the past when constructing his recovery program. As Elliot A. Rosen notes: "The suggestion of recent scholarship that Herbert Hoover pioneered the New Deal, or at the very least deserves recognition as a 'forgotten progressive,' rends the delicate fabric of history beyond recognition and affords the Great Engineer's views a disservice. Hoover qualifies as a progressive in the postwar era only in the sense that business conservatives and reactionaries dressed their views in the language of that movement." Rosen draws on the contrast that has become the common wisdom in discussing the New Deal: "Whereas Roosevelt and the Brains Trust broadened the social contract to include an economic constitutional order, Hoover persisted in traditionalist views that restricted the federal government and its functions and insisted on reliance upon local and state government, as well as private voluntary (associative) endeavor, in the depression crisis."[2]

Of course, the argument thus far is neither that Hoover was the author of the New Deal nor that he was a closet statist. Indeed, there is little one could do to support such assertions short of cynically recasting the historical record. However, one may still assert that Hoover *and* Roosevelt viewed the calamity of the Great Depression from the perspective of active participants in the war mobilization effort, and each in his own way sought to apply the lessons of war to the events of the depression. It is interesting to note that the explicit distinction that many have drawn between Hoover (the enemy of intervention) and Roosevelt (the statist) was not at all evident to contemporary critics. For example, in reviewing the results of the 1932 election and comparing Hoover's defeat to his victory four years earlier, Elmer Davis remarked: "Hoover, who in 1928 was denouncing his unnamed 'opponents' . . . for plotting to introduce state socialism, was compelled to ask for reelection in 1932 as a reward for his own success in introducing state socialism."[3] As shown in the last chapter, the vision of Hoover as the champion of laissez-faire did not resonate with those who had experienced the Hoover presidency and his failure to provide solutions to the crisis of the depression.

This is not to say that the earlier associationalist experiments were adopted wholesale by the New Deal without alterations. In truth, the Roosevelt administration made significant changes that were foreclosed to Hoover for po-

---

2. Eliot A. Rosen, *Hoover, Roosevelt, and the Brains Trust: From Depression to New Deal* (New York: Columbia University Press, 1977), 329.

3. Elmer Davis, "Hoover and Hubris," *New Republic,* November 16, 1932, 9.

litical and ideological reasons. Hoover and other advocates of associationalism were careful not to exceed certain ideologically defined thresholds with respect to the role of the state in the new system (see Chapter 4). Officials could facilitate group formation and create a context in which groups could engage in a form of self-regulation. However, they could not place the state in a position of financially supporting participants or promoting activities that might directly circumvent the price system. At least this was the original position, one that became less rigid as Hoover witnessed the collapse of associationalism and embraced the Reconstruction Finance Corporation. Roosevelt was not similarly bound. With the justification of a crisis, he could rationalize a far more central role for the state than that envisioned by Hoover. In several policy areas, the New Deal initiatives were designed to promote market stability and profitability via various cartelizing mechanisms and direct supports remarkably similar to (and often borrowed directly from) those which had been introduced during the war and refined during the 1920s. Where Hoover saw fascism or socialism, Roosevelt saw the opportunity for experimentation. In the end, the problems that emerged from these experiments were similar to those which had arisen out of the war effort, albeit with more significant consequences for the budget and the evolution of state-economy relations. Indeed, they became the source of serious concern in the latter half of the 1930s, as many within the New Deal grew suspicious of this model of "planning" and turned to a far different model of the state.

A New Deal for an Old Model

The intellectual and political foundations of what I have referred to as the Associational Regime were essentially in place by the close of the 1920s.[4] The accumulated experience of the war, the associationalism and New Era economics of the 1920s, and the economic associations working in close proximity to government agencies created new resources for managing crises. The key question was whether they would be effectively engaged. The 1932 campaign provided few indicators that the presidential election would mark a significant change in policy: the Democratic platform was economically conservative, and Roosevelt freely vacillated between planning and expanded an-

4. See Marc Allen Eisner, *Regulatory Politics in Transition* (Baltimore: Johns Hopkins University Press, 1993).

titrust enforcement. As Raymond Moley recalled, Roosevelt "lurch[ed]
between the philosophy of controlling bigness and the philosophy of destroying bigness, between the belief in a partnership between government and
industry and the belief in trustbusting. . . . Roosevelt had not the slightest
comprehension of the differences between the two sets of beliefs. . . . Not even
the realization that he was playing ninepins with the skulls and thighbones of
economic orthodoxy seemed to worry him."[5]

Despite Roosevelt's philosophical ambiguities and internal contradictions,
which were evident to members of the Brain Trust, he won a decisive victory
over Hoover. Yet, as the *New Republic* noted immediately following the 1932
election: "If Franklin D. Roosevelt has the least trace of common sense, he
ceased being elated concerning the magnitude of his victory almost one hour
after the returns rolled in. Even from the point of view of the practical politi-
cian, it is a sobering thought that Hoover also had an overwhelming victory
four years ago. All informed observers agree that the country did not vote for
Roosevelt; it voted against Hoover." In sum, "this is an election in which we
can find more satisfaction in rejoicing at defeats than at victories."[6] Lindsay
Rogers worried that Roosevelt's campaign had consisted of promises "directed
toward luring as many [Republican] progressives as possible into his camp.
At the same time he was so guarded in his public promises to these recruits
that the conservative wing of his party was not definitively alienated. That
was wise campaign strategy, but when action becomes necessary the day of
reckoning will be at hand."[7] Setting aside the popularized image of the New
Deal, there is little evidence that Roosevelt assumed office with anything
resembling a comprehensive program. In the worlds of a contemporary observer, during his campaign "Roosevelt studiously avoided taking any clearly
defined position on economic policy." As a result, "he received the votes of all
sorts and conditions of people, with the most variegated economic beliefs,"
but had "no well organized, educated and convinced body of opinion behind
his New Deal program."[8] Similarly, his key advisers were themselves divided
over what might constitute a coherent and effective recovery program.[9] In
this environment of chaos and ambiguity, the war and events of the past
several years had a profound impact. The war provided a common reference
point and suggested a potential response to the collapse of the economy while

5. Raymond Moley, *After Seven Years* (New York: Harper & Row, 1939), 189–90, 192.
6. *New Republic,* November 16, 1932, 1.
7. Lindsay Rogers, "Will the Democrats Turn Left?" *New Republic,* December 14, 1932, 121.
8. T. R. B., "Washington Notes," *New Republic,* August 9, 1933, 339.
9. See the contemporary account in "The Brain Trust," *New Republic,* June 7, 1933, 85–86.

offering a model of how diverse social interests might be incorporated into the administration of the recovery programs.

Roosevelt immediately began preparing the nation for a peacetime return to a war government. In his first inaugural address, he said that we must treat the task of recovery "as we would treat the emergency of war," and he promised that "the larger purposes will bind upon us all a sacred obligation with a unity of duty hitherto evoked only in a time of armed strife." He explained that he would have to ask Congress for "broad Executive power to wage a war against the enemy, as great as the power that would be given to me if we were in fact invaded by a foreign foe."[10] Under the conditions of crisis that prevailed in 1933, Congress provided the new president with the powers he requested in field after field. One observer remarked the stunning "speed with which the government of the United States has moved from democracy toward dictatorship," noting that "Mr. Roosevelt has, in some respects, more power than any other President under our Constitution ever had, except perhaps Mr. Wilson in wartime." As Roosevelt undoubtedly imagined, Congress's concerns over the "surrender of its constitutional rights" were muted by "the shadow of the national emergency."[11]

As Roosevelt freely appropriated the analogy of war to justify a dramatic expansion of executive power, former WIB chairman Bernard Baruch called for a restoration of the wartime system. In a speech before the Brookings Institution in May 1933, he repeated the message he had stressed since the market crash more than three years earlier: "A possible guide in this crisis may be found in the organization and methods of the War Industries Board."[12] The collection of war-inspired recovery plans combined well with the experiences of a number of Roosevelt's advisers, themselves veterans of the wartime agencies, and added credibility to the model of the WIB. But the references to war by Roosevelt, Baruch, and others were in some ways infelicitous given the very different nature of the economic problems at hand.[13] During the war, the challenge was to push production beyond the limits of the industrial plant while fighting inflation. In 1933, the goals were the opposite. Some means had to be found to stop deflation of prices and wages in an economy characterized by high unemployment and excess capacity. Nevertheless, the analogy

10. Franklin D. Roosevelt, "Inaugural Address, March 4, 1933," in *The Public Papers and Addresses of Franklin D. Roosevelt* (New York: Random House, 1938), 2:13, 14, 15.

11. "Washington Notes," *New Republic*, March 22, 1933, 156.

12. Bernard Baruch, quoted in Hugh S. Johnson, *The Blue Eagle: From Egg to Earth* (Garden City, N.Y.: Doubleday, Doran & Co., 1935), 153–54.

13. See George Soule, *The Coming American Revolution* (New York: Macmillan, 1934), 215, 184.

proved politically viable while providing all with a common reference point. Roosevelt's key advisers could provide theoretical justification for some form of planning. Tugwell, for example, pointed approvingly to the Soviet experiments in planning. The political utility of the programs, however, was paramount. They promised to forge a broad coalition uniting corporations, labor, and farmers, thereby transforming sources of potential opposition into clientele groups.[14]

Roosevelt and Baruch were not the only advocates of planning, nor was the model of the War Industries Board universally accepted as the correct reference point for constructing a recovery program. Different proposals reflected significant differences in the balance of power between the state and the corporate economy. As shown in Chapter 8, the idea of returning to something resembling the War Industries Board, albeit with a greater role for trade associations, was advocated by Henry I. Harriman of the Chamber of Commerce and General Electric's Gerald Swope during the Hoover administration, much to the dismay of the president. Their voices now joined with those of representatives of industries that had been exceptionally hard hit by the depression (e.g., oil, cotton). They appealed to the federal government to create or sanction a system that would allow trade associations to allocate production and stop deflation, particularly when their own systems of associational governance failed. Donald Richberg, a New Dealer of New Nationalist origins who drew heavily on the legacy of his mentor, Teddy Roosevelt, called for a national planning council to direct the activities of industry councils consisting of corporate managers, investors, and workers. This "democratization of industry" would mark the extension of democracy (as envisioned years earlier by Teddy Roosevelt) while providing a solution to the depression. Rexford Tugwell similarly advanced proposals that envisioned a far greater role for the state. In his *Industrial Discipline,* he called for the creation of a planning apparatus for each industry, operated through the related trade association. The plans of the individual associations would be combined and coordinated by an Industrial Integration Board. The strong resemblance to the War Industries Board was not a product of chance. Organized labor also entered the fray, albeit with far less enthusiasm for a system of planning that delegated authority to trade associations. The United Mine Workers' John L. Lewis, the Amalgamated Clothing Workers' Sidney Hillman, and even the American

14. William E. Leuchtenburg, "The New Deal and the Analogue of War," in *Change and Continuity in Twentieth-Century America,* ed. John Braeman, Robert H. Bremner, and Everett Walters (Columbus: Ohio University Press, 1964), 117, 129.

Federation of Labor called for planning, on the belief that labor would always be the first victim of depression, as corporations sought to preserve short-term profits by reducing wages and cutting the workforce. Despite labor's hopes of bypassing trade associations, the model that received the greatest support was that of the WIB, undoubtedly reflecting the nation's memory of the war and the active advocacy of WIB veterans.[15]

The model of the WIB and the involvement of Bernard Baruch carried some implications that concerned critics. There were fears that the industrial recovery plan, like the WIB before it, would be oriented toward business and that it would simply promote the inflation of prices and corporate profits without achieving overall recovery. Here, history was a good teacher: these were problems associated with the War Industries Board's brief experiment. As a contemporary critic noted when surveying the administration debates over industrial planning:

> There is a kind of "planning" wanted by certain advanced business leaders, and now being urged upon the administration, which is wholly unsound. This is planning by single industries to restrict output in the interests of raising prices, without more than formal supervision by the government and without real power or participation by labor. . . . Some few industries are victims of real over-production, but not all at once. Some prices are too low, but some prices, on the other hand, are too high. In any serious attempt at planning there ought to be a central agency to decide which products must be restricted and which must be expanded. It ought to have a price policy; it ought to know which prices to raise and which to cut. There should be power to increase output and lower prices as well as the reverse. All this implies that there must be strong representation, in the operation of any such scheme, for the interests of consumers as a whole, of industry as a whole, of labor as a whole. To turn planning over to separate groups of capitalist producers, each seeking to restrict output and raise prices, is to diminish the means of life for the whole nation.[16]

The key concern was that without a strong state presence and a commitment to planning on a far grander scale than conceived by the prevailing recovery plans, corporations would fix prices in their own interest, with scant

---

15. Arthur M. Schlesinger Jr., *The Coming of the New Deal* (Boston: Houghton Mifflin, 1958), 87–91, 92–94. Eisner, *Regulatory Politics in Transition,* 80–82, for a discussion of Tugwell.

16. "Roosevelt and Business: A Word of Warning," *New Republic,* May 10, 1933, 350–51.

thought of the larger issue of recovery. "It would be a bitter piece of irony if the 'new deal' turned out to be nothing in essence after all but turning the United States completely over to the big corporations."[17] Similarly, while the editors of the *Nation* believed Roosevelt's intentions to be good, they also predicted that corporations would quickly strive to use the National Recovery Administration to their advantage: "American business may for the moment present a docile and acquiescent appearance, but it is accustomed to rule and will attempt, as surely as it has attempted in the past, to dominate the government boards set up to rule it. . . . industrialists—whatever their present protestations—do not intend that any planned economy shall be allowed to do them out of opportunities to make as much money as possible."[18]

In 1933, it remained an open question whether the state would play a powerful independent role or the system would take the form of cartels controlling prices and outputs to increase the income of their members. However, the recovery legislation would mark "the acknowledged and legalized end of laissez-faire." Following its passage, the *New Republic* predicted "future struggles will not concern the question whether we are to have a system regulated automatically by 'economic laws,' or a system consciously administered. They will concern the immensely important questions of what kind of planning we shall have, what objectives it shall seek, what instruments it shall use and what classes shall control it."[19] As would become increasingly clear, the administrative model at the core of the National Industrial Recovery Act would provide a de facto answer to many of these questions insofar as it structured politics and policies much as it had in its earlier incarnations.

The National Recovery Administration

From the perspective of 1933, what was astounding was not the diversity of positions with respect to industrial recovery but rather the incredible convergence of opinion. Granted, there were spirited disagreements over the relative balance of the state and trade associations in any new system and over the kinds of provisions that would be necessary to protect labor. However, something of an elite consensus emerged around the conviction that a departure

17. Ibid., 351.
18. "Business Hops Aboard," *Nation,* June 28, 1933, 713.
19. "The Industrial Recovery Bill," *New Republic,* May 31, 1933, 58.

from existing patterns of economic activity was necessary for the preservation
of the system as a whole. Oddly enough, with this remarkable convergence
of opinion and a looming unemployment problem, Roosevelt did not turn
immediately to the question of industrial recovery. Rather, key industrial recovery legislation was delayed while the administration addressed banking
reform and the Agricultural Adjustment Act (see below). The administration
was forced into action, however, on April 16, 1933, when the Senate passed
Senator Hugo Black's thirty-hour bill, which would have spread the work to
the currently unemployed by imposing legal prohibitions on the interstate
shipment of goods produced by firms failing to adopt the thirty-hour week.
The Black-Connery bill and growing pressures for a public-works program
were sufficient to force action.[20]

Over the course of the next several weeks, two groups worked to create
industrial recovery proposals. One group, which relied heavily on Baruch con-
fidant and former WIB army representative Hugh Johnson, produced draft
legislation calling for a system of government licensing backed by tough sanctions. Donald Richberg, Raymond Moley, and Budget Director Lewis Douglas
supported the Johnson draft. A second and competing piece of legislation,
endorsed by Labor Secretary Frances Perkins, Jerome Frank, Undersecretary
of Commerce John Dickenson, and Senator Robert Wagner, placed a greater
emphasis on trade associations. In early May, Roosevelt directed both groups
to resolve any differences and present a single piece of legislation. The final
result was the National Industrial Recovery Act, which passed both houses
with minor revisions and was signed into law on June 16, 1933.[21]

Title I of the National Industrial Recovery Act created a system of govern-

20. The administration was initially sympathetic to the Black-Connery bill. Frances Perkins suggested that the bill would require a minimum-wages provision so that a reduction of hours would not
result in a comparable reduction in incomes. Likewise, she argued that the bill would have to provide
greater flexibility, particularly in seasonal industries. Organized labor supported Black-Connery even if
there were concerns that minimum wages might come to constitute maximum wages unless the bill also
contained provisions protecting collective bargaining. However, administration support was withdrawn on
May 1, 1933, partially as a response to business pressure. As Basil Rauch explains, "A hundred leading
industrialists met in Philadelphia on April 11 to protest against the Bill, and similar meetings were held
in other cities. . . . Leaders of the main organizations of business, including President Henry I. Harriman
of the Chamber of Commerce, President James A. Emery of the National Association of Manufacturers,
and Robert Lamont of the Iron and Steel Institute, appeared before the House Committee to register their
protest. Immediately, when the aggressive opposition of business began to be felt, the President directed
Moley to obtain plans from business groups which they would favor as substitutes." Soon thereafter, the
administration announced that it no longer supported the bill. See Basil Rauch, *The History of the New Deal,
1933–1938* (New York: Creative Age Press, 1944), 75–76.

21. Schlesinger, *The Coming of the New Deal*, 96–98. See Charles A. Gulick Jr., "Some Economic
Aspects of the NIRA," *Columbia Law Review* 33, no. 7 (1933): 1103–46.

ment-supervised self-regulation modeled directly on the War Industries Board and the pattern of state-economy relations it represented. As NRA administrator Hugh Johnson explained after reviewing the efforts of the WIB: "That experience, that organization, that method are of the very essence of the background of NRA and NIRA—the basic thought was, if Industry can thus act as a unit for the purpose of war, why cannot it also act as a unit for purposes of peace."[22] The parallels between the WIB and the NRA were not lost on contemporaries, as this excerpt from the *New Republic* shows:

> The fact is, of course, that the Industrial Recovery Act is a modernization of the system used by the War Industries Board under Mr. B. M. Baruch. The details are different, the scope is enlarged, and there is, of course, a new political philosophy underlying the act. But the scheme of operations will be mainly the same. The same sort of set-up will be required, and that is where General Johnson has his advantage, because it so happens that General Johnson was a member of that War Industries Board under Baruch and had more to do with devising and manipulating the war-industries machinery than any other man with the exception of Mr. Baruch himself. He has let it be known that his new job, so far as industries are concerned, will be managed along the same general lines.[23]

The newly created system of industrial "planning" vested power in "industry-dominated code authorities, most of which were simply trade associations in public garb."[24] The code authorities were empowered to establish codes of fair conduct under an antitrust exemption in order to impede deflation and ruinous competition. Drawing on the example of the National War Labor Board, section 7(a) of the NIRA required each code to acknowledge labor's "right to organize and bargain collectively through representatives of their own choosing . . . free from the interference, restraint, or coercion of employers of labor, or their agents." To prevent business interference, it stipulated "that no employee and no one seeking employment shall be required as a condition of employment to join any company union or to refrain from joining, organizing, or assisting a labor organization of his own choosing." Finally,

22. Johnson, *The Blue Eagle,* 114.
23. T. R. B., "Washington Notes," *New Republic,* June 21, 1933, 151.
24. Colin Gordon, *New Deals: Business, Labor, and Politics in America, 1920–1935* (Cambridge: Cambridge University Press, 1994), 177–78.

section 7(a) required employers to "comply with the maximum hours of labor, minimum rates of pay, and other conditions of employment."

Title I of the NIRA authorized the system of codes that would rely heavily on trade associations and code authorities. Title II, in contrast, addressed "Public Works and Construction Projects." It authorized the creation of a Public Works Administration with a $3.3 billion appropriation. An expansive public-works provision was deemed important by many involved in drafting the legislation, including Robert M. La Follette Jr. and Frances Perkins, the central proponent of public-works spending. But even Hugh Johnson argued that the two parts of the act were critical. Whereas Title I could potentially address the problem of deflation, Title II held the potential for stimulating the production of capital goods and raising purchasing power so as to limit or nullify the impact of higher wage levels on prices. The administration of the Title II public-works provisions was assigned to the Department of Interior on Roosevelt's judgment that industrial control would demand Johnson's full attention.[25]

In introducing the act, Roosevelt referred to the NIRA as "a great cooperative movement throughout all industry."[26] As the president explained when signing the NIRA, "Its goal is the assurance of a reasonable profit to industry and living wages for labor with the elimination of the piratical methods and practices which have not only harassed honest business but also contributed to the ills of labor."[27] The themes of cooperation and stabilization were stressed in Roosevelt's statements. Thus, he characterized the NIRA as "an industrial covenant" and "a great spontaneous cooperation." Corporations "in each trade [must] now band themselves together faithfully in their modern guilds—without exception—and agree to act together and at once." This would eliminate the "principles of unchecked competition," replacing them with cooperative agreements and government controls. Once again, the return to a system of wartime management was justified by the warlike emergency confronting the nation. The NRA was compared to "the great cooperation of 1917 and 1918," and FDR hoped that industry would "once more . . . join in our common peril." He concluded his lengthy statement on the NIRA with a stirring call for unity and patriotism: "As in the great crisis

25. Schlesinger, *The Coming of the New Deal*, 103.
26. Franklin D. Roosevelt, "A Recommendation to the Congress to Enact the National Industrial Recovery Act to Put the People Back to Work, May 17, 1933," in *The Public Papers and Addresses of Franklin D. Roosevelt*, 2:202.
27. Franklin D. Roosevelt, "The Goal of the National Industrial Recovery Act—A Statement by the President on Signing It, June 16, 1933," in *The Public Papers and Addresses of Franklin D. Roosevelt*, 2:246.

of the World War, [the NIRA] puts a whole people to the simple test: 'Must we go on in many groping, disorganized, separate units to defeat or shall we move as one great team to victory?'"[28]

Although business support for the NRA was widespread at the beginning, it was relatively thin. Much of the business community embraced the NRA and saw it as the direct outgrowth of the business-based plans that had circulated since the latter half of the Hoover presidency. Some rejected the Roosevelt initiative in the hope of "organizing without benefit of the National Recovery Administration, of getting together for the purpose of fixing prices and dividing markets on their own initiatives."[29] Others resisted the NRA's overtures in the belief that the "natural processes of recovery" or the intervention of the Court would render the program irrelevant. A series of editorials in *Forbes* placed the blame for the NRA squarely on business. The "dictatorship era" introduced with the NRA was a product of a business community "ready to grasp anything which promised to avert catastrophe and chaos" and "willing to obey any command—indeed, we clamored to have some one tell us, order us, what to do." American businessmen would have to "develop a type of leadership capable and worthy of guiding its own ship without undo interference from Government or bureaucracy." Unless business worked "to acquire quickly a new technique of adjusting through their own efforts the varied interests of owners, employers, consumers, competitors, the public, and the Government," the result would be inevitable: "business men [will] sink to serfdom, to niggardly dependence on the whims and prejudiced caprices of petty officeholders, to the close restraint of an ever tightening bondage of Washington Red Tape."[30]

The response of organized labor was, as one might predict, given the guarantees of section 7(a), less divided. Labor organizations were bound to flourish under the NRA. As William Green told the readers of the *American Federationist:* "Under the Recovery Act, organization is the order of the day— organization of employers in trade associations, workers in trade unions, and channels to reflect the interests and needs of consumers. Without the cooperation of labor, the National Recovery Administration would be fatally handicapped." With respect to the rights to organize and bargain collectively, "the terms of the Recovery Act are unmistakable." While he cautioned AFL mem-

28. Franklin D. Roosevelt, "Presidential Statement on N.I.R.A.—'To Put People Back to Work,' June 16, 1933," in *The Public Papers and Addresses of Franklin D. Roosevelt,* 2:252, 253, 256.

29. *Nation*, July 19, 1933, 57.

30. "Fascism Won't Fit Us: What Will Follow Dictators?" *Forbes,* August 1, 1933, 4; "Can Business Leaders Re-earn Leadership?" *Forbes,* July 1, 1933, 6.

bers that under these conditions of crisis "it is wise to avoid interferences with work," he sent a clear message to the administration concerning the limits of labor support: "When employers recognize this right [to organize] and provide true collective bargaining procedures for every stage of the relationship, workers will not need to strike. The only safe way to abolish strikes is to eliminate their causes."[31]

The NRA was placed under the direction of Hugh Johnson, but only after it became clear that Roosevelt's first choice, former WIB chairman Baruch, would not accept the position.[32] Johnson had worked closely with Raymond Moley in drafting the enabling legislation; his familiarity with the War Industries Board, the only comparable agency in U.S. history, was considered crucial.[33] Johnson used every opportunity to draw attention to the NRA and generate voluntary efforts to organize under codes. He explained that "the right of economic self-defense is narrowed to a ribbon. In such an environment, both industry and labor must organize or perish. That is one of the chief reasons for the Recovery Administration." The fundamental principle of the NRA was simple: "organization to the ultimate."[34] Business, in particular, took Johnson's message to heart, as waves of corporate representatives descended on Washington. As Paul Y. Anderson reported, the result was utter confusion: "The inauguration of the industrial-recovery program has precipitated a spectacle of chaos without a parallel, even in war time. . . . We see the dynamic General, with few competent assistants and no money, struggling to perfect his organization, discover his powers, determine his policies, and define his objectives—all within the space of a week. In short, we see him trying to complete in a few days a job that would normally require several months." One gets an even clearer picture of the situation when one "consider[s] the spectacle presented by industry itself," with "not less than 2,000 trade-association lawyers whipping up their respective clients to rush in with codes governing trade practices, wages, and working hours—all of them impelled solely by a desire to escape the operation of the federal anti-trust laws."[35]

Hugh Johnson, Donald Richberg, and the president used the threat of imposed codes and negative publicity to compel participation when recalcitrant corporations resisted the NRA following slight improvements in busi-

31. William Green, "Editorial," *American Federationist* 40, no. 9 (1933): 906, 907.
32. See Donald R. Richberg, *My Hero: The Indiscreet Memoirs of an Eventful but Unheroic Life* (New York: G.P. Putnam's, 1954), 165.
33. Moley, *After Seven Years,* 188.
34. Hugh S. Johnson, "The New Order," *American Federationist* 40, no. 11 (1933), 1182, 1180.
35. Paul Y. Anderson, "Government Without Congress," *Nation,* July 5, 1933, 11.

ness conditions and their growing realization that minimum wages and shorter working hours could carry costs that might not be fully absorbed by consumers.[36] To push the NRA forward in the face of this opposition, Johnson and the president released a "blanket code" in July 1933 that established a maximum work week of thirty-five hours and minimum wages for clerical and industrial workers. To increase support for the "voluntary" blanket code, the NRA used the fanfare of a national campaign "designed to arouse mass opinion to wartime fervor," complete with "nationwide radio appeals, campaign posters, public speeches, and other devices employed in the Liberty Loan drives." Using parades, the symbolism of the Blue Eagle, and an appeal to national sacrifice, the NRA secured the pledges of more than two million employers.[37] The publicity efforts were emphasized because of Johnson's fears that the National Industrial Recovery Act would be found unconstitutional. As Arthur M. Schlesinger explains: "Johnson . . . began to feel that he had no choice but to substitute social compulsion and thus to gamble on a voluntary approach to industrial planning. . . . everything else had to be subordinated to winning the uncoerced assent of major industries to the codes. In this way, he could bypass the constitutional issue. NRA could not therefore be an agency of direction. It had to be a forum of bargaining. The licensing powers written so hopefully into the bill could not be invoked (and, indeed, never were)."[38] Here, as in the case of the War Industries Board and the wartime mobilization agencies more broadly conceived, the NRA had to discover means of securing voluntary cooperation. Roosevelt had to offer business incentives because legal sanctions were, at best, thin. Planning was hampered to the extent that those who were subject to the dictates of the agency were able to resist or exit the relationship altogether, most likely with the support of the Court, which, at least until 1937, was still unwilling to sacrifice the interstate-commerce clause and allow a seemingly endless expansion of national state authority.

Arriving at acceptable codes in major industries was trying. In a number of industries, codes were put into place only after protracted negotiations or the threat of force. When the petroleum industry proved incapable of organizing itself, for example, Johnson imposed a code and gave the industry twenty-four hours to comment on its provisions. In the auto industry, the problem

36. T. R. B. "Washington Notes," *New Republic,* July 26, 1933, 287–88.
37. Paul Y. Anderson, "Roosevelt Turns Left," *Nation,* August 2, 1933, 120; William E. Leuchtenburg, *Franklin D. Roosevelt and the New Deal, 1932–1940* (New York: Harper & Row, 1963), 65–66. *Nation,* August 2, 1933, 113.
38. Schlesinger, *The Coming of the New Deal,* 108–9.

wasn't one of disorganization and internal conflicts but the intransigence of
Henry Ford, whose unwillingness to abide by section 7(a) collective-bargaining provisions yielded the unfortunate situation in which all of the industry
actors except Ford were organized under the code. Difficulties existed in coal
mining as well, once again over the issue of labor. Though unwilling to support section 7(a), mine owners themselves failed to provide a code, even following the personal intervention of the president and Johnson. When violence
flared between the mine owners and the United Mine Workers, Roosevelt
gave the industry twenty-four hours to approve a code, resulting in a bitumi-
nous-coal code on September 18, 1933.[39] However, backed with waves of
public support, the threats identified above, and clear economic incentives,
the NRA moved with great rapidity, particularly in light of its limited resources. In less than two years, the NRA approved 557 basic and 189 supple-
mentary codes, covering 95 percent of the industrial workforce.

Yet, there were at least two immediate problems. First, the decision to
move with such speed meant that many questionable codes were approved
without much scrutiny. Code authorities were dominated by the industries in
question (only 51 of 546 had labor representatives, and only 10 had consumer
representatives),[40] and codes frequently were designed to promote profitability of the dominant actors. As one observer noted: "The plain intent of the
law to promote balance in industry has been obscured in administration. . . .
Bad codes were approved because the Administration thought it better to
approve what the industry would concede rather than delay."[41] When divisions within an industry threatened to delay the voluntary acceptance of a
code, the NRA frequently promoted separate codes for a single industry and
justified the different treatments by identifying factors that allowed one to
view the codes as addressing easily distinguished lines of business.

Second, the power to administer the codes was vested in the industries
themselves, with only the nominal supervision of the NRA, which relied on a
network of local compliance boards, which in their turn were, by all accounts,
far less than what was needed for the task. By late 1933, *Forbes* reported,
Johnson and his compatriots had assumed "a less bellicose, more co-operative,
more conciliatory stance" toward business, thereby providing every indication
that the "NRA intends to grant industry a reasonable measure of self-government . . . and that it will step in only in instances where self-government

39. Ibid., 116–18.
40. Ellis W. Hawley, *The New Deal and the Problem of Monopoly* (Princeton, N.J.: Princeton University Press, 1966), 61.
41. *American Federationist* 41, no. 7 (1934): 697.

becomes impotent."[42] Despite the well-orchestrated demonstrations of support for the NRA in 1933, most observers reported widespread evasion. While optimists may have seen the delegation of code making and enforcement as unproblematic, it was clear that businesses were intent on using the authority to promote their own profitability. This fact was not lost on participants. As Howard S. Blood, president of Norge Corporation, noted: "Through cooperative self-government, industries can now eliminate many of the competitive evils which have caused commercial practices to degenerate into nonprofitable rackets." Similarly, Continental Can Company president O. C. Huffaman remarked that "adoption of the NRA code is simply a short cut to the end toward which the responsible and far-seeing elements of industry have been working for years."[43]

The results, in any event, should have been predictable. Codes commonly favored the larger corporations, already overrepresented in the code authorities, while creating impediments for smaller businesses. Complaints were filed in ever greater numbers, raising the concern of antimonopoly progressives in the Congress, particularly William Borah and Gerald Nye, the latter of whom claimed to have received over eighteen thousand letters from small businesses and their representatives detailing how the code authorities, dominated by large concerns and providing them little representation, were promoting price-fixing, selling below costs, and other practices that would only enhance the power of monopoly under the NRA's antitrust exemptions. Senators Hugo Black and Robert Wagner joined in the critique of the NRA, noting that price-fixing was increasing the profitability of the largest businesses while transferring income from the consumers and maintaining downward pressure on wages. In March 1934, the complaints over the NRA and concerns over its extension led Roosevelt to create a National Recovery Review Board, chaired by Clarence S. Darrow.[44] The board was given the mandate of reviewing codes to determine whether they contributed to monopoly and worked to the detriment of small business, assessing the merits of the voluminous complaints, and suggesting code revisions.[45] In the end, the board's report cited ample evidence that the NRA codes were promoting monopolistic prac-

42. "Are We Getting Over the Blue Eagle Blues?" *Forbes*, January 1, 1934, 18.

43. Quoted in "What the Codes Will Mean to Business Life," *Forbes*, September 1933, 10.

44. See Raymond Willoughby, "Small Business and the NRA," *Nation's Business* 22, no. 5 (1934): 31–32, 80–85.

45. See Theodore Rosenof, *Dogma, Depression, and the New Deal: The Debate of Political Leaders over Economic Recovery* (Port Washington, N.Y.: Kennikat Press, 1975), 85–91; Albert U. Romasco, *The Politics of Recovery* (New York: Oxford University Press, 1983), 210–15.

tices. Indeed, in its June 1934 report, the board concluded that all of the codes it had considered provided "an opportunity for the more powerful and more profitable interests to seize control of an industry or to augment and extend control already obtained."[46]

The NRA, indicted by the National Recovery Review Board and a growing bloc of opposition in the Senate, increasingly lost the support of its business constituents as well. As one business critic observed in August of 1934: "A year ago Washington hotels were crowded with business men come to request Codes for their own industries. To-day to mention the word 'code' in a business group is like striking a match in a room filled with explosive vapors. [The NRA] stands in the minds of many for petty tyranny, for bureaucracy, for economic fallacy, for monopoly by others, for unfair restrictions, and business ruin."[47] In August, Roosevelt began his efforts to end Johnson's chairmanship, a feat that was ultimately completed in October. The NRA was placed under the direction of a National Industrial Recovery Board. Through the spring of 1935, Roosevelt sought to identify reforms that would assuage NRA critics and allow for the extension of the recovery act. The Chamber of Commerce, earlier a great supporter of the National Industrial Recovery Act, argued that the NRA should be allowed to die and that Congress should pass a new bill "to permit voluntary codes of fair competition" and "agreements between competitors which, upon receiving governmental approval, would be free from penalties of the antitrust laws."[48] As one might guess, Roosevelt rejected the Chamber's plan. With mounting business defections from the NRA and little hope of Senate support, the May 1935 *Schechter* decision delivered a constitutional coup de grace.

The Performance of the NRA

To what extent was the NRA a success? Although it is difficult to answer this question directly, it is clear that the economic free fall that had consumed the Hoover presidency had ended and that there actually were modest movements toward recovery. The gross national product (in 1929 dollars) increased

46. Quoted in Rhonda F. Levine, *Class Struggle and the New Deal: Industrial Labor, Industrial Capital, and the State* (Lawrence: University Press of Kansas, 1988), 96.

47. "After the NRA—What?" *Forbes,* February 1, 1934, 10.

48. Warren Bishop, "Business Drafts a Plan," *Nation's Business* 23, no. 6 (1935): 16. See also Otis L. Graham Jr., *Toward a Planned Economy: From Roosevelt to Nixon* (New York: Oxford University Press, 1976), 30; Anthony J. Badger, *The New Deal: The Depression Years, 1933–1940* (New York: Hill & Wang, 1989), 88–92; Gerald Swope, "Planning and Economic Organization," *The Proceedings of the Academy of Political Science* 15, no. 4 (1934): 452–57; Leuchtenburg, *Franklin D. Roosevelt and the New Deal,* 84–90.

from $74.2 billion in 1933 to $91.4 billion in 1935. The unemployment rate
fell from a 1933 high of 24.9 percent to 20.1 percent in 1935, the last year
of the NRA. New jobs were being created, and existing work was being
spread around. Thus, average weekly hours in manufacturing fell from 38.1
in 1933 to 34.6 and 36.6 hours in the next two years. Under the NRA codes,
compensation in manufacturing increased from an average of 44¢ per hour to
55¢ per hour during the period in question. In nominal terms, weekly wages
increased, even if, in most cases, these increases were more than absorbed by
rising prices.[49] Beyond the wage and employment figures, labor made gains
in levels of unionization. The number of unionized nonagricultural workers
grew from 3.1 million in 1932 to 3.6 million by 1935, accounting for 13.4
percent of the workforce.[50]

At the same time, there were significant increases in corporate incomes.
Corporate profits rose significantly during the NRA's tenure. However, what
is equally apparent is that the greatest gains were realized by the largest
corporations, as indicated in the relative performance of small corporations
(with total assets of under $1 million), medium corporations (with total assets
between $1 million and $9,999,999), and large corporations (with total assets
$10 million and above). According to Internal Revenue Service data, pretax
profits increased dramatically for the largest firms. In 1932, the 2,565 largest
corporations suffered a loss of $163 million—the only year during the Great
Depression when the aggregate of large firms recorded a loss. By 1935, the
3,135 corporations that fell into this classification realized $4.3 billion in
profits. Medium-sized firms had witnessed a reversal of fortunes as well. In
1932, the 19,147 firms in this classification absorbed losses of $1.2 billion.
By 1935, the number of medium-sized firms had increased to 21,176. When
combined, their profits stood at $1 billion, approximately one-quarter of the
profits realized by corporations with assets over $10 million. In contrast, the
smallest firms faired quite poorly. In 1932, the 370,309 corporations with
assets of under $1 million weathered $2.2 billion in losses. The losses continued in 1933 ($908 million) and 1934 ($249 million). In 1935, however, the
372,792 firms in this group finally realized $189 million in profits, though
this represented only 4.4 percent of those realized by the largest firms. Taking
these data into account, it is clear that small-business complaints concerning
the big-business bias of the NRA may have been well founded.[51]

49. *Statistical History of the United States, Colonial Times to Present,* series D-47, D-626, 627, and F-3,
4. See "Hours and Wages Under the NRA," *American Federationist* 41, no. 6 (1934): 584–90.

50. *Statistical History of the United States,* series D 743.

51. Calculations by the author, using data from *Statistical History of the United States,* series V 125.

In all probability, there will never be a clear conclusion regarding the proportion of the changes noted above that can be attributed to the NRA rather than the cyclical forces in the economy and other factors. There is, however, sufficient evidence that the NRA's efforts were riddled with serious administrative problems. Despite the high participation rates, the codes and the process of code making and enforcement created many problems that might have been anticipated, given the performance of the WIB and many of the associational experiments of the 1920s. First, the NRA was in a difficult position by virtue of its tenuous legal authority and a lack of real tools—a constraining factor that was similar to that which faced the WIB (see Chapter 3). With fears that a court challenge could prove deadly, "the process of code-making turned from an exercise in overhead government planning into a series of protracted bilateral negotiations. And in these government was handicapped by a difficult bargaining position."[52]

By extension, second, the code-making process in many cases involved a significant delegation of authority. As Ralph E. Flanders observed in 1933: "Congress worked out no technique of recovery. It simply forged an instrument of power and placed it in the hands of the President. . . . the President has very wisely declined to initiate the innumerable details of industrial policy which it is his right to determine. He has extended that power to the National Recovery Administration, organized for the purpose. Through it, industry has been invited to exercise the initiative."[53] Lacking the necessary expertise to create the codes in the first place, the NRA vested responsibility in the business-dominated code authorities, afterward having to acknowledge that it also lacked the time and resources to assess the impact of industry agreements. This was a clear case of compensatory state building, with all the attendant vulnerabilities. In this case, extreme delegation was combined with an inability on the part of the administration to monitor performance. As George Soule explained: "You could look in vain in Washington for a board of experts, of men trained in economics, statistics, or engineering, whose sole business was to assess what was going on, to record concrete objectives, and judge concrete progress made toward them." As with the earlier war agencies and the associationalist enclaves of the 1920s, the NRA was highly dependent on the information corporations chose to provide: "[P]rivate industry . . . did not want the government to exercise any authority over output or prices, or to

<hr>

52. Schlesinger, *The Coming of the New Deal*, 110.
53. Ralph E. Flanders, "Business Looks at the N.R.A.," *Atlantic Monthly*, 152, no. 5 (1933): 625.

know anything about the codes and profits of individual enterprises. And the administration let it have its way."[54]

Why did the NRA prove to have so many deficiencies? It is useful to consider this question from an economic and political perspective. As economic policy, the NIRA had problems that were distinct from its political and administrative difficulties. The central economic strategy associated with the NRA was to increase purchasing power by increasing wages and limiting the work week, thereby employing ever greater numbers, who, with their higher incomes, would stimulate recovery. To that end, the NRA imposed and approved codes that specified, among other things, wages and hours. The "blanket code" of 1933 became something of a exemplar with respect to these issues, and Hugh Johnson predicted that, as a consequence of its enactment, six million people would join the workforce by Labor Day 1933. However, as Albert Evans noted: "[T]his assumption might have had some plausibility in 1928 or 1929, when the average hours of work per week exceeded forty-eight, [but] it has no such implications in 1933, when the average weekly working hours in manufacturing industries during the year's first five months were only 34.7."[55] Moreover, as Evans also explained, there was evidence that employers were speeding up the process and fully employing underused assets to meet new demand, thus failing to translate improvements in industrial production into commensurate increases in employment or payrolls. With respect to white-collar workers, where the blanket code presented a forty-hour week and a wage of $11–$15 per week, many businesses were already abiding by standards that were better than those prescribed by the administration. What of those workers who were formerly paid less than the NRA required? As Evans correctly predicted: "Employers will discover before long that many of those who were formerly considered cheap and inefficient workers are really endowed with considerable talent and can do almost as good work as was done formerly by employees who received twice or more the minimum wages specified in the codes."[56] In sum, there was little reason to believe that the NRA would have its intended effect of increasing purchasing power and reducing unemployment through the simple expedient of imposing minimum wages and maximum hours.

Of course, the labor provisions were but one part of the NRA recovery

54. Soule, *The Coming American Revolution,* 229, 231.
55. Albert Evans, "Can the NRA Succeed?" *Nation,* September 27, 1933, 345.
56. Ibid., 346.

program. The NRA was an experiment in compensatory state building, an effort to erect a system of government-supervised self-regulation plainly modeled on the War Industries Board. Beyond the political expediency, the core model of the NRA was designed to introduce stability into an industrial economy that was highly unstable and deflationary. It is here that economic and political failures dovetailed. One might suppose that the early support of business coupled with high levels of delegation and staff experience with the earlier mobilization apparatus would have contributed to the NRA's success. However, the reliance on trade associations translated into a reliance on the largest industrial interests, which would play a central role in their activities. This, when combined with the limited administrative capacities of the NRA, would have important consequences for performance. As Evans explained:

> Sophisticated industrialists . . . have been willing to surrender some of their laissez faire privileges for the greater advantage of the abolition of the anti-trust laws and the regulation of competition. The industrial codes not only give them this long-hoped-for opportunity, but definitely select trade associations, which are naturally dominated by the largest corporations, to regulate their own houses. The trade associations are to establish the definitions of fair competition and fair prices. The government's partnership will prove meaningless, since it will take many years of study before a government administrator will be able to determine what each industry's new problems really are in order to decide what "unfair" competition and "fair" prices are.[57]

As seen in the chapters in Part II of this book, an associationalist strategy carries with it a great vulnerability particularly under conditions of peace. Recall that the associational model, with its reliance on business voluntarism and cooperation, must provide the economic or moral incentives to guarantee participation. Absent the crisis of war, it can be difficult to foist the sacrifice of profitability onto business in the hopes of reaching broader social objectives. Indeed, this is the conclusion that Donald Brand derives from his fine study of the NRA, *Corporatism and the Rule of Law*. He writes:

> It had attempted too much. The NRA was an attempt to fashion a societal corporatist social peace treaty. . . . It was an attempt to replace conflict rooted in self-interest with cooperation and self-sacrifice

57. Ibid., 347.

rooted in a new social ethics. The self-sacrifice would have been forthcoming only if the NRA had been viewed as the moral equivalent of
war, yet despite Johnson's best efforts to sell the NRA on those
grounds, the NRA had soon lapsed into bitter struggles between labor
and business as they jockeyed for a relatively advantageous position
beneath the rhetoric of self-restraint. Unlike the war, the depression
had not been perceived as a sufficient national danger for groups to
lay aside their particular and conflicting interests on behalf of an overarching national purpose. The moral prerequisites for a societal corporatist peace treaty simply did not exist.[58]

In the end, Roosevelt discovered what his predecessor had discovered: in dealing with private associations, sacrifice and cooperation were difficult to secure
even when the nation faced "the moral equivalent of war"—that is, depression. However, there were ways in which the basic model could be applied
without as severe a set of problems as encountered in the NRA.

Although the Supreme Court struck down the National Industrial Recovery Act, the model survived. New Deal initiatives were implemented to extend regulations to a number of industries, including communications, stock
exchanges, the trucking industry, public-utility holding companies, commercial air transportation, and securities dealers. In some cases, new agencies were
rightly described as "small NRAs," given the fact that NRA codes provided
the starting point in regulatory design (e.g., investment-banking regulation).
Oftentimes, the initiatives were justified as efforts to hold business account-
able and protect unwary consumers, a point to be explored later in this chapter. In other cases (e.g., aeronautics, stock-market regulations), the goal was
to promote stability as a means of reducing future economic fluctuations.
Regardless of the justification, there was a common model adopted for integrating interests into the new regulatory system. With some minor exceptions,
regulatory initiatives created systems of government-supervised self-regulation where maximum authority was delegated to the parties in question. As
with other applications of this model of compensatory state building, the
regulated interests often provided regulators with access to expertise and participated in making decisions regarding entry, exit, and pricing.[59]

Postwar analysts would attribute the poor performance of the key regulatory initiatives to a host of factors. Some would portray it as the intentional

58. Donald R. Brand, *Corporatism and the Rule of Law: A Study of the National Recovery Administration*
(Ithaca, N.Y.: Cornell University Press, 1988), 289.
59. See Eisner, *Regulatory Politics in Transition*, 89–117.

product of corporate liberalism or the unintended consequence of agency capture at a particular point in an agency's life cycle.[60] Others would see it as the logical consequence of excessive delegation or the rent-seeking behavior of firms that could offer political resources to regulators in return for their services as cartel managers.[61] However, to the extent that these regulatory initiatives were a direct application of the model developed under conditions of war, one can attribute policy failure to the weaknesses inherent in compensatory state building. The extreme delegation of authority to regulated interests, the bias in support of the largest interests, and the rigidity of the opposition to technological dynamism would each become central characteristics of the modern regulatory state. Three decades after the close of the New Deal, these problems would lead critics on the Left and the Right to call for competitive deregulation and regulatory reform, ultimately eliminating much of the regulatory legacy of the New Deal.

The passing of the NRA was welcomed by many, even if its basic structure was preserved in a number of regulatory initiatives. While the National Industrial Recovery Act was quickly discounted as a mistake by many New Dealers and critics alike, the Agricultural Adjustment Act was viewed as a success. Whereas the former failed to achieve its goals under anything but the most partisan reading, the latter was widely interpreted as having improved farm incomes and the stability of the agricultural economy. It is thus useful to examine the Agricultural Adjustment Administration (AAA) and consider the National Recovery Administration's difficulties in light of its successes.

The Agricultural Adjustment Administration

The 1920s was a fertile decade with respect to the debates concerning the agricultural economy. Declining farm incomes following the heady days of the war, when combined with new levels of political organization and a growing stock of expertise in the USDA concerning agricultural regulation, created

60. See Gabriel Kolko, *The Triumph of Conservatism: A Reinterpretation of American History, 1900–1916* (New York: Free Press, 1963); Grant McConnell, *Private Power and American Democracy* (New York: Alfred A. Knopf, 1966); and Marver H. Bernstein, *Regulating Business by Independent Commission* (Princeton, N.J.: Princeton University Press, 1955).

61. See Theodore Lowi, *The End of Liberalism*, 2d ed. (New York: W.W. Norton, 1979), and George J. Stigler, "The Theory of Economic Regulation," *Bell Journal of Economics and Management Science*, 2, no. 1 (1971): 3–21.

a context that was well-suited for experimentation. As shown in Chapter 6, several competing farm-policy proposals emerged during the New Era. Hoover's agricultural policy, as embodied in the Agricultural Marketing Act of 1929, stressed the private organization of commodity groups and cooperatives as a means of self-regulation. The state facilitated self-regulation by providing start-up funds for some associations and making loans for purchasing and storing surpluses. However, it had little to offer in support of farm incomes. Beyond this associationalist approach, other, more ambitious plans attracted a great deal of attention. George Peek and Hugh Johnson had popularized the "two-price plan," under which the government would purchase surpluses to raise prices to a level that would return farmers to parity, disposing of surpluses on international markets at the lower prices. McNary-Haugen received the support of the Farm Bloc and many key agricultural groups. A competing approach, the domestic allotment plan, developed and refined through the activities of several agricultural economists, including W. J. Spillman, John D. Black, and Beardsley Ruml, found its clearest and most influential expression in the proposal of M. L. Wilson, an agricultural economics professor at Montana State College and a veteran of the USDA's Bureau of Agricultural Economics. Under Wilson's "voluntary domestic allotment plan," a processing tax roughly equal to the amount of the tariff would be collected and distributed among participating farmers on a pro rata basis. Participating farmers would have access to the funds upon signing a contract restricting the size of the crop. Both McNary-Haugen and the voluntary domestic allotment plan were designed to create scarcity in agricultural commodities and thus to raise prices and farm incomes, albeit using different mechanisms to achieve artificial scarcity and different incentives to farmers to inveigle their support.

Of course, the Hoover administration had relied on cooperation and the tariff. Under the provisions of the Agricultural Marketing Act of 1929, a Federal Farm Board doled out low-interest loans to stimulate the formation of new cooperatives and commodity-stabilization corporations. In theory, the commodity-stabilization corporations could reduce fluctuations in the price of key commodities by holding surpluses during periods of overproduction. However, without any capacity to force a reduction in acreage or impose long-term plans for the farm sector, any gains would be temporary and contingent on the performance of the industrial economy. Unfortunately, circumstances changed with sufficient rapidity to undermine the cooperative system and the Farm Board. As the economy collapsed, bringing with it agricultural demand, the stabilization funds were rapidly depleted. Commodity surpluses had to be disposed of by whatever means available. In the end, "losses from the stabilization program totaled over $300 million, a figure hardly compatible with big business's desire for low federal expenditures."[62]

The tariff proved equally problematic as a response to the agricultural crisis. Although it was initially introduced as an agricultural recovery measure, Smoot-Hawley raised rates on agricultural imports and nonagricultural goods alike. Although Hoover continued to advocate the Smoot-Hawley tariff during the 1932 presidential campaign, arguing that an elimination of the tariff would result in a flood of Argentinean corn and Mexican cattle, the tariff lost its appeal among farmers for some rather plain reasons. First, as Wayne Gard explained: "Most of our agricultural tariffs are of the 'gold-brick' variety. Since in the case of nearly every farm product the United States is an exporter rather than an importer, the tariffs on such products generally are ineffective; there are no imports against which they can be charged." Indeed, the agricultural tariff merely legitimized the demands of those seeking to ratchet up industrial tariff rates. Although the tariff provided no real benefits to the farmer due to the export orientation of the agricultural economy, the farmer suffered "infinite harm from the high rates on manufactured goods," while "retaliatory tariffs, embargoes, and favorable trade arrangements with rival nations" effectively foreclosed markets.[63]

With the desperate conditions in agriculture and the failure of the Republican agricultural policy, farmers looked to the Roosevelt administration, hoping for a much different response. Roosevelt and his advisers accepted the premise that agricultural recovery was an essential component of recovery broadly understood. In the words of two contemporary witnesses, Farnsworth Jennings and Robert Sullivan: "The derangement of farming has resulted in the gradual diminishing of the farmers' purchasing power, to the hurt of manufacturers and their employees. Until the purchasing power of the farmer is restored, the recovery of industry will be seriously retarded."[64]

Rexford Tugwell was an advocate of the voluntary domestic allotment plan, as was economist M. L. Wilson, who accompanied Tugwell into Roosevelt's camp and successfully converted the presidential candidate to his cause. However, as Roosevelt actively courted the farm vote on the campaign trail,

62. Kenneth Finegold, "From Agrarianism to Adjustment: The Political Origins of New Deal Agricultural Policy," *Politics and Society*, 11, no. 1 (1982): 16.

63. Wayne Gard, "The Farmer and the Tariff," *Nation*, February 8, 1933, 147.

64. Farnsworth L. Jennings and Robert C. Sullivan, "Legal Planning for Agriculture," *Yale Law Journal* 42, no. 6 (1933): 881. See Murray R. Benedict, *Can We Solve the Farm Problem? An Analysis of Federal Aid to Agriculture* (New York: Twentieth Century Fund, 1955), 226.

he was ambiguous in his support for the plan largely because so many farmers
and farm associations had promoted McNary-Haugen for nearly a decade.
Like other Roosevelt campaign declarations, farm-policy statements never
achieved the specificity of policy proposals but rather stood as testimony to a
pro-farmer orientation that was enticing enough to attract support and nebu-
lous enough to veil any indications of his specific preferences for one or another of the competing plans. Following the Roosevelt victory, Secretary of
Agriculture Henry Wallace, himself convinced by Wilson's advocacy of the
voluntary domestic allotment plan, framed a new farm bill that authorized
broad discretion in addressing the farm crisis. "[T]he Act was a piece of enabling legislation that gave the Secretary of Agriculture discretion to choose
from a number of alternative policies. Aside from entering agreements with
growers of basic commodities to pay them to reduce their acreage, the Secretary could also negotiate marketing agreements by which processors would
pay farmers a minimum price for their produce; he could give cotton growers
the option of buying government stored cotton in return for cutting production and could subsidise agricultural exports."[65]

Because many farmers and associations remained advocates of McNary-
Haugen, the first challenge was to mobilize farmers behind a plan that had
left them cold in the past. Roosevelt clearly stated his support for the voluntary domestic allotment plan to a meeting of farm leaders in March 1933.
However, it was necessary for the administration to enlist the support of farm
organizations and farmers for the AAA to be successful. Here, the administration was already employing the agricultural associations as clientele groups.
As Kenneth Finegold explains: "The role of farmer organizations in the establishment of the AAA was rather the reverse of that suggested by pluralist
theory. . . . it was the president-elect and his advisors who were able to use
the ties developed with the farm organizations during the campaign to 'impose' their preference for a policy of production controls upon the organizations. The farm organizations, in turn, won the consent of their members for
the new direction in federal farm policy."[66] Of course, the worsening farm
economy, the growing reality of farm foreclosures, and the potential for a
national farmers' strike created a context in which any significant effort to
bolster farm incomes would be greeted warmly.[67]

The New Deal's agricultural relief proposal, while seemingly bold in con-

65. Badger, The New Deal, 152.
66. Finegold, "From Agrarianism to Adjustment," 23.
67. See Leuchtenburg, Franklin D. Roosevelt and the New Deal, 48–52.

trast to the actions of the earlier administration, still received a fair amount of criticism. The *Nation,* for example, came out strongly in opposition to the new farm legislation, predicting that this "mere resurrection of the allotment and parity plans, with a few dubious amendments," would "prove to be the most harmful piece of legislation adopted in many years, not even excluding the Smoot-Hawley tariff." Noting that there was nothing "sacrosanct and 'right' about the price relationship that happened to exist from 1909 to 1914," it called on Congress to consider "the most fundamental changes in supply and demand and in relative costs of production" that have occurred in the intervening decades. The belief that the policy would increase farm purchasing power was described as "almost completely fallacious," since "exactly as much purchasing power would be taken away from consumers."[68] Indeed, the redistributive features of the agricultural adjustment legislation were the most problematic:

> Stripped to its essentials, it is a bill to take away a billion or so dollars a year from three-fourths of the population and pay it over to the other fourth. Even this could be defended if it could be shown that practically all of the three-fourths from whom the funds were taken were better off than practically all of the one-fourth to whom they were given, and if the three-fourths were taxed in some relation to their individual ability to pay and the one-fourth were subsidized in some relation to their individual need. The measure makes no pretense, however, of fulfilling any of these conditions. . . . the larger the farm, that is, the wealthier the farmer, the larger the bonus. The other three-fourths are to be taxed by the most indefensible tax ever levied by any government in modern times. . . . If a subsidy is to be paid to one-fourth of our population, the one demand that must be made in common decency is that it be raised by an increase in the income, inheritance, and corporation taxes, and not by a tax that must fall on underpaid workers and the unemployed.[69]

The *Nation* concluded that "the new farm bill . . . marks a return on an unparalleled scale to the subsidy methods that broke down when they were attempted under the Farm Board and under the old loan policy of the Reconstruction Finance Corporation." Lower tariffs and the exportation of surpluses,

---

68. *Nation,* March 29, 1933, 329–30. See the sharply negative critique in B. H. Hibbard, "Will the Farm Bill Work?" *Nation,* April 5, 1933, 366–67.

69. "The Farm Subsidy," *Nation,* April 12, 1933, 387.

it was argued, rather than a new subsidy program, were deemed essential for true agricultural relief.[70]

According to the Agricultural Adjustment Act, the central goal of the policy was "to establish and maintain such balance between the production and consumption of agricultural commodities, and such marketing conditions therefor, as will re-establish prices to farmers at a level that will give agricultural commodities a purchasing power with respect to articles that farmers buy, equivalent to the purchasing power of agricultural commodities in the base period" (i.e., 1909–14, for all commodities other than tobacco, which was pegged to the period 1919–29). This goal of achieving parity had taken on great significance for the advocates of agricultural relief in the 1920s. The regulatory authority given to the newly created Agricultural Adjustment Administration extended, in the first instance, to limiting production and increasing farm income. To this end, the AAA was authorized to reduce acreage under cultivation via voluntary agreements backed with benefit payments (i.e., "rental fees" at rates deemed "fair and reasonable") and nonrecourse loans made in advance on commodities. This system was to be financed through processing taxes that reflected "the difference between the current average farm price for the commodity and the fair exchange value of the commodity" (i.e., what would be needed to achieve parity). Production controls initially limited to corn, cotton, hogs, milk, rice, and tobacco were extended the next year to include barley, beef, flax, grain sorghums, peanuts, rye, sugar beets, and sugar cane. The AAA was also authorized to enter into marketing agreements with producers and processors to control prices, production levels, and the profit margins of handlers and processors. This authorization came complete with an antitrust exemption. In order to regulate processors and associations that might drive down prices through their purchasing, the act authorized the AAA to license them and to use the licensing process to stop "unfair practices of charges that prevent or tend to prevent the . . . restoration of normal economic conditions." In addition to the processing tax noted above, Congress authorized an appropriation of $100 million to cover administration and expenses incurred at the beginning of the program.[71]

In October 1933, Roosevelt directed the agriculture secretary to incorporate a Commodity Credit Corporation (CCC). This government corporation was created as the primary agency responsible for price supports and the

70. *Nation,* March 29, 1933, 330.
71. Benedict, *Can We Solve the Farm Problem?* 228–30. See Paul J. Kern, "Federal Farm Legislation: A Factual Appraisal," *Columbia Law Review* 33, no. 6 (1933): 985–1012.

purchase/sale of agricultural commodities. At first, the CCC was run essentially as an extension of the Reconstruction Finance Corporation, which provided most of its funds (the CCC was ultimately transferred to the USDA in July 1939, under Reorganization Plan No. 1). The CCC supported prices by setting a floor price for commodities and making loans and loan guarantees at that price for parties that participated in the set-aside program. Under such nonrecourse loans, floor prices could be set above the market price, and loans could be made with the realization that should the floor price be higher than the market price, the farmer could surrender his or her collateral (i.e., the specific portion of the farm production) to the CCC. In essence, nonrecourse loans provided a fine means of supplementing farm income immediately while compelling much higher levels of participation in the "voluntary" set-aside program. The CCC also resorted to the emergency purchase of pork in 1933–34 and cattle and sheep the next year to reduce surpluses.[72]

It appears that the AAA was remarkably effective, although it is difficult to separate its impact from that of the droughts in 1934–36, which created such scarcity in some key commodities, like wheat, that the nation actually depended on imports. The effectiveness of the AAA's programs was enhanced by the density of coverage. Between 93 and 98 percent of the corn acreage in top corn-producing states, along with some 89 percent of the wheat, was covered by the agreements. Over 75 percent of the cotton acreage was controlled through AAA contracts. The high participation rates resulted in the elimination of surpluses and an increase in farm incomes. Agricultural cash income, which stood at $.4 billion in 1932, exceeded $7.2 billion in 1935. At the same time, interest on mortgage debt fell from 9.6 percent of gross income to 4.5 percent.[73] In large part, the improvement of farm incomes was a product of the high levels of transfer payments, which reached $573 million by 1935. As a result of this performance record, the basic features of the AAA were reconstituted after the Supreme Court overturned the processing-tax provisions in *U.S. v. Butler* (1936).[74]

Almost immediately following the Court decision in *Butler,* Congress passed new legislation that continued the system of agricultural regulation, albeit with some notable modifications. The Soil Conservation and Domestic

---

72. Merle Fainsod, Lincoln Gordon, and Joseph C. Palamountain Jr., *Government in the American Economy,* 3d ed. (New York: W.W. Norton, 1959), 134.

73. M. R. Benedict, "An Appraisal of Aspects of the Transition Program for Agriculture," *Journal of Farm Economics* 19, no. 1 (1937): 32.

74. Badger, *The New Deal,* 159, and Fainsod, Gordon, and Palamountain, *Government in the American Economy,* 135.

Allotment Act of 1936 provided direct federal payments (rather than funds collected through a processor tax) to farmers for replacing "soil-depleting" crops with "soil-conserving" crops. While this new emphasis reflected the debates over land use within the AAA, it was essentially a new package for an old policy. "This was a shift from the plan of making payments for not planting certain crops to making payments for planting types of crops that were considered desirable from the standpoint of soil conservation. Since the crops defined as soil-depleting were essentially those previously referred to as basic crops, this was in effect another way of paying for reducing the acreages of the principal cash crops."[75] The act also authorized benefit payments to farmers raising basic crops, albeit only on the portion that constituted the farm's prorated share of the crop consumed domestically. In the end, the impact of the new legislation was essentially the same as that of the Agricultural Adjustment Act of 1933: farmers were paid to reduce acres devoted to basic (surplus-prone) crops. The key difference, of course, came in the source of the benefit payments.

Congress supplemented the Soil Conservation and Domestic Allotment Act with the passage of a second Agricultural Adjustment Act in 1938. Under the Soil Conservation and Domestic Allotment Act, support payments were drawn directly from congressional appropriations and were smaller than those previously. Fortuitously small harvests in 1936 allowed the market to make up some of the difference in farm commodity prices. However, favorable weather, expanded planting driven by the high prices of the previous season, and the lack of a working system of set-asides promised a large harvest for 1937. Roosevelt urged Congress for new farm legislation that would provide a permanent replacement for the 1933 act. Under the Agricultural Adjustment Act of 1938, a system of nonrecourse loans, parity payments, and marketing agreements was combined with acreage allotments to prevent overproduction and thus bring the farm economy toward the established goal of parity. The secretary of agriculture was directed to establish marketing quotas to control surpluses of key commodities, subject to the approval of producers controlling two-thirds of the commodity in question.

The new farm legislation carried two important features that would structure agricultural politics in the future. First, whereas the initial AAA was designed as an emergency measure, the new legislation created a permanent system. As J. S. Davis remarked in 1937: "Huge federal subsidies to farmers, however camouflaged, are one thing in years of extreme agricultural distress

75. Benedict, *Can We Solve the Farm Problem?* 252.

and quite another in the general run of years. The grave emergency which the Agricultural Adjustment Act was ostensibly designed to meet has passed." Under this permanent policy, "farmers have been taught that 'parity prices' as legally defined are their just due, and that Congressional recognition of this 'right' marks a new epoch in our agricultural policy."[76] Second, whereas the first Agricultural Adjustment Act vested AAA bureaucrats with a tremendous amount of discretion in designing agricultural policy and arriving at decisions concerning levels of support and production on a commodity-by-commodity basis, these details were now incorporated directly into legislation. Henceforth, Congress would be the key player in determining levels of support, with obvious implications for Congress–interest-group relations and USDA autonomy. With significant political capital to be extracted from farm bills, Congress claimed the power over subsidy levels that was formerly vested in the USDA, thereby giving rise to the long history of farm bills that stretches to this day.[77]

Superficially, it would appear that the AAA was nothing more than an NRA for the farm economy. Why, then, did the AAA succeed, whereas the NRA nearly collapsed? An adequate response to this question has four components. First, farmers and farm associations had been actively advocating a system of government supports directed toward the goal of parity for more than a decade. The AAA provided an opportunity to realize this goal. The sectoral and regional divisions that prevented comparable business efforts were less pronounced in agriculture. Second, the AAA provided farmers with direct subsidies, thus creating greater incentives for participation than those which existed on the industrial side, where a return of profitability led businesses to entertain defection from the NRA. Such a system of subsidies, firmly rejected by Commerce Secretary and President Hoover over the 1920s, did not encounter the same ideological barriers a decade later. As a result, one of the central weaknesses of any associational scheme—the need to entice cooperation with profitability—was used to strengthen the relationship between the state and economic groups. Certainly, the lack of a viable alternative to the benefits provided by the state meant that participation was necessary for survival. Third, farmers had a good deal of experience working with government officials. The USDA had long served important functions for the farmer, providing technical support via the dissemination of new tech-

76. J. S. Davis, "Observations on Agricultural Policy," *Journal of Farm Economics* 19, no. 4 (1937): 864, 871.
77. Badger, *The New Deal*, 161–63, 168.

nologies and information on market conditions. To be certain, many corporate executives had gained some experience working with the Commerce Department, the Federal Trade Commission, and other agencies over the course of the last several decades. But these agencies provided a context for corporate cooperation instead of serving a directly promotional function. Finally, the AAA could draw on the expertise of USDA bureaucrats. As noted in Chapter 6, the USDA had more scientists on staff than the rest of the government combined. They were experienced in the direct application of intellectual innovations to the problems confronted in agriculture. They proved to be an indispensable asset for the recovery program. Indeed, Theda Skocpol and Kenneth Finegold use the close relationship between farmers and the USDA, and the stock of bureaucratic expertise, to explain the relative success of the AAA.[78]

Despite this positive record, the AAA suffered from several problems, some of which were common to other New Deal initiatives. First, the AAA's reliance on processor taxes inflated consumer prices, thereby creating a system that transferred wealth from the population as a whole to those participating in the AAA. Regulation, in this case, constituted a means of redistributing wealth from consumers to producers. The difficulties in this transfer were even greater when the problem was one of underconsumption rather than oversupply. Many consumers found that the prices for meat, dairy products, and vegetables increased precisely when they could least afford it, thus leading to a reduction in the consumption of life's necessities. Second, the AAA placed a disproportionate emphasis on large farm and producer groups to create a stable coalition and exploit the existing relationships between the USDA and large farms. One result of this emphasis was that "extension agents worked only with the more prosperous farmers and did not have the time, the inclination, or the techniques to work with the low-income and poverty-stricken rural groups."[79] Another result was the channeling of support payments to the most successful farms rather than poverty-stricken tenant farms, a bias that continues to this day. When seen in this light, the large-scale redistribution of income is most difficult to justify as a reform measure, although it makes perfect sense when interpreted as a cost of coalition maintenance.

Relatedly, third, the corporatism of the AAA undermined attempts to use agricultural policy to address rural poverty and promote long-term economic

78. See Theda Skocpol and Kenneth Finegold, "State Capacity and Economic Intervention in the Early New Deal," *Political Science Quarterly* 97, no. 2 (1982): 255–78.
79. M. L. Wilson, "Problem of Poverty in Agriculture," *Journal of Farm Economics* 22, no. 1 (1940): 10.

reforms. Much evidence at the time suggested that farm policy was actually working to the detriment of the tenants and share-croppers, who were being forced off of land that was to be left fallow, only for the landowner to collect parity and conservation payments. At the same time, the continuing dissemination of new technologies (e.g., motorization of farm power) was displacing farm laborers.[80] A number of New Dealers, including Jerome Frank and Rexford Tugwell, promoted a more activist orientation to agricultural planning, one aimed at addressing broad issues of economic justice. However, such promotion threatened to undermine the close relationship between major commodity producers and the AAA. The Roosevelt administration chose to nurture its relationship with major producers; Jerome Frank and other advocates of social-policy reform were purged from the AAA in 1935. In the end, rural poverty would receive the attention of the Resettlement Administration and, after 1937, the Farm Security Administration, neither of which had a fraction of the resources that the AAA had devoted to the pursuit of parity.[81]

Beyond Welfare Capitalism

Before the New Deal, there were a few significant advances toward greater recognition of, and protection for, organized labor. As shown in Chapter 5, the National War Labor Board of World War I had gone far in implementing the basic principles developed by the U.S. Commission on Industrial Relations. The right to organize and engage in collective bargaining had become the cornerstone of war labor policy. However, the progress made under the National War Labor Board was temporary. In this case, the failure of policy makers in the 1920s to extend the legacy of World War I was critical. In the absence of a system of industrial relations in which the state played a role comparable to that played in several regulatory arenas, many corporations provided a host of welfare benefits and internal mechanisms of labor representation in hopes of limiting the appeal of independent unions. With the abdication of state authority, the power to make decisions regarding labor relations and the extent to which profits would translate into worker incomes rested,

80. Ibid., 10–11. See Theodore Saloutos and John D. Hicks, *Agricultural Discontent in the Middle West, 1900–1939* (Madison: University of Wisconsin Press, 1951), 515–17.

81. See Leuchtenburg, *Franklin D. Roosevelt and the New Deal*, 75–76, and Romasco, *The Politics of Recovery*, 165–67. Saloutos and Hicks, *Agricultural Discontent in the Middle West*, 510.

by default, with corporate managers. As the events of the Hoover presidency suggest, associationalism in labor relations depended heavily on positive economic performance. Partnerships forged in prosperity would be forsaken in times of economic hardship, when corporations found the system far too expensive to maintain.[82]

The New Deal brought unparalleled advances for organized labor and stood as a logical culmination of the earlier war experience. The new regulatory system promoted the organization of workers and compelled corporate managers to engage in collective bargaining. No longer could there be any reasonable expectation that corporate policies would guarantee the welfare of workers. As noted earlier, the New Deal industrial recovery program was premised on the belief that the economy would be prone to industrial disruption absent the creation of a system of collective bargaining. Of course, whether employers bargained with independent unions or company unions was not a critical issue for many of the New Dealers (including Hugh Johnson), as exhibited, for example, in the iron and steel codes, which contained provisions for company unions and internal mechanisms for adjudicating disputes.[83] While section 7(a) of the National Industrial Recovery Act recognized some of the historical demands of labor and essentially reestablished the operating principle of the National War Labor Board, the elimination of the NRA created a regulatory vacuum. Heightened labor expectations and employer intransigence resulted in a new wave of industrial militancy. Thus, 1935 witnessed 2,014 work stoppages—the largest number since the wave of strikes in 1920–21—involving some 1.12 million workers.[84] Following the *Schechter* decision, Congress moved promptly to pass a new National Labor Relations Act.

Before examining the National Labor Relations Act in detail, it is important to consider the NRA's contribution to the labor movement. Although the movement toward unionization increased dramatically following the passage of the National Industrial Recovery Act, contemporary observers ques-

82. Foster Rhea Dulles and Melvyn Dubofsky, *Labor in America: A History,* 4th ed. (Arlington Heights, Ill.: Harlan Davidson, 1984), 241–42, 253–54. Milton Derber, "The New Deal and Labor," in *The New Deal: The National Level,* ed. John Braeman, Robert H. Bremner, and David Brody (Columbus: Ohio State University Press, 1975), 116–17.

83. See Johnson's statement in "The New Order," 1187. See William Green, "Labor States Its Case at Iron and Steel Code Hearings," *American Federationist* 40, no. 9 (1933): 914–23. The code, proposed by the American Iron and Steel Institute, allowed for the nomination and election of representatives on the premises of the employer, required that the representatives be chosen from among employees, and established internal mechanisms of appeal for labor disputes.

84. *Statistical History of the United States,* series D 764.

tioned whether the act would have genuinely positive fruits or whether, alternatively, it would subvert the historical demands of organized labor. In a contemporary critique of New Deal labor policy, Herbert Rabinowitz interpreted the act as having very conservative implications for the evolution of labor relations: "Section 7-a, as officially interpreted, aims to confer upon labor the privilege to organize and bargain collectively, but denies every effective use of this privilege. Far from enlarging labor's most essential rights, the New Deal actually endangers them." Rabinowitz explained:

> Under the new dispensation, as envisaged by General Johnson, unions are to survive not as militant organizations of workers, as in the past, but merely as the necessary machinery to insure that the arrangements entered into by labor leaders under central, government-dominated auspices will be observed by the millions of the rank and file. . . . It is not difficult to see in these developments the foreshadowing of an attempt to bring about universal compulsory arbitration, for which machinery is already being evolved. Labor is to be fed—and tamed. It is to be given a comfortable cage, but its claws are to be clipped and its teeth filed.[85]

While this assessment of section 7(a) of the NIRA seems extreme at first glance, one need only consider the underlying approach to labor relations, particularly as it evolved following the *Schechter* decision and the passage of the Wagner Act.

The new labor-relations bill was proposed by Senator Wagner, head of the NRA's National Labor Relations Board (NLRB). First introduced in the Senate on February 21, 1935, the bill was drafted without much consultation with the administration and received Roosevelt's endorsement a few days before *Schechter,* and then only after it was clear that the bill would pass both chambers of Congress.[86] The act created a new National Labor Relations Board composed of three individuals appointed by the president and confirmed by the Senate. Expanding upon the provisions of the National Industrial Recovery Act, the new legislation established the right of workers to elect via majority rule their own exclusive representatives. Employee representation would take the place of the company unions that had been a central element of welfare capitalism: they were effectively outlawed. The act explicitly pro-

85. Herbert Rabinowitz, "Amend Section 7-a!" *Nation,* December 27, 1933, 732.
86. See James A. Gross, *The Making of the National Labor Relations Board: A Study in Economics, Politics, and the Law* (Albany: State University of New York Press, 1974), vol. 1, chap. 4.

hibited a number of unfair labor practices and placed great power in the new NLRB. It was, for example, empowered to determine the appropriate unit for elections and representation, which in turn would significantly determine the shape of organized labor in the United States. The NLRB was also authorized to issue cease and desist orders and to appeal for court injunctions in response to the violations of these orders.[87] While the new NLRB was in many ways similar to the National War Labor Board, there was an important difference, as Melvyn Dubofsky correctly notes, "[U]nlike its World War I precursor . . . the NLRB had real coercive power."[88]

The National Labor Relations Act drew on the legacy of the NRA and the NWLB. It created a system of collective bargaining in which representatives of labor and management negotiated over the various dimensions of the employment relationship, albeit within narrow legal parameters. Once unions were certified, management had a duty to bargain. This promoted stability in industrial relations via the regulation of the adversarial relationship between labor and management. This system of collective bargaining also minimized direct state intervention and restricted the scope of conflict by reinforcing several important presumptions. First, management had a distinct interest in making all the key decisions within the business enterprise (e.g., decisions on production, capital investment, technology, workplace organization). Second, labor unions had a distinct interest in negotiating over the impact that management decisions would have on a relatively narrow set of issues (e.g., wages, hours, and working conditions). Thus, private-property rights and the contract rights of business were preserved, labor's right to association was legally acknowledged, and a framework was established in which the state played a limited role of supervising the collective-bargaining process without entering into substantive decision making.[89]

As the asymmetries of power in the industrial relations system suggest, the administration's goal was more to promote industrial stability than to advocate the expansive demands of labor or completely equalize the power of the two partners in the wage bargain. Roosevelt procrastinated in his support for the Wagner Act. He was ambivalent over the question of proportional representation in unionization, despite the obvious conclusion that any movement away from monopolistic representation would severely compromise the

87. See Fainsod, Gordon, and Palamountain, *Government and the American Economy*, 190–91.

88. Melvyn Dubofsky, *The State and Labor in Modern America* (Chapel Hill: University of North Carolina Press, 1994), 166.

89. Thomas A. Kochan, Harry C. Katz, and Robert B. McKersie, *The Transformation of American Industrial Relations* (New York: Basic Books, 1986), 24, 27.

bargaining power of workers. He repudiated the sit-down strike, which, he believed, undermined the collective-bargaining process. The goal of promoting stability was also evident in Roosevelt's response to concerns that the NLRB was biased in support of the Congress of Industrial Organization. Board member Edwin Smith and the board secretary, Nathan Witt, alleged Communists and close associates of CIO general counsel Lee Pressman, actively promoted a seemingly boundless interpretation of the NLRB's mandate. At the very least, this compromised the NLRB's neutrality; and at the worst, it would place the NLRB in the position of planning the evolution of capital-labor relations, thereby sacrificing business support for the NLRB. Roosevelt appointed William M. Leiserson to the board and directed him to "clean up" the situation, a strategy that resulted, ultimately, in the resignation of a number of NLRB officials and procedural changes that enhanced the neutrality of the board.[90]

This intervention to preserve the NLRB's neutrality was believed essential: the perception of neutrality would determine whether business would accept the board as a legitimate intermediary in industrial relations. Any doubts concerning NLRB neutrality could embroil the board in endless appeals that would absorb all of its resources. To promote neutrality, the administration had decided at an early point to professionalize the NLRB with attorneys, representatives of a profession that values procedural propriety and conflict resolution within a neutral legal system. Legal norms could invest the NLRB with a sense of impartiality. Because the law could address a limited set of issues—precisely those that did not threaten the distribution of economic power—it could contribute to the stability of industrial relations and set parameters on industrial conflict.[91] This strategy of legal professionalization and strict neutrality was successful: the new labor policy was ruled constitutional in *NLRB v. Jones and Laughlin Steel Corporation* (1937).[92] Subsequently, the Economic Division was removed altogether. Members of the division had proved too willing to move beyond a technical-support function to engage in

90. Derber, "The New Deal and Labor," 115–16; Christopher L. Tomlins, *The State and the Unions: Labor Relations, Law, and the Organized Labor Movement in America, 1880–1960* (Cambridge: Cambridge University Press, 1985), 201–24.

91. See Terry M. Moe, "Interests, Institutions, and Positive Theory: The Politics of the NLRB," *Studies in American Political Development* 2 (1987): 236–99; Tomlins, *The State and the Unions,* 154. Contrast Tomlins's position with that in Dubofsky, *The State and Labor in Modern America,* 131.

92. *National Labor Relations Board v. Jones and Laughlin Steel Corporation,* 301 U.S. 1 (1937); Peter H. Irons, *The New Deal Lawyers* (Princeton: Princeton University Press, 1982), 236–40; and J. Warren Madden, "The Birth of the Board," in *The Wagner Act After Ten Years,* ed. Louis G. Silverberg (Washington, D.C.: Bureau of National Affairs, 1945).

long-term planning. By 1940, when hostile House hearings led to allegations that division head David Saposs had Communist links and that the division as a whole carried a planning bias into its activities, the fate of the economists had been sealed.[93]

Under the system created by the National Labor Relations Act, the NLRB played a central role in holding elections for union representation. To a great extent, the growth of union membership during the period was a product of NLRB policies and an indicator of agency performance. By the end of 1939, over twenty-five thousand cases involving nearly six million workers had been filed with the NLRB. The NLRB had conducted twenty-five hundred elections for union representation and settled two thousand strikes. In many instances, the NLRB was decisive in resolving conflicts between the AFL and the CIO by determining the correct unit of representation. The NLRB provided an orderly mechanism for resolving these conflicts, thus allowing for gains in union density as the two organizations competed for new affiliates. This role, in turn, opened the board to the criticism of its chief beneficiaries. As a result of this competition and the new mechanisms put in place by the NLRB, union membership almost doubled in the four years following the passage of the Wagner Act, increasing from some 3.75 million to over 6.55 million.[94]

The NLRB brought far greater stability to industrial relations and allowed for union gains without the open industrial warfare that had marred the history of industrial relations. However, as Herbert Rabinowitz's earlier comments suggest, some feared that these benefits came at a colossal cost. Labor contracts and industrial relations were recast in highly legalistic terms; disputes were resolved in quasi-judicial hearings rather than on the shop floor. The highly complex legal discourse that now dominated industrial relations effectively banished rank-and-file union members from the debates over labor contracts. This exclusion would only intensify in the post–World War II period, when complicated multiyear agreements covering all aspects of the wage bargain became routine. New Deal regulation of industrial relations introduced a greater conservatism into the labor movement: narrowly circumscribed discussions of wages, hours, and benefits foreclosed the debates over workplace control that had raged earlier in the decade. The detailed multiyear contracts of the early postwar period created new sources of rigidity in the

93. See Gross, *The Making of the National Labor Relations Board,* 176–79, 237.

94. Derber, "The New Deal and Labor," 114; Tomlins, *The State and the Unions,* 148, 156; Dulles and Dubofsky, *Labor in America,* 288.

production process. In the end, the labor initiatives had an impact similar to those of other regulatory policies: by creating a system of government-supervised self-regulation that integrated associations into the policy process, stability could be achieved, albeit with a residue of rigidity that would impede dynamism in the future.

From Welfare Capitalism to the Welfare State

The events of the 1920s and early 1930s had provided a cruelly clear lesson: progressive corporations would assume expanded responsibility for the welfare of their workers by providing a host of quasi-welfare-state benefits only to the extent that such expenditures could be funded out of revenues. As the depression cut into sales and the economy entered long-term decline, corporations began to cut their labor forces, thus marking an end to welfare capitalism. The advances in social welfare allowed for a decisive movement from a system of welfare capitalism to a system of guaranteed entitlements. The National Labor Relations Act's prohibitions on company unions completed the transformation of labor policy.

Once in office, Roosevelt moved quickly to provide relief to the unemployed and support for the starved state and local welfare agencies. The Federal Emergency Relief Act of 1933 appropriated $500 million for direct relief, to be administered by the Federal Emergency Relief Administration (FERA), under the direction of Harry Hopkins. On arrival of winter 1933, the Civil Works Administration (CWA) was created to implement an emergency works program for the unemployed. Through the combined efforts of FERA, CWA, and the Civilian Conservation Corps, some twenty-eight million people—more than 22 percent of the population—received some form of relief at this time.[95] Concerns over the cost of the CWA led Roosevelt to disband it, leaving the FERA as the primary relief agency. Unlike the CWA, the FERA required recipients to complete a means test. Moreover, it provided much lower levels of benefits. By the end of 1934, some twenty million people remained on relief, suggesting that the need for relief was far greater than anticipated by the administration.[96] Congress passed the Emergency Relief Appropriation Act of 1935, authorizing the president to spend $5 billion on various forms of relief. Of this money, some $1.4 billion went to the Works Progress Administration (WPA), a new public-works agency that replaced the FERA and

95. James T. Patterson, *America's Struggle Against Poverty, 1900–1985* (Cambridge: Harvard University Press, 1986), 57.

96. Leuchtenburg, *Franklin D. Roosevelt and the New Deal,* 121–24.

was placed, once again, under the direction of Hopkins. It targeted projects that would be useful (without competing with private-sector activity), labor intensive, and located in areas of high unemployment. As an incentive to leave the public-works projects when opportunities presented themselves, the WPA provided a "security wage" below what would be available in private-sector employment.[97]

In at least two ways, the New Deal relief programs were connected to the events examined earlier in this chapter. First, through reliance on public works, Roosevelt and his advisers reached back to the option promoted vigorously by the Unemployment Conference of 1921. Labor Secretary Frances Perkins noted that much of what was learned in the Unemployment Conference regarding the role of public investment and stabilization was used in designing the public-works programs.[98] More important, the chief relief agencies—including the Public Works Administration and the Federal Emergency Relief Administration—were initially part of Hoover's RFC (a reincarnation of the War Finance Corporation), which had provided relief funds to the states during the final months of the Hoover administration.[99]

New Deal relief and public-works programs were unprecedented in scope and size. They were also designed to be temporary, reflecting the president's fears that relief would wear down work incentives and give rise to long-term dependence. In his famous 1935 message to Congress—a statement that could be drawn from the welfare-reform debates of the 1990s—Roosevelt warned: "The lessons of history, confirmed by the evidence immediately before me, show conclusively that continued dependence upon relief induces a spiritual and moral disintegration fundamentally destructive to the national fiber. To dole out relief in this way is to administer a narcotic, a subtle destroyer of the human spirit. It is inimical to the dictates of sound policy. It is in violation of the traditions of America. . . . The Federal Government must and shall quit this business of relief."[100] Roosevelt's main legacy, the Social Security Act of 1935, was designed to replace relief with a permanent contributory system of social insurance. It maximized states' autonomy in the program design and implementation out of fear that stringent national standards would threaten well-entrenched state programs and violate states' rights—a

97. Ibid., 124–30; Patterson, *America's Struggle Against Poverty*, 63–64.

98. Frances Perkins, *People at Work* (New York: John Day, 1934), 189.

99. Olson, *Herbert Hoover and the Reconstruction Finance Corporation*, 88–90.

100. Franklin D. Roosevelt, "Annual Message to the Congress, January 4, 1935," in *Poverty and Public Policy in Modern America*, ed. Donald T. Critchlow and Ellis W. Hawley (Chicago: Dorsey Press, 1989), 152–53.

particularly salient issue in the South.[101] With the death of welfare capitalism under the company-union prohibitions of the Wagner Act, the timing could not have been more fortuitous.

The Social Security Act, however, was flawed in many ways. The only truly national portion of the act—the old-age pensions—was based on a regressive payroll tax and excluded entire categories of domestic and agricultural workers, as a concession to Southern Democrats. The problems were not limited to the pension system, however. Unemployment compensation and the various categorical aid programs were characterized by painfully low payment levels and great local variation in program design and payment levels. Although states were required to provide benefits that would allow for "reasonable subsistence compatible with decency and health," in practice this meant little. Yet, the Social Security Act compelled corporations to contribute to the welfare of their workers. Thus, the voluntary system of welfare capitalism that emerged in the 1920s to provide employer benevolence in times of economic expansion was replaced by mandatory programs under the aegis of the state. This new system would prove far more robust in its ability to withstand economic fluctuations. While coverage was by no means universal, it was far greater than anything that had previously existed.[102]

Economic Management, Structural Reform, and Compensatory Policy

During the last depression, the president's Unemployment Conference had produced some rather sophisticated recommendations for managing the business cycle. For Hoover, a system of countercyclical public works and corporate investments directed by statistical indicators of economic performance would allow for a scientific management of the economy and, hopefully, an end to prolonged periods of unemployment. Hoover retained a strong belief in the need for balanced budgets over the business cycle; spending during downturns would be financed by surplus funds created during periods of expansion. He was skeptical that the federal government could play a direct role in

101. Ann Shola Orloff, "The Political Origins of America's Belated Welfare State," in *The Politics of Social Policy in the United States*, ed. Margaret Weir, Ann Shola Orloff, and Theda Skocpol (Princeton, N.J.: Princeton University Press, 1988), 65–80.

102. See Badger, *The New Deal*, 231; Patterson, *America's Struggle Against Poverty*, 68–73.

relief, however, given the limited fiscal resources of the state and his ongoing commitment to voluntarism and associational governance. As president, Hoover was more willing to promote federal expenditures, as revealed by his early endorsement of a $3 billion fund for public construction. However, he remained hopeful that the private-sector investment that he had advocated since 1921 would materialize. As the depression eroded tax receipts and voluntary investment, Hoover expedited the release of funds for construction projects and ultimately promoted the Reconstruction Finance Corporation. Direct federal funding of relief remained an impossibility, however, as revealed by the conflicts surrounding the definition of the RFC's duties.

As governor, Roosevelt had been similarly disposed to budgetary restraint. As candidate, he resorted to the old-time religion of balanced budgets. During the campaign, he had denounced his adversary for his reckless forays into the world of deficit spending and governmental sprawl. Indeed, a major plank of his economic platform was an economy drive designed to reduce the size of the federal government by one-quarter. However, as Elliot Rosen explains, "Hoover and Roosevelt differed on the public-works/relief issue and the balanced budget, as on so many others, not in principle but in the squire's willingness to jettison received dogma when reality dictated its abandonment. Hoover refused to alter his fundamental position . . . for fear that direct relief would lead to 'socialism and collectivism with its destruction of human liberty.' Roosevelt had no such ideological fears."[103] In the area of fiscal policy, as in the design of relief programs for industry and agriculture, Roosevelt was willing to sanction a far greater role for the state than was Hoover. The creed of American individualism was less a religion, than a bias, for Roosevelt.

There is little evidence that Roosevelt appreciated the ramifications of the Unemployment Conference for the Great Depression, even if the Department of Interior under Harold Ickes had promoted a number of public-work projects, such as the Tennessee Valley Authority, many of which could have positive implications for employment and long-term growth. Given his political commitments from the campaign and his fear that excessive spending might cast him in the same light as he had cast Hoover, Roosevelt was slow to embrace a policy of fiscal stimulation. One critic noted "the ludicrous position in which the Administration places itself when it urges employers of all kinds to raise wages and increase employment, while at the same time it sets the contrary example by cutting wages and dismissing workers! . . . The whole tragic farce is a hangover from the panicky days when Ogden Mills and a

103. Rosen, *Hoover, Roosevelt, and the Brains Trust,* 351.

majority of the newspapers were clamoring for 'a balanced budget'—as if a really balanced budget were possible in such times as these! What is needed is not so much a balanced budget as a balanced outlook."[104] While Roosevelt would run deficits out of necessity, this belief in balanced budgets would place limits on the size of the deficits and the rapidity of recovery.

With fiscal policy initially tied to the goal of economy and budgetary restraint, the administration's recovery efforts emphasized structural reforms such as the NRA and the AAA, and a number of regulatory initiatives were promoted, in part, on the belief that they would contribute to economic stability. However, on the basis of these measures alone, it was highly questionable that recovery would be forthcoming. What was required was a stronger connection between these "reforms" and a broad macroeconomic program. William F. Ogburn noted this fact in 1933:

> The theory runs that we can pay these higher wages out of sales of goods to ourselves. But the payment of wages comes before sales, and at this point assistance is needed from the banks, which can help by the expansion of bank credit. Industry figures it can pay higher wages and higher prices. Higher wages can be paid if we have higher prices, but to buy at higher prices we shall have to have still higher wages. These alternately increasing prices and wages can be met if we can increase the volume of money and credit. Such is the process of inflation, and indeed also of recovery from depressions. The progress of recovery, once it begins, will be aided by the fact that prices have dropped so low; purchasing power will increase more rapidly than wage rates because of the increase of employment and the demand for raw materials and producers' goods.[105]

In sum, the success of recovery along the lines suggested by the NRA would depend on the underlying macroeconomic policy. Absent a sufficient expansion of credit, the NRA could simply stimulate an inflation that would fail to have the desired impact on recovery.

Initially, Roosevelt and his key advisers were cautious in their use of fiscal policy. To be certain, Keynes, who had taken a personal interest in the New Deal, provided a theoretical justification for expansionary fiscal policy as a means of battling aggregate-demand failure. Alvin Hansen had made compa-

104. Anderson, "Roosevelt Turns Left," 121.
105. William F. Ogburn, "The Consumer and the NRA," *Nation,* September 20, 1933, 318.

rable arguments, focusing on the tendencies toward stagnation in a mature capitalist economy. In the short run, Roosevelt promoted emergency relief and a host of recovery programs and was willing to tolerate the deficits that resulted from the combination of relief and a depression-related drop in revenues. However, at the same time, he advocated raising corporate taxes and estate taxes and eliminating tax expenditures wherever possible. He also promoted, albeit unsuccessfully, a permanent federal inheritance tax and an undistributed-profits tax.[106] Drawing on the support of Treasury Secretary Henry Morgenthau Jr. and other balanced-budget hawks, Roosevelt resorted to taxation as a means of reducing the deficits. Thus, in 1936 the Roosevelt administration successfully secured tax increases. The next year, the new Social Security taxes were implemented for the first time. The new taxes combined with the absence of a one-time veterans bonus paid in 1936 pushed the economy into a free fall: between July 1937 and May 1938, industrial production fell by 33 percent—the most rapid economic decline to that point in U.S. history—thereby expunging most of the advances of the past few years. At the same time, the new crisis heightened the president's responsiveness to members of the administration and academic economists who had arrived at proto-Keynesian conclusions through their practical experience.[107] In March 1938, following the economic collapse, Fed chairman Marriner Eccles mobilized an influential group of New Dealers, including Henry Wallace, Harold Ickes, Harry Hopkins, Leon Henderson, Lauchlin Currie, Beardsley Ruml, and Mordecai Ezekiel, to convince Roosevelt of the virtues of a countercyclical stimulus program. Following his Warm Springs conversion, Roosevelt called on Congress for a $5 billion stimulus package, combining funding for additional public works and credit.[108]

This movement toward countercyclical demand management did not occur in a vacuum, however, but was part of a larger rethinking of the role of the state. The model of government-supervised self-regulation—the model at

106. See John F. Witte, *The Politics and Development of the Federal Income Tax* (Madison: University of Wisconsin Press, 1985), 96–109.

107. See Walter S. Salant, "The Spread of Keynesian Doctrines and Practices in the United States," in *The Political Power of Ideas: Keynesianism Across Nations,* ed. Peter Hall (Princeton, N.J.: Princeton University Press, 1989). See also William J. Barber, *Designs Within Disorder: Franklin D. Roosevelt, the Economists, and the Shaping of American Economic Policy, 1933–1945* (Cambridge: Cambridge University Press, 1996), for detailed discussion of economic policy debates.

108. See the account in David Brinkley, "The New Deal and the Idea of the State," in *The Rise and Fall of the New Deal Order, 1930–1980,* ed. Steve Fraser and Gary Gerstle (Princeton, N.J.: Princeton University Press, 1989), 95–97, and Herbert Stein, *The Fiscal Revolution in America* (Washington, D.C.: AEI Press, 1990), 91–130.

the heart of the NRA and the chief legacy of wartime mobilization—lived on after the Supreme Court overturned the National Industrial Recovery Act. As noted earlier, it was rapidly disseminated through a host of New Deal initiatives, giving great continuity to the policies, agencies, and patterns of state-economy relations that constituted the Associational Regime. As regulations were expanded to include investment banking, industrial relations, trucking, and civil aeronautics, key features of the emergency measures were given new life. Even if many of these regulatory agencies would ultimately function as cartel managers, they were created with a very different end in mind. Within the Roosevelt administration, there was growing skepticism regarding the virtues of the old associational doctrines, which seemed, in the wake of the NRA experience, to support little more than a form of corporate-dominated planning under the protective auspices of the state. This position solidified after the fall into recession, when a host of new New Dealers actively advocated a different role for the state.[109] Increasingly, the state's role would be viewed less as orchestrating a corporatist concert of interests—the model at the heart of the associational regime—and more as promoting the public interest. Thurman Arnold, Thomas Corcoran, Benjamin Cohen, Leon Henderson, Jerome Frank, William O. Douglas, and James Landis, among others, argued that policy should focus on forcing heightened corporate accountability and consumer welfare. In some instances, this would require a closer regulation of corporate behavior. In other instances, such as antitrust, it would require an active state role in breaking up the economic bottlenecks that appeared to many, including Roosevelt's new antitrust enforcer, Thurman Arnold, to be causally connected to the slow pace of recovery. In the most extreme case, public utilities, it required nothing short of the forcible reorganization and deconcentration of an entire industry.

Yale law professor Thurman Arnold was appointed assistant attorney general for antitrust in 1938. His tenure exemplifies the shift in administration policy away from the earlier associationalism. For Arnold, the large industrial interests that had been so dominant under the NRA were a source of grave concern because they acted as private governments, exercising power over society and extracting its wealth without a modicum of accountability. Past antitrust enforcement had been largely a symbolic effort. It had "made business less ruthless and more polite" while allowing corporations systematically to create economic bottlenecks that misallocated society's wealth and limited

109. See Brinkley, "The New Deal and the Idea of the State."

the potential for growth.[110] However, Arnold argued that enforcement, rather than attack size alone, had to address "the use of organized power to restrain trade unreasonably, without justification in terms of greater distribution of goods. . . . Size in itself is not an evil, but it does give power to those who control it."[111] As the Antitrust Division reported its new enforcement philosophy: "The answer to the monopoly problem . . . does not consist of destroying the efficiency of organized industry whenever that efficiency is passed on to the consumer." Rather, policy must "break down the obstacles to production created by dominant groups."[112] The Antitrust Division's budget more than doubled in two years, allowing for a significant increase in antitrust prosecutions, many of which were announced with great fanfare and publicity and aimed at the very practices and intercorporate relations that had been promoted under the NRA. During Arnold's five-year tenure, he was responsible for nearly one-half of all the antitrust cases filed since the passage of the Sherman Act.[113]

Despite the support for more vigorous antitrust enforcement and the investigations of the Temporary National Economic Committee, Roosevelt retained a residual faith in the earlier model of planning. In a press conference of January 1938, he recalled that "under NRA it was perfectly legal for the heads of all the companies in a given industry to sit down around a table with the Government, and, from their own statistics and the statistics of their trade associations and the statistics given them by the Government, figure out much more clearly than they ever had before, as an industry, what the probable demand of the country would be for a period of six months or a year ahead . . . so that they won't overproduce." Roosevelt announced that this kind of activity appeared "perfectly legitimate," and he expressed a hope that antitrust revisions might make it "a completely legal thing to do."[114] Nevertheless, the model of the NRA had been discredited within the administration and an increasingly antagonistic Congress. More activist antitrust measures, new regulations designed to promote corporate accountability, higher levels of fiscal stimulation, and the social security old-age pensions, it was believed, would provide the key to recovery. Taken together, they could

110. Thurman W. Arnold, "Antitrust Enforcement: Past and Future," *Law and Contemporary Problems* 7, no. 1 (1940): 9.

111. Thurman W. Arnold, *Bottlenecks of Business* (New York: Reynal & Hitchcock, 1940), 125.

112. U.S. Justice Department, *Annual Report of the Attorney General of the United States* (Washington, D.C.: Government Printing Office, 1941), 60.

113. See Marc Allen Eisner, *Antitrust and the Triumph of Economics: Institutions, Expertise, and Policy Change* (Chapel Hill: University of North Carolina Press, 1991), 77–83.

114. Quoted in Stein, *Fiscal Revolution in America,* 103–4.

open channels of commerce, create new opportunities for expansion, and provide a source of compensatory financing to overcome the lack of aggregate
demand.

In the end, Roosevelt's 1938 conversion to fiscal activism came far too
late, and the level of stimulation remained anemic. Between 1933 and 1939,
cash deficits equaled approximately $21 billion. These deficits were not suffi-
cient to stimulate recovery, particularly when combined with sharp spending
reductions at the state and local levels.[115] As a result, by the end of 1939
unemployment stood at 17.2 percent, and the economy had not yet returned
to its predepression level of output.[116] In the end, World War II would provide the engine for economic recovery. It rapidly eliminated the most harmful
depression in American history. In so doing, it revealed that an active fiscal
policy along Keynesian lines could secure the full employment that had been
such an elusive goal during the past decade, as unemployment fell from 17.2
percent on the eve of the war to 1.2 percent in 1944.[117] The rapid progress
from depression to overemployment suggested that Keynesianism might hold
great promise for future economic management, particularly in a period in
which large-scale unemployment was believed endemic to a mature capitalist
economy.

World War II placed new demands on the American state, reintroducing a
dynamic that had been evident in the last war to end all wars. Once again, it
became clear that the demands of total war were far greater than could be
met with existing public resources, despite the swelling of the state over the
course of the New Deal. Once again, the model of compensatory state building would be embraced as a means of meeting the challenge. By May 1940,
the advisory commission of the Council of National Defense had been resurrected, followed by the proliferation of war agencies, the influx of dollar-a-
year men, and the creation of industrial advisory committees providing a
dense network of corporate representation in every phase of domestic economic mobilization. The problems of excessive delegation, limited political
control and accountability, and corporate profiteering in munitions reared

115. Herbert Stein, *Presidential Economics: The Making of Economic Policy from Roosevelt to Reagan and
Beyond* (New York: Simon & Schuster, 1985), 38. Susan Previant Lee and Peter Passell, *A New Economic
View of American History* (New York: W.W. Norton, 1979), 386–88.
116. See Herbert Stein, *Fiscal Revolution in America*, 88–115, and Salant, "The Spread of Keynesian
Doctrines and Practices in the United States," 42–45.
117. Robert M. Collins, *The Business Response to Keynes, 1929–1964* (New York: Columbia University
Press, 1981), 79.

their heads. In the latter half of the 1930s, many of the New Dealers had become critical of the model of state building integral to the NRA, hoping to replace this model with a new set of reform measures. They were skeptical that such a model could be applied without creating all of the problems inherent in compensatory state building. In the end, this skepticism became but another victim of war. Just as World War I had elevated New Nationalist conceptions of the state and rendered the New Freedom irrelevant, World War II forced a return to the models that had become the object of concern. The historic moment had passed.

10

The Great War, New Battles, and the Limits of the Modern State

> [T]he War was a calamity, though with compensations. . . . We have learned
> things, as men must from any great experience; but too often we seem to
> have learned the wrong things. And we might have had better experiences to
> learn from. Perhaps all we can be sure of is that nothing has remained
> untouched by the War. Everything that has happened has happened
> differently because of it.   —John Maurice Clark, 1931

In his 1933 book entitled *The Roosevelt Revolution,* Ernest K. Lindley could not have presented the election of Roosevelt in grander terms: "The word 'revolution' sprang naturally to the lips. No other word seems strong enough to describe a change so swift and so fundamental. The United States had embarked on an experiment in new economic relationships of revolutionary audacity and magnitude." Although Lindley could not doubt that the New Deal was revolutionary, "the revolution was thoroughly saturated with cherished American ideals. Its objectives were security, happiness, self-respect, a decent standard of living for the ordinary man, the idea of generally distributed well-being expressed in the Declaration of Independence, or in any other summary of the aspiration of a democratic or socialistic state."[1] One cannot fault Lindley's sense of excitement given the severity of the Great Depression and the promise of the new administration. Yet, a half century later, the conclusion that the New Deal was a revolution in public policy and institutional forms remains a popular—if increasingly frayed—position.

The New Deal is often presented as a watershed in American history, a

---

1. Ernest K. Lindley, *The Roosevelt Revolution: First Phase* (New York: Viking Press, 1933), 4, 5.

point at which the traditional American state was transformed into a modern
structure with modern functions. As Albert U. Romasco notes: "[T]he entire
sweep of the New Deal, if it is visualized as an object on the American historical landscape, appears as a mammoth waterfall cascading with an endless din
and viewed with an enduring fascination."[2] This fascination comes at a cost,
however. Anthony Badger explains: "Historians . . . have often appeared to
be trapped in a cycle of lamentation or celebration of the New Deal: they
have spent more time denigrating or championing it than explaining it."[3]
The past several chapters have challenged the assertion that the New Deal
constituted a revolution; and they have done so, not because of any devalua-
tion of the accomplishments and aspirations of the Roosevelt presidency, but
because of concerns over the broader issue of how best to situate this episode
in the broader development of the American state and political economy.

Our understanding of political development is very often driven by the
search for crises followed by the establishment of new equilibriums. We assume, explicitly or implicitly, that various crises have brought clear breaks
with the past. New political eras are thus inaugurated complete with new
institutions, public policies, and prevailing public philosophies. We structure
our very understanding of American political history with a succession of
orders, as the Jacksonian Era, the Gilded Age, the Progressive Era, the New
Era, and the New Deal follow each other, separated one from another by
crises that revealed the weaknesses of the old and dictated in one way or
another the distinctive features of the new. Popular periodization may provide
a useful shorthand for referring to a cluster of related political-historical phenomena. Yet, it may simultaneously distort our understanding of political
change to the extent that it places too great a premium on disjunction and
discontinuity.

In Chapter 1, a number of elements of an evolutionary institutional perspective were presented to guide the development of the study in subsequent
chapters. It was argued that bounded rationality, information scarcity, and
institutional inertia constrain the pace of change. Institutional evolution is
largely path-dependent in that the administrative capacities, policy tools,
stocks of bureaucratic expertise, and established patterns of state-society relations that exist in a given period place limitations on the options subsequently
open to officials. Although gradual incremental adjustments to new situations

---

2. Albert U. Romasco, *The Politics of Recovery* (New York: Oxford University Press, 1983), vii.
3. Anthony J. Badger, *The New Deal: The Depression Years, 1933–1940* (New York: Hill & Wang, 1989), 2.

tend to be the norm, periods of relative stability are from time to time punctuated by periods of discontinuous evolution—that is, rapid, substantial, institutional changes that recast basic rules, roles, policy tools, and patterns of state-society relations. Often, this discontinuous evolution is a consequence of profound exogenous shocks. Here are the crises that loom so large in historical periodization, those events that separate one era from the next.

Yet, even when periods of rapid change occur, there are strands of continuity with the past. Consider one of the core concepts applied in this book: the regime. As noted in Chapter 1, a regime of a given period comprises policies and institutions that share a set of goals, values, models of administration, and patterns of state-society relations. As related innovations are introduced to deal with different problems, a certain continuity across policy areas emerges that gives the initiatives of a period a certain coherence. When new crises emerge, officials commonly search for appropriate responses by drawing on prevailing political-economic ideas that describe what might appear to be an appropriate role for the state. The doctrines commonly suggest new administrative models and new means of integrating organized interests into the policy process. The immediate suitability of these doctrines rests on several factors, including officials' experiences with similar problems in the past, earlier investment and staffing decisions within relevant agencies, the earlier development of applicable policy tools, the organization of private-sector actors, and established patterns of state-group relations. In short, the availability of potential innovations will be conditioned by the extent to which they can be reconciled with what has come before. Political-institutional development is path-dependent, even if the path rarely takes the form of a straight line passing through historical time.

As the chapters in Part II of this book revealed, the war had a significant impact in shaping events in a number of policy areas. In each case, the organization of economic interests had been changed as a result of the war. In each case, the war gave rise to new expectations concerning the role of the state in promoting stability and rising incomes. In each case, policy makers and group representatives could draw on the experiences of war to suggest new ways of designing peacetime policies and reconfiguring patterns of state-group relations. Granted, there were differences in the extent to which the lessons of war were applied in peace. However, the experiences of war, as they shaped the politics, policies, and institutions of the New Era, provided the raw materials from which a new regime would be constructed. This regime, which began to take form during the Hoover presidency, came into full fruition during the New Deal. To seek to provide an account of the New Deal separate from the events of war and the 1920s is to miss the impact of the past and the limitations in the historical legacy inherited by the Roosevelt administration.

The role that the past plays in this saga raises some serious concerns. If, as suggested throughout, actors seek to manage uncertainty by drawing analogies to problems for which policies and institutions have already been designed, the room for error is great. Problem definition is more art than science. As Deborah A. Stone reminds us: "Policy stories are tools of strategy. Policymakers often create problems (in the artistic sense) as a context for the actions they want to take. . . . they *represent* the world in such a way as to make themselves, their skills, and their favorite course of action necessary."[4] Murray Edelman makes a similar point when he notes that "a crisis . . . is a creation of the language used to depict it; the appearance of a crisis is a political act, not a recognition of a fact or of a rare situation."[5] When officials make policy and institutional decisions by analogizing to past problems and events, when they use prevailing political-economic ideas not to recast the world anew but to extend the reach of existing institutions, policies, and patterns of state-group relations, they partially resolve the problems of uncertainty. At the same time, they may draw on solutions that are not fully appropriate to the challenges at hand. Analogies carry costs, some hidden, some intentional. All "policy metaphors imply prescription" and thus simultaneously constitute advocacy for a given set of policies, institutions, and patterns of state-economy relations.[6] The analogy of war—the exact analogy adopted by the Roosevelt administration when seeking to address the crisis of the Great Depression—justified the demand that greater power be invested in the regime. At the same time, it suggested that certain policies, institutions, and patterns of state-economy relations could be reconfigured to address the new crisis.

When reflecting on the performance of the New Deal, it is easy to identify serious deficiencies. One might cite the failed fiscal policy even following Roosevelt's 1938 Warm Springs conversion to Keynesianism, when the fiscal record was one of restraint. The federal government, after all, ran a deficit of $3.862 billion in 1939, less that the $4.435 billion deficit of 1936—two years before Roosevelt's supposed conversion. Of course, these deficits pale in comparison with the $13.362 billion deficit of 1919 or the $9.032 billion

4. Deborah A. Stone, *Policy Paradox and Political Reason* (Glenview, Ill.: Scott, Foresman & Co., 1988), 116. See also John W. Kingdon, *Agendas, Alternatives, and Public Policies* (Glenview, Ill.: Scott, Foresman & Co., 1984), 186.

5. Murray Edelman, *Constructing the Political Spectacle* (Chicago: University of Chicago Press, 1988), 31–32.

6. Stone, *Policy Paradox and Political Reason*, 118.

incurred the year before.[7] In the area of fiscal policy, Roosevelt never truly adopted the analogy of war. One might also cite the failure to introduce the kind of planning mechanisms that many members of the administration viewed as essential to the new state role, and the resulting limits of reform and income redistribution. The compensatory-state-building model that was at the heart of the New Deal planning experiments carried serious weaknesses that limited what planners could accomplish. In these areas and others, the gaps between promise and performance were great.

Yet, one must be careful not to let the deficiencies of the New Deal undermine an appreciation for the long-term significance of the Roosevelt presidency. Many contemporary students of "big government" would be quick to note that the New Deal brought a momentous increase in the size of government. The small state that had historically characterized the United States was replaced by a much larger enterprise. Here the statistics are unambiguous. In terms of civilian employment, the federal government was 158 percent as large on the eve of World War II as it had been in 1933—an increase from 603,587 to 953,891 employees. In six short years, Roosevelt had added as many employees to the public payroll as had been added from 1901 to his inauguration.[8] As one might expect, this increase in the number of employees was outpaced by levels of government expenditures, which by 1939 stood at 192 percent of their 1933 level. Stated another way, federal expenditures had increased from 7 percent of GDP to 10.2 percent. This was the beginning of what would be a long-term trajectory. In terms of civilian employees and overall expenditures, the New Deal state would appear quite small in comparison with that which existed in the decades after World War II. By 1949, public-sector civilian employment was 220 percent its 1939 level; expenditures had increased from 10.2 percent of GDP to 16.2 percent in the same period.[9]

The size of government is of far less significance than the scope of governmental authority, although the two are certainly correlated. The New Deal brought a consequential and lasting expansion in the regulatory and redistributive activities of the state. After the crisis of depression had passed, public authority remained far greater than it had in the years before the collapse of the economy—an example of the ratchet effect that accompanies many cri-

7. *Statistical History of the United States,* series Y-256.
8. *Statistical History of the United States,* series Y-241.
9. Author's calculations from data in *Statistical History of the United States,* series Y-255 and Y-241. Expenditures as a percentage of GDP from table A-3 of Herbert Stein, *Presidential Economics,* 3d ed. (Washington, D.C.: American Enterprise Institute, 1994).

ses.[10] New regulatory policies were introduced or extended to cover several industries, including air and surface transportation, communications, commercial banking, corporate finance, agriculture, and industrial relations. The New Deal regulatory policies initiated under the banner of structural reform were far greater in number and impact than those introduced in the decades since the passage of the Interstate Commerce Act. Whereas associational arrangements fortified with a modest state presence had been common in the 1920s, the new regulatory policies placed the state in a stronger position, thoroughly transforming the nature of the regulatory state. Whereas many policies before the period had been designed to preserve markets or compensate for their absence, the new policies were established in most cases to maintain industrial stability and elevate the incomes of the regulated. Although the regulatory policies had powerful redistributive implications insofar as they transferred national income toward the regulated parties, the greatest efforts at income redistribution were found in the new welfare policies. Beyond the emergency measures that accompanied the first New Deal, the Social Security Act of 1935 established what would become the largest entitlement programs in the nation's history. As with regulation, there were precedents before the New Deal, most clearly in the case of Civil War pensions.[11] Yet, it is in the scope of the state's redistributive efforts that the New Deal stands out as a genuine watershed in U.S. history.

In addition, there were critical political and institutional legacies. The New Deal completed the transition to a president-centered political system. As noted in Chapter 2, the transfer of power from the legislative to the executive can be understood as an important component in the expansion of administrative capacity. Under the emergency conditions prevailing during the New Deal, Congress delegated much authority to the president. This authority, in turn, was delegated to the growing number of administrative agencies charged with implementing policies. To some extent, the delegation of authority could be justified on the grounds that the administrative agencies (many of which were professionalized) and the groups they integrated into the administrative apparatus had the concentration of expertise and experience necessary to make detailed policies addressing the problems in question. Unlike Congress, which was highly responsive to the unstructured interaction

10. For a discussion of the ratchet, see Robert Higgs, *Crisis and Leviathan: Critical Episodes in the Growth of American Government* (New York: Oxford University Press, 1987), chap. 4.

11. See Ann Shola Orloff, "The Political Origins of America's Belated Welfare State," in *The Politics of Social Policy in the United States,* ed. Margaret Weir, Ann Shola Orloff, and Theda Skocpol (Princeton, N.J.: Princeton University Press, 1988).

with mobilized interests, these administrative units at least had the potential to limit access to sites of decision making and thus make policies that were more than an aggregate of group demands.

The centralization of authority in the executive and the vesting of power in administrative agencies presumably dense with expertise and experience should have strong positive implications for the expansion of administrative capacity. The government of courts and parties that prevailed through the nineteenth century had, unquestionably, given way to a state that was identifiably modern.[12] As an exercise in compensatory state building, however, the system increasingly depended on a peculiar system of interest representation, something that Theodore Lowi has captured with the concept of "interest-group liberalism." Under interest-group liberalism, representation is built "upon the oligopolistic character of interest groups, reducing the number of competitors, favoring the best organized competitors, specializing politics around agencies, ultimately limiting participation to channels provided by pre-existing groups."[13] Such a system of representation thrives on and demands broad delegations of authority. As interest groups are integrated into the administrative agencies to create a system of government-supervised self-regulation, they are given a key role in determining the substance of public policy. Needless to say, groups will remain integrated in such a system only as long as it serves their self-interest. Officials will tailor policies to meet the needs of the regulated, even if this entails creating a system of regressive redistribution and regulatory barriers that has largely negative consequences for social welfare and the overall dynamism of the economy. As a result, the exercise of power is linked, intimately, to the welfare of those parties selected for inclusion.

The limitations of compensatory state building are both practical and normative. On the practical side, excessive delegation leads inexorably to a loss of control. Policy is shaped by those groups engaged in the policy process, often with minimal official direction. Because decisions occur at the fringes of the organization—that netherworld where the public and private become impossible to differentiate—those at upper levels in the organization can find it difficult to monitor and direct the evolution of policy. Second, excessive delegation significantly reduces the capacity to impose costs on regulated parties and usually has the opposite effect. Those who are integrated into the

12. See Stephen Skowronek, *Building a New American State: The Expansion of National Administrative Capacities, 1877–1920* (Cambridge: Cambridge University Press, 1982).
13. Theodore Lowi, *The End of Liberalism: The Second Republic of the United States*, 2d ed. (New York: W. W. Norton, 1979), 63.

administrative apparatus participate in the expectation that such participation
will provide material benefits such as fixed prices, guaranteed incomes, and
barriers to the entry of new competitors.[14] Officials who might seek to impose
costs may witness the defection of parties who discover that it is easier to exit
than it is to protest. This incapacity to impose costs seriously limits the ability
to plan and use policies for the realization of long-term objectives. It introduces a conservatism into the process such that it is difficult to enact truly
innovative policies that might challenge existing distributions of power and
authority. The exercise of public authority becomes an exercise in transfer-
seeking.

On the normative side, government-supervised self-regulation does serious
damage to democratic governance. As Theodore Lowi correctly notes, such a
system "possesses the mentality of a world universalized ticket-fixing. Destroy
privilege by universalizing it. Reduce conflict by yielding to it. Redistribute
power by the maxim of each according to his claim. Purchase support for the
regime by reserving an official place for every major structure of power." By
delegating significant authority to administrative agencies where decisions are
made through bargaining, the system opposes "privilege in policy formulation
only to foster it quite systematically in the implementation of policy."[15] In
the end, the violation of democratic norms becomes widespread, even if hidden from view. Accountability becomes a chimera. Whatever democratic decision rules officially exist within majoritarian bodies become little more than
formalities when introduced into the world of administration.

To the extent that these costs were understood in World War I, they
were deemed acceptable given the lack of alternative means of mobilizing the
economy for war. Likewise, one might understand the attraction of this model
for institutional design in the dark days of 1933. The state remained underdeveloped and administratively weak. The only way to secure the allegiance of
large organized interests and create a planning capacity was to extend sovereignty and material benefits, much as had been done in the past. Key agencies, policies, and patterns of state-group relations had been inherited from
the experience of war mobilization. In some cases, old initiatives were simply
resurrected or repackaged under the label of the New Deal. Roosevelt and so
many of his advisers had participated in the war mobilization activities and
must have had firsthand knowledge of the difficulties that emerged as consequences of compensatory state building.

14. See George J. Stigler, "The Theory of Economic Regulation," *Bell Journal of Economics and Management Science* 2, no. 1 (1971): 3–21.

15. Lowi, *The End of Liberalism*, 297.

By 1935, and certainly by 1937–38, a large and growing number of New Dealers had rejected the model that was at the core of the early recovery efforts and disseminated through the "little NRAs." They could clearly see the costs, both economic and political, of what has been referred to here as compensatory state building. They saw associationalism and its more statist descendants as providing little more than an opportunity and justification for business cartelization. They envisioned a transition to a state that would use its power to eliminate the bottlenecks that impeded recovery and to provide new sources of countercyclical stimulation through the new system of entitlements, public works, and fiscal policy. But much as World War I engulfed the New Freedom progressives and forced a de facto acceptance of the New Nationalist model, so also would World War II quash this critique and give new support to a model that had been discredited by the events of the first New Deal.

It is difficult to predict how far the reform sentiments of the second New Deal would have gone absent the interference of war. But World War II resulted, once again, in the proliferation of mobilization agencies and the extreme delegation of power to business-dominated associations and dollar-a-year men. The War Production Board, under the direction of Donald Nelson (vice-president of Sears), essentially re-created the decentralized system used a generation earlier by the War Industries Board. A network of industrial advisory committees was established to work with the board's industrial divisions. There were, to be certain, concerns about the extreme delegation of authority, as expressed in the hearings held by the Senate's Truman Committee. However, Nelson fielded these concerns much as Baruch had in the previous war, by arguing that rapid mobilization would be an impossibility without the experience, expertise, and connections of the dollar-a-year men.[16] Indeed, the reliance on this business network was substantial. As Nelson explained in his *Arsenal of Democracy:* "[I]t wasn't up to me or to WPB to tell industry how to do its job; it was our function to show industry what had to be done, and then do everything in our power to enable industry to do it, placing our chief reliance on the limitless energy and skill of American manufacturers." As part of this reliance on industry, "no order or directive affecting industry could be issued by WPB which was not submitted in advance to the Industry Committees and discussed by them."[17] Working under certificates of immunity from

16. Gregory Hooks, *Forging the Military-Industrial Complex: World War II's Battle of the Potomac* (Urbana: University of Illinois Press, 1991), 109.

17. Donald M. Nelson, *Arsenal of Democracy: The Story of American War Production* (New York: Harcourt, Brace & Co., 1946), 208, 345.

antitrust prosecutions and with an expectation of profitable war contracts, the committee members were more than willing to lend their assistance. Compensatory state building became, once again, the order of the day.

To be certain, the experiences of World War I led the new generation of mobilizers to avoid many difficulties. Price-fixing, labor regulations, and funding of the war effort were all far smoother than one might have expected. Moreover, far more consideration was given to reconversion, which became a dominant focus of discussion after 1943. Yet, particularly in reconversion, the biases associated with compensatory state building once again had an impact on events. A decision to free up resources in the final stages of the war would have permitted many of the smaller firms, which were no longer profiting from war production, to make a transition into civilian production, thus providing the structural preconditions for a decentralized competitive economy after the war. Yet, early reconversion was opposed by the larger industrial concerns, who had great influence in the war mobilization agencies (particularly the Office of War Mobilization) and the Joint Chiefs of Staff. In the end, gradual reconversion was derailed, and small firms were left to languish until the end of the war. Many found it impossible to compete with the larger firms, which entered the postwar economy with large reserves of capital derived from war contracts. Many had no options other than bankruptcy or acquisition. The large firms quickly secured new defense contracts and were given preferential status in acquiring the facilities and stockpiles the government had financed, often at fire-sale prices. As Gregory Hooks notes, they were "turned over to [the large firms] at such low prices" that they "represented a 'capital subsidy,' making it even more difficult for smaller and newer producers to compete."[18] The expanded facilities of the chief corporate beneficiaries of the war allowed them preferential access to postwar markets as well, thus cementing in their capacity to generate wealth.

Funded by a growing number of lucrative defense contracts, regulated by agencies that would function as de facto cartel managers, large corporations would find in the postwar decades a close connection between their ongoing profitability and the role of the state. The critics of excessive delegation, regulatory capture, and the elite dominance of American institutions would find much evidence upon which to base their critiques, while others would seek to understand how the more progressive full-employment goals associated with the new postwar macroeconomic policy system could be discarded in the Employment Act, thereby giving rise to a system that stressed price stability

18. Hooks, *Forging the Military-Industrial Complex,* 210.

over the elimination of joblessness. If there had been a genuine revolution only a few decades earlier, it was concluded, it must have been incomplete, betrayed, or derailed—a fate common to all revolutions. Yet, an examination of compensatory state building—the model that provided the core of this "revolution"—and a consideration of the evolutionary trajectory connecting World War I to the contemporary era reveal that this fate was largely predictable.

Index